EMERGENCE
OF A
FREE PRESS

EMERGENCE
OF A
FREE PRESS

LEONARD W. LEVY

IVAN R. DEE

Chicago

Library of Congress Cataloging-in-Publication Data:
Levy, Leonard Williams, 1923–
  Emergence of a free press / Leonard W. Levy.
      p. cm.
Originally published: Oxford ; New York : Oxford University Press, 1985.
Includes bibliographical references and index.
ISBN 1-56663-560-8 (alk. paper)
1. Freedom of the press—United States—History. I. Title.
KF4774.L48 2004
342.7308'53—dc22
                                                                          2004041404

To Elyse
who likes this one
—with deepest love—

Preface

When this book was first published in 1960, I called it revisionist history. What was then a heresy became a new orthodoxy and, like any orthodoxy, generated dissent. I myself have long had a dissident view of the 1960 book. In a letter of 1976 to a friend, Max Lerner, I remarked that I had exaggerated the thesis and wanted to rewrite the book after an extended examination of newspaper sources. *Emergence of a Free Press*, a substantially expanded and revised version of *Legacy of Suppression*, is the result. This new edition, sixty percent larger than the original, is also revisionist history: I am revising myself. I no longer believe that history supports some of my original conclusions. Although I continue to endorse others, including the major conclusion, I prefer to mute the sledgehammer phrasing of some. Having done additional research, found new evidence, and listened to criticism, I reject the provocative thesis expressed in the original title and therefore have had to scrap that title for a neutral one.

Legacy of Suppression was not a book I had planned to write. It was the result of chance and, I regret to say, spite. In 1957 I had a Guggenheim fellowship for the purpose of exploring the origins of the Fifth Amendment, specifically, the right against compulsory self-incrimination. But, at that time an opportunity presented itself to write for money—$1000 for about six weeks of work. That seemed an enormous amount because the Guggenheim, the sole source of my support, then paid $4000 for the year. Thanks to Henry Steele Commager's influence, The Fund for the Republic Inc., which later called itself The Center for Democratic Institutions, commissioned me to write a memorandum on the original meanings of the First Amendment's clauses.

Robert M. Hutchins, who headed The Fund, liked to hold formal conferences with the nation's leading intellectuals on urgent problems of the times, and he thought that a scholarly memorandum on the historical background of the First Amendment would be useful to have at hand in the event that a historical question arose in the course of some discussion. My own opinion was that Zechariah Chafee's *Free Speech in the United States* and Anson Phelps Stokes's *Church and State in the United States* provided all the data needed to resolve a question concerning the intentions of the Framers of the First Amendment. But, Hutchins preferred a more convenient packaging of the information based on a fresh look at the primary sources. Despite my strong liberal opinions on the First Amendment, I felt obligated to give an objective statement of the evidence and of the conclusions that they dictated. I wrote a memorandum of about seventy-five pages, two-thirds of which dealt with the clauses on religion and bore out what all liberals knew, namely, that the Framers intended a high wall of separation between church and state and guaranteed liberty of conscience even for non-Christians and non-believers; but the twenty-five pages or so on the free speech–free press clause flatly contradicted liberal assumptions and their champions such as Chafee and Justices Oliver Wendell Holmes, Louis D. Brandeis, Hugo L. Black, and William O. Douglas. To my surprise, I discovered that the Framers had a constricted view of the scope of permissible political expression.

The Fund was enthusiastic about my work on the church-state and religious liberty clauses, but not the rest. I was summoned to New York for a discussion. Officials of The Fund wanted me to polish the work on the religion clauses, and they would publish it as a handsome pamphlet in their series called Basic Issues. But, Hutchins clearly disapproved of my work on the speech-press clause. He made it clear to me that the pamphlet would not include that section of the work.

Perhaps I was overly sensitive, but I felt that I was being subjected to censorship by one of the nation's foremost strongholds of civil liberties. My fellow liberals seemed to be suppressing scholarship that did not support their presuppositions. I was angry and decided to strike back by giving what I thought would be maximum publicity to the material that The Fund rejected. Deferring my research on the book that became *The Origins of the Fifth Amendment*, I decided to write an article of approximately fifty pages on the original meaning of the free speech–press clause. I planned to submit it to the *Harvard Law Review*.

I deepened my research on that clause and wrote the article, but before submitting it for publication I sent copies to Commager and to

Mark Howe at Harvard Law School, a masterly legal historian. Commager, who was distressed by my findings, worried whether they provided scholarly ammunition for misuse by McCarthyites. Above all, however, he thought I should not rush into print; he argued that if I continued digging into the sources I very likely would find countervailing evidence that would support the Holmes-Chafee traditional liberal position.

Howe too believed that I should continue my research. He asked me questions about matters that I had not explored, about colonial English backgrounds that I had slighted, and about assumptions underlying some of the positions which I had taken. In effect he was asking me to expand the article.

So I went back to further research, and instead of producing a law review article I found myself writing a book, which turned out to be *Legacy of Suppression: Freedom of Speech and Press in Early American History*. In my acknowledgments I maliciously thanked The Fund for the Republic for having helped make the book possible, and it was not until 1972, in a book collecting various of my own essays, that I published for the first time the piece called "No Establishment of Religion: The Original Understanding," which constituted the rest of the original memorandum The Fund had liked. Thus I wrote *Legacy of Suppression* to spite Hutchins and The Fund and as a result of a chance opportunity to explore the subject.

The title I chose and the rather strong theme I developed in that book reflected both my shock at discovering the neglected evidence and my indignation at Hutchins and The Fund for attempting to suppress my work. As a result I overdid it. I had a novel position, which I overstated. I summarized my findings as follows in the 1960 preface.

This book presents a revisionist interpretation of the origins and original understanding of the First Amendment's clause on freedom of speech and press. I have been reluctantly forced to conclude that the generation which adopted the Constitution and the Bill of Rights did not believe in a broad scope for freedom of expression, particularly in the realm of politics.

I find that libertarian theory from the time of Milton to the ratification of the First Amendment substantially accepted the right of the state to suppress seditious libel. I find also that the American experience with freedom of political expression was as slight as the theoretical inheritance was narrow. Indeed, the American legislatures, especially during the colonial period, were far more oppressive than the supposedly tyrannous common-law courts. The evidence drawn particularly from the period 1776 to 1791 indicates that the generation that framed the first state declarations of rights and the First Amendment was hardly as libertarian as we have traditionally assumed. They did not intend to give free rein to criticism of the government that might be deemed seditious libel, although the concept of seditious libel was—and still is—the principal basis of muzzling political dissent. There is even reason to believe that the Bill of Rights was more the chance product of political expediency on all sides than of principled commitment to personal liberties. A broad libertarian theory of freedom of speech and press did not emerge in the United States until the Jeffersonians, when a minority party, were forced to defend themselves against the Federalist Sedition Act of 1798. In power, however, the Jeffersonians were not much more tolerant of their political critics than the Federalists had been.

I was wrong in asserting that the American experience with freedom of political expression was as slight as the conceptual and legal understanding was narrow. Indeed, elsewhere in the 1960 preface I contradicted myself when more accurately stating that the common law did not in fact "actually prevent the widespread discussion of affairs of state by the common people." At several points in the book, but only in passing, I noted the discrepancy between theory and practice. Chapter One, for example, concluded with the observations that an "astonishing degree" of open political discussion existed, considering the legal restraints, and that "the law in the books and the law in life" must be distinguished. At best I was inconsistent. From a far more thorough reading of American newspapers of the eighteenth century I now know that the American experience with a free press was as broad as the theoretical inheritance was narrow.

My original interest lay with law and theory; I had paid little attention to press practices. I had searched the newspapers only for statements on the meaning of freedom of the press and had ignored the nearly epidemic degree of seditious libel that infected American newspapers after Independence. Press criticism of government policies and politicians, on both state and national levels, during the war and in the peaceful years of the 1780s and 1790s, raged as contemptuously and scorchingly as it had against Great Britain in the period between the Stamp Act and the battle of Lexington. Some states gave written constitutional protection to freedom of the press after Independence; others did not. Whether they did or did not, their presses operated as if the law of seditious libel did not exist. To one whose prime concern was law and theory, a legacy of suppression came into focus; to one who looks at newspaper judgments on public men and measures, the revolutionary controversy spurred an expanding legacy of liberty.

If the press freely aspersed on matters of public concern for a generation before 1798, the broad new libertarianism that emerged after the enactment of the Sedition Act formed a continuum linking prior experience with subsequent theory. If a legacy of suppression had existed at all, the realms of law and theory had perpetuated it, not the realm of practice. In effect the concern for freedom of political expression continually evolved, as the American reaction to the Sedition Act illustrated. In England, Fox's Libel Act of 1792, which merely allowed a jury to decide the criminality of a defendant's words, met with popular acclaim and enjoys the historical reputation of having been a libertarian reform. England did not, however, allow a defendant in a criminal libel case to plead truth as a defense until Lord Campbell's Act of 1843. By comparison the Sedition Act of 1798 should resonate as a truly libertarian achievement because it represented the final triumph of the principles of the Zenger case: it emulated Fox's Libel Act and preceded Lord Campbell's by forty-five years, and additionally, it required proof of malice. Its reformist character notwithstanding, the Sedition Act had a notorious reputation in its own time as well as during the subsequent course of American history, showing that Americans respected freedom of political expression far more than theoreticians and legalists had acknowledged before 1798.

I disagree with *Legacy of Suppression* in one other respect. In several places I gave the misleading impression that freedom of the press meant to the Framers merely the absence of prior restraints. Similarly, I sometimes declared that they shared Blackstone's view, as I still deliberately do. Whether referring to that oracle of the common law or to freedom of the press as freedom from prior restraints, I mean, first, that the criminal law held people responsible for abuse of that freedom. Second, I mean not to exhaust the meanings of freedom of the press by identifying it as, at the least, freedom from prior restraint. The Supreme Court was right when declaring in 1936, "It is impossible to concede that by the words 'freedom of the press' the framers of the first amendment intended to adopt merely the narrow view then reflected by the law of England that such freedom consisted only in immunity from previous censorship; for this abuse had then permanently disappeared from English practice."[1] The test for the criminal abuse of freedom of the press constituted the real problem, not the imposition of subsequent punishment for that abuse. In any case, freedom of the press merely began with its immunity from previous restraints.

[1] *Grosjean v. American Press Co.*, 297 U.S. 233, 248 (1936).

Freedom of the press also meant that the press had achieved a special status as an unofficial fourth branch of government, "the Fourth Estate," whose function was to check the three official branches by exposing misdeeds and policies contrary to the public interest. Additionally, freedom of the press had come to mean that the system of popular government could not effectively operate unless the press discharged its obligations to the electorate by judging officeholders and candidates for office. The relationship between the press and the electoral process had become so close that popular government and political parties depended upon the existence of a free press. Some theorists even contended that a free press, by virtue of its watchdog function, also served as the matrix for the perpetuation of all other personal liberties protected by the Bill of Rights.

I am still convinced, however, that the revolutionary generation did not seek to wipe out the core idea of seditious libel, that the government may be criminally assaulted by mere words; that the legislatures were more suppressive than the courts; that the theory of freedom of political expression remained quite narrow until 1798, except for a few aberrant statements; that English libertarian theory was usually in the vanguard of the American; that the Bill of Rights in its immediate history was in large measure a lucky political accident; and that the First Amendment was as much an expression of federalism as of libertarianism. I also still contend that tarring and feathering a Tory editor because of his opinions showed a rather restricted meaning and scope of freedom of the press. Indeed, one may ask whether there was free speech during the revolutionary era if only the speech of freedom was free. And one may receive the same answers from people as different as Herbert Marcuse[2] and Richard Buel[3] that only truth deserves a right to be broadcast, or that those who oppose the truth don't deserve freedom of speech, or that if truth's enemies control the government, extralegal means including violence may justifiably be employed by truth's out-of-power advocates. I regard anyone who takes that viewpoint as hostile to free political discussion.

My principal thesis remains unchanged. I still aim to demolish the proposition formerly accepted in both law and history that it was the intent of the American Revolution or the Framers of the First Amendment to abolish the common law of seditious libel. James

---

[2] Marcuse, "Repressive Tolerance," in Robert Paul Wolff *et al.*, *A Critique of Pure Tolerance* (Boston, 1965), 81-117.

[3] Buel, "Freedom of the Press in Revolutionary America: The Evolution of Libertarianism, 1760-1820," in Bernard Bailyn and John B. Hench, eds., *The Press and the American Revolution* (Worcester, Mass., 1980), 59-98.

Madison himself, the "father" of the Constitution and of the Bill of Rights, explicitly argued that proposition,[4] and it has been reiterated in our own time by our greatest judges, as well as by distinguished constitutional scholars.

Justice Holmes, for example, with Justice Brandeis concurring, declared, "I wholly disagree with the argument . . . that the First Amendment left the common law as to seditious libel in force. History seems to me against the notion."[5] Subsequently Justices Black and Douglas stated, "But the First Amendment repudiated seditious libel for this country."[6] More recently Justice William Brennan for a unanimous Court asserted that by the verdict of subsequent history the Sedition Act of 1798 was unconstitutional on First Amendment grounds.[7] The scholarship upon which the Holmesian view rests derives from the original and influential essay on freedom of the press in the United States by Henry Schofield, who noted that under the English common law many political publications in the colonies before the American Revolution were considered seditious and even treasonable. "One of the objects of the Revolution," Schofield concluded, in a statement quoted with approval by the Supreme Court, "was to get rid of the English common law on liberty of speech and of the press."[8] Justice Black for the Court added, "There are no contrary implications in any part of the history of the period in which the First Amendment was framed and adopted."[9] Professor Chafee, the author of the classic work on freedom of speech, alleged, "The First Amendment was written by men to whom Wilkes and Junius were household words, who intended to wipe out the common law of sedition, and make further prosecutions for criticism of the government, without any incitement to law-breaking, forever impossible in

[4] "Madison's Report on the Virginia Resolutions" (1799-1800), in Jonathan Elliot, ed., *The Debates in the Several State Conventions on the Adoption of the Federal Constitution . . . and Other Illustrations of the Constitution* (Philadelphia, 1941, 2nd ed. rev.), 4:561-67.

[5] *Abrams v. United States*, 250 U.S. 616, 630 (1919).

[6] *Beauharnais v. Illinois*, 343 U.S. 250, 272 (1951). See also the opinion of Justice Jackson in the same case at 289.

[7] *New York Times Co. v. Sullivan*, 376 U.S. 254 (1964).

[8] Henry Schofield, *Essays on Constitutional Law and Equity* (Boston, 1921), 2:521-22, reprinting the essay, "Freedom of the Press in the United States," originally published in *Proceedings* of the American Sociological Society, 11: 67-116 (1914).

[9] For the opinion of the Supreme Court, see *Bridges v. Cal.*, 314 U.S. 252, 264 (1941). Justice Black's remark followed a quotation from Madison's Report of 1799-1800 which argued the unconstitutionality of the Sedition Act. One might think that the statute constituted a "contrary implication."

the United States of America."[10] Numerous others supported the same proposition.[11] They have, however, in Mrs. Malaprop's phrase, "anticipated the past" by succumbing to an impulse to re-create it so that its image may be seen in a manner consistent with our rhetorical tradition of freedom, thereby yielding a message that will instruct the present. The evidence suggests that the proposition is suppositious and unprovable.[12]

[10] Zechariah Chafee, Jr., *Free Speech in the United States* (Cambridge, Mass., 1948), 21.

[11] See, for example, Theodore Schroeder, *Constitutional Free Speech* (New York, 1919), 98; Leon Whipple, *Our Ancient Liberties* (New York, 1927), 93-94; Giles J. Patterson, *Free Speech and a Free Press* (Boston, 1939), 101-2, 125-28; Osmond K. Fraenkel, *Our Civil Liberties* (New York, 1944), 64-65; Francis Biddle, *The Fear of Freedom* (New York, 1951), 55-56; James Morton Smith, *Freedom's Fetters: The Alien and Sedition Laws and American Civil Liberties* (Ithaca, 1956), 427-31; John Kelly, "Criminal Libel and Free Speech," *Kansas Law Review* 6(1958):310; and C. Herman Pritchett, *The American Constitution* (New York, 1959), 430. For a similar view by an older and very eminent authority, Judge Thomas M. Cooley, see his *Treatise on the Constitutional Limitations Which Rest Upon the Legislative Power of the States*, ed. V. H. Lane (Boston, 1903, 7th ed.), 613-15. Such views became infrequent after the publication of *Legacy of Suppression.* For explicit disagreements, see George Anastaplo, review of *Legacy of Suppression*, in *New York University Law Review* 39(1964):735-41, and in George Anastaplo, *The Constitutionalist: Notes on the First Amendment* (Dallas, 1971), consult index for entries under my name and under the heading Sedition; David A. Anderson, "The Origins of the Press Clause," *U.C.L.A. Law Review* 30(1983):456-540; and William T. Mayton, "Seditious Libel and the Lost Guarantee of a Freedom of Expression," *Columbia Law Review*, 84(1984):91-142, which I read in typescript. After publication of *Legacy*, most authors who had occasion to pass judgment on the question whether the First Amendment superseded the common law of seditious libel chose to ignore the question as antiquarian or irrelevant. Thomas I. Emerson, in his magnificent book *The System of Freedom of Expression* (New York, 1970), noted the difference between Chafee and Levy and asserted that an "ambiguity" exists about the meaning of the First Amendment because of "historical dispute" on the question whether the Framers intended to abolish "the English law of seditious libel." Emerson, who is not strong on history, did not even get Fox's Libel Act correct (Emerson, p. 99). Edward G. Hudon, *Freedom of Speech and Press in America* (Washington, D.C., 1963), took higher ground; he listed *Legacy* in a bibliography to his preface and thereafter ignored it, thus avoiding altogether the need to cope with it. More characteristic were the responses of those who deprecated the values of history on learning that the Framers did not support their arguments. Alexander Meiklejohn, for example, in "The First Amendment Is an Absolute," *1961 The Supreme Court Review* (Chicago, 1961), 263-64, tolerantly accepted *Legacy* but declared that it did not deal with First Amendment problems "which now especially concern us." More crudely, Martin Shapiro, *Freedom of Speech: The Supreme Court and Judicial Review* (Englewood Cliffs, N.J., 1966), 93, dismissed *Legacy* as "irrelevant. As with all other constitutional provisions, it is not the founders' intentions but our intentions that count."

[12] A few older writers, whose articles were forerunners of *Legacy of Suppression*, agreed with this conclusion, but their differences with the Holmes-

We may even have to confront the possibility that the intentions of the Framers were not the most libertarian and their insights on the subject of freedom of expression not the most edifying. But this should be expected because the Framers were nurtured on the crabbed historicism of Coke and the narrow conservatism of Blackstone, as well as Zenger's case. The ways of thought of a lifetime are not easily broken. The Declaration of Independence severed the political connection with England but the American states continued the English common-law system except as explicitly rejected by statute. If the Revolution produced any radical libertarians on the meaning of freedom of speech and press, they were not present at the Constitutional Convention or the First Congress, which drafted the Bill of Rights. Scholars and judges have betrayed a penchant for what John P. Roche called "retrospective symmetry," by giving to present convictions a patriotic lineage and tradition[13]—in this case, the fatherhood of the "Framers." But this is no reason to be distressed. We may miss the comforting assurance of having the past's original intentions coincide with present preferences. Yet the case for civil liberties is so powerfully grounded in political philosophy's wisest principles, as well as the wisest policies drawn from experience, that it need not be anchored to the past. What passed for wisdom in the era of the Framers may very well have passed out-of-date with the growth of libertarianism in America.

My acknowledgment that the press of the new nation functioned as if the law of criminal libel hardly mattered is not entirely graceful. I refuse to *prove* the existence of unfettered press practices by giving illustrations of savage press criticisms of government policies or vicious character assassinations of American politicians. I am not intent on measuring the degree of freedom that Americans enjoyed. I am interested, to use an analogy, in defining the concept of crime, and therefore do not find crime-rate statistics to be helpful. In our own

---

Chafee-Schofield thesis seem equally presuppositious because they offered no or slight evidence to support their view. See Edward S. Corwin, "Freedom of Speech and Press under the First Amendment: A Resumé," in *Selected Essays on Constitutional Law*, Douglas B. Maggs et al., ed. (Chicago, 1938), 2:1060-63; W. R. Vance, "Freedom of Speech and of the Press," *Minnesota Law Review* 2(1918):259; and Thomas F. Carroll, "Freedom of Speech and of the Press in the Federalist Period: The Sedition Act," *Michigan Law Review* 18(1920): 636-37, 649-50.

[13] Roche, "American Liberty: An Examination of the 'Tradition' of Freedom," in M. R. Konvitz and C. Rossiter, eds., *Aspects of Liberty* (Ithaca, 1958), 130.

time, obscenity is still illegal, though we live in a society saturated by it and witness few prosecutions; their paucity does not illumine the meaning of obscenity. So, too, the rarity of prosecutions for seditious libel, and the existence of an unfettered press do not illumine the scope and meaning of freedom of the press or the law on freedom of the press. The argument that freedom of political expression existed as a fact and therefore undermined the old thesis of a legacy of suppression is an odd one in some respects. That argument seems to be on all fours with the proposition that the existence of so many heretics during the reign of Bloody Mary proves there was a great degree of freedom of religion, despite the fires at Smithfield; or, that there was freedom of the press, a century later, because Lilburne, while in prison for his political opinion, was able to smuggle out a series of seditious tracts for publication. More to the point, perhaps, would be the experience of the Jeffersonian press during the Sedition Act period. The fact that the Philadelphia *Aurora* appeared regularly while William Duane, its editor, was under indictment for violation of the Act, strikes me as poor evidence that freedom of the press, as a matter of practice, was really secure at the time. Although the *Aurora* never ceased its scathing comments on the Administration, I believe that the prosecution of its editor for his opinions demonstrated a stunted concept of a free press; and I cannot accept the view that freedom of the press was safe despite the Sedition Act.

James Morton Smith lent his authority to the view that a wider degree of freedom existed than I originally indicated.[14] He was right. Professor Smith, in his own closely related study that I think is first-rate even if wrong at points, quotes approvingly Sir James Fitzjames Stephen's observation that the enforcement of the *law* of seditious libel in England "was wholly inconsistent with any serious public discussion of political affairs." Smith concludes: "As long as it was recognized as the law of the land, any political discussion existed by sufferance of the government."[15] I agree and maintain that the law of seditious libel, which was not superseded by either the Revolution or the First Amendment, made political discussion in this country dependent upon government sufferance. I find it difficult to believe that meaningful freedom of the press could exist in that condition. That so many courageous and irresponsible editors daily risked imprisonment amazes me.

[14] James Morton Smith, review of *Legacy of Suppression*, in *William and Mary Quarterly* 20(1963):156-59.
[15] James Morton Smith, *Freedom's Fetters: The Alien and Sedition Laws and American Civil Liberties* (Ithaca, 1956), 425.

I wrote *Legacy of Suppression* and this revision in the unshakable belief that the concept of seditious libel and freedom of the press are incompatible. So long as the press *may* be subjected to government control, whether or not that control is exercised, the press cannot be free—or is not as free as it should be. Freedom of the press cannot thrive as it should if closeted with a time bomb, the concept of seditious libel, ticking away in the law. The number or frequency of detonations does not matter. The Sedition Act of 1798, the Sedition Act of 1918, and the Smith Act of 1940, together with the prosecutions under them, are unendurable. One case is too many. Harry Kalven best made the point when he wrote:

> The concept of seditious libel strikes at the very heart of democracy. Political freedom ends when government can use its powers and its courts to silence its critics. My point is not the tepid one that there should be leeway for criticism of the government. It is rather that defamation of the government is an impossible notion for a democracy. In brief, I suggest, that the presence or absence in the law of the concept of seditious libel defines the society. A society may or may not treat obscenity or contempt by publication as legal offenses without altering its basic nature. If, however, it makes seditious libel an offense, it is not a free society no matter what its other characteristics.[16]

I believe that and am therefore puzzled by the paradox in the following pages of nearly unfettered press practices in a system characterized by legal fetters and the absence of a theory of political expression that justified those press practices.

The publication of *Legacy of Suppression* appalled some liberals. I myself was a little apologetic about it for fear, as Henry Commager predicted, that the wicked forces of reaction might capitalize on the discovery that the Framers gave their paternal blessing to suppressive impulses. "No citizen," I sonorously intoned, "and certainly no jurist worthy of his position, would or should conclude his judgment on either a constitutional question or a matter of public policy by an antiquarian examination of the original meaning of the freedom of speech-and-press clause."[17] Justice Hugo L. Black, the passionate and self-proclaimed absolutist on free speech and press issues, who was

[16] "The New York Times Case: A Note on 'The Central Meaning of the First Amendment,'" *1964 The Supreme Court Review*, ed. Philip Kurland (Chicago, 1964), 205.

[17] Commager wrote a handsome review of the book, *New York Times Book Review*, Nov. 13, 1960.

innocent of history when he did not distort it or invent it, assigned one of his law clerks to check out every fact and investigate every source in his search for errors in the book. Years later, in 1976, the clerk told me he had spent an entire summer on the task but found no mistakes. Justice Black, who heavily annotated his copy of the book, told me that he refused to read my next book, because of its subtitle: "The Darker Side." A close friend of Black, Professor Edmond Cahn of New York University Law School, tried to persuade him that *Legacy of Suppression* had some merit. Cahn had reviewed the book very favorably[18] and recommended it to Black. In the first draft of his reply to Cahn, Black wrote of *Legacy*, "In brief my judgment is that it is probably one of the most devastating blows that has been delivered against civil liberty in America for a long time." I am not sure whether Black ranked me above or below Joe McCarthy as an enemy of civil liberty. Probably below because he regretted that Levy, "a great libertarian" according to Cahn, had "seen fit to take this completely reactionary view of the First Amendment's purposes." Cahn sought to assure Black that First Amendment libertarianism would survive my book, but the justice moodily replied, "I hope you are right but I am afraid you are not in believing that Dean Levy's book has done no damage to the First Amendment."

Justice Black believed that the book would provide an armory of support for people who wanted the Amendment to mean less than he and Professor Cahn thought that it meant. As proof, Black wondered if Cahn had read the favorable review of the book in the *New Republic* by Alexander Bickel of Yale Law School, who was closely associated with Frankfurter, Black's antagonist on the Court.[19] Black's view of the book showed how selectively and very subjectively one can read. If Black had not read with his absolutist convictions dominating his understanding, he would have seen why Cahn and Commager could appreciate the book, though not necessarily agreeing with all of it. Black would have seen how it was possible for Willmore Kendall and Walter Berns to assault the book from the right.[20] Incidentally, though the book has been cited in several Supreme Court opinions, not even conservative judges have used it to support the results that Black so strongly feared.

[18] *New York Herald Tribune Book Section*, Oct. 16, 1960.
[19] *New Republic*, July 18, 1960.
[20] Kendall's weird review of *Legacy*, in his *Willmore Kendall: Contra Mundum*, Nellie D. Kendall, ed., 290-92, appeared originally in the *Stanford Law Review* for May 1964 and purported to be a review of my *Jefferson and Civil Liberties*. Citations to Berns's three essays on *Legacy* may be found below, in the bibliography; see index under Berns for discussion.

On the contrary, I find delicious irony in the fact that the Supreme Court, speaking through Justice William Brennan, relied on *Legacy* to reach one of its foremost libertarian decisions in a 1964 free-press case. In a turgid yet critical passage, Brennan declared, "If neither factual error nor defamatory content suffices to remove the constitutional shield from criticism of official conduct, the combination of the two elements is no less adequate. This is the lesson to be drawn from the great controversy over the Sedition Act of 1798, 1 Stat. 586, which first crystallized a national awareness of the central meaning of the First Amendment. See Levy *Legacy of Suppression* (1960) at 258 et seq."[21] Brennan said nothing about the Revolution or the First Amendment overturning the common law of seditious libel. His point, rather, was that the First Amendment protected mistaken opinions and even defamation of public officials, and that the proof consisted in the later emergence of a broad new libertarianism which repudiated the Sedition Act. The original intentions of the Framers and the original meaning of the First Amendment meant nothing to the Court; what counted in giving the Amendment content was subsequent opinion: "The central meaning" of the Amendment undermined the Sedition Act because "the attack upon its validity has carried the day in the court of history."[22] Another irony is that the Sedition Act, which played the villainous role here, was far more libertarian than the *Croswell* test,[23] which really carried the day in the court of history until *New York Times v. Sullivan.*

Leonard W. Levy
Andrew W. Mellon Professor of
Humanities and Chairman, Graduate
Faculty of History, Claremont Graduate
School, Claremont, California.

[21] *N.Y. Times Co. v. Sullivan*, 376 U.S. 254 at 273.
[22] *Ibid.*, 276. Justices Goldberg and Douglas, concurring, agreed, *ibid.*, 298 n.1.
[23] On the *Croswell* test, see below, pp. 338-39

Acknowledgements

Because this book is based on *Legacy of Suppression* I have a continuing obligation to acknowledge that Paul Freund and the late Mark Howe, both of Harvard Law School, and my former Brandeis University colleague, John P. Roche, now of Tufts University, read the original version in typescript; their criticisms helped me to improve it. Henry Steele Commager of Amherst College made suggestions that proved to be a lot wiser than I understood at the time. Felix Frankfurter and Max Lerner also offered considerable encouragement.

I have accumulated no comparable debts for *Emergence of a Free Press*. People who borrow their opinions from others can scarcely repay their debts. Fortunately I have none. I must, however, acknowledge that I have read and considered the criticisms that *Legacy* has continued to engender for almost a quarter of a century. A writer in a 1980 issue of *Journalism History* (vol. 7, p. 114), greeting a new book as the latest challenge to *Legacy*, concluded that I had "generated about as much scholarship as anyone in recent memory." Despite the gross exaggeration, *Legacy* has provoked enough criticism for some of it to have been instructive or to require a response. Harold L. Nelson of the University of Wisconsin School of Journalism, the author of a pioneer article on the colonial history of the press (published too late for my use in *Legacy*), used to require his graduate students to write critiques of some aspect of *Legacy* as part of their training. For many years they produced seminar papers, journal articles, master's theses, and doctoral dissertations purporting to challenge *Legacy*. The work of a Nelson protégé, Dwight L. Teeter, now of the University of Texas at Austin helped shape this revision, even though I reject much of what he says. The same may be said of the work of David A.

Anderson, of the University of Texas Law School at Austin, who had the benefit of a reading by both Nelson and Teeter.

Kenneth L. Karst of UCLA Law School helped make this book possible in a different way. At a critical time he assumed many of my duties as editor of our joint project, *The Encyclopedia of the American Constitution* (to be published in 1987), thereby freeing me to write this book. Four others aided more directly. David Gordon typed *Legacy* into the word-processor. Michael DeGolyer, the best research assistant I've ever had the pleasure of working with, brought me books and microforms as needed and typed into the word-processor the revisions and new material that I wrote with a fountain pen. Patrick Delana compiled the bibliography and index, relieving me of those stupefying tasks and earning my gratitude. DeGolyer and Delana worked the word-processor under the supervision of Dennis Mahoney, assistant editor of the Encyclopedia, who occasionally made acerbic comments of considerable value. I could not have finished this book on schedule without the contributions of those named in this paragraph. I have saved for last the name of Lelah Mullican, my secretary, because she did not have to assist but deserves to see her name in print.

Wendy and Leslie, who long ago abandoned interest in helping me, have thoughtfully produced Aaron and Natalie to replace them at a future time.

Contents

EMERGENCE
OF A
FREE PRESS

CHAPTER I

Seditious Libel versus Freedom of Expression

The phrase "freedom of speech" originated in Anglo-American history during the struggle of Parliament to achieve the privilege of free debate, and in that sense it has a history separate from the history of free speech as a civil liberty. Until the last quarter of the eighteenth century, freedom of speech referred not to a civil right but primarily to a parliamentary right: the legislator's immunity from punishment for anything said by him in his official capacity during a legislative session.[1] The citizen's personal right of freedom of speech evolved as an offshoot of freedom of the press and of freedom of religion—the freedom to speak openly on religious matters. The right to speak one's mind freely about government and religion developed very late. To be sure, one can go all the way back to the ancients, especially the Athenians and the Romans of the early Republic, and discover a few statements favoring a broad liberty of expression. The plays of Euripides, for example, are a storehouse of allusions to the glories and values of free speech. The hero of *Ion*, to cite an instance, hopes that his unknown mother may be Athenian so that "by my mother may free speech be mine," else he "bears a bondman's tongue"; and a passage between Jocasta and Polyneices, in *The Pheonissae*, demonstrates the Greek understanding that unwise government results from a curb

---

[1] On the parliamentary right, see J. E. Neale, "The Commons' Privilege of Free Speech in Parliament," in R. W. Seton-Watson, ed., *Tudor Studies* (London, 1924), 257-86; Zechariah Chafee, Jr., *Three Human Rights in the Constitution of 1787* (Lawrence, Kan., 1956), 4-89; Harold Hulme, "The Winning of Freedom of Speech by the House of Commons," *American Historical Review* 61:825-53 (July 1956); and Harold Hulme, *The Life of Sir John Eliot* (New York, 1957), 47-48, 59-60, 248-52, 307-38, and 365-68.

3

on citizens' tongues. Demosthenes declared that no greater calamity could befall a people than "the privation of free speech." Yet there is no evidence that even the most libertarian among the Greeks suffered oral or written sedition to exist with impunity. Plato's account of the punishment of Socrates by the freedom-loving Athenians for the crime of blasphemous or subversive utterances is the best-known case of its kind in history.[2] Machiavelli might have been echoing the ancients as well as representing the best thought of the Renaissance when he qualified the right of every man to "think all things, speak all things, write all things," by pointing out that popular governments are aspersed because the people are free to "speak ill" of them, whereas Princes, though wise to allow the citizen a "liberty to have and sustain the opinions which please him best," must be "talked of with Reserve and Respect."[3]

The phrase "freedom of speech" appeared in a "Proclamation," issued by King James I in 1620, "against excess of Lavish and Licentious Speech of matters of State"; but, the King's point was that "freedome of speech" did not extend to matters of state, which "are no Theames, or subjects fit for vulgar persons, or common meetings. . . ."[4] In 1644 William Walwyn, the Leveller leader, advocated "freedom of discourse" and John Milton "freedom of speaking." Milton in 1673 referred to "freedom of speech" in the sense of a personal rather than a parliamentarian's right. In the eighteenth century this usage, although more common, was still unusual before 1776. Among those who employed it were "Tory Author" and "A Young Gentleman of the Temple" in 1712, John Trenchard and Thomas Gordon collaborating as "Cato" in 1721, an anonymous defender of "Craftsman" in 1731, James Alexander in 1737, James Parker in 1740, Bishop Thomas Hayter in the late 1750s, William Bollan in 1766, and the *Boston Gazette* in 1767.[5]

[2] On Demosthenes, see Thomas Erskine May, *The Constitutional History of England* (New York, 1880), 2:102 n. 1. See generally, Max Radin, "Freedom of Speech in Ancient Athens," *American Journal of Philology* 48:215-30 (1927); and Laura Robinson, *Free Speech in the Roman Republic* (Baltimore, 1940). On Periclean Athens and freedom of expression, see Leonard W. Levy, *Treason Against God: A History of the Offense of Blasphemy* (New York, 1980), 7-15.

[3] Quoted in [Joseph Addison?], *The Thoughts of A Tory Author Concerning the Press: With the Opinion of the Ancients and Moderns, about Freedom of SPEECH and WRITING* (London, 1712), 7, 8.

[4] Dec. 24, 1620, in Frederick S. Siebert, ed., *Documents Relating to the Development of the Relations Between Press and Government in England in the XVIth and XVIIth Centuries* (East Lansing, n.d., multilithed vol.) Chap. III, 37-38, citing British Museum, 21. h1 (6).

[5] All these, together with citations, will be discussed in Chapters Three and Four, below.

Speaking "with Reserve and Respect," as Machiavelli put it, is not speaking freely. Free speech as we understand the term had some basis in everyday experience but remained nearly unknown to legal or constitutional history and to libertarian thought on either side of the Atlantic before 1776. In that year Pennsylvania's Declaration of Rights elevated freedom of speech to constitutional status, but of the original thirteen states only Pennsylvania acted to protect free speech. The First Amendment's guarantee that freedom of speech shall not be abridged was therefore almost without precedent.

Neither freedom of speech nor freedom of press could become a civil liberty until people believed that the truth of their opinions, especially their religious opinions, was relative rather than absolute; until kings and parliaments felt sufficiently strong and stable to be able to ignore political criticism; and until the people considered themselves as the source of sovereignty, the masters rather than the servants of the government. There could be no toleration of dissent when Catholics, Anglicans, and Puritans profoundly believed that the precise shade of belief that each respectively professed must be established as England's only true religion and that all be compelled to accept it for their own salvation as well as for the good of God and the nation. Heresy and nonconformity, severely prosecuted as crimes from the time the Inquisition arrived in England, continued to be crimes after the nationalization of the church under Henry VIII. Whether Catholics or Protestants, or Anglicans or Puritans, controlled the government, the compulsion of conscience for the sake of uniformity necessitated restraints on freedom of speech and press regarding religion. The Reformation, moreover, by making the monarch the head of the established church, converted every religious question into a political one and suffused government policies with religious overtones. As a result, nonconformity and heresy became virtually indistinguishable from sedition and treason. Criticism of the church affected the state and vice versa. Not only did that make criticism dangerous; it made it necessarily wrong when emanating from inferior subjects against their masters. The danger was particularly great for several centuries following the emergence of the national state, when the life of the monarch was in jeopardy, the peace and security of the state precarious. Freedom of religious and political expression was feared as a means of triggering conspiracies, internal disorders, wars, revolutions, or some other disastrous train of events that might pull down church and state.

Just as many torts or private wrongs became crimes, or offenses against the king's peace, so too certain libels became the objects of criminal retribution. As early as 1275 Parliament outlawed "any slanderous News . . . or *false* News or Tales where by discord or occasion of discord or slander may grow between the King and his people or the great men of the Realm . . ." Parliament re-enacted the statute in 1379 for the prevention of the "subversion and destruction of the said realm" by means of false speech.[6] The king's council, which later became the Court of Star Chamber, meted out punishment. These were the earliest statutes making dangerous utterances a crime, and together with the ecclesiastical laws against heresy, blasphemy, and other religious crimes intensified the long history of suppression of opinions deemed pernicious.

The invention of printing, of course, magnified the danger of such opinions. The Crown claimed an authority to control printing presses as a right of prerogative. Henry VIII took over a system for the censorship of heretical manuscripts, long established by the English church and approved by Parliament, and soon applied it to writings on any subject. The manuscript of any work intended for publication had to be submitted to royal officials empowered to censor objectionable passages and to approve or deny a license for the printing of the work. Anything published without an *imprimatur* was criminal. Under Elizabeth the government elaborated the system of prior restraints upon the press, dividing the administration of the complex licensing system among three Crown agencies: the Stationers' Company, a guild of master publishers chartered to monopolize the presses and vested with extraordinary powers of search and seizure; the Court of High Commission, the highest ecclesiastical tribunal, which controlled the Stationers' Company and did the actual licensing; and the Court of Star Chamber which issued decrees defining criminal matter and shared with the Court of High Commission jurisdiction over the trial of offenders. The agencies for enforcement changed during the Puritan Revolution, but the licensing system continued. Under the Restoration, the system was based principally on an act of Parliament, rather than royal prerogative; it continued until 1694.[7] But the expiration of the system at that time did not remotely mean that the press had become free. It remained subject to the restraints of the common law, so-called because it was the law shared in common throughout the realm to distinguish it from local law. The common law was a national or centralized body of non-statutory ("un-

---

[6] Van Vechten Veeder, "History of the Law of Defamation," in *Select Essays in Anglo-American Legal History*, comp. and ed. by a Committee of the Association of American Law Schools (Boston, 1909, 3 vols.), 3:453-54.

[7] For an excellent discussion of the licensing system from its origins in England to its demise in 1694, see Frederick S. Siebert, *Freedom of the Press in England, 1476-1776* (Urbana, 1952), chaps. 2-3, 6-12.

written") and uncodified law devised mainly by the king's royal courts of record in London, especially the Court of Common Pleas (civil jurisdiction) and the Court of King's Bench (criminal jurisdiction), and applied in a supposedly uniform manner by royal judges who served everywhere in the realm.[8]

One might publish without a license, but he did so at the peril of being punished for libel. The point of departure for the modern law of criminal libels was Sir Edward Coke's report of *De Libellis Famosis*, a Star Chamber case of 1606, in which the following propositions were stated. A libel against a private person might be punished criminally on the theory that it provokes revenge and therefore tends, however remotely, to a breach of the peace. But a libel against a government official comprises an even greater offense "for it concerns not only the breach of the peace, but also the scandal of government . . ."[9] The medieval statutes fixed the falsity of the libel as the essence of the crime, but the Star Chamber ruled in 1606 that truth or falsity was not material, because a true statement that damages the reputation of the government or an official is the more dangerous to the public peace. The Star Chamber also ruled that the common law courts possessed concurrent jurisdiction over criminal libels. After Parliament abolished the Star Chamber in 1642, the common-law courts had exclusive jurisdiction and applied Star Chamber doctrines in libel prosecutions.

Four major classes of criminal libel emerged from subsequent decisions in the common-law courts. Blasphemous libel or defamation of religion, together with laws against heresy and the establishment of a state church, made freedom of religious expression a risk.[10] The law of obscene libel protected public morality but crimped literary, artistic, and other forms of personal expression.[11] The law of private libel protected individual reputations by making possible civil suits for damages; but the state could prosecute a gross private libel to prevent supposed bad tendencies toward breach of the peace. The use of the criminal law to avenge the defamation of a person made the libel, in such a case, to be known as a "criminal libel," although the

---

[8] On the common law, see Theodore F. T. Plucknett, *Concise History of the Common Law* (Boston, 1956, 5th ed.); Frederick Pollock and Frederic W. Maitland, *History of English Law Before the Times of Edward I* (Cambridge, Eng. 1895, 2 vols.); William S. Holdsworth, *A History of English Law* (London, 1938-66, 16 vols.); A. K. R. Kiralfy, *Potter's Historical Introduction to English Law and Its Institutions* (London, 1962, 4th ed.).

[9] *De Libellis Famosis*, 3 Coke's *Reports* 254 (1606). See Sir James Fitzjames Stephen, *A History of the Criminal Law of England* (London, 1883, 3 vols.), 2:304-5.

[10] See Levy, *Treason Against God*.

[11] See Norman St. John Stevas, *Obscenity and the Law* (London, 1956).

same term referred collectively to four classes of libel. Thus criminal libel was a redundant subcategory of the broad offense of criminal libel.

By far the most repressive class of libel was seditious libel. It can be defined in a quite elaborate and technical manner in order to take into account the malicious or criminal intent of the accused, the bad tendency of his remarks, and their truth or falsity. But the crime has never been satisfactorily or consistently defined, the necessary result of its inherent vagueness. Seditious libel has always been an accordion-like concept, expandable or contractible at the whim of judges. Judged by actual prosecutions, the crime consisted of defaming or contemning or ridiculing the government: its form, constitution, officers, laws, conduct, or policies, to the jeopardy of the public peace. In effect, any malicious criticism about the government that could be construed to have the bad tendency of lowering it in the public's esteem, holding it up to contempt or hatred, or of disturbing the peace was seditious libel, exposing the speaker or writer to criminal prosecution. Words damaging to the government that tended, however remotely, to cause a breach of the peace, constituted seditious libel according to the courts, but such reasoning explained nothing because *every* crime theoretically breached the king's peace. Criticism of the government that went too far, not the tendency of the words to breach the peace, distinguished the crime of seditious libel, although loose judicial language sometimes suggested otherwise. Loose language invariably characterized the crime, because the government always alleged that the defendant spoke or wrote maliciously, falsely, scandalously, scurrilously, and seditiously, or some combination thereof.

Sergeant William Hawkins, whose chapter on libels in his influential treatise of 1716 became a standard authority, declared,

> Nor can there be any doubt but that a writing which defames a private person only is as much a libel as that which defames persons entrusted in a public capacity, in as much as it manifestly tends to create ill blood, and to cause a disturbance of the public peace; however, it is certain that it is a very high aggravation of a libel that it tends to scandalize the government, by reflecting on those who are entrusted with the administration of public affairs, which does not only endanger the public peace, as all other libels do, by stirring up the parties immediately concerned in it to acts of revenge, but also has a direct tendency to breed in the people a dislike of their governors, and incline them to faction and sedition.[12]

[12] Hawkins, *A Treatise of the Pleas of the Crown* (London, 1716). In the eighteenth century there were reprintings in 1724, 1739, 1762, 1771, 1787, and 1795.

The fact that seditious libel was a crime did not make criticism of the government illegal or even risky. By the early eighteenth century, partisanship and polemics characterized the English press. The press teemed with seditious libels, according to judicial standards, but suffered little from prosecutions. As a matter of practice it was remarkably free and unrestrained; prosecutions tended to be selective and exemplary. Judicial standards probably did not coincide with popular ones; juries sometimes rebelled against judicial instructions, refusing to return verdicts of guilty. Moreover, libelous writers frequently had the protection of powerful factional leaders.

Chief Justice John Holt in Tuchin's case (1704) explained the rationale underlying the concept of seditious libel: "a reflection on the government" must be punished because, "If people should not be called to account for possessing the people with an ill opinion of the government, no government can subsist. For it is very necessary for all governments that the people should have a good opinion of it. And nothing can be worse to any government than to endeavour to procure animosities as to the management of it; this has always been looked upon as a crime, and no government can be safe without it."[13]

Through the seventeenth century, certain seditious libels that could be construed as revealing an intention to "compass" or imagine the death of the king were punished as treason. In 1663 William Twyn, for printing a book that endorsed the right of revolution, was held to have compassed the king's death; Twyn was sentenced to be hanged, cut down while still alive, and then emasculated, disemboweled, quartered, and beheaded—the standard punishment for treason.[14] Algernon Sidney also paid the penalty for treason; his offense was the writing of an unpublished treatise on government discovered in his study.[15] Treason as a purely verbal crime, unconnected with some overt act beyond the words themselves, died out after the execution of John Matthews in 1720, convicted under a special statute rather than at common law.[16] Utterances once held to be treasonable became wholly assimilated within the concept of seditious libel. As a lesser crime or misdemeanor, seditious libel merited less severe punishment: imprisonment, fines, the pillory, and whipping.

But prosecution for seditious libel became the government's prin-

---

[13] *Rex v. Tuchin*, in Thomas Bayly Howell, comp., *A Complete Collection of State Trials to 1783*, continued by T. J. Howell to 1820 (London, 1816-28, 34 vols.), 14:1095, 1128 (1704), quoted in Stephen, *History of the Criminal Law in England*, 2:318.

[14] *Rex v. Twyn*, in Howell, *State Trials*, 6:513, 536 (1663).

[15] *Rex v. Sidney*, in Howell, *State Trials*, 9:818 (1683), discussed by Stephen, *History of the Criminal Law in England*, 2:409-11.

[16] *Rex v. Mathews*, Howell, *State Trials*, 15:1323 (1719).

cipal instrument for controlling the press. According to Frederick S. Siebert's excellent study of freedom of the press in England, "convictions for seditious libel ran into the hundreds" in both the seventeenth and eighteenth centuries.[17] That probably exaggerated the number of eighteenth-century convictions for seditious libel. Of the period 1700-1730, Siebert said, "Only occasionally was it necessary for the government to crack the whip of seditious libel to remind printers and publishers of their proper function." Of the period 1730-60, he said, it "witnessed the beginning of the revolt of juries and the failure of prosecutions. . . ." A conviction in 1754 he described as "the first to be obtained from a London jury in twenty-seven years."[18] A wide disparity existed between the number of informations filed for seditious libel and the actual number of prosecutions; there was also a disparity between the number of prosecutions and the actual number of convictions. The number of informations undoubtedly "ran into the hundreds." Being arrested, called into court, and forced to pay costs on the dismissal of the information could have an intimidating effect even if the prosecution proceeded no further. In other words, trials, let alone convictions, were not necessary for the law of seditious libel to operate oppressively. One prosecutorial trick was to charge a person with seditious libel, persuade him to leave the country in order to avoid trial, and then outlaw him if he left, thereby preventing his return.[19]

The procedure in prosecuting a seditious libel was extremely objectionable to libertarian theorists, more so than the fact that the ac-

[17] Siebert, *Freedom of the Press*, 365.

[18] Siebert, *Freedom of the Press*, 381-83. The 1754 case was *Rex* v. *Nutt*, referred to by Chief Justice Mansfield in *Rex* v. *Dean of St. Asaph* as the first conviction in twenty-seven years, Howell, *State Trials*, 21:847, 1038 (1783).

[19] Lucyle Werkmeister, *The London Daily Press, 1772-1792* (Lincoln, Neb., 1963), 318-19. Reliance on Howell, *State Trials* to determine either the number of cases of seditious libel or the number of indictments explicitly using the term "seditious libel" is amateurish. Gerald J. Baldasty, "A Theory of Press Freedom: Massachusetts Newspapers and Law, 1782-1791," unpublished M.A. Thesis, University of Wisconsin, 1974, counted twenty-eight cases in Howell between 1588 and 1770 in only eleven of which the word "seditious" appeared in the indictments, but in twenty-five of which "breach of the peace" or an equivalent appeared. Baldasty concluded that "seditious libel" is a misnomer for the cases and that criminal defamation of the government was punishable because it breached the peace of the realm. Apart from the fact that all crimes breached the peace, at least in theory, the fact is that most cases of seditious libel were not reported in Howell, *State Trials*. I have examined several pamphlets with the same or similar title, *The Proceedings in* [or *of*] *the Old Bailey* [various spellings], covering the years 1683-98, in which there are references to more than eleven prosecutions for "seditious libel." For many more such prosecutions of the 1790s not reported by Howell, see Werkmeister, *London Daily Press*, 325-77.

cused could be punished for words alone.[20] From 1662 until a century
later the secretary of state possessed the power of ferreting out seditious libels by issuing warrants that authorized a search of the homes
and offices of all suspects and the arrest of anyone on the mere suspicion of being implicated in the writing, publishing, or circulation
of such libels. General warrants, the use of which was severely restricted in felony cases, were employed promiscuously in cases of
seditious libel, a misdemeanor. Search, seizure, and arrest were used
to harass anti-administration writers and editors against whom the
evidence might not warrant a trial. But the government did not remain restricted to trying only those indicted or presented by a grand
jury. Alternatively, the attorney-general might proceed against all
misdemeanors by an information, that is, by determining the libelous
character of a publication, bringing it to the attention of the Court
of the King's Bench, and securing a warrant for the arrest and trial
of the offender. Prosecuting by information rather than by indictment bypassed the Englishman's beloved institution, the grand jury,
which in felony cases stood between him and the government.

At the trial of a seditious libel, the defendant was not even judged
by his peers in any meaningful way. Despite the ambiguity of earlier
practice, judges in the eighteenth century permitted juries to decide
only the fact of the publication. That is, the only question that the
jury passed upon was whether the defendant did or did not publish
the remarks charged against him and whether they carried the innuendo as alleged. The judges reserved exclusively for themselves as
a matter of law the decision on the crucial question whether the defendant's remarks were seditious because maliciously intended and
of a bad tendency. In 1731 in the case of *Rex v. Francklin*, for example, Chief Justice Thomas Raymond said in his charge to the jury
that

> . . . in this information for libel there are three things to be con-
> sidered, whereof two by you the jury, and one by the court. The
> first thing under your consideration is whether the defendant Mr.
> Francklin is guilty of the publication of this Craftsman or not? The

[20] My account of the law of seditious libel and the procedure of prosecution
is based on a great number of the tracts and books discussed in Chapters Three
and Four. Particularly useful were [Anon.], *State Law: Or, the Doctrine of
Libels, Discussed and Examined* (London, n.d. [1729], 2nd ed.), 136 pp; (John
Raynor), *A Digest of the Law concerning Libels. By a Gentleman of the Inner-
Temple* (Dublin, 1778), 139 pp.; and Father of Candor, *A Letter Concerning
Libels, Warrants, the Seizure of Papers and Sureties for the Peace of Behaviour*
(London, 1771, 7th ed.), reprinted in *A Collection of Interesting Political
Tracts* (probably edited by J. Almon) (London, 1773), 1:1-164.

second is, whether the expressions in that letter refer to his present majesty and his principal officers and ministers of state, and are applicable to them or not? . . . But then there is a third thing, to wit, whether these defamatory expressions amount to a libel or not? This does not belong to the office of the jury, but to the office of the Court; because it is a matter of law, and not of fact; . . . and there is redress to be had in another place if either of the parties are not satisfied; for we are not to invade one another's province, as is now of late a notion among some people who ought to know better.[21]

The judges also refused to permit the defendant to plead the truth as a defense.[22] Indeed, they proceeded on the theory that the truth of a libel made it even worse because it was more provocative, thereby increasing the tendency to breach of the peace or exacerbating the scandal against the government. As a result of these rules applicable to criminal or crown libels, a man might be arrested on a general warrant, prosecuted on an information without the consent of a grand jury, and convicted for his political opinions by judges appointed by the government he had aspersed.

Thus the disappearance of the prior restraints that had been imposed by the licensing system until 1694 did not meaningfully free the press. Theoretically one might say or print what he pleased, but he was responsible to the common law for allegedly malicious, scurrilous, scandalous, or derogatory utterances which supposedly tended towards the contempt, ridicule, hatred, scorn, or disrepute of other persons, religion, government, or morality. Blackstone, the oracle of the common law in the minds of the American Framers, summarized the law of Crown libels as follows:

Where blasphemous, immoral, treasonable, schismatical, seditious, or scandalous libels are punished by the English law . . . the liberty of the press, properly understood, is by no means infringed or violated. The *liberty of the press* is indeed essential to the nature of a free state; but this consists in laying no *previous* restraints upon publications, and not in freedom from censure for criminal matter when published. Every freeman has an undoubted right to lay what sentiments he pleases before the public: to forbid this is to destroy

[21] Howell, *State Trials*, 17:626, 671, 672.
[22] In the case of *Rex* v. *Owen* in Howell, *State Trials*, 18:1203 (1752), the court instructed the jury to bring in a verdict of guilty, but the jury rebelled and decided on a "not guilty" verdict based on their judgment that the allegedly seditious words did not constitute a libel as matter of law or fact. In another report of the same case, the jury "thought there was truth and reason in the pamphlet before them, which had been deemed a libel; and therefore . . . brought in the bookseller not guilty." *Ibid.*, 21:853.

the freedom of the press: but if he publishes what is improper, mischievous, or illegal, he must take the consequences of his own temerity. . . . But to punish (as the law does at present) any dangerous or offensive writings, which, when published, shall on a fair and impartial trial[23] be adjudged of a pernicious tendency, is necessary for the preservation of peace and good order, a government and religion, the only solid foundations of civil liberty. Thus the will of individuals is still left free; the abuse only of that free-will is the object of legal punishment. Neither is any restraint hereby laid upon freedom of thought or enquiry: liberty of private sentiment is still left; the disseminating, or making public, of bad sentiments, destructive of the ends of society, is the crime which society corrects.[24]

Samuel Johnson believed the law too liberal. "It seems not more reasonable," he complained, "to leave the right of printing unrestrained, because writers may be afterwards restrained, than it would be to sleep with doors unbolted, because by our laws, we can hang a thief."[25]

The common law's definition of freedom of the press meant merely the absence of censorship in advance of publication. But the presence of punishment afterwards, for "bad sentiments," oral or published, had an effect similar to a law authorizing previous restraints. A man who may be whipped and jailed for what he says or prints is not likely to feel free to express his opinions even if he does not need a government license to do so. The common-law definition of freedom of the press left the press at the mercy of the Crown's prosecutors and judges. Freedom of discussion and the law of libel simply conflicted; the first could not conceptually coexist with the second.

Parliament restrained speech and press as did the common-law courts. Both Lords and Commons combined the functions of prosecutor, judge, and jury, with the result that prosecutions before either house could be more effective than in the courts. In the Woodfall case, for example, the defendant, prosecuted on an information for seditious libel, was saved from a conviction when the jury returned a verdict of "guilty of printing and publishing *only*"; but the Com-

---

[23] Blackstone's endorsement of a "fair and impartial" trial was meaningless to the libertarians of the time, since he explicitly repudiated one of their two major gauges of fairness, the right of the defendant to prove the truth of his alleged libel; moreover, Blackstone ignored the other libertarian gauge of fairness at a time when it was the principal issue of contention: the right of the jury rather than of the judge to decide the criminality of the alleged libel.

[24] Sir William Blackstone, *Commentaries on the Laws of England* (London, 1765-69), book 4, chap. II, 151-152. Reprinted in Leonard W. Levy, ed., *Freedom of the Press from Zenger to Jefferson* (Indianapolis, 1966), 104-5.

[25] Quoted by Robert R. Rea, *The English Press in Politics, 1760-1774* (Lincoln, Neb., 1963), 6.

mons, prosecuting him in 1774 for the same offense, imprisoned him and exacted costs of 72 pounds.[26] Theoretically, Parliament did not prosecute for the common-law crime of libel; it directed its punitive powers against contempt of its authority or reputation resulting from a breach of its privileges. In practice, however, the distinction between a verbal contempt, breaching parliamentary privilege, and the crime of seditious libel could be negligible.

"Parliamentary privilege," an omnibus term, referred to a bundle of rights that each house claimed and exercised.[27] Among these were freedom from arrest, access to the executive, passing upon the credentials of members, freedom of speech, and the power of punishing both members and nonmembers for violations of privileges. The English Bill of Rights of 1689 secured to members their freedom of speech, after more than a century of struggle highlighted by the martyrdom of Sir John Eliot. After 1689 the problem was not that the Crown infringed on Parliament's free speech, but that Parliament did not permit freedom of speech to nonmembers. It prohibited the unauthorized reporting of parliamentary proceedings. Reflections on either house or any of its members or on the government generally, in other words, seditious libels, fell subject to prosecution by the house itself. The guilty parties were summoned, examined, and tried in a summary fashion; their criminal publications were burned by the hangman at the order of the house, the party humiliated, usually on his knees, and forced to pay costs. He could also be imprisoned indefinitely by the Lords, but only for the life of the session by the Commons. Commons and Lords, wrote Frederick Siebert, after about 1730 were the "principal deterrents to free and open discussion of political questions through the power to punish a printer for what today would be considered harmless discussions of public issues. . . . All in all, Parliament seems to have exerted almost as great a pressure on printers and publishers in the eighteenth century as did the common-law courts."[28] In the colonies, the assemblies menaced freedom of discussion far more than the common-law courts.[29]

[26] *Rex* v. *Woodfall*, Howell, *State Trials*, 20:895 (1770), and Siebert, *Freedom of the Press*, 371-72.

[27] See, generally, Mary Patterson Clarke, *Parliamentary Privilege in the American Colonies* (New Haven, 1943), and Carl Wittke, *The History of English Parliamentary Privilege* (Columbus: Ohio State University Bulletin, vol. 26, no. 2, 1921).

[28] Siebert, *Freedom of the Press*, 368. But in the last quarter of the eighteenth century, Parliament "quietly abdicated its functions as a prosecutor and judge of seditious libels in favor of the attorney general and common-law courts." *Ibid.*, 374.

[29] This point is largely the subject of Chapter Two, below.

Prosecutions for breach of parliamentary privilege and for criminal utterances certainly fettered speech and press, but could not suppress criticism of the government. In England and her colonies, the king's subjects were so interested in politics and so convinced by their glorious, if largely rhetorical, traditions of freedom that an astonishing degree of open and robust discussion existed, considering the restraints. Law in the books and law in practice, one must always remember, were not the same. Even a flurry of actual prosecutions could have only a lingering rather than an enduring effect, as in the case of persecution for the cause of conscience. It would be an exaggeration to say that speech and press were free as a matter of common experience, although fettered by the law. It would be closer to the truth to say that the concept of freedom of speech or of the press was so little known that even libertarian theory regarded the right to express seditious sentiments as an intolerable indulgence in licentiousness.

CHAPTER II

The American Colonial Experience

The presistent image of colonial America as a society in which freedom of expression was cherished is an hallucination of sentiment that ignores history. The evidence provides little comfort for the notion that the colonies hospitably received advocates of obnoxious or detestable ideas on matters that counted. Nor is there reason to believe that rambunctious unorthodoxies suffered only from Puritan bigots and tyrannous royal judges. The American people simply did not believe or understand that freedom of thought and expression means equal freedom for the other person, especially the one with hated ideas.

To be sure, the utmost freedom often existed on the frontier, but the test of free speech is not the right to soliloquize or shout outrageous ideas from the top of a lonely mountain; it is, rather, the right to speak openly and with impunity among neighbors. Colonial America was the scene of the most extraordinary diversity of opinion on religion, politics, social structure, and other vital subjects, but every community, particularly outside of the few "cities," tended to be a tight little island clutching its own respective orthodoxy and too eager to banish or extralegally punish unwelcome dissidents. As John P. Roche said so strikingly, "Colonial America was an open society dotted with closed enclaves, and one could generally settle with his co-believers in safety and comfort and exercise the right of oppression."[1]

---

[1] Roche, "American Liberty: An Examination of the 'Tradition' of Freedom," in M. R. Konvitz and C. Rossiter, eds., *Aspects of Liberty* (Ithaca, 1958), 137.

Where the community suffered vigorously expressed nonconformist opinions to exist, they were likely to run afoul of the law. In
colonial America, as in England, the common law of criminal libel
was strung out like a chicken wire of constraint against the captious
and the chancy, making the open discussion of public issues potentially hazardous except when public opinion opposed administration
policy. However, the judiciary in America, particularly in the eighteenth century, was not the agency that menaced those who would
disturb an acquiescent public opinion. It is an old saw, of course, and
an inaccurate one, that "Colonial times were rife with a continuing
struggle between the royal judges and American writers and printers,
who demanded freedom to criticize."[2] There may have been hundreds of trials for seditious libel in England during both the seventeenth and eighteenth centuries, but in America before the Revolution, the number was insignificant, probably not more than half a
dozen. The notoriety of the Zenger trial derives in part because it was
so isolated a phenomenon. The Zenger case was the last of its kind
under the royal judges, excepting the aborted trial of Alexander Mc-
Dougall in 1771.[3] On the eve of the Revolution some zealous prosecutors and judges sought indictments, but grand juries, representing
public opinion, thwarted them. Thus, "Court trials for seditious libel
ended as a serious threat to printers in the American colonies with
the Zenger case," as Harold L. Nelson pointed out.[4]

The traditionally maligned judges, as a matter of fact, behaved
virtually as angels of self-restraint when compared with the intolerance of community opinion or the tyranny of governors who, acting
in a quasi-judicial capacity with their Councils, were a much more
dreaded and active instrument of suppression than the common-law
courts. Yet the most suppressive body by far, surpassing even the
prerogative court of governor-and-council, was that acclaimed bas-
tion of the people's liberties: the popularly elected assembly. That
the law bore down harshly on verbal crimes in colonial America was
mainly the result of the inquisitorial propensities of the nonjudicial
branches, which ferreted out slights on the government. The law of
seditious libel, particularly in the eighteenth century, was enforced
in America chiefly by the provincial legislatures exercising their
power of punishing alleged breaches of parliamentary privilege, secondly, by the executive officers in concert with the upper houses,

[2] John Kelly, "Criminal Libel and Free Speech," *Kansas Law Review* 6 (1958):
306.
[3] See below, pp. 75-81.
[4] Harold L. Nelson, "Seditious Libel in Colonial America," *American Journal
of Legal History* 3(1959):160-72, a pathbreaking article; quotation at p. 164.

and lastly, a poor third, by the common-law courts. The courts gathered a very few seditious scalps and lost as many to acquittals; but the assemblies, like the House of Commons which they emulated, needing no grand jury to indict and no petty jury to convict, racked up a far larger score. The power of the legislature to punish breach of privilege or contempts, as Nelson said, was "the most efficacious of all colonial controls."[5]

Zealously pursuing its prerogative of being immune to criticism, an Assembly might summon, interrogate, and fix criminal penalties against anyone who had supposedly libeled its members, proceedings, or the government generally. Any words, written, printed, or spoken, that were imagined to have a tendency of impeaching an assembly's behavior, questioning its authority, derogating from its honor, affronting its dignity, or defaming its members, individually or together, were regarded as a seditious scandal against the government, punishable as a breach of privilege. The historian of *Parliamentary Privilege in the American Colonies* concluded, in guarded understatement, "Literally scores of persons, probably hundreds, throughout the colonies were tracked down by the various messengers and sergeants and brought into the house to make inglorious submission for words spoken in the heat of anger or for writings which intentionally or otherwise had given offense."[6]

The practice began with the first assembly that ever met on American soil, when the Virginia House of Burgesses, in 1620, adjudged a Captain Henry Spellman guilty of "treasonable words" and stripped him of his rank.[7] Cavalier Virginia simply did not tolerate dissent. Governor William Berkeley's often quoted statement of 1671 suggests the attitude of the Old Dominion's government. Replying to a query put to him by the Lords Commissioners of Foreign Plantations on the state of religion, he wrote that it might be better and added, "But, I thank God, there are no free schools nor *printing*, and I hope we shall not have these hundred years; for *learning* has brought disobedience, and heresy, and sects into the world, and *printing* has divulged them, and libels against the best government. God keep us from both."[8]

In 1660 the House of Burgesses had committed a man for "scan-

---

[5] *Ibid.*, 163-64.

[6] Mary Patterson Clarke, *Parliamentary Privilege in the American Colonies* (New Haven, 1943), 117.

[7] H. R. McIlwaine and J. P. Kennedy, eds., *Journals of the House of Burgesses of Virginia, 1619-1776* (Richmond, 1905-15), vol. 1(1619-1659):15.

[8] Quoted in William Waller Hening, *The Statutes at Large Being a Collection of All the Laws of Virginia (1619-1792)* (Richmond, 1809-23), 2:517.

dalous, mutinous, and seditious" words; he had criticized the House
on a tax matter.[9] Even a member of the governor's Council was wise
to curb his tongue. Colonel Philip Ludwell, who thoughtlessly called
Governor Herbert Jeffreys a lawbreaker, was convicted and heavily
fined in 1678 by his fellow councillors for scandalizing the government.[10] In 1682 a printer named Buckner who had the temerity to
publish unlicensed the laws of the colony was forced to post a bond
of 100 pounds to be forfeit should he ever print anything in the
future.[11] In 1685 the governor, Francis Lord Howard of Effingham,
issued a proclamation condemning the "over lycentiousnesse of the
People in their discourses" and reminded the public that any remark
tending to sedition was criminal.[12] A proclamation of 1690 ordered
grand juries to indict as a seditious person anyone who spoke contemptuously about the laws. Because seditious utterances were ordi-
narily tried before local justices of the peace, there is no way of
estimating the frequency of prosecutions. Only cases seriously affecting the state were brought to the attention of either the House of
Burgesses or the Council. In 1693 Thomas Rooke was convicted by
the House for having spoken abusively against it. The burgesses
forced him to kneel before them and beg forgiveness, yet imprisoned
him anyway after his abject apology.[13] In a case of 1699 the Council
deputized one of its members to arrest and subject to "condign punishment" four individuals alleged to have stirred up sedition by
spreading an "evill opinion" of the government.[14] In 1702 the Council accused William Byrd of spreading "seditious" reports and turned
him over to the burgesses to vindicate the honor of the government.
Byrd was forced to humble himself before the bar of the House.[15]
In 1704 a grand jury refused to indict Robert Beverly, even though
his remarks were "false, scandalous, and malitious." The jurors, convinced that the people were loyal to the government, could not believe that Beverly threatened the public peace. The case was unique;

[9] *Ibid.*, 2:15. Case of Edward Prescotte, 1660. For related events of an earlier
date, see 1:360-361 and 380. For a 1666 case see Philip A. Bruce, *Institutional
History of Virginia in the Seventeenth Century* (New York, 1910, 2 vols.),
2:448, involving Thomas Folkes.

[10] H. R. McIlwaine and W. L. Hall, eds., *Executive Journals of the Council
of Colonial Virginia, 1680-1754* (Richmond, 1925-45), 1:468-78.

[11] William Waller Hening, ed. *The Statutes at Large, Being a Collection of
All the Laws of Virginia*, 2:518, Proclamation of 12 Oct. 1685.

[12] McIlwaine, ed., *Executive Journals of the Council*, 1:75.

[13] *Bruce, Institutional History*, 2:449.

[14] *Ibid.*, 1:438.

[15] Beverly Fleet, compiler, *Virginia Colonial Abstracts* (Richmond, 1937-52,
34 vols.), 7:23-24.

never before or after was a criminal utterance said to have no tendency to breach of the peace. Beverly merely lost his job as a court clerk.[16]

In the same year occurred the strange case of the Reverend John Munro. Andrew Hamilton, John Peter Zenger's counsel in 1735, had Munro's case in mind when vividly describing to a New York jury the first prosecution in America for libeling a governor. Munro's story was that he had the misfortune to meet Governor Francis Nicholson on a road, only to be abused without reason. When the parson was asked why he had not ridden away, he replied that the governor, who was known to have killed men in cold blood, was armed and would have shot him. In another conversation Munro cast other "odious reflections" on the governor. For Munro's remarks, the attorney general of Virginia accused him of stirring sedition. Somehow an order from England ended the prosecution when Nicholson was recalled.[17] Shortly after, Benjamin Cartwright was convicted for his opprobrious language about public officials. He was sentenced to be lashed and pay costs. By recanting he escaped corporal punishment.[18]

In neighboring Maryland during the seventeenth century there was as little freedom of expression as in Virginia. A man who vilified the government in 1666 received thirty-nine lashes. Such cases were not unusual.[19] In 1689 a disaffected group calling itself the Protestant Association, led by John Coode, who had been tried earlier for seditious speech and blasphemy, revolted against Lord Baltimore's proprietary government. In their declaration of reasons for taking up arms, the rebels specified a grievance that suggests that open political debate had been scotched in Maryland. Referring to harsh laws that had been severely enforced, they singled out "especially one that against all Sense, Equity, Reason, and Law Punishes all Speeches, Practices, and Attempts relating to his Lordship and Government, that shall be thought Mutinous and Seditious. . . ." Among the punishments actually meted out had been "Whipping, Branding, Boreing

[16] *Ibid.*, 7:404.

[17] *Ibid.*, 7:42. Hamilton's description of the unnamed case, narrated with amusing embellishments, appears in Stanley Nider Katz, ed., *A Brief Narrative of the Case and Trial of John Peter Zenger* (Cambridge, Mass. 1970, 2nd ed.), 93-94. At pp. 228-29 n. 49, Katz surmised that the case involved a clergyman named John Gourdon in 1699 and credited me with informing him that Hamilton had in mind the case of Francis Makemie, discussed below, pp. 35-36. Without doubt Munro's case was the right one.

[18] Fleet, comp., *Virginia Colonial Abstracts*, 11:3.

[19] See William Hand Browne, *et al.*, eds., *Archives of Maryland* (Baltimore, 1883-), 2:55, 4:309 and 321; 65:15-16.

through the Tongue, Fine, Imprisonment, Banishment, or Death," making unsafe the "Words and Actions" of everyone.[20] In 1696 a man who verbally abused the Maryland Assembly was fined a thousand pounds' worth of tobacco.[21] In 1698 Gerard Slye and Philip Clark, former associates of Coode, were again in trouble for aspersing Governor Francis Nicholson. The governor's Council issued warrants for their arrest, charging them with extravagant and scandalous words that disturbed the government. Clark, a member of the Assembly and a "mighty pretender to law, especially Magna Carta," was convicted, after trial, and sentenced to imprisonment for six months. Although Slye confessed his guilt before the Council, he was bound over for trial. He then compounded his offense by writing fresh articles against the governor, deemed by that official to be "part false, part scandalous, and all malicious." When Slye heard his sentence, after conviction, of a fine plus five months in prison, he again confessed, pleaded for mercy, and made a public submission. He made bond for good behavior, paid his fine, and had his imprisonment remitted. The Assembly resented the sentence of Clark, one of its members, as a breach of parliamentary privilege, but the governor's Council rejected the Assembly's appeal as based on pretended authority. Clark was not just a convicted felon, according to the Council; he was a rebel against government, because rebellions began when disaffected people scandalized and rendered odious those in authority.[22]

A glance at New York and Pennsylvania indicates that speech and press were as unfree there during the seventeenth century as in the South. Prosecutions for "speaking seditious words" began in New York under the first governor and were continuing at the close of the century. In the case of one Peter Chocke, who had denied the governor's authority and called him the worst in the history of the province, the Quarter Sessions Court of Westchester decided that the "words vented by the said Chocke" were so "highly Criminall" as to warrant being tried by the highest court of the province.[23]

[20] "The Declaration of the Reasons and Motives for the Present Appearing in Arms of Their Majesties Protestant Subjects in the Province of Maryland," 1689, in Charles M. Andrews, ed., *Narratives of the Insurrections, 1675-1690* (New York, 1915), 309.

[21] Browne, ed., *Archives of Maryland*, 19:368.

[22] J. W. Fortescue, ed., *Calendar of State Papers, Colonial Series, America and the West Indies* (27 Oct. 1697 to 31 Dec. 1698), preserved in the Public Records Office (London, 1905), 392, 399, 412-13, 503, 525.

[23] Julius Goebel, Jr., and T. Raymond Naughton, *Law Enforcement in Colonial New York* (New York, 1944), 152. For other references to cases of seditious speech, see p. 62 nn. 12 and 13, and p. 99 n. 178.

Prior censorship, of course, rigorously restrained the press. Until the appointment of Governor William Burnet, in 1719, every governor from Thomas Dongan's time had been instructed to permit no press, book, pamphlets, or other printed matter "without your especial leave & license first obtained."[24] In 1685, three years after the first settlement under Penn's propietorship, John Curtis of Philadelphia was prosecuted for "speaking treasonable words."[25]

A year later Pennsylvania's troubles began with its first printer, William Bradford. His initial publication, an almanac, was censored while still in manuscript, and he was warned "not to print anything but what shall have Lycence from ye Councill."[26] Penn himself had presided over a Council meeting in 1683 when it was ordered that the laws of the colony should not be printed.[27] In 1689 Bradford found himself in trouble for having printed at the request of Joseph Growdon, a councillor, a copy of the "Frame of Government" of 1682, with comments by Growdon. The latter, on being interrogated by Governor John Blackwell at a session of the Council, refused, even under threat of censure, to answer any questions concerning the un-licensed publication "of a dangerous nature."[28] Blackwell, knowing Bradford to be the printer, for there were no others south of Boston, summoned him next, only to find him as intractable as Councillor Growdon. Repeatedly invoking the common-law privilege against self-incrimination, as had Growdon, Bradford resisted the governor's alternating cajolery and threats. At one point the suspect stated that he knew of no one's having been appointed Imprimatur, whereupon Blackwell burst out, "Sir, I am 'Imprimatur'; and that you shall know." A moment later he added, "Sir, I have particular order from Governor Penn for the suppressing of printing here, and narrowly to look after your press, and I will search your house, look after your press, and make you give in five hundred pounds security to print nothing but what I allow, or I'll lay you fast."[29] Whether Bradford

[24] "Instructions to Governor Dongan," 1686, in E. B. O'Callaghan and B. Fernow, eds., *Documents Relative to the Colonial History of the State of New York* (Albany, 1856-87), 3:375. See also 5:142.

[25] David Paul Brown, *The Forum: Or, Forty Years Full Practice at the Philadelphia Bar* (Philadelphia, 1856), 1:267.

[26] *Minutes of the Provincial Council of Pennsylvania* (Harrisburg, 1838-40), 1:115.

[27] *Ibid.*, 1:18.

[28] *Ibid.*, 1:278.

[29] "The examination of William Bradford before Governor Blackwell, at Philadelphia, the 9th of the Second month, 1689, concerning printing the Charter," Framed MS hung in hall of New York Historical Society. Reprinted in Brown, *The Forum*, 1:276-79, and in John William Wallace, *An Address Delivered at the Celebration by the New York Historical Society, May 20,*

was forced to post bond in so high an amount is unknown, but he was sufficiently discouraged to give up and return to England. Shortly, however, he was back in Pennsylvania. A year later, his press seized by the government, he was in jail, charged with seditious libel and awaiting trial as a defendant in what was one of the earliest criminal trials in America involving freedom of the press.[30]

Bradford had supported a separatist faction among the Quakers led by George Keith, whose heretical views caused his dismissal as headmaster of the Friends' school in Philadelphia. Forbidden to speak at Quaker meetings, he and a follower, Thomas Budd, publicized their position through a number of tracts published by Bradford, although without his name on them. In one of these, *An Appeal from the twenty-eight Judges to the Spirit of Truth*, Keith predicted that the name of Deputy Governor Thomas Lloyd "would stink"; he also contended that ministers should not be magistrates and accused them of monopolizing the magisterial power. As a result, Keith, Budd, Bradford, and several of their faction were arrested in 1692. The warrant for their commitment alleged their guilt for "Publishing, Uttering, & Spreading a Malitious and Seditious paper . . . Tending to the Disturbance of the Peace and Subversion of the present Government."[31] The prisoners were summarily convicted "without All Hearing or Tryal" by a court composed of eight magistrates, six of whom were the very ministers accused by Keith. He and the other defendants, excepting Bradford and a MacComb who had circulated the tract, were sentenced to humiliation in the public market place, there to be proclaimed by the common crier as seditious persons, dis-

---

1863, of the Two Hundredth Birth Day of Mr. William Bradford (Albany, 1863), 49-52. No record of the examination appears in the *Minutes of the Provincial Council of Pennsylvania.*

[30] Matt Bushnell Jones, *Thomas Maule, The Salem Quaker and Free Speech in Massachusetts Bay* (Salem, 1936, 42 pp.; reprinted from Essex Institute Historical Collections, vol. 72, no. 1, Jan. 1936), 13, mistakenly claimed that Maule's trial of 1696, reviewed below, was "the first criminal action involving freedom of the press to be tried in the American colonies." In all likelihood there were probably similar trials before Bradford's. As a matter of fact, there were much earlier trials, such as Wheelwright's in 1637, mentioned below, involving freedom of speech, as contrasted with freedom of the press, but raising the same broad issues.

[31] The characterization of Lloyd is at p. 6 and the warrant, dated Aug. 24, 1692, is reproduced at p. 4 of *New England's Spirit of Persecution Transmitted to Pennsylvania, And the Pretended Quaker found persecuting the True Christian-Quaker, in the Tryal of Peter Boss, George Keith, Thomas Budd and William Bradford . . . 1693. Giving an Account of the most Arbitrary Procedure of that Court* (Philadelphia, 1693, printed by William Bradford), 38 pp. Ascribed to George Keith and Thomas Budd.

turbers of the peace, subverters of the government, and enemies to the king.[32] Bradford and MacComb escaped sentence by demanding their rights under Magna Carta to a trial by jury. The judges reluctantly consented, although one of them observed that the prisoners deserved to have their backs lashed instead.[33]

After four months in jail, Bradford came to trial at the end of 1692. Keith and his associates were also defendants, new presentments having been made against them for the same tracts under a statute prohibiting defamation of the magistrates. Tried separately, after the others were convicted and fined five pounds each, Bradford managed his case with considerable skill and daring. He immediately challenged two of the jurors on the ground of having prejudged his case, because they had been overheard expressing the opinion that Keith and his followers were enemies of the government. One of the two jurors, acknowledging the statement attributed to him, requested to be discharged, but the court, the same Quaker magistrates who had presided at the earlier stage of the case, refused. The prosecutor then demanded of Bradford whether he had ever heard any of the jurors say that he had printed the seditious tract, "for that is only what they are to find."[34] In reply, Bradford, for the first time in an American libel trial, raised the contention that the jury was to try the whole of the matter, the criminality of the publication as well as the defendant's responsibility for it.

> BRADFORD. "That is not only what they are to find, they are to find also, whether this be a seditious paper, or not, & whether it does tend to the weakening of the hands of the Magistrate."
> ATTORNEY. "No, that is matter of Law, which the Jury is not to meddle with, but find whether W.B. printed it or not, and the Bench is to judge whether it be a seditious Paper or not; for the Law has determined what is a Breach of the Peace, and the penalty, which the Bench only is to give judgment on."
> JUDGE JENNINGS. "You are only to try, whether W.B. printed it, or not."
> BRADFORD. "That is wrong; for the Jury are Judges in Law, as well as in matter of Fact."[35]

Unable to get a favorable ruling from the court, Bradford continued his own defense, arguing that the tract had not been seditious

---

[32] Proclamation read by the crier, *ibid.*, 6.

[33] *Ibid.*, 10.

[34] *Ibid.*, 33. The trials were held Dec. 6-10, 1692.

[35] *Ibid.*, 33-34. Page 33 is misnumbered as p. 31 in the rare tract reporting the trial.

and that there was no evidence to show that he had been the printer. When the prosecution introduced the frame or form containing the pages set in type, which the sheriff had seized in Bradford's office, the printer demanded that evidence be adduced to prove he had set the type. Thus, Bradford's defense, unlike the later Zenger defense, did not rest on an admission of his responsibility for the printing, counterbalanced by a claim that he had a right to print what he pleased if truthful. In other words, the charge of seditious printing raised an issue of freedom of the press that was not argued.

Judge Samuel Jennings, in instructing the jury, surprisingly accepted Bradford's point that they might find whether the tract was seditious as well as the fact of his responsibility.[36] The jury deadlocked at nine to three for a conviction, and after forty-eight hours were discharged without having reached a verdict. There is a story that Bradford was saved by a sympathetic juror who, while examining the typeform that was used to print the tract, accidentally shoved the bottom of the form with his cane, whereupon it came apart and all the type collapsed to the floor, and with it, the prosecution's case.[37]

Bradford asked the court for a release from prison with his printing tools restored, but he was recommitted to await a new trial. After about a year had passed from the time of his arrest, he was suddenly released without a second trial. His rescuer was Governor Benjamin Fletcher of New York, who, on the suspension of Penn's charter, had been given control of Pennsylvania. Fletcher, needing an official press in New York, prevailed upon the Pennsylvania Council to restore Bradford's liberty and property,[38] and he promptly left the City of Brotherly Love for a new career as a royal printer. In his new home, he established the *New-York Gazette*, which was the province's only newspaper until the appearance in 1733 of Zenger's *Journal*. Chastened by his experiences in Pennsylvania, Bradford allowed his paper to be a licensed administration organ. When Zenger was prosecuted for seditious libel, old William Bradford condemned him for having published "pieces tending to set the province in a flame, and to raise sedition and tumults."[39] Bradford may have been the first American martyr to the cause of a free press and the earliest advocate of the jury's power to decide the law in libel cases; but there is nothing in

[36] *Ibid.*, 36.

[37] Brown, *The Forum*, 1:282 and Wallace, *An Address*, 56-57, both relying on Isaiah Thomas, *The History of Printing in America* (Worcester, Mass., 1810), 2:12. The only primary source for the case, *New England's Spirit of Persecution*, does not mention this incident.

[38] *Minutes of the Provincial Council of Pennsylvania*, 1:326-27.

[39] Quoted in Thomas, *History of Printing in America*, 2:97.

his career of consistently failing to champion freedom of the press that justifies awarding him the palm as a doughty exponent of the cause for which he once suffered.

The absence of freedom of speech in seventeenth-century Massachusetts, especially on religious subjects, is so familiar a fact that a mere reminder should suffice. Beginning in 1635 when the legislature, sitting as a court, banished Roger Williams for the crime of disseminating "newe & dangerous opinions" against the authority of the magistrates,[40] the government kept busy by punishing dissidents for sedition, heresy, or both. Between 1637 and 1647, John Wheelwright, Anne Hutchinson, a half-dozen or more of their Antinomian followers, Peter Hobart and others involved in the Hingham affair, Robert Child and his six associates, and Samuel Gorton were all convicted for seditious sermons, petitions, or remonstrances against the civil authority.[41] In 1652 William Pynchon, an assistant, by escaping to England missed the distinction of being the first person to be prosecuted for opinions expressed in print. His tract, which had been licensed in England, was adjudged "erronyous and hereticale" by the legislature, which commanded it to be burned by the public executioner.[42] There had been several earlier cases of unpublished manuscript works having been censored or burned.[43] In 1654 the respected first president of Harvard, Henry Dunster, was indicted by a grand jury and convicted for breaching the peace by delivering a sermon on infant baptism.[44] He was the first person prosecuted under common-law process for a religious speech. In 1661 the legislature humiliated another distinguished person, John Eliot, by forcing him to retract "such expressions as doe too manifestly scandalize" the

---

[40] Nathaniel B. Shurtleff, ed., *Records of the Governor and Company of the Massachusetts Bay in New England (1628-86)* (Boston, 1853-54), 1:160.

[41] For a convenient compilation of the original sources concerning all those named but Gorton, see Mark DeWolfe Howe, ed., *Readings in American Legal History* (Cambridge, Mass., 1949), 144-79 and 189-208, especially 148-53, 157, 164, 179, 190, 197, and 202. The original sources on Gorton are Edward Winslow, *Hypocrasie Unmasked, A True Relation of the Proceedings of the Governor and Company of the Massachusetts Bay against Samuel Gorton of Rhode Island* (1646), ed. Howard Millar Chapin (Providence, 1916); and Gorton's "Simplicities Defence against Seven-Headed Policy" (1646), in Peter Force, ed., *Tracts and Other Papers Relating Principally to the Origin . . . of the Colonies in North America* (New York, 1947 ed.), vol. 4, no. 6. John Winthrop, *The History of New England from 1630 to 1649*, ed. James Savage (Boston, 1853), has data on all the cases.

[42] Clyde Augustus Duniway, *The Development of Freedom of the Press in Massachusetts* (New York, 1906), 32-33.

[43] *Ibid.*, 19, 20, 24, and 29, for the cases of Stoughton, Smyth, Lechford, and Saltonstall.

[44] *Ibid.*, 34-35.

government of England, and ordered his book, *The Christian Commonwealth*, which advocated that rulers should be elected, to be "totally suppressed."[45] The government's persecutions of the Baptists and Quakers that began in the 1650s and lasted through the century were religiously inspired but legally grounded in part on the victims' censure of the government and their tendency to disturb the peace, which was synonymous with seditious utterance.[46] John Wise, "the first great American democrat," with five associates who were named, plus an unspecified number of others identified only as "evil minded and disaffected persons," were tried and convicted for seditious libel in 1687. They had seditiously brought the king's government into hatred and contempt in the minds of the people by daring to declare that a tax not levied by the Assembly was contrary to Magna Carta and did not have to be paid. Wise's punishment was suspension from the ministry, a fine of fifty pounds, and the posting of a bond in the extravagant sum of one thousand pounds to guarantee his good behavior for a year.[47] In late 1689 the Massachusetts General Court warned, "Whereas many papers have been lately printed and dispersed tending to the disturbance of peace and subversion of the government," malefactors would be treated "with uttermost Severity" as enemies of the Crown.[48]

One Massachusetts case deserving more extended notice was that of Thomas Maule, the irascible Quaker merchant of Salem who has been credited as having won the "first victory for freedom of the press in America," an honor that belonged to William Bradford.[49] Maule in 1695 published a book, licensed and printed in New York, which was so aspersive a commentary on the civil and ecclesiastical rulers of Massachusetts that he was promptly arrested for "wicked Lyes and Slanders . . . upon Government, and likewise divers corrupt and pernicious Doctrines utterly subversive of the true Christian religion and professed faith."[50] The sheriff seized all available copies of his

[45] *Ibid.*, 34-35.
[46] See, for example, the statute of 1656 against the Quakers, quoted in Peleg W. Chandler, ed., *American Criminal Trials* (Boston, 1844), 1:35, and the discussion therein following.
[47] "Proceedings Agt. Wise and Others of Ipswich for Misdemeanors," in Robert Noxon Toppan, ed., *Edward Randolph* (Boston, 1898-1909), 4:171-82. For the phrase characterizing Wise, see Clinton Rossiter, *Seedtime of the Republic* (New York, 1953), 206-25.
[48] Duniway, *Freedom of the Press*, 67-68.
[49] Jones, *Thomas Maule*, 25.
[50] Theo. Philanthes [Thomas Maule], *New-England Persecutors Mauld With their own Weapons . . . Together with a brief Account of the Imprisonment and Tryal of Thomas Maule of Salem, for publishing a Book, entitled, Truth held forth and maintained, &c.* (New York, 1697, 62 pp.), 53.

book, and brought Maule before the lieutenant-governor and Council in Boston, "who," he wrote, "put divers Insnaring Questions to
said *Maule*," which he refused to answer.[51] The Council ordered his
books to be burned but conceded his demand that he be tried by a
jury of his local peers. His bond, however, was placed at an astro-
nomical figure, thereby ensuring his safekeeping in jail. Conducting
his own defense in a most aggressive manner before three judges, all
members of the Council, Maule repeated in court the bitter charges
he had made in his book. When he was interrupted by one of the
judges who denounced him as a "horrible Lyar" and admonished him
to silence, he declared fearlessly that he spoke only the truth and did
not fear their punishments because he had been imprisoned on five
former occasions and twice whipped.[52] His statements in court caused
a postponement of the trial so that he might be reindicted for verbal
crimes against the judges in addition to his published libels.

    In late 1696, after nearly a year in jail from the time of his arrest,
he was finally tried. The presiding judge asked the jury to return a
verdict of guilty on ground that the defendant's book tended to the
overthrow of the Commonwealth and the church. Maule, in his defense, said nothing about freedom of the press. Instead, he made a
technically adroit attack on the insufficiency of the evidence against
him, combined with a clever appeal to the jury's emotional reaction
against the recent witchcraft trials with which he compared the case
against him. He concluded, like Bradford had at his trial, by calling
upon the jury to decide the law over the heads of the judges, his
accusers.[53] The jury, much to the court's dismay, returned a verdict
of not guilty. The foreman, when asked to explain the verdict, declared that the jury believed that the prosecution should have been
an ecclesiastical rather than a civil affair, a matter to be decided by a
"Jury of divines."[54] Neither the arguments of the defense nor the
jury's explanation of the verdict showed any concern for freedom
of the press. Although this was the first criminal trial in Massachusetts
for a printed libel and has been hailed as a precursor of the Zenger
case, the participants regarded the cause as a matter of conscience
rather than that of a free press. This case and the others which have
been reviewed indicate that on points that cut to the sinews, liberty
of expression barely existed in principle or practice in the American
colonies during the seventeenth century.

[51] *Ibid.*, 55.
[52] *Ibid.*, 56-57.
[53] *Ibid.*, 51-62.
[54] *Ibid.*, 62.

By 1763 the situation was substantially unchanged but for the disappearance of the licensing system. A continuation of the case of Massachusetts will illustrate. In 1719, when the governor was still empowered to exercise prior censorship, John Checkley, the most prominent Anglican minister in the Bay Colony, was prevented from publishing a tract critical of Calvinist doctrines.[55] The legislature then enacted a statute, aimed at Checkley, compelling any person "suspected to be disaffected to his Majesty or to his Government" to swear an oath of loyalty. Checkley refused the oath on grounds of conscience and a resentment against being the only person singled out, without any act of disloyalty on his part. For his contumacy he was convicted in 1720, fined six pounds, and bound to good behavior.[56] After a stay in England, Checkley returned to Boston with a stock of his writings defending episcopacy, including the book that he had been forbidden to publish in 1719. The Council declared that the book reflected on the ministers of the Commonwealth and contained "sundry vile insinuations against His Majestys rightfull and lawfull authority & the constitution of the Government of Great Britain." He was indicted in 1724 for having libelously published "false Seditious & wicked words," convicted, and fined fifty pounds. On appeal to the Superior Court of Judicature, he was quickly retried and convicted again. The jury returned only a special verdict, finding that he had published the book; the court, reserving to itself determination of the criminality of the book, ruled as a matter of law that Checkley had published a seditious libel. He was fined fifty pounds and costs and obligated to post a bond of double that sum for his future good behavior.[57]

Several printers at about this time were hounded by the government, reminding critics that the indefinable line between liberty of the press and licentiousness made discretion the better part of safety. John Colman in 1720 published a tract on the reasons for the economic distress of the province, with the result that the governor and Council ordered his arrest and prosecution on ground that the tract contained many passages "reflecting upon the Acts & Laws of the Province, & other proceedings of the Government and has a Tendency to Disturb the Administration of the Government, as well as

[55] Duniway, *Freedom of the Press*, 84-86.
[56] Edmund F. Slafter, *John Checkley; or, the Evolution of Religious Tolerance in Massachusetts Bay* (Boston, 1897), 1:34-37.
[57] *Ibid.*, 1:56-66. The case is also reviewed by Duniway, *Freedom of the Press*, 107-10 and 166-71; and Thomas, *History of Printing in America*, 2: 427-28.

the Publick Peace."[58] The prosecution was dropped without explanation after Colman had been harassed by the necessity of court ap-
pearances and the posting of bonds.

A similar incident involved Benjamin Gray the next year when
he published an unlicensed tract arguing for bills of credit. The
Council voted that he had employed "many Vile, Scandalous, and
very Abusive Expressions" reflecting on the government and ordered
his prosecution.[59] This time, however, the Council did not proceed by
an information, as in Colman's case; it trusted a grand jury to return
an indictment, but the jurors, upon hearing Gray's contrite expressions of sorrow for his misdeed and his allegations that he had not
intended to affront the government, found no true bill.[60]

At this time, 1721, effective censorship by licensing ended in
Massachusetts. Governor Shute, disturbed about the growing licentiousness of the press, attempted to obtain from the House of Representatives of the General Court endorsement of his instructions from
the king that no printed matter be permitted without his prior license.
The House, however, rejected the proposed censorship law, though
not because of any solicitude for freedom of the press. In their reply
to the governor, the representatives agreed that seditious libel should
meet with condign punishment, but chided the executive for having
permitted libels against the House. The House's reply showed that it
rejected the proposed legislation because to have vested the executive
with an exclusive licensing power might have made it difficult for
the representatives to publish before the people their own criticisms
of his policies. Although freedom of the press benefited from this
blow against the licensing system, the House was motivated only by
a desire to strengthen its own position against executive domination.[61]

The final attempt to enforce prior restraints in Massachusetts ended
in failure in 1723. James Franklin of Boston, who founded the unlicensed *New England Courant* and made it a vehicle of political and
religious satire, was the unwilling hero of the episode. In 1722, when
his paper was less than a year old, he ran a brief notice that the government was outfitting a ship to go after coastal pirates "sometime
this month, wind and weather permitting." The insinuation that
effective action was not being adopted as speedily as possible was
galling to the General Court. The Council promptly arrested him and
after a *pro forma* hearing resolved that he had committed "a High

[58] Duniway, *Freedom of the Press*, 92.
[59] Thomas, *History of Printing in America*, 2:425.
[60] Duniway, *Freedom of the Press*, 94.
[61] *Ibid.*, 94-96.

affront to this Government"; whereupon the House, concurring, ordered his immediate imprisonment for the remaining month of the legislative session. This summary punishment was a striking instance of the exercise of parliamentary privilege, a legislative revenge for an imagined insult. After a week of close confinement, Franklin humbly petitioned the General Court for the privilege of using the prison yard, pleading illness and being "heartily sorry" for his offense. His petition was granted, but he served out the month.[62]

The experience did not, however, temper his journalistic satire. Upon his release the *Courant* continued its policy of mockery and innuendo. Moreover, Franklin felt incensed because the House had condemned him without affording him a fair trial. He wrote a scathing denunciation of the House's exercise of parliamentary privilege. He invoked Magna Carta and the rights of an Englishman, complaining that he had been denied the judgment of his peers and "due Process of Law." He concluded a second essay on the same subject by daring to challenge the House's authority to try him. Inevitably, when the General Court met in its next session, members read the *New-England Courant* looking for a pretext to silence Franklin.[63] They did not read anything about freedom of the press. But several stinging pieces in early 1723 provoked the General Court to deal with Franklin once again.

A joint committee was appointed to consider measures of restraint. The report of the committee, adopted by both houses, censured the publisher for having offended the government by injurious reflections which disturbed the public peace. He was then ordered never to print the *Courant* or any pamphlet or paper "Except it be first Supervised, by the Secretary of this Province," and he was to post bond to insure his compliance. The irrepressible Franklin disregarded the orders of the General Court by bringing out the next issue of the *Courant* without license and with a fresh aspersion; but he discreetly went into hiding to escape the inevitable warrant for his arrest on a charge of contempt of the General Court. At this point, Franklin made his young brother Ben the new publisher of the paper in order to circumvent obedience to the legislature's command that James Franklin print nothing unlicensed. Upon his eventual capture and imprisonment, the legislature, confident of its case against him, per-

[62] Thomas, *History of Printing in America*, 2:217, reprints the offensive passage; the orders of the General Court and the prisoner's petition are duplicated in Duniway, *Freedom of the Press*, 99, 163.

[63] *New-England Courant*, July 16 and 30, 1722, copies supplied by Professor Jeffery A. Smith.

mitted his release under bond and requested an indictment from a grand jury. That was the government's mistake. It should have held him in jail under authority of the General Court for breach of privilege, because the grand jury, probably motivated by a detestation of the licensing system which had ended a generation earlier in England, returned the bill ignoramus. Thus, Franklin went luckily free, and prior restraint of the press was at an end in Massachusetts.[64] Within a year, however, Franklin, chastened by his bouts with prison, ceased making his newspaper a provocative journal of opinion. It became "dull" and safe. Within a decade he was publishing a noncontroversial newspaper in Newport.[65]

Despite the disappearance of prior restraint, the press was not free. Only the next year John Checkley was convicted for seditious libel. The law of criminal publications remained unaltered; subsequent punishment awaited anyone who "abused" his right to publish his sentiments without license. Thomas Fleet, publisher of *The Evening Post* in Boston, was the next victim. His paper was remarkably candid in its comments on a variety of subjects and was denounced as a "sink of sedition, error, and heresy" by the clergy in particular, although he was careful not to asperse government policies. In 1742, however, he printed an item that he had picked up in conversation with a naval officer. Parliament, he reported "had called for all the Papers relating to the war [between England and Spain], and 'twas expected the Right Hon. Sir Robert Walpole would be taken into custody in a very few days." The Council immediately ordered the attorney-general to file an information against Fleet, circumventing a grand jury, and to prosecute him for his "libelous Reflection upon his Majesty's administration" tending to "inflame the minds of his Majesty's subjects here and disaffect them to his Government." Fleet, however, immediately produced five respectable witnesses to attest to the truth of the news item, and events quickly proved its accuracy. As a result, the prosecution was dropped.[66] The government had not been obligated by law to allow Fleet the privilege of proving the truth of his statement as a defense to a charge of seditious libel, but it would have

[64] Thomas, *History of Printing in America*, 2:219-22, and Duniway, *Freedom of the Press*, 101-3.

[65] Stephen Botein, "'Meer Mechanics' and an Open Press: The Business and Political Strategies of Colonial American Printers," in Donald Fleming and Bernard Bailyn, eds., *Perspectives in American History* 9:208-09 (1975).

[66] *Boston Evening Post*, March 8 and 15, 1742. See also Thomas, *History of Printing in America*, 2:473 and 234; Duniway, *Freedom of the Press*, 112-15; and Mary Ann Yodelis, "Boston's First Major Newspaper War: A 'Great Awakening' of Freedom," *Journalism Quarterly* 51(1974):211-12.

flouted public opinion had it persisted in the prosecution, especially after Walpole fell from power. The government's intention to circumscribe political reportage was surely evident, though, and newspapers were alerted to the fact that literal accuracy bounded their freedom.

Fleet himself "may have felt intimidated by threats against his freedom to publish," according to one scholar. He refused to publish an article submitted to him even though he shared the author's "opinion." Truth, he declared, could not always be safely printed. He seemed not afraid of the fact that the law did not allow truth as a defense. That had not stopped him in the matter involving Walpole, because there he confidently knew he could prove the facts of what he had printed. In this instance, however, he realized that he might be criminally liable if he printed an "opinion" whose truth or falsity was unprovable.[67]

In 1754 the General Court demonstrated once again its power to restrain the press by punishing public criticism as a breach of privilege. A pamphlet with the intriguing title "The Monster of Monsters" had been anonymously published satirizing the House's debate on a recently enacted and unpopular excise bill—the allegorical monster. The House angrily resolved that the unknown author had perpetrated "a false, scandalous Libel reflecting upon the Proceedings of the House in general, and on many worthy Members in particular, in breach of the privileges thereof."[68] The hangman was ordered to burn a copy of the offensive pamphlet, while warrants went out for the arrest of Daniel Fowle, suspected as the printer, and his apprentice Joseph Russell. Brought to the bar of the House, the two were easily trapped into confessing their complicity as distributors of the pamphlet. Fowle also implicated his brother, who was also a printer, and a Mr. Royal Tyler, a prominent merchant who later became a member of the Council. Fowle's brother, Zechariah, was arrested but escaped punishment because of illness. Tyler, the probable author, on being interrogated by the speaker of the House, unsuccessfully demanded a lawyer and answered all questions by referring to his privilege against self-incrimination. He was thrown in jail and denied bail, but was unaccountably released after two days, as was Daniel Fowle's apprentice. The House regarded Daniel as the chief culprit and

---

[67] Yodelis, "Boston's First Major Newspaper War," 212. The quotation is from Yodelis's unpublished Ph.D. dissertation, "Boston's Second Major Paper War" (University of Wisconsin, 1971), 21.

[68] Quoted in Daniel Fowle, *A Total Eclipse of Liberty* (Boston, 1755, 32 pp.), 11.

treated him accordingly. He was imprisoned incommunicado, denied even the privilege of writing a censored letter to his wife. Although writing materials were prohibited to him, the jailer negligently failed to search his person. He spent the first night on the floor of the bedless, stinking, unheated cell composing a narrative of his suffering. Having caught a "prodigious cold," he was moved to a better cell in the company of "Murderers, Thieves, Common-Cheats, Pick-Pockets, &c." His confinement all the while was grounded merely on a charge of being "suspected of being guilty."

After five days of rough treatment, Fowle was brought before the bar of the House again where he was severely reprimanded by the speaker for having published a seditious libel and then was returned to his cell until he should pay the costs of his case. On the sixth day of imprisonment, when the affair had become "the chief Topik of Conversation in Town," Fowle petitioned the speaker for a discharge so that he might nurse his sick wife. The petition was granted on condition that he return when summoned, but public sympathy being with Fowle, the House dropped its charges and let him alone even after he published his tract, *A Total Eclipse of Liberty*,[69] which in pathos and anger told the world about his troubles. The oddest aspect of the whole affair is that the supposedly esteemed liberty of the press did not seem to be at stake in the minds of any of the participants. Fowle himself regarded the whole affair as a gross violation of Magna Carta's guarantee of personal liberty and due process of law. Vigorously condemning the proceedings against him as unjust and arbitrary, he quoted Montesquieu to prove the tyranny of one body being accuser, judge, and jury. But he never mentioned liberty of the press or any aspect of freedom of discussion. His complaint was not that his words were deemed criminal, but that he had been treated harshly and denied trial.

Nursing his inflamed sense of injustice, Fowle persistently petitioned for redress of grievance. He did not challenge the power of the House to punish for breach of parliamentary privilege but insisted that he had been innocent. In 1764 the General Court remitted the costs that had been exacted from him to pay for his prosecution and imprisonment, but Fowle was not satisfied. He petitioned again, and in 1766 the General Court, sympathetic to one who had suffered

[69] My account of Fowle's case is based mainly on this tract, cited in the note above. The quoted phrases are at pp. 19, 24, and 26. See also *Journals of the House of Representatives of Massachusetts 1754-55* (Boston, 1956), 63-64, 67, and 72.

the loss of his liberty perhaps unjustly, awarded Fowle twenty pounds in damages. By then Fowle had long since mended his ways. He had given up his paper in Boston, founded one in Portsmouth, New Hampshire, and had become a government printer, eschewing political criticism and supporting the established authorities.[70]

In the neighboring colony of New York the open expression of opinion was esteemed as little as in Massachusetts. Early in the eighteenth century occurred the trial of Colonel Nicholas Bayard, a leader of the aristocratic party who had been instrumental in securing the conviction and execution of Jacob Leisler. The appointment of a new governor, Lord Cornbury, kindled Bayard's hope of returning to power against the Leislerians, who then controlled the government. In an effort to ingratiate himself with Cornbury, Bayard drew up addresses to him, the king, and Parliament, accusing Lieutenant-Governor John Nanfan, the chief justice, and members of the Council, of nefarious actions ranging from bribery to oppression. Among those whose signatures Bayard procured were members of the local garrison. Nanfan immediately retaliated by arresting the author of the derogatory addresses on a charge of treason under a statute of 1691 loosely drawn by Bayard himself against Leisler. It provided that anyone who by arms "or otherwise" endeavored to "disturbe the peace" should be deemed a traitor. Bayard was hoisted by his own petard; instead of confronting a charge of seditious libel, a mere misdemeanor, he found himself, in 1702, on trial for his life along with his henchman, Alderman John Hutchins. The indictment alleged their attempt to procure the mutiny of the garrison by inducing the soldiers to sign false and scandalous lies against the government, rendering it "cheap and vile" in the eyes of people. From indictment to conviction, the case was a travesty of common-law procedure, a fact which saved the prisoners' heads, for the prosecution was condemned as illegal on appeal to the Privy Council. Had the government of New York been content with a charge of seditious libel, it could have made the conviction stick.[71]

The government had even less luck with its prosecution of Francis Makemie and John Hampton, Presbyterian ministers who were arrested for unlicensed preaching with intent to "spread their *Perni-*

---

[70] Duniway, *Freedom of the Press*, 118-19 and 171-73. Botein, "'Meer Mechanics'," 211.

[71] *Rex v. Bayard*, Thomas Bayly Howell, comp., *A Complete Collection of State Trials to 1783*, continued by T. J. Howell to 1820 (London, 1816-28), 14: 471-516 (1702).

cious Doctrine and *Principles*, to the disturbance of the Church by *Law Established*, and of the *Government* of this *Province*."[72] Although Hampton was imprisoned with Makemie, he was not presented to the grand jury by the attorney-general, probably because he had not aggravated the offense, as had Makemie, by publishing his unlicensed sermon which was "reputed a Libel" by the governor. While the two were in jail, they applied for a release to the courts, stating that Cornbury had refused to recognize their legal documents from Virginia and Maryland certifying that they had complied with the provisions of the 1689 Act of Toleration. The judiciary, however, never received their petition; the attorney-general pocketed it, "asserting it to be a Libel against Ld. Cornbury." At the trial, the prosecution presented a case of seditious and unlicensed preaching, while the defense argued that the Act of Toleration extended to the colonies and protected the rights of conscience. The jury of New Yorkers returned a verdict of not guilty, influenced very possibly by the popular opposition to the assumption in the indictment that the Church of England was the established church of the province.[73]

The acquittal scored a victory for religious toleration and freedom of religious speech. But no speech reprehending the government was tolerated, at least not before the Zenger case. Before then the Assembly showed its mettle by punishing for breach of privilege the occasional hardy critic who dared to scandalize its dignity by offensive comment. Between 1706 and 1720 there were four such cases, one of which involved the arrest of nine citizens and another of seventeen grand jurors for seditious reflections on the Assembly.[74] In two of these four cases the victim of the Assembly's wrath was one of its own members, Lewis Morris in 1710, and Samuel Mulford in 1720. Representative Mulford's troubles began in 1716 when he was first expelled from the Assembly for a speech against unequal representation in which he asked whether the government was carried on for the benefit of the people or was arbitrary, illegal, and oppressive. Governor Robert Hunter, the object of some of Mulford's choicest adjectives, instituted a common-law prosecution against him for "a

[72] *A Narrative of a New and Unusual American Imprisonment of Two Presbyterian Ministers: And Prosecution of Mr. Francis Makemie*, 1707, by a Learner of Law, and Lover of Liberty. Reprinted in Force, ed., *Tracts and Other Papers*, vol. 4, no. 4, p. 24. The anonymous author was probably Makemie himself.

[73] On this point, see Sanford H. Cobb, *The Rise of Religious Liberty in America* (New York, 1902), 337-41.

[74] *Journal of the Votes and Proceedings of the General Assembly of the Colony of New-York, 1691-1765* (New York, 1764-66), 1:211 (1706), 1:283 (1710), 1:411 (1717), and 1:443 (1720).

false and Malitious Libel, against the Government . . . tending to alienate the affections of the Subjects from the Government."[75] The Assembly then relented and petitioned the governor to quash the prosecution on the theory that a speech on the floor was privileged—except of course when the member aspersed the Assembly, in which case it alone might take appropriate action. Hunter replied that the prosecution was not for the speech in the Assembly but for its publication by Mulford. The case, however, never came to trial. Mulford went directly to England where he secured from the Lords of Trade an order commanding Hunter to cease the criminal proceedings against him.[76] In 1720 Mulford was back in the Assembly, where he again unburdened himself in an accusation that the representatives had gotten the colony deeply in debt and ought to be cleaned out by the people. His "rash Expression" was solemnly deemed to be a reflection upon the House, which after examining him before its bar voted that he be summarily expelled. Mulford's case indicates that free speech, which originated as a parliamentary privilege, did not extend to criticism of the legislature even by a member. The year before, in neighboring New Jersey, the House convicted two men who could not prove the truth of their charge that a member of the Assembly had drunk a toast to the damnation of the governor.[77]

The Zenger case in 1735 gave the press freedom to print as far as the truth carried and a jury's emotions sympathetically swayed, if the truth was directed away from the Assembly. Nevertheless, the verdict of history is correct in regarding this case as a watershed in the evolution of freedom of the press, not because it set a legal precedent, for it set none, but because the jury's verdict resonated with popular opinion. The widely read and frequently reprinted report of the case strengthened a widespread belief that the law of seditious libel derived from Star Chamber doctrines, belied common sense by denying truth as a defense, and denigrated the role of juries, thus jeopardizing the honest expression of opinions. The Zenger verdict made people exult both in liberty and the relationship of liberty of the press to liberty itself. Just as people understood the difference between gods and God, so too this case gave them a lucid understanding of what they knew instinctively, that a gulf existed between legal liberties and liberty. It invigorated their understanding that citizens—and Zenger's attorney spoke of "citizens," not just subjects—should distrust an

[75] The sources are printed in O'Callaghan and Fernow, eds., *Documents Relative to the Colonial History of New York*, 3:363-71, which includes Mulford's speech; his defense in court begins at p. 372.

[76] *Ibid.*, 3:383 and 5:505.

[77] Clarke, *Parliamentary Privilege*, 119.

unjust government that sought to overawe them. It fortified their conviction that in a season of tyranny, citizens must be forthright in their censure of that government and should enjoy impunity for their courage in speaking out truthfully. It made them believe that intemperance in governing justified intemperance in expression and that intemperate criticism of an arbitrary or corrupt administration, if true, should not be a crime. As a writer in the *Philadelphia Gazette* declared about the popular verdict, "if it is not law, it is better than law, it ought to be law, and will always be law wherever justice prevails."[78]

The Zenger case originated in a power struggle between New York's governor, William Cosby, and the political faction led by Lewis Morris, who determined to check Cosby's arrogant, mendacious, and illegal regime.[79] Soon after his arrival in New York in the summer of 1732, the royal governor antagonized the local establishment. Rip Van Dam, a leading merchant who was the senior member of the Council, had acted as governor until Cosby arrived. Cosby demanded half the salary that the Council voted for Van Dam. When Van Dam refused to pay, Cosby sued him in the provincial supreme court, after first authorizing its judges to sit as a court of equity, which functioned without a jury. Chief Justice Lewis Morris accepted the arguments of Van Dam's lawyers, James Alexander and William Smith, that an equity court created solely by the governor was illegal, but the other two judges, James DeLancey and Frederick Philipse, supported the governor. Cosby fired Morris and elevated DeLancey to the chief justiceship, without the Council's consent.

[78] *Philadelphia Gazette,* May 18, 1738.

[79] My account of the Zenger case is based primarily on Livingston Rutherfurd, *John Peter Zenger, His Press, His Trial and a Bibliography of Zenger Imprints. Also a Reprint of the First Edition of the Trial* (New York, 1904), still the best and most detailed book, now rare. My own abridged version of the trial, based on Rutherfurd's literal reprint, is in Levy, ed. *Freedom of the Press from Zenger to Jefferson* (Indianapolis, 1966), 43-61. I have read every issue of Zenger's *New-York Weekly Journal.* The best modern account, which parallels Rutherfurd, is Stanley Nider Katz, ed., *A Brief Narrative of the Case and Trial of John Peter Zenger,* by James Alexander (Cambridge, Mass., 1972, 2nd ed.). Katz's introduction and critical annotations are excellent, and his volume includes valuable supplementary documents such as Alexander's brief. Because of the easy availability of Katz's modernized edition of the trial, I have referred to it in my notes. My own essay, "Did the Zenger Case Really Matter?" *William and Mary Quarterly,* 3rd ser., 17(1960):35-50, stressed the continued suppressive role of the popular Assembly of New York, a subject ignored by Paul Finkelman's putative reply, "The Zenger Case: Prototype of a Political Trial," an otherwise worthwhile essay, in Michal R. Belknap, ed., *American Political Trials* (Westport, Conn., 1981), 21-42. All background facts are from Livingston's prefatory chapters, pp. 3-132, as corroborated by Katz's introduction, pp. 1-38.

DeLancey's commission authorized his court to determine both civil and criminal cases. By contrast, in England the judges of the King's Bench, the supreme criminal court, possessed no civil jurisdiction, and the judges of the highest civil court, the Court of Common Pleas, exercised no criminal jurisdiction. Moreover, judges traditionally held office during "good behavior," but Cosby had appointed DeLancey and Philipse to serve at his "pleasure."

Morris, a nabob of New York, joined forces with Van Dam, Alexander and Smith, his two lawyers, Philip Livingston, and Cadwallader Colden, the colony's scientist-politician, and formed a "Popular Party" to challenge the judicial commissions, expose the arbitrary malfeasance of the governor, and regain political power. But the opposition faction needed a voice to shape and mobilize public opinion. Cosby controlled the sole newspaper of the province, the *New-York Gazette*, run by William Bradford, "The King's Printer." The solution was the founding of an opposition newspaper. Thus the *New-York Weekly Journal*, printed by John Peter Zenger, originated as a propaganda vehicle for the Morris faction. Zenger himself, a poorly educated German immigrant, was neither the editor nor writer of his paper; he was merely the printer and had scant understanding of politics or of the opinions that filled the columns of his newspaper. In effect James Alexander was the managing editor and chief editorial writer; Morris, Smith, and Colden, as well as Alexander, posing as pseudonymous readers, contributed letters to the editor scalding the governor and his appointees as villains who had no respect for law, liberty, or private property. Even the advertisements in the newspaper ridiculed the Cosbyites.

The *Weekly Journal* also published extracts from Whig theorists, chief among them John Trenchard and Thomas Gordon, the authors of *Cato's Letters: Or Essays on Liberty, Civil and Religious.*[80] Zenger's paper, as the first independent and truly free press in America, engaging weekly in the dangerous practice of opposing the administration of the province, needed a theory to legitimate its editorial practices. The reading public as well as Crown officers had to be educated. *Cato's Letters* served to castigate Cosby, to broadcast Whig theory, and to rationalize freedom of the press.

In the second issue of the newspaper, in late 1733, Alexander wrote the first of several essays in which he developed a libertarian theory of freedom of the press to justify the newspaper's actual practice of that freedom. At the same time Alexander excoriated Cosby by in-

---

[80] Discussed below, Chapter Three.

nuendo. Explaining why freedom of the press was a necessary part of the British constitution, Alexander observed that some people believed that might made right, and "if such an over grown Criminal, or an impudent Monster in Iniquity, cannot immediately be come at by ordinary Justice, let him yet receive the lash of satire, let the glaring truth of his ill administration . . . render his actions odious to all honest minds." Two months later the *Weekly Journal* referred to a governor who had turned "rogue."[81]

Cosby decided to stop Zenger's press by imprisoning the printer for his seditious libels. Chief Justice DeLancey failed, however, to convince a grand jury to indict, and he failed again nine months later in October 1734, despite a strong charge on the meaning and dangers of seditious libel.[82] Cosby's Council then urged the Assembly to concur in an order that certain issues of Zenger's newspaper be burned by the common hangman, that a reward be offered for the authors of the libels, and that the printer be prosecuted. The Assembly refused, as did the city's Court of Quarter Sessions. The Council then commanded the sheriff to see to the burning of the papers. On November 17, 1735, Zenger was imprisoned on a warrant issued by the Council charging him with having published "several seditious libels . . . tending to raise factions . . . among the people . . . inflaming their minds with contempt of His Majesty's government, and greatly disturbing the peace thereof."[83]

Although Zenger had the best lawyers in the colony, James Alexander and William Smith, they could not prevent the chief justice from setting bail impossibly high, thus keeping his prisoner in jail. In January 1735 DeLancey failed for a third time to obtain a grand jury indictment. Richard Bradley, the attorney general, then charged Zenger by an information for having published "false, scandalous, malicious, and seditious" libels.[84] That is, on his authority as prosecutor, the attorney general bypassed the grand jury system and single-handedly preferred charges, an "information" against Zenger before the court, which then ordered a trial. Prosecution by information was legal, though unpopular. Fortunately for Zenger, Bradley's information contained the word "false," which ultimately proved to be the key to his defense. Zenger's lawyers, knowing that a court consisting of DeLancey and Philipse was biased against their client,

---

[81] *New-York Weekly Journal*, Nov. 12, 1733, essay reprinted in Levy, ed. *Freedom of the Press*, 26-32, quotation at p. 28. For "rogue," *Weekly Journal*, Jan. 21, 1734.

[82] For the charge, see Katz, ed. *Brief Narrative*, 41-42.

[83] *Ibid.*, 45.

[84] *Ibid.*, 50.

challenged the legality of the commissions of the judges. DeLancey, outraged, summarily disbarred Alexander and Smith. In their place he appointed a young but able lawyer, John Chambers, to defend Zenger. Chambers, although an opponent of the Morris faction, pleaded Zenger not guilty and diligently challenged prejudiced jurors. The original panel of jurors included Cosby appointees, enemies of Morris, and Cosby's "baker, tailor, shoemaker, candlemaker, joiner, etc." DeLancey, confident that the prosecutor could easily prove that Zenger had published the libels, supported Chambers's motions, with the result that a neutral jury was impaneled to try the case.[85] Meanwhile, as Zenger spent nine months in prison awaiting his trial, his wife tended his press and Alexander supervised the continued publication of the *Weekly Journal*.

August 4, 1735, was the day of the trial. After the attorney general opened the prosecution's case, Andrew Hamilton of Philadelphia surprised the court when he rose in the audience and introduced himself as Zenger's counsel. Chambers yielded. James Alexander had engaged Hamilton, an old friend, to defend the printer and in so doing obtained the services of a man reputed to be the best advocate in America. Hamilton had been attorney general of Pennsylvania and at the time of the trial was speaker of the Pennsylvania Assembly. His case was ready-made for him, because Alexander had prepared a masterful brief.[86]

Hamilton opened the defense with Alexander's daring gambit of confessing Zenger's responsibility for the allegedly libelous articles. Hamilton added, however, that Zenger had a right to publish the truth. The attorney general, believing that the confession virtually awarded the verdict to the prosecution, accurately declared that because Zenger had admitted the publications, "the jury must find a verdict for the King, for supposing they were true . . . the law says their being true is an aggravation of the crime."[87] Hamilton disagreed; for the publications to be libelous, he argued, they must be false. Bradley, thinking to impress the jury, reviewed the publications against the governor, concluding that they stirred up sedition and disturbance of the peace by disquieting the minds of the people. Hamilton insisted, however, that the charges against Zenger included the word "false," without proof of which no libel existed; only if the

[85] *Ibid.*, 51-54, 56.
[86] On Hamilton, see Burton Alva Konkle, *The Life of Andrew Hamilton, 1676-1741* (Philadelphia, 1941). The briefs of both Alexander and Chambers are in Katz, ed., *Brief Narrative*, 139-51.
[87] Katz, ed., *Brief Narrative*, 62.

Crown proved the falsehood would he concede the libel. When the Crown attorney refused to offer such proof, on ground that he was not obliged to do so, Hamilton shrewdly offered to prove that the alleged libels were true, knowing that if he persuaded the jury, Cosby in effect would have been convicted. Accordingly the chief justice swiftly intervened: "You cannot be admitted, Mr. Hamilton, to give the truth of a libel in evidence," because it was a libel even if true. "The law was clear," DeLancey correctly stated, "that you cannot justify a libel," and for the second time he quoted Sergeant William Hawkins's authoritative book, *Pleas of the Crown*, in support of his ruling.[88]

Hamilton retorted that the court's law derived from the tyrannical Court of Star Chamber, long since dead, to the good fortune of English liberty; he squeezed precedents to buttress his view of the law that it permitted truth as a defense to a charge of libel. Hamilton could not satisfy DeLancey, because the great legal luminaries of England—Coke, Hale, Holt, and Hawkins—had proved that the common-law courts perpetuated and accepted Star Chamber doctrine. Nevertheless, Hamilton managed to exploit the doubt in the minds of the jurors whether the law made good sense. Mercilessly Hamilton scored the doctrine that truth aggravated a libel; were the jurors supposed to believe that "truth is a greater sin than falsehood"?[89]

When DeLancey stopped Hamilton from arguing further that truth was a defense to a charge of libel, Hamilton necessarily abandoned his reliance on Alexander's brief and shifted his strategy. "Then, gentlemen of the jury," he declared, "it is to you we must now appeal for witnesses to the truth of the facts . . . and are denied the liberty to prove." Boldly he played to the jury over the head of the court, concocting an argument that was destined to survive first in public opinion and ultimately in the law itself. He reminded the jurors that as citizens of New York, they knew the facts concerning the supposed libels about the governor's administration. The facts, he declared, were "notoriously known to be true."[90] When a difference arose as to whether Zenger's words should be understood as malicious, seditious, and tending to breach the peace, DeLancey remarked that those who had to judge would understand the words properly. Hamilton told the jurors that they, not the court, were the judges; if they

---

[88] *Ibid.*, 69-70, for the quotation, and pp. 41-42 and 74 for the reliance on Hawkins. See William Hawkins, *A Treatise of the Pleas of the Crown* (London, 1716, 2 vols.), 1:184.

[89] Katz, ed. *Brief Narrative*, 70-74.

[90] *Ibid.*, 75.

did not understand the words to be false, the publications were not criminal. DeLancey then ruled that the jury's only task was "to find that Zenger printed and published those papers, and leave it to the Court to judge whether they are libelous . . . it is in the nature of a special verdict where the jury leave the matter of law to the Court."[91]

Hamilton, addressing the jury, then launched into an argument of several hours. The court's rule, he said, "renders juries useless," a result he again traced to rulings of the "terrible Court of Star Chamber." A free people, having a sense of justice, knew when a governor abused power. They would protect the innocent from him because they were not obliged "to support a governor who goes about to destroy a province . . . or their privileges." Legal restraints on the right of freemen to protest extended only to "what is false." Hamilton admitted that although truth alone could excuse complaints about a bad administration, "nothing ought to excuse a man who raises a false charge or accusation, even against a private person, and that no manner of allowance ought to be made to him who does so against a public magistrate." The attorney general, Hamilton reminded the jury, regarded government as above criticism and insisted that licentiousness could not be tolerated, because it brought rulers into popular contempt. Hamilton did not disagree except that he did not regard truth as licentious. He called attention to the fact that government officials who abused power caused injustice and oppression, thereby deserving the contempt of the people. Thus, if the jury believed that Zenger had published the truth, the verdict should be in his favor.[92]

Hamilton knew that the law was against him and that Zenger was guilty as a matter of law. So he had used the jury as a court of public opinion and turned the case into a trial of Cosby. Hamilton's best defense turned out to be an aggressive assault. Summoning his forensic gifts, he then turned his case into one that would endure as long as people cherished liberty and trusted juries. Ascending the heights of eloquence, he declared in his peroration that Zenger's was not a "small" case:

> . . . the question before the Court and you gentlemen of the jury is not of small nor private concern, it is not the cause of a poor printer, nor of New York alone, which you are now trying. No! It may in its consequences affect every freeman that lives under a British government on the main of America. It is the best cause. It is the cause of liberty; and I make no doubt but that your upright conduct this day will not only entitle you to the love and esteem of your fellow

[91] *Ibid.*, 78.
[92] *Ibid.*, 78-79, 84, 96.

citizens; but every man who prefers freedom to a life of slavery will bless and honor you as men who have baffled the attempt of tyranny; and by an impartial and uncorrupt verdict, have laid a noble foundation for securing to ourselves, our posterity, and our neighbors that to which nature and the laws of our country have given us a right—the liberty—both of exposing and opposing arbitrary power (in these parts of the world, at least) by speaking and writing truth.[93]

Although both the attorney general and chief justice again reminded the jury that scandalous reflection on the government that stirred popular odium was a crime, Hamilton got in a parting shot. He apologized for having been carried away in the cause of freedom. The jury had heard enough. After withdrawing "a short time," they returned a general verdict of not guilty, "upon which there were three huzzas in the hall, which was crowded with people." Zenger left the courtroom a free man.[94]

Within a couple of years, Cosby was dead, Lewis Morris was speaker of the Assembly, and Zenger, prosperous from government contracts, printed an establishment newspaper whose seditious fires were banked. The report of Zenger's trial, however, was enormously popular, in England even more than in America. It had an undeniable attraction for printers, lawyers, and politicians, who quoted it or excerpted it or republished it when it suited their causes. In England, however, it had no noticeable effect. In America its effect was significant even though it had no impact on the law; a jury's verdict does not alter law. But common-law prosecutions petered out after Zenger's case. An obscure New Yorker was tried in 1745 for "singing in praise of the Pretender," and a legislature's prosecution in Virginia at about the same time ended in an acquittal when a printer, William Parks, received the privilege of proving the truth of his charges.[95] It was a revocable privilege, because the law remained the same as it had been in England and the colonies, although occasionally, even a legislature trying some individual for aspersive remarks that breached parliamentary privilege granted the defendant an opportunity to prove the truth of his comments. Moreover the record of the Zenger case kept aloft the standard of truth as a defense, despite the unchanging law. The last case of a common law trial for seditious libel occurred,

---

[93] *Ibid.*, 99.

[94] *Ibid.*, 101.

[95] Julius Goebel, Jr., and T. Raymond Naughton, *Law Enforcement in Colonial New York* (New York, 1944), 99 n. 178, citing *MS* Minutes, N.Y. Court of Quarter Sessions, 1732-62, p. 181, from the New York case. Parks's case is discussed below, p. 60.

abortively, in New York in 1770-71 when Alexander McDougall verbally assaulted the New York Assembly. He was indicted and would have been convicted but for the death of the prosecution's star witness; however, when the common-law prosecution failed, the legislature, having no regard for the truth as a defense, convicted and imprisoned him for seditious libel in the form of breach of privilege.[96]

Had John Peter Zenger attacked the New York Assembly instead of a despised royal governor, he would have been summarily convicted at the bar of the house, jailed, and in all likelihood, forgotten by posterity. Instead, he was tried by a jury and acquitted because he symbolized a popular cause. The Assembly had refused to support the prosecution and so had the Court of Quarter Sessions, the upper house of the city's legislature consisting of the mayor, recorder, and aldermen sitting in a judicial capacity. That body, dominated by the partisans of Lewis Morris, believed itself bound to preserve "as much as they can, the liberties of the press, and the people of the Province, since an Assembly of the Province and several Grand Juries have refused to meddle with the papers."[97]

That the Zenger case did not emancipate the press in colonial New York is suggested by subsequent events. The power of the legislature to punish anyone for breach of privilege could humble offenders. Long after the right to publish without first gaining government approval or license had been won, the colonial legislatures continued to regard the unlicensed publication of their votes and proceedings as a breach of privilege. Information of the most vital public interest could be printed only after first being submitted to the Speaker of the House for his examination and signature. Beginning in 1754 the order for official approval for reporting the Assembly's activities was repeated at each session down to the Revolution.[98]

The governor, too, was finicky about publications concerning him, as James Parker, the official printer, came to know. During King George's War, in 1747, Governor George Clinton sharply criticized the Assembly for its insufficient appropriation of defense funds, and the Assembly, angrily retorting that his remarks tended to the "subversion" of its rights, drew up a long remonstrance in its defense. Clinton then commanded Parker not to print the remonstrance in the proceedings of the Assembly because it scandalized him. The printer, caught between contending forces either of which could destroy him, helplessly turned to the House for instructions, giving

[96] McDougall's case is discussed below, pp. 75-81.
[97] Katz, ed., *Brief Narrative*, 46.
[98] *Journal of Votes and Proceedings*, 2:65.

it a rare opportunity to masquerade as the self-appointed defender of the free press. Unanimously the legislators voted

> That it is the undoubted Right of the People of this Colony, to know the Proceedings of their Representatives . . . That any Attempt to prohibit the printing or re-printing, any of the Proceedings of this House, is an infringement of the Privileges of this House, and of the People they represent . . . That his Excellency's Order to forbid the printing or re-printing the said Remonstrance, is unwarrantable, arbitrary and illegal, and . . . tends to the utter subversion of all the Rights and Liberties of this House, and of the People they represent.[99]

The Assembly then ordered Parker to print its remonstrance and deliver ten copies to each member so that the people might be apprised of their representatives' "firm Resolution to preserve the Liberty of the Press. . . ."[100] Confronted by this popular stand, Clinton shrewdly took no action against Parker; there was no sense in further antagonizing the Assembly from which adequate defense measures had still to be wheedled.

The legislature's professed commitment to the principle of a free press was abandoned a few years later, in 1753, when the printer, Hugh Gaine, deeming the king's instructions to the new governor and the latter's speech to the Assembly a matter of public interest, published them in his *New York Mercury*. The Assembly, upon learning that Gaine had "presumed" to print part of its proceedings without license, summoned him to its bar and demanded to know by what authority he had dared to breach its privileges. Gaine, who was apparently astonished and intimidated by the turn of events, most abjectly humbled himself. He had done wrong, he claimed, only out of ignorance but was profusely sorry for having given offense and "humbly asked their pardon." Mollified by this proper display of contrition, the Assembly magnanimously released him after censure, a warning, and exaction of the costs of the case.[101]

In 1756 James Parker, who had been the center of the earlier episode when the Assembly's conflict with the governor dictated the tactic of posturing as a friend of liberty of the press, was the next victim of parliamentary privilege. He had published in his *New-York Gazette* an article on the distressed condition of the people in Orange

---

[99] *Ibid.*, 2:193; see also pp. 173 and 192.
[100] *Ibid.*, 2:198.
[101] *Ibid.*, 2:358-59. On Gaine, see Alfred Lawrence Lorenz, *Hugh Gaine* (Carbondale, Ill., 1972), not useful on freedom of press.

and Ulster Counties which the House took to be "greatly reflecting" upon it and calculated "to irritate the People of this Colony against their Representatives." Parker and his associate, William Weyman, were voted to be guilty of a "high misdemeanor" and contempt of authority. Taken into custody by the sergeant-at-arms of the House, they were interrogated before the bar. A most cooperative witness, Parker revealed that the offensive article had been written by the Reverend Hezekiah Watkins of Newburg. The publishers confessed their fault for printing the article, denied any intention of giving affront, promised to be more circumspect in the future, and humbly begged the pardon of the honorable House. Notwithstanding this submission to authority, the Assembly kept the prisoners in jail for a week before discharging them. The Reverend Mr. Watkins, who was promptly arrested, admitted his authorship but pleaded that he had acted out of a mistaken zeal for the welfare of the people rather than from disrespect for the House. He was heartily sorry and pleaded to be forgiven, but was jailed anyway. The next day, however, he was formally reprimanded before the bar of the House and discharged after paying the costs.[102]

In 1758 the speaker of the House received a letter from one Samuel Townsend, a justice of the peace in Queen's County, asking legislative relief for certain refugees quartered on Long Island. The speaker, presenting the House with the letter, termed it "insolent," whereupon that body commanded Townsend's appearance. When he daringly failed to show up, the House cited him for contempt and issued a warrant for his arrest. Hauled before the bar of the House he was examined in the usual intimidating fashion, but he showed no signs of repentance. The House then voted that because his letter reflected on its "Honour, Justice and Authority," he was guilty of a "high Misdemeanour and a most daring Insult." The gloomy prison provoked Townsend to reconsider his position. He forthwith sent the House a petition expressing his deep sorrow for having written the letter by which he had inadvertently cast reflection on the House. He promised faithfully to avoid every occasion of exposing himself to such misdeeds in the future and asked for the House's "Compassion." Moved by this respectful submission from a judge, the House immediately released him from jail and discharged him after an official reprimand from the speaker.[103]

As New York approached the revolutionary controversy, its press was only as free as its legislature permitted. In practice, all political

[102] *Journal of Votes and Proceedings*, 2:487-89.
[103] *Ibid.*, 2:551-55 *passim*.

comment was tolerated as long as criticism did not affront the people's representatives. The failure of the common-law prosecutions against Bayard, Makemie, and Zenger made the courts a mere formal threat against unfettered discussion. The actively suppressive power was exercised by an unlimited discretion in the legislature to move against supposed breaches of parliamentary privilege. The frequency of the cases and the incidence of punishment were scarcely great enough to suggest tyranny; indeed prosecutions for breach of privilege were merely sporadic. But the arbitrary exercise of legislative prerogative was sufficiently restrictive to have a dampening effect on the free expression of opinion on legislative measures and matters.

All libertarian theorists had been united on the salutary influence of freedom of speech and press as a check on evil or incompetent rulers and on the stimulus to responsible government provided by open discussion. But in New York, as in Massachusetts, the legislature did not allow this libertarian theory to be put into practice. A royal governor, his policies, and his administration were almost always fair game for popular disapprobation; the Zenger case proved that. In the struggle of the colonial assembly for independence from the governor, most anti-administration criticism played into the hands of the legislature and the popular party. Freedom of the press was, in other words, a useful instrument for the expansion of legislative prerogative, but in any clash between parliamentary privilege and liberty of discussion, the former was the unexceptioned superior. This fact recalls the statement of the popular party representatives, John Morin Scott and William Livingston, in their New York journal printed by James Parker: any publication that they deemed injurious to the country verged on treason, making "groundless and trifling" the plea of freedom of the press.[104] Parker himself summarized the matter when he wrote that one might say anything on condition that he did so with a just regard for the laws[105]—and the laws provided for the punishment of seditious libel and breach of parliamentary privilege. The scope of permissible free expression was recognized as so narrow that none of the several defendants before the New York General Assembly even attempted to justify himself by reference to liberty of the press. Perhaps they realized the claim would have been "groundless and trifling."

The experience with freedom of speech and press in Pennsylvania was hardly different from New York's. Licensing lasted till at least 1722 as the case of Andrew Bradford indicates. He had followed his

[104] See below, pp. 138-40.
[105] *Ibid.*

father, old William Bradford, into the printing business and founded Pennsylvania's first newspaper, the Philadelphia *American Weekly Mercury*. Shortly after the second anniversary of the paper, in 1722, he printed a brief pamphlet by an anonymous author and then carried it as an article in his paper. The subject was the "dying Credit of the Province." Summoned by the Council to explain the aspersive innuendos against the government, Bradford lamely declared that he had no knowledge of the offensive piece which must have been accepted and run off by one of his journeyman printers without his knowledge. If freedom of the press mattered, the way to defend it was not to state how "very sorry" he was for the publication of the piece "and for which he humbly submitted himself and ask'd Pardon of the Govr. and the Board." On behalf of the Council, the governor ordered, "That he must not for the future presume to publish anything relating to or concerning the Affairs of this Government, or the Government of any other of his Majesty's Colonies, without the permission of the Governour or Secretary of this province."[106] There was an interesting sidelight to the incident. Among the members of the Council laying down this order, which was utterly irreconcilable with any principle of a free press, was the man who later gained fame as the stalwart defender of the press, Zenger's counsel, Andrew Hamilton.

A year later one of those rare common-law prosecutions for seditious speech occurred. Two men were arrested for derogatory comments about the king. One added to his contempt by affronting the magistrates in a declaration that he was not bound to obey either the House of Hanover or the House of Hanover's judges. The first prisoner confessed his guilt, but the second was contumacious, and his sedition had to be proved at a trial. Judge Robert Asheton informed the jury that "it is greatly imprudent and presumptuous, for private persons to intermeddle with matters of so high a nature; and it will be impossible to preserve the peace, unless subjects will quietly submit themselves to those whom Providence has placed over them . . . what severity can be too harsh for those who thus despise dominions, and speak evil of dignitaries? who curse, asperse, and deny their supreme, true, and lawful and *undoubted* sovereign." Upon conviction the individual who had confessed was sentenced to two hours in the pillory with a paper fixed on his breast and another on his back with the words: "I stand here for speaking contemptuously against my sovereign Lord, King George." He was also fined twenty

[106] *Minutes of the Provincial Council of Pennsylvania*, 1:143.

marks sterling and costs. The other defendant was sentenced to the
pillory for two hours on each of two days and afterwards, on each
day, "you *shall be tied to the tail of a cart, and be drawn round two
of this city squares,* and then you shall be *whipped on your bare back,
with forty-one lashes,* and be imprisoned till you have paid the
charges of prosecution."[107] A sentence like this did not have to be
repeated to have a lingering cautionary effect on the tongues of
citizens.

Andrew Bradford was again in trouble with the Council in 1729.
His *Mercury,* it seems, had published a letter, signed "Brutus," which
the authorities considered to be a reflection on the king and the government of Great Britain, calculated "to incite the Inhabitants of this
Province to throw off all subjection to the regular and established
powers of Government." The Council added that the letter constituted "a wicked & seditious Libell" that had been published under
mistaken notions of liberty. Bradford was jailed, his home and printing shop searched for evidence of the author's identity, and the
attorney-general was ordered to commence a prosecution against the
printer. He saved his skin, however, by naming the author as a
Parson Campbell of Long Island and pleaded sheer innocency of the
bad tendency of the letter signed "Brutus." Although he was recommitted to jail, there to ponder the perils of publishing, his cooperation
with the authorities and his abject apologies won his discharge. The
records do not indicate the fate of the mysterious Long Island parson.[108] They do indicate, however, that the recorder of the Council,
and one of those who conducted the examination of Bradford and
committed him to prison, was Andrew Hamilton.

Bradford and Hamilton were, as a matter of fact, enemies for years
and attacked each other through the pages of the *Mercury* and
Franklin's *Pennsylvania Gazette.*[109] During the Zenger trial, Andrew
Bradford had good reason to emulate his father, Zenger's rival and
publisher of the administration organ, the *New-York Gazette,* in
applauding the prosecution. The younger Bradford was also the
American publisher of "Remarks on Zenger's Tryal" by the West
Indian lawyers who attacked the validity of Hamilton's argument for
the defense.[110] Bradford did his best to disabuse the public of the

[107] Quoted in Brown, *The Forum,* 1:262-65 *passim.* Brown cites no primary
source in the case, nor have I been able to locate one.
[108] *Ibid.,* 1:285-86, and *Minutes of the Provincial Council of Pennsylvania,*
3:392.
[109] See Anna Janney DeArmond, *Andrew Bradford, Colonial Journalist*
(Newark, Del., 1949), chap. 4, "The Bradford-Hamilton Controversy."
[110] See below, pp. 130-31.

notion that Hamilton deserved his reputation as a champion of a free press. A "single Attempt on the side of Liberty," he editorialized, should not obscure a long record of enmity to the cause of the press. Bradford had more in mind than Hamilton's participation in the Council orders that had restrained him. Replying to a "Panegyrick" on Hamilton that appeared in Franklin's paper, Bradford accused him of hypocrisy and added the following tale to the evidence:

> A Person that has cruelly harassed and imprisoned a Printer, and again caused him to be assaulted and knock'd down in the open Street, meerly for copying an English Print, or inserting in his News-Paper, some general Invectives against a particular Vice, which by a foreign Innuendo, or consciousness of Guilt, the Person applied to himself, can no more merit the Character of a sincere Advocate for the Liberty of the Press, than a venal Hireling for a fulsome Harangue does the Name of a Cato. . . .[111]

The Council, or upper house, by no means outdid the Assembly as a defender of the proper bounds of freedom of the press. The most glaring instance of the Assembly's exercise of its punitive powers occurred in 1758 in relation to the Smith-Moore case.[112] William Moore, the Anglican chief judge of the Court of Common Pleas for Chester County, had a record of angry opposition to Quaker principles on the subject of defensive war. In late 1757, on the charge that he had been unjust in his capacity as judge, the Quaker-dominated Assembly summoned him for examination. Moore iterated his innocence and denied the authority of the House to try him for his conduct as a judge, particularly because the charges against him were cognizable at common law, thus creating the possibility of double jeopardy. The Assembly continued its investigation anyway, and in an address to Governor William Denny, published in the *Pennsylvania Gazette*, demanded Moore's removal from office on ground of oppression and corruption. The judge, having been accused in the public press, prepared a defense which he asked the *Gazette* to publish. The printer of the *Gazette*, William Hall, a partner of Ben Franklin, discreetly requested and received permission from the Speaker of the House and other leading politicians to run Moore's reply. They advised that

[111] *American Weekly Mercury*, April 13, 1738, quoted in DeArmond, *Bradford*, 106; see also pp. 110-11.
[112] Reported at great length in *Votes and Proceedings of the House of Representatives of the Province of Pennsylvania (1682-1776)*, in Gertrude MacKinney and Charles F. Hoban, eds., *Pennsylvania Archives*, 8th ser. (n.p., 1931-35), vol. 6, chiefly at pp. 4677-4716. For another case involving scandalous reflection on the Assembly, see 6:4615.

they opposed "restraining the press."[113] Hall's report of Moore's article was also published by the other Philadelphia newspaper, the *Pennsylvania Journal*, which William Bradford printed. Moore then approached his friend and future son-in-law, the Reverend William
Smith, for help. Smith, one of the most prominent Anglicans in the
province and president of the University of Pennsylvania, or, more
properly, provost of the College and Academy of Philadelphia as it
was then called, was an extremely influential person among the large
German-speaking population of the city. He had been instrumental
in founding a German-language newspaper, the *Philadelphia Zeitung*,
and Moore requested Smith's good offices in seeing to the translation
and publication of his reply to the legislature. Smith's compliance
was his undoing, for the members of the House had been waiting for
a pretext to revenge themselves upon him for his outspoken advocacy of a more aggressive campaign against the French. Early in
1758 the sergeant-at-arms of the incoming Assembly arrested both
Smith and Moore for their crimes against the preceding Assembly.[114]
David Hall and William Bradford, who printed the same article in
English, were not touched by the law. No member of the Assembly
explained why "restraining the Press" was inadvisable in the case of
Hall and Bradford but advisable as to Smith's German language
newspaper.

Three of Smith's friends were summoned to testify on his complicity in publishing Moore's newspaper account. The first examined,
Dr. Phineas Bond, refused to answer any questions. He was assured
that the Assembly was not seeking to incriminate him, yet he re-

[113] Leonard W. Labaree, ed., *The Papers of Benjamin Franklin* (New Haven,
1959–), 8:37 (1965).

[114] MacKinney, ed., *Votes and Proceedings*, 6:4619-20, 4637, 4645, and
4677-78. See also Horace Wemyss Smith, *Life and Correspondence of the Reverend William Smith* (Philadelphia, 1879), who discusses the case at 1:167-87,
an account valuable for data on the background of the case and for its reproduction of Smith's letters and other primary sources. Clarke, *Parliamentary
Privilege*, pp. 240-46, is good on legal points. William Renwick Riddell, "Libel
on the Assembly: A Prerevolutionary Episode," *The Pennsylvania Magazine of
History and Biography*, 52(1928):176-92, 249-79, and 342-60, is chiefly concerned with the antagonism between the House and the governor and also
with the legal power of the House to imprison for contempt. The account in
Albert Frank Gegenheimer, *William Smith* (Philadelphia, 1943), 139-48, contains nothing of value and is undocumented. The best account is in George
Dargo, *Roots of the Republic: A New Perspective on Early American Constitutionalism* (New York, 1974), 118-26. Professor Jeffery Smith of the University of Iowa sent me a copy of the invaluable contemporary accounts by the
Smith-Moore faction that appeared in *The American Magazine* (Philadelphia),
issues of Jan. 1758, pp. 199-200 and Feb. 1758, pp. 210-15. William Smith edited
The American Magazine.

mained obstinate. Finally he was offered immunity against prosecution for any testimony he might offer in relation to the alleged seditious libel by Smith and Moore. When Bond persisted in his role as a silent witness, the Assembly voted him to be in "high Contempt" and committed him to jail for an indefinite period. After a few hours behind bars Bond reconsidered his position and informed the Assembly that he proposed to disclose that which "he had apprehended himself obliged by the Ties of Honour and Friendship to conceal." He and Smith's other friends then gave damaging testimony and were discharged.[115]

Judge Moore, after five days of imprisonment, was summoned to the bar of the House for a hearing. He admitted his authorship of the newspaper address against the Assembly, but denied its competency to try him, particularly on the charges relating to his conduct as a magistrate. He was tried anyway, on two counts: judicial misconduct and libeling the House, the constitution, and the government. Upon conviction for the second count, he was pronounced guilty of "false, scandalous, virulent and seditious Libel," the common hangman was commanded to burn copies of his offensive publication, and the sheriff was ordered to hold him in jail indefinitely or until such time as the Assembly might authorize his discharge. The sheriff was additionally commanded that "he do not obey any Writ or *Habeas Corpus*, or other Writ whatsoever, that may come to his Hands for Bailing and Discharging the said *William Moore.*"[116]

This suspension of the writ of habeas corpus was as arbitrary a deprivation of personal liberty as any American legislature might dare attempt. If the word tyranny seems too harsh to describe the case, it is only because in England no writ covered a commitment by either house of Parliament. But the Pennsylvania Assembly was not Parliament, even though it aped the empire's great legislature. Parliament literally and constitutionally possessed unlimited powers. *Lex parliamenti* superseded *lex terrae*. In America, however, the very concept of constitutionalism meant a government of regularized and distinctly limited powers, invalidating the notion of legislative prerogative. The constitutional theory underlying the American Revolution denied that the highest authority in the land was a legislature from whose acts no appeals could be had. The Assembly's absolute denial of habeas corpus, especially as to the misdemeanor of a seditious libel in the form of a breach of privilege, comported more with the conduct of a Stuart despot than with supposed American principles of law

[115] MacKinney, ed., *Votes and Proceedings*, 6:4678-80, 4681-82.
[116] *Ibid.*, 6:4683-89. The quotation is at 6:4689.

and government that antedated the revolution by at least a century.

With Judge Moore in jail, the Assembly turned to the provost of the college. He was brought before the bar of the House and formally charged with "being a Promoter and Abettor of the Writing and Publishing a Libel, entitled, *The humble Address of William Moore*." Smith requested counsel, a copy of the charges against him, and discharge from prison so that he might prepare his defense. He was permitted counsel, a copy of the charges, and time to prepare his defense, but was denied liberty even under bond.[117] Governor Denny and the Assembly, meanwhile, exchanged a series of long, recriminatory messages on the justice and legality of the Assembly's prosecutions of Smith and Moore. At one point the governor raised the question whether the present Assembly might take cognizance of a libel addressed to the previous one, but the Assembly aggressively repudiated all challenges to its authority.[118] To buttress its case against Smith, it summoned Anthony Armbruster, the printer of the German-language paper that had published the libel. For seeming prevarication and refusal to answer certain questions repeatedly put to him, Armbruster was committed to jail, to be held indefinitely in close confinement. After one day of imprisonment, he docilely submitted to the will of the Assembly, begging its pardon and giving direct answers to all questions. The Assembly then voted, *before* Smith's trial commenced, "Resolved, by a great Majority, That the said William Smith is guilty of promoting and publishing the libellous Paper entitled, *The Address of* William Moore *to Governor* Denny."[119]

The mock trial before a kangaroo court, acting as accuser, judge, and jury, began almost a week later and was marked by extraordinary procedure even for a legislature, a body not noted for judicial regularity. Libertarian theorists had raised the cry of "Star Chamber law" when royal judges reserved to themselves the question whether a publication was libelous. But not even under Star Chamber procedure was the question of libel decided in advance of the trial. The nearest analogy to the procedure in Smith's case occurs in Wonderland at the trial of the Knave of Hearts for stealing the tarts; the sentence "Off with his head!" preceded both trial and verdict. To make certain that there could be no slip-up, the Pennsylvania Assembly also decided prior to the trial that the prisoner would not be per-

[117] *Ibid.*, 6:4691-92.
[118] *Ibid.*, 6:4649-54, 4680-81, 4683-85, 4693-96, 4697-98, 4708-14.
[119] *Ibid.*, 6:4704-5.

mitted to dispute its power and authority to punish persons guilty of "Libels against the Government," nor to argue that Moore's publication was not a libel. Smith's counsel requested and was denied leave to argue that a libel on one assembly could not be punished by a succeeding one, or to enquire whether the publication charged did constitute libel. Smith was permitted only to defend himself against the charge on which he had already been adjudged guilty: abetting that libel.[120]

The trial ran its course to a predetermined end. Smith was sentenced to jail until he should give "Satisfaction" to the Assembly for his offense. His counsel immediately moved that he be allowed the privilege of an appeal to the king, that he be furnished with transcripts of the proceedings of the Assembly, and that he be released on bail pending decision on the appeal. But the Assembly refused the motion, answering that appeals could be had to the king and Privy Council only from "inferior Courts" but never from the "Judgments of the House of Assembly, relating to Breach of Privilege, and Contempt to the House."[121] Smith had only to purge himself of his offense by due submission to the authority of the Assembly and confess his error, if he desired his freedom, declared the speaker. At this point the prisoner arose and replied with deep feeling that he was innocent of any crime and "could not in Conscience make any Acknowledgments, or profess Sorrow and Contrition to the House for his Conduct; and, striking his Hand upon his Breast, assured them, no Punishment they could inflict, would be half so terrible to him, as the suffering his Tongue to give his Heart the Lie."[122] He also thought it was his duty "to keep the Dutch press as *free* as any other in the province"; he also invoked, at least in passing, freedom of the press in his defense.[123] He was the only American with the temerity or imagination to confront a legislature with that defense on a charge of breach of privilege. Smith's impassioned statement moved several persons in the audience to stamp their feet and applaud him. The Assembly, taking offense, arrested several of Smith's supporters and convicted them of breach of privilege. They were later released after being forced to ask the Assembly's pardon.[124] But Smith himself was

[120] *Ibid.*, 6:4703-4.
[121] *Ibid.*, 6:4715.
[122] *Ibid.*
[123] The remark appeared in *The American Magazine*, Jan. 1758, p. 196.
[124] MacKinney, ed., *Votes and Proceedings*, 6:4715-25 *passim;* Theodore Thayer, *Pennsylvania Politics and the Growth of Democracy 1740-1776* (Harrisburg, 1953), 68-71.

returned to prison, committed indefinitely; and the Assembly commanded the sheriff that he should not, at his peril, obey a writ of habeas corpus.

In jail Smith proved his mettle by attacking the Assembly in a series of articles that William Bradford, grandson of the first Pennsylvania printer, fearlessly published in his *Pennsylvania Journal*. In the first of these articles Smith challenged the authority of the Assembly to try him. A legislative trial, he argued, violated due process and Magna Carta. He also invoked the Habeas Corpus Act of 1679 and freedom of speech and press against the Assembly. "But to call people to account for freedom of Speech or Printing, and sit as Judges, Juries, and Prosecutions in their own Cause, has never been attempted by them [the House of Commons]." Smith was wrong in saying that and wrong again in adding, "In such cases they [Commons] always order a Prosecution in the Court of Law, where the party may have the benefit of a fair Trial and incur the Penalties annexed to the Crime. There is nothing the Law of England is more tender than the *Freedom* of the *Press*, knowing it to be the great Bulwark of all *other freedom*." Smith than launched into a pastiche from *Cato's Letters*, starting with an extract from Number 15, "Of Freedom of Speech."[125] In his third essay Smith condemned the legislature's "uncommon endeavours, used for a number of years past, to overawe the *Press*, and to vilify and intimidate the advocates for impartial Enquiry."[126] Moore's account of his case, which Smith edited, was more restrained. Liberty of the press, Moore claimed, entitled him to "animadvert freely" on topics of government, but always use that liberty, he said, "within the bounds of Moderation and Law."[127]

The prisoners, Smith and Moore, vainly petitioned the chief justice of the highest court of the province for a writ of habeas corpus. The court ruled that the petitioners, having been committed by the House for a breach of privilege, could not be granted the writ nor be bailed during the sitting of the House. The governor also refused to intercede. Not until the Assembly recessed were the prisoners freed, after more than three months of imprisonment. But when the Assembly reconvened within three weeks, they were again arrested and imprisoned. Fortunately for them the Assembly shortly adjourned for the summer. Governor Denny, who had repeatedly resisted requests from the Assembly to remove Judge Moore from office, now con-

---

[125] *Pennsylvania Journal* (Philadelphia), Feb. 23, 1758 (copy supplied by Jeffery A. Smith).
[126] *The American Magazine*, April 1758, p. 308.
[127] *Ibid.*, Feb. 1758, p. 210.

vened his Council for a full hearing of the charges; the Council unanimously ruled that Moore was "perfectly innocent." But when the Assembly met once again in the fall, it characterized the action of the governor and Council as a "Design to overthrow the Constitution, and enslave the People, by depriving their Representatives of their most essential Rights, Powers, and Privileges." A week after this statement, the Assembly continued its unprecedented behavior by re-ordering the imprisonment of both Smith and Moore, but the sergeant-at-arms failed to find either. Two months later an incoming Assembly convened and promptly demonstrated that it had been infected by its predecessor's contagion of harassment. Moore, from somewhere in hiding, had published another libel on the representatives, and an order went out for his arrest and Smith's, on a warrant from the speaker. The sergeant-at-arms eventually reported that Moore had "absconded" while Smith had "lately embarked for England." Undaunted, the Assembly for the fifth time ordered Moore's arrest.[128]

Smith had fled to England to appeal his cause to the Privy Council. His efforts to obtain justice there were opposed by the official agent of the Pennsylvania Assembly, Benjamin Franklin. Franklin actively managed the case against Smith and Moore and decisively supported the Assembly. Able lawyers presented the case before the Privy Council, but Franklin planned the strategy and tactics. He wrote a refutation of every point of Smith's petition and supplied counsel with precedents from breach of privilege cases in Massachusetts, New York, and Virginia. Franklin maintained that a representative legislature could try and imprison for "Breaches of Privilege, Contempts, false and libellous charges, etc." He condemned Moore's article as "highly reflecting" on the government and derogatory to the privileges of the Assembly. He declared that Smith had suffered not at all by the "Censure of the House for publishing a Libel, he having been long considered as a common Scribbler of Libels against Publick Bodies." And he argued that no appeal could be taken from the judgment of the Assembly. Thus spoke America's foremost printer and reputed champion of freedom of the press. He was not just doing his job. He believed in the position he represented.[129]

When the Privy Council finally moved on the case, in 1759, it decided that Moore's published statement had indeed been a seditious

---

[128] MacKinney, ed., *Votes and Proceedings*, 6:4792, 4799, 4805, 4839, 4894, 4930. See also Riddell, "Libel on the Assembly," *Pennsylvania Magazine* 52:251, 262 *et passim*; Smith, *Life of Smith*, 1:180, 187.
[129] Labaree, ed., *Papers of Franklin*, 8:28-40, 87-88.

libel upon the Assembly; but, since it had been published after the adjournment of the Assembly against which it had been directed, no subsequent Assembly had jurisdiction to consider the offense. Only the Assembly that had been libeled might take action during the life of its session. In addition, the Privy Council ruled that the power of the House of Commons to imprison for contempt in the form of a libel or breach of privilege was not possessed by "these inferior Assemblies in America"; nor could they suspend the writ of habeas corpus in such cases without invading both "his Majesty's Royal Prerogative, and the Liberties of the People." The latest warrants for the rearrest of Smith and Moore were thus rendered void, enabling them to return to Philadelphia in safety, eighteen months after their nightmare had begun.[130] So ended an episode which together with others of a similar nature[131] demonstrated the American legislature's regard for freedom of the press and civil liberty generally. Incidentally, the future conduct of "these inferior Assemblies in America" indicated that they had an equal regard for the opinion of the Privy Council on the point that they possessed no powers of imprisoning for seditious contempt.

In the South, conditions were about the same as in the Middle and the New England colonies. The cast of characters differed in the Southern cases but the plot did not change except in one respect. There were fewer cases, but not because a greater freedom prevailed. On the contrary, there seems to have been more acquiescence and less press activity. Virginia, for example, had no press until 1729 and no newspaper until 1733. Printing came to the Carolinas and Georgia even later and everywhere in the South was introduced under government auspices, closely controlled until the outbreak of the revolutionary controversy in the 1760s. The government press in Virginia had no competitor until 1766.[132] Therefore, the early Southern cases

---

[130] MacKinney, ed., *Votes and Proceedings*, 6:5092, Riddell, "Libel on the Assembly," *Pennsylvania Magazine*, 52:263, 342, 343; Gegenheimer, *William Smith*, 148; and Joseph Henry Smith, *Appeals to the Privy Council from the American Plantations* (New York, 1965), 646-49.

[131] In addition to the earlier cases which have been reviewed, there were others contemporary with the Smith-Moore affair. See Clarke, *Parliamentary Privilege*, p. 120, citing a manuscript journal of the Rhode Island legislature, for the imprisonment by both Houses of a citizen who damned the Assembly. The New Hampshire Assembly also jailed a man for the same offense in 1754. See Clarke, p. 120, citing *New Hampshire Provincial Papers*, 6:240-241. Clarke, at p. 107 and again at p. 120, refers to earlier New Hampshire cases involving breach of privilege by scandalous utterance.

[132] See Thomas, *History of Printing in America*, vol. 2, under the heads of the individual colonies.

involved seditious utterances of a spoken nature, as when a man in 1666 accused the speaker of the House of Burgesses of being an atheist, or when a man in 1695 accused the South Carolina speaker of misappropriating funds. Instances of such cases, wrote the historian of parliamentary privilege in the colonies, "could be multiplied indefinitely with endless variety."[133]

In South Carolina in 1741 the attorney general initiated a common-law prosecution for criminal libel against George Whitefield, the famous evangelist; Hugh Bryan, his follower; and Peter Timothy, the printer of the *South Carolina Gazette* who published their article calumniating the established church in Charleston. The three men were freed on bail and, for unknown reasons, the government dropped the prosecution even before a grand jury could consider an indictment against them.[134] In 1747 Peter Timothy satirized Governor John Glen's plan to enforce Sunday laws, with the result that someone, probably a clergyman of the Church of England, anonymously requested the Charleston grand jury to indict him. The grand jury announced that an indictment would be "destructive of the liberty of the press, a privilege we enjoy, and has been so justly contended for by our ancestors."[135] That statement gave some backbone to hackneyed panegyrics about a free press.

In 1750 Governor Glen's frontier and Indian policies provoked a controversy that resulted in threats of prosecution. James Adair, an Indian trader, wrote a letter insulting the government, whose Council, finding the letter "very Scurilous [*sic*] and Scandlous [*sic*]," turned it over to the attorney general. Adair was arrested on a charge of seditious libel, but the case did not go to trial. In the related case of Matthew Roche, the House censured him for a "Seditious paper, tending to create a Division between his Majesty's Governor, and the people." The House also regarded Roche's paper as an insulting breach of privilege.[136] And yet Roche's prosecution too was dropped, inexplicably. Peter Timothy's involvement ended in a similar way. Twice a grand jury refused to indict him for his printed attacks on the governor's land and Indian policies. The records do not show whether he made a deal to behave discreetly in return for his free-

---

[133] Clarke, *Parliamentary Privilege*, 118, 119.

[134] *Ibid.*, 2:156, and Jeffery A. Smith, "Impartiality and Revolutionary Ideology: Editorial Policies of the *South Carolina Gazette*, 1732-1775," *Journal of Southern History*, 49 (Nov. 1983), 516-17.

[135] Smith, "Impartiality," p. 520, citing *South Carolina Gazette*, March 30, 1747.

[136] R. Nicholas Olsberg, ed., *The Journal of the Commons House of Assembly, 1750-1751* (Columbia, S.C., 1974), 9-11, 156, 161-62.

dom. He quietly reported his vindication by the grand jury by saying that he would make no remarks "on liberty, etc. on libels, etc. on indictments."[137] A year later when the same issues agitated the public, Timothy's paper failed to report essential news; replying to a query about his silence, he cautiously declared, "We hope it may be permitted us to answer we *were not permitted to do it*."[138] Thus the grand jury's statement about freedom of the press faded into insignificance compared with the printer's deliberate refusal to publish news of vital interest to the public and his declaration that "we were not permitted."

Although the royal judges in the South compiled no record of suppressing criminal utterances, the governors, Councils, and lower houses did better. The House of Burgesses of Virginia, for example, punished ten men in 1705 for signing a seditious paper and would have taken punitive action again in 1710 had an anonymous author been located.[139] Governor Alexander Spotswood of Virginia made his bid against the disseminators of "Seditious principles . . . or other Insinuations tending to the disturbance of the peace" when he issued a proclamation in 1711 threatening "the Loss of Life or Member" or imprisonment for anyone daring to commit the heinous crime.[140] The Council in 1714 prosecuted a justice of the peace for "many Seditious Speeches" and in 1720 a minister charged with "uttering false and Scandalous Speeches" against the Crown.[141]

In the 1740s William Parks, the royal printer of the Virginia *Gazette*, published a sensational story about the conviction years earlier of a member of the House of Burgesses for the crime of sheep stealing. Outraged by the affront to one of its members, the House summoned Parks for a legislative trial on a charge of criminal libel. He had scandalized "the government by reflecting on those who are entrusted with the administration of public affairs." Because Parks's accusation against the representatives was either true or false, the House accorded him the privilege of truth as a defense. The production of judicial records bore out his accusation, resulting in an acquittal. Once again, the Zengerian principle that truth cannot be a libel

[137] Smith, "Impartiality and Revolutionary Ideology," citing *South Carolina Gazette*, Nov. 26, 1750.
[138] *Ibid.*, citing *Gazette*, Oct. 3, 1751.
[139] *Journals of the House of Burgesses of Virginia*, vol. 1702-1712, pp. 148 and 230.
[140] McIlwaine, ed., *Executive Journals of the Council of Colonial Virginia*, 3:586-587.
[141] *Ibid.*, 3:364 and 527.

triumphed, contrary to the common-law principle that in a criminal case, truth aggravated the libel.[142]

Similarly, in 1758, in North Carolina, Joshua Bailey escaped the House's punishment, except for his trial and assessment of costs, when he proved the truth of his allegation that a member of the House had lied.[143] In 1758, when the Pennsylvania Assembly moved against the provost of the provincial college, the House of Burgesses in Virginia also wielded its power to punish a breach of privilege, this time against a professor of philosophy of the College of William and Mary. Professor Rowe had indiscreetly declared at a friend's house, unaware that another of the guests was a member of the legislature, that as a minister of the Anglican Church he would refuse to administer sacraments to any "Scoundrels" in the legislature who would vote for settling the salaries of the clergy in cash instead of tobacco. For his "scandalous and malicious" utterances that highly reflected on the honor of the House of Burgesses, Rowe was arrested, forced to beg pardon, and discharged on paying costs.[144] None of the available evidence for the South, or elsewhere, for that matter, suggests that freedom of speech or press flourished before the revolutionary controversy.

[142] Thomas, *History of Printing*, 2:142-44.
[143] William L. Saunders, ed., *The Colonial Records of North Carolina* (*1662-1776*), (*Raleigh*, 1886-90, 10 vols.), 5:1039 and 7:624.
[144] *Journals of the House of Burgesses of Virginia*, vol. 1758-1761, pp. 16, 17-18.

CHAPTER III

A Free Press in the Controversy with Britain

No cause was more honored by rhetorical declamation and dishonored in practice than that of freedom of expression during the revolutionary period, from the 1760s through the cessation of hostilities. The irony of the period might best be portrayed by a cartoon depicting the tarring and feathering of a Tory speaker under a banner run up by the patriots inscribed, "In Liberty's Cause." Yankee Doodle's Liberty Boys vociferously claimed for themselves the right to free expression that they denied their opponents, if they could.

The revolutionary controversy with England did wonders for the expansion and vitality of the colonial press, because the patriot leaders discovered the secret of propaganda as well as the uses of coercion and the powers of factionalism. The press along with pulpit, platform, and parliamentary forum, became an enormously effective vehicle for advertising the Whig position, and so long as England maintained control of the situation, the revolutionary journalists, whose newspapers doubled in number between 1763 and 1775, unceasingly urged the value of open debate. "Cato," Zenger, Andrew Hamilton and John Wilkes became continental heroes, extolled for their defense of virtually unfettered political discussion. Colonial patriots identified the royal judges and their common law of seditious libel with Star Chamber tyranny on the slightest suggestion from government supporters that patriot propagandists were licentiously abusing their privileges of free speech and press. With the instruments for the administration of justice in the hands of the Crown, Whig leaders employed extralegal instruments, particularly threats and mob violence, to checkmate any efforts of the government to suppress seditious libel.[1]

Not that the royal governors, usually with the support of their councils, did not have legitimate cause for retreating in self-defense to the royal courts. Colonists treated royal authority and parliamentary measures with a merciless contempt and abuse that passed all bounds of fair debate. Fair debate was, however, a prized value for the revolutionary party. Josiah Quincy, Jr., writing as "Nedham," laid down its standard when he endorsed "propriety of language" by asserting that the man who acts from principle will "treat all villains with words and actions correspondent to their crimes." Knaves could not be dignified by civility. "FACT is a test of just sentiment. TRUTH is an external standard of propriety in language." Then, in a demonstration of his own adherence to this standard, Quincy declared, "Thus I have considered Mr. Hutchinson as degrading the highest station in the law to the lowest office of the inquisition; as descending from the rank of CHIEF JUSTICE to that of a COMMON INFORMER: an informer against 'particular persons and the province in general;'—yes,—the dark assassin of private characters and HIS NATIVE COUNTRY." The piece concluded with an invective describing Governor Thomas Hutchinson as "the first, the most malignant and *insatiable* enemy" of America who had "committed greater public crimes, than his life can repair or his death satisfy."[2] Little wonder that the royal authorities wistfully hoped that a few convictions for seditious libel might have a salutary effect in restraining an extravagance of language that exacerbated an incendiary situation.

The royal courts, however, proved even more futile in the crisis than they had been in the preceding decades. Except for the convictions of Bayard in 1702, reversed on appeal, of the two Philadelphians who had repudiated the House of Hanover in 1723, and of Checkley in 1724, no common-law prosecutions for seditious utterance succeeded in the eighteenth century. Even in the preceding century, the defendants in the two most notable cases that involved freedom of the press, Bradford and Maule, had not been convicted. It is no sur-

[1] For detailed treatments of the subject of this paragraph, see generally Philip Davidson, *Propaganda and the American Revolution, 1763-1783* (Chapel Hill, N.C., 1941); and Arthur M. Schlesinger, *Prelude to Independence: The Newspaper War on Britain, 1764-1776* (New York, 1958).

[2] Quoted in Joseph T. Buckingham, *Specimens of Newspaper Literature* (Boston, 1852), 1:187 and 191.

prise, then, that during the crisis years preceding the battle of Lexington, only one indictment could be wrangled from a grand jury—and it came to nothing.[3] The authorities tried to do better, but only half-heartedly. The danger of touching off a riot because of an unpopular prosecution posed too great a risk. In New York after the passage of the Stamp Act, Lieutenant-Governor Cadwallader Colden informed Secretary Conway in England that the provincial newspapers brimmed with a hate "exciting the people to disobedience of the Laws and to Sedition." But he agreed with his Council "that considering the present temper of the people this is not a proper time to prosecute the printers and Publishers of the Seditious Papers. The Attorney General likewise told me that he does not think himself safe to commence any such Prosecution."[4] A month later Colden reported that James Parker was suspected to be the printer of an incendiary paper but to make an inquiry into the matter might be imprudent for fear of "raising the Mob which it is thought proper by all means to avoid."[5] By way of contrast the Assembly never doubted its power to suppress seditious publications. At the height of the Stamp Act crisis, a letter purporting to come from anonymous members of the Sons of Liberty, signing themselves "Freedom," was delivered to the clerk of the House instructing the members on the measures to be taken and accusing them of not supporting "public Liberty." The Assembly, with the support of the radical leaders,[6] promptly voting the letter to be "Libellous, Scandalous, and Seditious," called upon the governor to offer a reward of fifty pounds for the discovery of the author or authors.[7] Fortunately for the authors, they escaped capture.

Nowhere did the common-law process more evidently fail than

[3] McDougall's case, discussed below, pp. 76-81. James Morton Smith, *Freedom's Fetters: The Alien and Sedition Laws and American Civil Liberties* (Ithaca, 1956), at pp. 426-27 claims that a "method used to crush colonial opposition to ministerial policies was an accelerated use of the law of seditious libel." Aside from the fact that colonial opposition to ministerial policies was not crushed at all, none of Smith's authorities offers evidence to support his generalization.

[4] Sept. 23, 1765, in E. B. O'Callaghan and B. Fernow, ed., *Documents Relative to the Colonial History of New York* (Albany, 1856-87), 7:759.

[5] Oct. 12, 1765, to Conway, *ibid.*, 7:767.

[6] Carl Lotus Becker, *The History of Political Parties in the Province of New York 1760-1776* (Madison, 1909), 39.

[7] *Journal of the Votes and Proceedings of the General Assembly of the Colony of New-York, 1691-1765* (New York, 1764-66), 2:787. Becker, p. 40, explained that although the Assembly opposed the Stamp Act and had approved of the resolutions of the Stamp Act Congress, "it was especially opposed to having political matters referred to the unenfranchised for decision." It was even more opposed to being criticized.

in Massachusetts where Chief Justice Hutchinson doggedly sought to persuade grand juries to return indictments for seditious libel.[8] In one charge, early in 1767, he urged a grand jury to take note of the fact that libeling a person in public print constituted a crime of high nature, "and it is more mischievous still, when its rulers were slandered and the authority of the government despised." The grand jury ignored him.[9] Later in 1767, the chief justice undertook to define freedom of the press, stating:

> Pretty high Notions of the Liberty of the Press, I am sensible, have prevailed of late among us, but it is very dangerous to meddle with, and strike at this Court. The Liberty of the Press is doubtless a very great Blessing, but this liberty means no more than a Freedom for every Thing to pass from the Press without Licence,—That is, you shall not be obliged to obtain a Licence from any Authority before the Emission of Things from the Press. Unlicenced Printing was never thought to mean a liberty of reviling and calumniating all Ranks and Degrees of Men with Impunity, all Authority with Ignominy.—To carry this absurd Notion of the Liberty of the Press to the Length some would have it—to print every Thing that is Libellous and Slanderous—is truly astonishing, and of the most dangerous Tendency.[10]

Hutchinson's definition of freedom of the press was not only accurate and orthodox; it was the standard definition in Anglo-American thought and law.

The *Boston Gazette*, published by Benjamin Edes and John Gill, spokesmen for Sam Adams and the radical party, replied to Hutchinson by quoting Cato's celebrated letter on "Freedom of Speech,"[11] but Cato's libertarianism had consisted of his philosophical exposition of the values of freedom of expression and his wise advice that al-

[8] Mary Ann Yodelis's unpublished dissertation, "Boston's Second Major Newspaper War: Economics, Politics and the Theory and Practice of Political Expression in the Press, 1763-1775" (University of Wisconsin, 1971), purports to be a repudiation of *Legacy of Suppression*, but the five pounds of typescript supply in staggering detail proof of the thesis advanced here that during the prerevolutionary controversy the Boston newspapers published whatever they pleased with impunity, as if the law of seditious libel had never existed. For a summary statement, see Yodelis, "Courts, Counting House and Streets: Attempts at Press Control, 1763-1775," *Journalism History* 1:11-15 (1974).

[9] Josiah Quincy, Jr., ed., *Reports of Cases Argued and Adjudged in the Superior Court of Judicature of the Province of Massachusetts Bay, Between 1761 and 1772* (Boston, 1865), 236-37.

[10] *Ibid.*, 244-45. Charge to the Grand Jury, August term, 1767.

[11] Schlesinger, *Prelude to Independence*, 96. Cato is discussed below, at pp. 109-14.

though seditious libels were base, unlawful, and punishable, prosecutions endangered liberty more than its abuse imperiled the state. He and other libertarians understood freedom of the press very differently from Hutchinson but had differed not at all in their understanding of its legal responsibility. The *Boston Gazette* itself, in an essay by "Freeborn American," had offered the following statement only a few months earlier: "Political liberty consists in a freedom of speech and action, so far as the laws of a community will permit and no farther: all beyond is criminal, and tends to the destruction of Liberty itself.—That Society whose laws least restrain the words and actions of its members, is most free.—There is no nation on the earth, where freedom of speech is more extensive than among the English."[12] Hutchinson, Blackstone, or Mansfield could have written that; it bears repeating that the newspaper of the radical patriot faction published it.

In early 1768 the *Gazette* ran an unsigned piece, written by Dr. Joseph Warren, that vilified Governor Francis Bernard in an effort to hold him up to the public as a hated enemy of the province.[13] The Council unanimously agreed that the article was a seditious libel placing the governor "in the most odious light."[14] With this support Bernard appealed to the lower house, hoping for an endorsement of his plan to turn the matter over to a grand jury, but that house, in control of the radicals, simply expressed its regrets to the governor, declared itself unwilling to take any additional notice of the matter, and resolved for the first time in its history that "The Liberty of the Press is a great bulwark of the Liberty of the People: It is, therefore, the incumbent Duty of those who are constituted the Guardians of the People's Rights to defend and maintain it."[15] Bernard, ignoring the advice of the House to go no further, turned to the courts for help.

Chief Justice Hutchinson, charging the grand jury, explained the tendency of criminal libels to disturb the peace and warned that their increased prevalence "threatens the Subversion of all Rule among us." Indeed, they came close to "high treason." Once again he defined the true meaning of freedom of the press; formerly, he recalled, no man could print his thoughts without a license. "When this Restraint was taken off, then was the true Liberty of the Press. Every Man who

[12] *Boston Gazette,* March 9, 1767. The entire essay is available in Levy, ed., *Freedom of the Press,* 94-97.
[13] Quincy, ed., *Reports of Cases,* reprints the article at pp. 271-72.
[14] *Ibid.,* 273.
[15] *Ibid.,* 275. The House vote was 39 to 30. *Journals of the House of Representatives of Massachusetts, 1767-1768* (Boston, 1975), 206-7, 210-11.

prints, prints at his Peril." He then demanded of the grand jurors indictments against those responsible for the seditious statements in the
Gazette, but they found no true bill, inspiring the newspaper, in articles written by Dr. Warren and Sam Adams, to toast the House and
the grand jury for vindicating the freedom of the press. Adams also
ridiculed the "absurd doctrine, *the more true, the more libellous.*"
Josiah Quincy, Jr., who had been present at Hutchinson's charge,
added a personal note to his report of it, vaguely challenging "some
Points of Law" on the authority of "Bollan on the Freedom of Speech
and Writing upon Publick Affairs. . . ."[16] At a later session in 1768
the chief justice again tried and failed to get a grand jury to indict for
"inflammatory, seditious Libels upon Government or the Rulers in
Government, which tend to destroy all civil Peace, and strike at the
Root of all Order and Government."[17] Boston juries believed Sam
Adams who wrote this encomium on freedom of the press for the
Boston Gazette:

> THERE is nothing so *fretting* and *vexatious;* nothing so justly
> TERRIBLE to tyrants, and their tools and abettors, as a FREE
> PRESS. The reason is obvious; namely, Because it is, as it has been
> very justly observ'd in a *spirited* answer to a *spirited speech, "the*
> *bulwark of the People's Liberties."* For this reason, it is ever
> watched by those who are forming plans for the destruction of the
> people's liberties, with an *envious* and *malignant* eye.[18]

By the spring of 1769 Hutchinson declared sorrowfully to a grand
jury that although the "atrocious Crime" was fast multiplying, his
repeated charges on the subject had been "entirely neglected," and as
a result "I do not mention the Matter of Libels to you, Gentlemen—
I am discouraged!"[19] The law of seditious libel simply had no meaning any longer. The uninhibited practices of a free press, supported
by public opinion and reinforced by tactics of intimidation employed
by patriot leaders and their street followers, dissolved all legal restraints and sanctions. Complete freedom for the radical position
gained impregnability from roughhouse methods. In the spring of
1769 when the radicals exulted in their limitless expression, John
Mein, the loyalist printer of the *Chronicle,* scrawled this note to
Hutchinson:

[16] Quincy, ed., *Reports of Cases* 263, 266, 270, 277, and 278. On Bollan, see
below, at pp. 154-55.
[17] Quincy, ed., *Reports of Cases,* 305.
[18] Adams, *Boston Gazette,* March 14, 1768.
[19] Quincy, ed., *Reports of Cases,* 309.

I informed you in a Conversation some days since the probability of my being attacked: It just now happened by a Number of People . . . upwards of twenty, armed with a Spade, Canes, and Clubs. I luckily got into the Guardroom, where I now am: I write to your Honour to know what protection the Law can afford to a person in my Situation; and the Names of the Officers of the Law, who will put that Law into execution. About two hundred People are before the Guard and in Kingstreet: the Case requires immediate Steps to be taken. . . .[20]

With law and order as well as the common-law process and substance breaking down entirely, Governor Bernard appealed for help to the ministry in England. Edes and Gill, he recommended, should be seized and forced to identify their "treasonable and seditious" contributors; responsibility for appropriate action must, however, devolve upon the home government. But the ministry did nothing except to pass the responsibility to the provincial government for permitting seditious libels to go unpunished. The Governor's Council, replying through William Bollan—its agent in England whom Quincy had mistaken as an authority opposed to Hutchinson's exposition of the common law—hurled a resentful "tu quoque" at the Privy Council and House of Lords for being even far more lax than Massachusetts in countenancing defamation of the government. For every "seditious and libellous publication" in the Bay Colony "there are fifty in England," declared Bollan, alluding to the supporters of Wilkes and Junius. The governor's Council, he asserted, simply had no power to try a case.[21] He must have known, of course, that this was not true; he meant in all probability that the Council under the circumstances dared not act against the lower house or bypass the jury system.

By the end of 1771 the Council could not even enforce its own authority. Its members, elected by the House, which had cleaned out most of the leading Tories as early as 1766, were led by James Bowdoin and were "just as much dominated by the popular or democratic party as was the House."[22] Yet in late 1771 and 1772 the Council

[20] Chapter 5, "From the Courts to the Streets," pp. 316-64 of Yodelis's dissertation, documents the use of extralegal coercion against the government press and its supporters. The quotation from Mein is in Yodelis's article, "Courts, Counting House," p. 11.

[21] Schlesinger, *Prelude to Independence*, 310-11. The quoted material is from Duniway, *Freedom of the Press*, 129.

[22] Robert E. Brown, *Middle-Class Democracy and the Revolution in Massachusetts, 1691-1780* (Ithaca, 1955), 230. See also pp. 229 and 333. For detailed discussion of the Council's evolution toward radicalism, see Francis J. Walett, "The Massachusetts Council, 1766-1774," *William and Mary Quarterly*, 3rd ser., 6:605-27 (1949).

stood foursquare with Hutchinson, now governor, in seeking to scotch incendiary writers. The explanation, perhaps, lies in the repeal of the Townshend duties, the breaking of the Nonimportation Agreement, and the upsurge of prosperity that accompanied a near collapse of the revolutionary movement until the Tea Act of 1773 rekindled it. Whatever the reason, the Council in late 1771 believed that Isaiah Thomas, publisher of the *Massachusetts Spy*, known as "The Sedition Foundry," had passed the threshold of tolerable limits. Thomas, the most recklessly radical printer in America, regarded his unrestrained press as a blessing to mankind because he defended the glorious cause of liberty and exposed miscreants who betrayed it. The particular article that nettled the Council boasted the signature of that noble Roman, "Mucius Scaevola," who was suspected to be Joseph Green-leaf, a justice of the peace. Scaevola had flatly announced that Lieu-tenant-Governor Andrew Oliver "stood recorded as a perjured trai-tor" while Governor Hutchinson "ought to be dismissed and punished as a usurper."[23] The Council promptly summoned Thomas to answer for this libel, but with colossal nerve he refused to comply with the order. As he related the story, he instructed the Council's messenger to notify the governor and their honors that he could not wait upon them since he was "busily employed in his office."[24]

In the halcyon days before the revolutionary controversy, when the thought of mobs did not intimidate the government, the Council would have stunned such impudence by summarily imprisoning the party. But the imperative of acting through popular agencies forced the unanimous Council to content itself with ordering the attorney-general to prosecute Thomas at common law. He replied by attack-ing the Star Chamber doctrine of libels, called upon Hamilton's Zenger argument to prove that truth was a defense against seditious libel—had not Scaevola written only the truth?—and quoted William Bollan, the Council's own agent in London, on the values of free discussion. Thomas vigorously advocated the truth-as-defense doc-trine of the Zenger defense, which he publicized; moreover he in-sisted that a jury in any case of seditious libel must decide whether the author composed the piece "falsely, seditiously, and maliciously" and then render a general verdict on the law as well as the fact.[25]

On the other side, the unwavering position of the "friends of the

---

[23] *Massachusetts Spy*, Nov. 14, 1771.
[24] Isaiah Thomas, *The History of Printing in America* (Worcester 1810), 1:380; *Massachusetts Spy*, Nov. 14, 1771, and Jan. 3, 1772.
[25] *Massachusetts Spy*, Dec. 26, 1771; Schlesinger, *Prelude to Independence*, 140-41.

government," according to Philanthrop, Jr., who was probably Jonathan Sewell, remained Blackstonian; although a printer could freely print what he pleased, he was "not exempt from Law."[26] In fact, however, the government had lost control of the law. "Honestus," another government supporter, complained:

> True Liberty is the *uncontrouled* exercise of every privilege which we derive from the Laws of our Country. When I reflect on the Tyranny of Patriotism, I think any other despotism a state of comparative felicity. Bad as our present Ministers are universally represented to be by the News Papers, they still allow us some degree of Freedom; they suffer us to think, to talk, and to write as we please, but the Patriots allow us no such indulgence. Unless we think, talk, and write as they would have us, we are Traitors to the State, we are infamous Hirelings to the Government.[27]

At the following term of the Supreme Court, in February of 1772, the chief justice dwelt on the horrors of seditious libel, but the grand jury blithely refused to indict Thomas. At this point the Council took what was a daring risk in Boston at that time by ordering the attorney-general to prosecute by an information, thereby avoiding the consent of a grand jury. But the popular party so vehemently attacked this plan as a violation of the liberties of the subject and of freedom of the press that the government dropped the prosecution. Stymied, the Council took petty revenge against Joseph Greenleaf, who had also refused to obey a summons; they dismissed him as a justice of the peace.[28] In the fall of that year, Thomas outdid himself by publishing an attack upon George III, accusing him of having corrupted the government by the appointment of "every dirty booby who was thought a convenient tool."[29] The apoplectic Hutchinson urged that Thomas be prosecuted by information, but the Council, recalling the public fury against an attempt to do that very thing earlier in the year, advised a popular but futile approach: indictment by grand jury. That body, of course, refused to return a true bill. By that time even the Ministry advised Hutchinson that "in the present temper of the times, prosecutions will be of no effect." Thomas himself exulted but menacingly warned that if the press were ever fettered, the next step would be "padlocks on our lips." He knew about

---

[26] *Boston News-Letter*, April 9, 1772.

[27] *Ibid.*, Dec. 17, 1771.

[28] Thomas, *History of Printing in America*, 2:380-83 and 475-76. See also Schlesinger, *Prelude to Independence*, 140-42.

[29] Quoted in Schlesinger, *Prelude to Independence*, 148.

fetters and padlocks because he quoted Blackstone on the freedom of the press as well as Cato and Alexander.[30]

The point of course is that the press was not fettered during the revolutionary controversy, at least not the patriot press. The patriot newspapers did not exercise a monopoly. Some Loyalist printers remained in business, although their number steadily diminished. Even in Boston some newspapers continued to support Britain, free, of course, from government restraint but not free from sanctions and threats from the patriot faction. The Fleet brothers, Thomas and John, courageously pursued an old policy of nonpartisanship, opening the columns of their *Boston Evening Press* to both the savage critics and apologetic supporters of Britain. As a result of their neutrality the Fleets antagonized both sides, lost subscribers, and closed down. The tradition of a free press as an impartial press that had no pronounced editorial policies could not survive the polarized politics engendered by the controversy with Britain. When the British regained control, even temporarily, they reasserted dominance of the press. In 1775, for example, when the redcoats occupied Boston, most of the patriot printers fled. The British caught and imprisoned John Gill of the seditious pair, Edes and Gill, for printing "sedition, treason, and rebellion."[31]

If any fetters or padlocks were forged for the press during the controversy with Britain, only one body possessed the actual power as well as authority, and that was the Assembly, always the most effective repressor. In Virginia where a grand jury declined to indict three publishers in 1766,[32] the House of Burgesses in 1767 demonstrated how to handle those who abused the liberty of the press. A man named James Pride, either out of naivete or foolish courage, served a writ on a member during the session of the House, an act which that body took as an affront to its collective dignity. Summoned to explain himself, Pride multiplied the affront by failing to obey the summons because of ill health; the House deemed the letter, which he sent by way of explanation, scandalous and a high breach of privilege. The Assembly displayed its mood by commanding its sergeant-at-arms to take Pride into custody by any means necessary, even if he had to break open doors and muster a posse. But a medical certificate arrived from Pride's doctor in time to prevent strong-arm measures. The suspicious House immediately commanded two

---

[30] *Ibid.; Massachusetts Spy*, July 22, 1773.

[31] Peter Force, ed., *American Archives: Consisting of a Collection of Authentic Records* (Washington, 1837ff.), 4th ser., 3:712.

[32] Thomas, *History of Printing in America*, 2:148.

physicians of its own choosing to examine Pride; they reported him without fever and able to attend on the Burgesses. This time the sergeant-at-arms brought in the malefactor, who, without even an interrogation, was delivered to the jailer on a warrant from the speaker to hold him "until discharged, by Order of the House." The prisoner was also assessed twelve pounds sixpence for the services of the Assembly's physician and sergeant.

After nine days of imprisonment without a hearing, Pride took a drastic step. He wrote an account of his case, revealing to the public the harsh treatment he was receiving, and he sent the manuscript by a friend to the Virginia *Gazette* for publication. William Rind, the printer, had the foresight to check with the authorities before running Pride's piece. The Assembly then resolved that their prisoner's act was a seditious insult. For the first and only time he was summoned, from jail, before the bar of the house, there to receive a censure instead of a hearing. On turning him over to the jailer again, the House ordered that he be kept "in close confinement, without the Use of Pen, Ink, or Paper; and that he be fed on Bread only, and allowed no Liquor whatever." Luck rode on Pride's side, however; only two days after his latest punishment the governor prorogued the House of Burgesses, making Pride eligible for habeas corpus. When finally free he discovered that he had lost his post as a naval officer.[33]

The North Carolina Assembly knew how to treat licentious use of the press, too. The victim was Hermon Husband, one of the leaders of the Regulators, a group of debtor farmers from the back country who had elected him to the Assembly. Late in 1770 the North Carolina *Gazette*, which sympathized with the Regulators, published an article accusing a judge of having unjustly treated debtors. The newspaper also chided members of the Assembly for not doing what was in their power to ameliorate the condition of the people. Affronted, the Assembly voted the article to be a "false, seditious, and Malicious Libel," and turned upon Husband as the suspected author. Summoned to the bar for examination, he denied responsibility for the publication. But the Assembly charged him with "prevarication." Even though he had been acquitted after trial on the charge of having incited a riot the preceding year, the Assembly condemned him as "a principal mover and promoter of the late riots and seditions," and on

---

[33] H. R. McIlwaine and J. P. Kennedy, eds., *Journals of the House of Burgesses of Virginia, 1619-1776* (Richmond, 1905-15), vol. 1766-1769, pp. 91, 97, 98-99, 100, 103, 110, 120, 121, 125. The sentence against Pride, quoted above, is at p. 121.

the theory that leopards do not change their spots assumed him to be the culprit responsible for the seditious piece in the *Gazette*. When Husband declared that the people would free him if he were jailed, the Assembly regarded him as being additionally guilty of a bold insult and an attempt to intimidate the members from a due discharge of their duties. A final resolution expelled him from his seat in the House.[34] He was then arrested and held in jail for a couple of months to await the action of a grand jury which ultimately failed to indict.[35] The refusal of grand juries to indict for seditious libel in Massachusetts and the two Carolinas suggests a growing popular repugnance for the doctrine of crown libels.

In Pennsylvania a clawless legislature failed to rake William Goddard, the irresponsible printer of the *Philadelphia Chronicle*. In 1771, in an article signed "Friend of Liberty," Goddard charged that Joseph Galloway, the speaker of the Pennsylvania Assembly, sought "to destroy the liberty of his country" and "enslave and ruin his countrymen." The Assembly adopted a resolution censuring the article as "false, scandalous, and malicious, a daring Insult to, and a Breach of the Privileges of the House." But instead of summoning and trying Goddard, the Assembly merely ordered that his newspaper and the others in the city publish the resolution of censure. Goddard complied but did not change his libelous practices. William Bradford's *Philadelphia Gazette* also complied, but Bradford added: "For my part, I not only consider it [the resolution] disgraceful, but dangerous, as it may be a Precedent hereafter to intimidate the Press, and infringe the Liberties of the Subject." Neither Bradford nor Goddard showed the least sign of intimidation. Two years later, in 1773, Goddard's *Chronicle* reported Galloway's reelection to the speakership as a public disgrace, remarking that "Perjury, Subornation, and the Basest Treachery . . . are sometimes no Disqualifications to a Place of Trust." The pusillanimous Assembly ignored the gross seditious libel; Goddard, who left the newspaper in his sister's charge, moved to Baltimore where he founded the *Maryland Journal*.[36]

The credo of Goddard's new paper was conventional although partisan: ". . . the Freedom of the Press shall be maintained, the utmost Impartiality observed, and every well-written Piece admitted, without Scruple, that does not tend to destroy or impair our excellent

[34] William L. Saunders, ed., *The Colonial Records of North Carolina (1662-1776)* (Raleigh, 1886-90), 8:331.

[35] See J. G. de R. Hamilton's article on Husband in the *Dictionary of American Biography*.

[36] Ward L. Miner, *William Goddard, Newspaperman* (Durham, N.C., 1962), 101-2, 109.

Constitution, injure the Cause of Liberty, disturb the Repose of Society, give Offense to Modesty, or, in any Shape, reflect Scandal on a News-Paper." Soon after, however, in 1779, Goddard, who could be vicious, published an extremely conservative defense of freedom of the press: "Restraints on the Press in any Cases, except Libels and Treason, narrow and debase the liberal sentiments of the Soul, and curb the rising Efforts of Genius. It is a Mockery of the Understanding to call that Country free, where this Restraint is tolerated, approved of, and supported." The qualifying clause, "except Libels and Treason," accepted the principle of the common law that a printer was criminally responsible for abusing his freedom. Goddard did not believe subsequent punishment improper or libel prosecutions incompatible with freedom. He managed to escape conflict with the Maryland authorities, although he was mobbed in 1779 for publishing an article critical of George Washington.[37]

In neighboring South Carolina the relations of the upper and lower houses of the legislature ruptured over an issue initially involving freedom of the press. Thomas Powell printed in his *South Carolina Gazette* a digest of the proceedings of the Council at the request of a member, William Henry Drayton. The Council summoned the publisher for questioning and concluded that he had contemptuously breached its privileges. This occurred in August of 1773, when the unlicensed publication of legislative proceedings was still a crime. Powell apologized but stubbornly refused to ask for pardon, provoking the Council to subject him to a formal trial at which it acted as prosecutor, judge, and jury. Drayton, coming to the publisher's defense, acknowledged that without intending any affront to the Council he had sent him a copy of part of the journals with a request that they be printed. Powell, condemned anyway for a breach of privileges and contempt, was committed to the Charleston jail. He was released two days later on a writ of habeas corpus issued by two judges who happened also to be the speaker of the Assembly and a member of it, Rawlins Lowndes and George G. Powell. They accepted the arguments of young Edmund Rutledge that the printer had a right to publish an accurate statement of the Council's proceedings at the request of one of its members, and secondly, that the Council, being an executive rather than a legislative body, possessed no authority to commit anyone for breach of parliamentary privilege. Powell, the printer, immediately issued a special issue of his paper notifying the public of the affair. Triumphantly lambasting the

[37] *Ibid.*, 139, 172.

Council, he declared that the restoration of his freedom "defeated the most violent attempt that had ever been made in this Province upon the Liberty of the Subject—probably intended to controul the Liberty of the Press."[38] The Council responded by ruling him guilty of seditious libel. A committee of the Council, including the chief justice of the province, then reported that Speaker Lowndes and Representative Powell, by discharging a prisoner committed by order of the Council in defense of its authority and dignity, stood "guilty of the most atrocious contempt of this house" and had "subverted the constitution of this government." The Council, accepting this report, notified the Assembly that it expected the proper steps to be taken against the two members for their crime.

By now freedom of the press had been completely lost as an issue in the case. The Assembly, refusing to comply with the Council's demands, cared only about justifying the conduct of its speaker and asserted its independence against the Council, which it denied to be a parliamentary body. Each house protested to the government in England that the other had unwarrantedly interfered in its affairs. The appeals not yet having been decided when the war broke out, the issues remained unresolved. The point which emerges most clearly from the affair is that the press in South Carolina remained at the mercy of the legislature. Had the *Gazette*'s publication concerning the Council not been politically useful to the Assembly in its struggle of long standing against the Council, the printer would have remained in jail at the Council's pleasure.[39]

In New York the Assembly, which had intimidated a printer and his journeymen in 1766 for inadvertently publishing an address of the

---

[38] *South Carolina Gazette*, Sept. 13, 1773, quoted by Sir Egerton Leigh, "Considerations on Certain Political Transactions of the Province of South Carolina" (London, 1774), reprinted in Jack P. Greene, ed., *The Nature of Colony Constitutions* (Columbia, S.C., 1970), 121 and 216 n. 91. Greene's book, which has a splendid introduction, contains invaluable contemporary documents. The judicial opinion by Lowndes is in *ibid.*, Arthur Lee, "Considerations," 177-81. Lee supported the lower house; Leigh, who was president of the Council, defended the upper house; he also defended himself by invoking freedom of the press to justify the resort to publication. *Ibid.*, 176, 201, and 205. *South Carolina Gazette*, Aug. 30, 1773, for the publication of the Council's records; Sept. 2, 1773 for Drayton's protest and the Council's order committing Powell; and Sept. 13, 1773, for Powell's trial before the Council. See also Thomas, *History of Printing in America*, 2:162-67; Edward McCrady, *The History of South Carolina under the Royal Government 1719-1776* (New York, 1899), 715-23; and David D. Wallace, *Constitutional History of South Carolina* (Abbeville, S.C., 1899), 80-88.

[39] Thomas, *History of Printing in America*, 2:162-67, and McCrady, *The History of South Carolina under the Royal Government 1719-1776*, 715-23.

House with two typographical errors,[40] proved itself capable of dealing effectively even with a radical of the patriot party. In December
of 1769, the Assembly had voted to supply provisions for the king's
troops in New York City, in return for Governor's Colden's signature to an act authorizing the emission of needed bills of credit.[41]
Three days later a handbill addressed "To the Betrayed Inhabitants
of New York," signed by a "Son of Liberty," blanketed the city.
The author condemned the Assembly for abandoning the liberties of
the people by passing the provisions bill, and he called upon the public to rise against unjust measures. The next day another broadside
appeared, over the name of "Legion," urging the public to attend a
mass protest meeting. Fourteen hundred turned out and were addressed by the radical agitator, John Lamb. The Assembly retaliated
by declaring each broadside to be "a false seditious and infamous
Libel" and called upon the governor to offer rewards for information
leading to the discovery of the author or authors. The Assembly had
passed the provisions bill by a bare majority, but unanimously passed
its resolves against the seditious writers. Governor Colden gladly
complied with the Assembly's request and issued proclamations offering one hundred and fifty pounds in reward money.[42]

Dazzled by so much money, a journeyman printer in the shop of
James Parker betrayed his employer as the printer of "To the Betrayed." Parker, who in 1756 had been jailed for a week by the Assembly for printing a reflection, now charged with having published
a seditious libel, suffered arrest and an inquiry by the governor and
Council. The sheriff took into custody all his apprentices and journeymen for questioning at the same time. Their testimony substan-
tiated that of the informer and also revealed that one Alexander
McDougall had corrected the proofs at the printing office. Parker
himself balked at naming the author, but he could not withstand the

[40] Thomas, *History of Printing in America*, 2:302-3.
[41] Becker, *Parties in New York*, 77-78.
[42] E. B. O'Callaghan, ed., *Documentary History of the State of New York*
(Albany, 1849-51), 3:528-36, reproduces the broadsides and Colden's proclamations which quote the Assembly's resolutions. According to the proclamations
the Assembly vote was unanimous. Isaac Q. Leake, *Memoir of the Life and
Times of General John Lamb* (Albany, 1850), 51, claimed that one member,
Philip Schuyler, voted against the resolutions. E. Wilder Spaulding, *His Excellency, George Clinton* (New York, 1938), 27, supported Leake. However,
the diary of William Smith, a member of the Council, also showed that the
Assembly's vote was unanimous. See William H. W. Sabine, ed., *Historical
Memoirs from 16 March 1763 to 9 July 1776 of William Smith* (New York,
1956), 71. The MS Journal, cited in the next note for Dec. 19, 1769, is con-
clusive; the vote was unanimous.

threats of imprisonment and dismissal from his post as comptroller of the post office. He made a deal with the Council, buying immunity against prosecution and loss of his post by identifying the author and pledging to appear against him as a government witness.[43]

Parker identified the man as Alexander McDougall, a local merchant who with Lamb and Isaac Sears was one of the commanders of the Sons of Liberty. Later McDougall would serve in both the First and Second Continental Congresses and as a major-general during the Revolution. He died in 1786 a pillar of conservatism, the first president of the Bank of New York and founder and head of the Society of Cincinnati in New York.[44] In February of 1770, he was arrested on a charge of seditious libel against the Assembly. With Parker as a witness of his authorship, the legislature had a sure-fire case and turned the prisoner over to the common-law courts. McDougall, on examination before Chief Justice Daniel Horsmanden, remained silent except to demand a trial by jury. The judge set bail at the inordinately high sum of five hundred pounds, which McDougall refused to pay, although Governor Colden called him "a person of some fortune." He preferred waiting in jail as a martyr while awaiting the action of the grand jury.[45]

McDougall remained in jail for two and a half months. His imprisonment did more to publicize the cause of liberty of the press than any event since Zenger's trial. Alexander's account of that trial was republished for the third time in New York, and Parker's paper and Holt's *New York Journal* courageously plumped for McDougall and freedom of discussion. The editor and the prisoner against whom

[43] For the McDougall case, I have read every issue of the *New York Journal,* the *New York Gazette, or Weekly Post-Boy* from December 1769 through March 1771, and the *New York Chronicle* through its last issue, Jan. 4, 1770. Another indispensable source was a microfilm copy of the manuscript *Journal of Votes and Proceedings of the General Assembly of the Colony of New-York* for the years 1769-71, obtained from the Public Records Office in London, Doc. #953. C.O. 5/1219. For additional accounts see "McDougall's Account," in a letter to the *New York Journal,* Feb. 15, 1770, and his statement in *ibid.,* Jan. 29, 1771. See also *Historical Memoirs of William Smith,* 73-75; Leake, *Lamb,* 60-61; Thomas, *History of Printing in America,* 2:479-81; and Dorothy Rita Dillon, *The New York Triumvirate* (New York, 1949), 106-7, and Roger J. Champagne, *Alexander McDougall and the American Revolution* (Schenectady, N.Y., 1975), 27-44.

[44] *Dictionary of American Biography.*

[45] "McDougall's Account," and Colden to Lord Hillsborough, Feb. 20, 1770, in Thomas Jones, *History of New York During the Revolutionary War* (New York, 1879, 2 vols.), 1:432-34. See also Thomas, *History of Printing in America,* 2:481; Julius Goebel, Jr., and T. Raymond Naughton, *Law Enforcement in Colonial New York* (New York, 1944), 506 n. 89.

he was to testify wrote hortatory articles urging all the colonies to enact statutes abolishing the "tyrannical Tenets" of the common law of seditious libel which was invariably associated with the infamous Star Chamber. Yet neither ever attacked the concept of seditious libel. They made no suggestion that government could not be criminally assaulted by its citizens' opinions. Beneath the epithetical rhetoric lay only the proposition that truth be accepted as a defense.[46] The *New York Mercury*, however, defended the common law and backed the Assembly against McDougall.[47] The editor of conservatism's voice was Hugh Gaine, who in 1753 had been forced by the Assembly to humble himself in order to avoid prosecution for having printed its proceedings without prior license.[48] Gaine's principal statement on freedom of the press was the following:

Among the Objections which to blind the Credulous, have been raised against this Prosecution, the most considerable are, that it is an Invasion of the *Liberty of the Press*, and of the *Right of the People to convass the Conduct of Government; and that the Paper itself is not offensive or criminal.* No man, 'till this Day of constitutional Light, has pretended, that the Press could sanctify every Production, however atrocious or malignant. Sufficient it is, that a *Printer* enjoys equal Privileges, with his fellow Citizens, as *they* have the Power to *act,* tho' they are punishable for their *Misconduct;* so ought *he* not to be under the Restraint of an *Imprimatur;* for then his Right of *private Judgment* would be suppressed, and his *Actions* rest on the Will of another. But if he abuses this *Independence,* to the Hurt of Society, or of Individuals, he ought not to be defended, for this would place him above *the Law,* which intends a general Security; and not to give to any, a *Dispensation* to be mischievous with Impunity. If there was no Check to Malice and Falsehood, Government must soon sink into Contempt, and the subject be stript of Protection. Political Writers have justly observed that the Principle of *Honour,* is not less the Strength of an *absolute* Throne, than *publick Virtue,* the Support of a *free State,* like that under which we live; often has it been predicted, that when the Body of the People, become tainted by Error and Corruption, a Dissolution of the Establishment will be unavoidable. What then

[46] See, for example, the *Post-Boy,* April 9, 1770, and *New York Journal,* March 15, 1770.

[47] Between April 9 and June 25, 1770, the *Mercury* published the twelve-part "Dougliad," a continuing attack on McDougall and a defense of the government and the prosecution. See also *Historical Memoirs of William Smith,* 75-76; Schlesinger, *Prelude to Independence,* 115-16; Dillon, *New York Triumvirate,* 112.

[48] See above, p. 46.

can have a more fatal Influence, to debauch our Principals, and estrange our Affections, than an *unrestrainted Licence*, to inculcate every wild and pernicious Tenet? To traduce and vilify those in Authority, to misrepresent their Conduct, to expose them to Odium and Contempt, and to excite a general Spirit of Jealousy and Distrust, must it not infallably lead to Faction, to revolt, and open Sedition?[49]

Notwithstanding Gaine's policy, the McDougall case as managed by the Sons of Liberty became America's equivalent of Wilkes's case in England. Indeed, McDougall himself consciously posed as the American Wilkes and turned his imprisonment into a theatrical triumph, while his supporters used the free press issue as an anti-administration weapon. Forty-five, the number of the *North Briton* that had earned Wilkes his conviction for seditious libel, became the talismanic symbol of libertarianism and of the American cause against England. On the forty-fifth day of the year, for example, forty-five Liberty Boys dined in honor of McDougall on forty-five pounds of beef from a forty-five-month-old bull, drank forty-five toasts to liberty of the press and its defenders, and after dinner marched to the city jail to salute McDougall with forty-five cheers. On one particularly festive liberty day, forty-five songs were sung to him by forty-five virgins, every one of whom, reported a damned Tory, was forty-five years old.[50]

At the end of April McDougall, attended by a mob of his partisans on the way from prison to court, finally appeared before the grand jury, which indicted him as the author of a seditious libel against the Assembly. The common-law indictment, the only one of its kind against a popular leader during the revolutionary controversy, was the first of its kind in twenty-five years. Yet the unique fact that every branch of the government, including the Assembly, supported the prosecution made the indictment understandable. So did the fact that the sheriff carefully picked the grand jurors, the "most . . . opulent & substantial gentlemen of the city." The court fixed the date of the trial for its next session in July, and McDougall, this time paying the huge bail assessed against him, quit prison. On July 2, just before the trial, James Parker, the star witness of the prosecution and the only one who could testify from personal knowledge that Mc-

[49] *New York Mercury*, April 26, 1770.
[50] Jones, *History of New York*, 1:27-28, 435; *New York Post-Boy*, Feb. 19, 1770, and *New York Journal*, March 22 and, for the Tory's letter, March 29, 1770; Leake, *Lamb*, 62 John C. Miller, *Origins of the American Revolution* (Boston, 1943), 306. On Wilkes, see below, pp. 144-47.

Dougall had written the seditious broadside, suddenly died. With his death the case against the defendant vanished. The trial was postponed till October and then again indefinitely. If McDougall gloated over the turn of events that promised him a discharge from the indictment, he failed to consider the power of a revengeful Assembly.[51]

With the collapse of the common-law prosecution, the Assembly resolved to punish McDougall on its own authority. Late in 1770 the speaker of the House ordered his arrest; after McDougall spent a week in jail the sergeant-at-arms brought him before the bar of the House. Speaker Henry Cruger then informed McDougall that he stood charged with having libeled the House and asked how he pleaded. McDougall refused to plead to the charge until, he declared, he learned of the identity of his accusers and the evidence against him. Cruger interrupted to threaten that he would be held in contempt for addressing the House without its prior leave, but George Clinton interceded on the prisoner's behalf, so that McDougall received permission to give his reasons for not pleading. He explained that he had no counsel, that the case still pended in the courts, and that the Assembly itself had already declared the broadside to be a seditious libel and its author guilty—in other words that he feared incriminating himself. Moreover, he added, the Assembly, having initiated the prosecution against him, now acted as his judge and jury which it had no power to do, particularly when it would be placing him under double jeopardy because he remained answerable at common law. For these reasons, McDougall declared, he would not answer the question whether he was guilty. Representative de Noyelles interjected that the House had the power to extort his answer and threatened infliction of *peine forte et dure,* a form of torture recognized in English law to force a suspect to plead one way or the other just so the trial might then proceed. One who stood mute, as McDougall, would be spread-eagled on the ground and have heavy metal weights placed upon his body; each day more weights would be added, while the prisoner was fed stale bread and stagnant water on alternate days. The "punishment hard and strong" continued until he either died or pleaded guilty or not guilty.[52] McDougall braved de

---

[51] Good accounts of the events leading to the aborted trial are in the *New York Post-Boy,* May 7, 1770; *New York Journal,* May 3, 1770; and *New York Mercury,* April 30, 1770.

[52] On *peine forte et dure,* see Sir James Fitzjames Stephen, *A History of the Criminal Law of England* (London, 1883), 1:297-99; E. M. Morgan, "The Privilege Against Self-Incrimination," *Minnesota Law Review* 34:12-14, 20-21 (1949). England abolished this barbaric practice by a statute of 1772 which provided that a refusal to plead was equivalent to a plea of guilty which, by a

Noyelles's barbaric threat obstinately refusing to plead to the charge, thereby stymying the proceedings.

The members fell to arguing among themselves whether they might coerce a prisoner to answer an incriminating question or even take jurisdiction of a case still pending in the courts. George Clinton, though he originally voted for the resolution to prosecute McDougall's seditious libel, now supported McDougall on technical grounds. Clinton admitted that if the Assembly were not a party to the common-law indictment it would have full pover over him and, if necessary, to make him plead might even throw him out of the window. The Assembly finally agreed to investigate the extent of its own powers in the case and ordered McDougall to state in writing his objections against entering a plea. His statement provoked Speaker Cruger to announce that he had reflected on the honor and dignity of the House. The members then voted that his fresh libels contemned their parliamentary privilege and demanded that he beg for pardon. His refusal prompted another vote sentencing him to an indeterminate period in prison. Only five members of the Assembly, including Clinton, opposed the sentence. As in Pennsylvania's Smith-Moore case, the Assembly ordered the sheriff not to honor a writ of habeas corpus. McDougall obtained a writ without avail, because the sheriff notified the court that the matter did not lie within its jurisdiction: the prisoner had been committed for breach of privilege. The court submitted to the legislature, and McDougall remained in jail. In the meantime the Assembly accepted a committee report, based on precedents of the House of Commons, supporting the lawfulness of its authority and actions in the case. Once more an American legislature endorsed the principle that it possessed an unbounded prerogative even in cases involving personal liberty and freedom of expression. After serving nearly three months in jail, McDougall finally got out when the legislative session ended. The common-law charge against him was dismissed, and America's Wilkes won his freedom.[53]

---

statute of 1827, was changed to a plea of not guilty. The only known instance of *peine* having been inflicted in the colonies occurred in Giles Corey's case in 1692 in Salem on a charge of witchcraft; he was pressed to death. Goebel, *Law Enforcement in Colonial New York*, 582, questionably assert that a "modification" of *peine* was used in 1691 when Jacob Leisler was ordered "tyed up and putt in irons" after his refusal to plead to a charge of treason. There is no record in England or America of *peine* having been used in a legislative trial; moreover at common law it might be used only in a felony case. Seditious libel was misdemeanor. Thus De Noyelles's threat was illegally based.

[53] For accounts of McDougall's appearance and trial before the Assembly, see *Journal of Votes and Proceedings*, Dec. 13, 1770, p. 8; and McDougall's own

Freedom, however, did not yet include a right to nettle a sensitive legislature. In 1773 George Rome, an Englishman who collected debts owed by Rhode Islanders to Rome's employers in London, enjoyed the status of the most unpopular person in the state. Rome reciprocated the feeling; he despised Rhode Island. In a private letter he excoriated the provincial government, including the Assembly and the judicial system, which he thought infected with corruption. In London Ben Franklin, who specialized in finding documents that could embarrass friends of parliamentary supremacy or royal prerogative, sent a copy of Rome's letter to patriots at home. The *Providence Gazette* published the letter. Although the Assembly needed the original copy before it could lawfully proceed, its rage overcame its legal scruples. The speaker of the Assembly summoned Rome before the bar of the house to account for his insults, but the defendant coolly observed that by the privilege of an Englishman he was under no obligation to answer a question that tended to incriminate him. The Assembly, recognizing no law but its own, ordered his imprisonment for the remainder of its session.[54]

The cases of Pride in Virginia, Husband in North Carolina, Powell in South Carolina, McDougall in New York, and Rome in Rhode Island demonstrated that parliamentary privilege was still a dread and active power on the eve of the Revolution. Legislative proceedings could not be published without prior license; the exercise of parliamentary privilege against fault-finders protected legislative measures. Legislatures could regard animadversion as subversion. Moreover, a verbal attack on government officials or policies that might be deemed an affront to the authority or honor of the legislature was subject to a power of repression from which not all the writs precious to the liberty of the subject could effect a rescue. In Massachusetts and Pennsylvania, however, public opinion so strongly backed the patriot party that it virtually immunized the grossest vituperation against supporters of Britain against any kind of legal retribution.

Some historians claim that the importance of the legislative power to punish for breach of parliamentary privilege has been exaggerated. Richard Buel, Jr., who offered no evidence, alleged that "after 1760

---

account in *New York Weekly Mercury* Dec. 24, 1770; and (New York) *Weekly Post-Boy* of the same date, reprinted in Leonard W. Levy, ed., *Freedom of the Press*, 117-27; McDougall's account is an invaluable source for the entire episode. See also Leake, *Lamb*, 71-73; Spaulding, *George Clinton*, 28-29; Thomas, *History of Printing in America*, 2:482-483; Dillon, *New York Triumvirate*, 119-121; Schlesinger, *Prelude to Independence*, 116.

[54] David S. Lovejoy, *Rhode Island Politics and the American Revolution* (Providence, 1958), 174-6.

the lower houses in patriot control largely abandoned the practice of punishing printers for breach of privilege."[55] That loaded proposition misleads, not just because "largely" is a weasel word but because the power to punish for breach of privilege applied to any insulting critic regardless of profession; that legislatures targeted few printers after 1760 is irrelevant to the consideration whether they used parliamentary privilege to punish people whose words offended legislative sensibilities. Legislatures in patriot control would not, of course, summon for trial a Benjamin Edes or Isaiah Thomas. The Pennsylvania legislature was not in patriot control, yet failed to humble Goddard. The Rhode Island legislature, which the patriots controlled, jailed Rome, an English bill collector, not a printer, and in doing so violated the constitution by showing no respect for the established right of a person not to accuse himself.[56] The New York Assembly, which the patriots did not control, jailed McDougall, but most patriots in the legislature voted with the DeLancey faction. The North Carolina legislature, which the patriots controlled, manhandled Husband.

When, however, the patriot mobs ran amok, smashing Loyalist presses, legislatures in patriot control had no need to exercise parliamentary privilege. Silencing the opposition press "gave apparent confirmation to the loyalist charge that in suppressing Tory opinion the colonists directly contradicted their professed ideals."[57] That indeed is the point: the patriots supported free speech and the liberty of the press for their side only. Moreover, if legislatures seldom used parliamentary privilege, the reason was, as Buel also said, that "Most printers had to cater to existing public sentiment if they wanted enough readers to keep them going, and nothing reflected that sentiment more faithfully than majority opinion in the legislature."[58] The legislatures in most colonies in fact remained dominant and posed the principal legal threat to freedom of expression, without having to use their judicial powers.

Another historian, Jeffery A. Smith, after looking at only a dozen cases, which he counted as twenty, and after botching his presentation of some of them, concluded "that the use of legislative privilege was sporadic, inconsistent, and largely ineffectual." It was indeed sporadic; it was inconsistent in the sense that the law is always incon-

---

[55] Richard Buel, Jr., "Freedom of the Press in Revolutionary America: The Evolution of Libertarianism, 1760-1820," in Bernard Bailyn and John B. Hench, eds., *The Press and the American Revolution* (Worcester, Mass., 1980), 60.

[56] Leonard W. Levy, *Origins of the Fifth Amendment: The Right Against Self-Incrimination* (New York, 1968), 368-432.

[57] Buel, "Freedom of the Press," 60.

[58] *Ibid.,* p. 75.

sistent by prosecuting selectively; but it was not ineffectual. Colonial printers, Smith added, "typically" stood on "their rights to due process and liberty of the press."[59] In fact they typically did not. Only in William Smith's case and in that of Thomas Powell did the defendants invoke freedom of the press; Isaiah Thomas, one of Jeffery Smith's "twenty," did so also, but he was not a victim of parliamentary privilege. Even in the Smith and Powell cases the free press issue was a minor one, clearly subordinated to the due process issue. The due process claim appeared in six cases at most, and in none was it successful. The Privy Council supported William Smith, in part, on other grounds.

The same historian, Jeffery A. Smith, believed that the use of parliamentary privilege was ineffectual because the legislatures failed to "silence or convert" their critics. Failure to convert is a fatuous yardstick of effectiveness. Failure to silence is not valid either, because the history of persecution for differences of opinion shows that victims are as likely to become obdurate as complaint. Moreover, the objective of a legislature in punishing for breach of privilege was not to "silence" or put a press out of business. And in all the cases, excepting that of Thomas who was not tried, the legislatures effectively subdued the printers. Also, to examine only cases involving printers in the pre-1776 period necessarily skewed the results. Freedom of speech was no less important than freedom of the press, the ordinary citizen as important as a printer. The author of *Parliamentary Privilege in the American Colonies* declared that for words tending to deny a legislature's authority, affront its honor, or slander any of its members, there were "scores of persons, probably hundreds," punished for breach of privilege; they had scandalized the government or seditiously libeled it.[60] Finally, parliamentary privilege did not disappear after Independence. As late as 1800 the United States Senate prosecuted William Duane, a printer, for his "high breach of the privileges of the Senate" resulting from his malicious and seditious publications about it.[61]

The patriot party used speedier and more effective means of silencing some opponents than the exercise of breach of privilege. Vigilan-

[59] Jeffery A. Smith, "Legislative Privilege and Colonial Journalism: a Reappraisal," scheduled for publication in *Journalism Quarterly*, Summer 1984. Professor Smith sent me a typescript of his forthcoming article; at the time of this writing he has resisted my efforts to convert him.

[60] Mary Patterson Clarke, 117.

[61] Daniel H. Hoffman, *Governmental Secrecy and the Founding Fathers: A Study in Constitutional Controls* (Westport, Conn., 1981), 207-8; Smith, *Freedom's Fetters*, 277-306.

tism may be a necessary ingredient in the making of a revolution, and there may even have been occasions when its existence among the patriots was understandably provoked. But it existed on a widespread scale, was always ugly, always a denial of due process, and always, before the outbreak of the war, directed not at an enemy but a fellow citizen whose opinions differed. On some occasions, that citizen was a staunch patriot whose judgment in the opinion of extremists needed correction by drastic methods for the good of the cause. John Holt, for example, the publisher of the *New York Gazette*, had vigorously opposed the Stamp Act and preferred to suspend publication of his newspaper rather than pay the tax. A letter from the Sons of Liberty notified him that he could best "promote the Cause" by continuing to publish without stamps in defiance of Parliament. Holt obeyed because the letter concluded with the threat that if he refused, "depend upon it, your House, Person and Effects, will be in imminent danger."[62]

Intimidation usually aimed at those who opposed "the Cause," like John Mein, publisher of the loyalist paper the *Boston Chronicle*. A mob smashed the windows of Mein's printing office, smeared his signs with filth, threatened his person with violence, and boycotted his paper, with the result that he went out of business and fled from Boston.[63] In New York, Isaac Sears, a bully-boy among the radical patriots, in the words of Dwight L. Teeter, "led attacks on newspaper offices on four different occasions, and headed a mob which kidnapped a prominent Tory clergyman-pamphleteer. Furthermore, he twice fomented riots over handbills which displeased . . . the Sons of Liberty. . . . Sears' activities suggest something of the power of the mob over printers and over the expression of unpopular political ideas in New York City from 1765 to 1776." Teeter, concluded, "Free expression was then reserved for opinions which coincided with those of Isaac 'King' Sears."[64]

The evidence forces the conclusion that Chief Justice Hutchinson had accurately summarized the situation when he acidly observed that the Adamses and their supporters contended "for an unlimited Freedom of Thought and Action, which they would confine wholly to themselves."[65] Free speech for one side only is not free speech at all, or at best is an extraordinarily narrow concept of it. That, in-

[62] Thomas, *History of Printing in America*, 2:297.
[63] Schlesinger, *Prelude to Independence*, 107-8.
[64] " 'King' Sears, the Mob and Freedom of the Press in New York, 1765-76," *Journalism Quarterly* 41 (1964):539, 544.
[65] Quincy, ed., *Reports of Cases*, 244.

deed, is the whole point: during the entire colonial period, from the time of the first settlements to the outbreak of the Revolution and the framing of the first bills of rights, America had had slight experience with freedom of speech or press as a meaningful condition of life.

The colonial press had tended to be bland, compliant, and noncontroversial. For a brief time James Franklin's *New-England Courant* flouted authority and exhibited a partisan tone; Zenger's *New-York Weekly Journal*, which for about four years functioned as an independent opposition newspaper, was a free press in the sense of being unencumbered by obligations to the government which it smartly attacked with regularity. Here and there other newspapers flirted briefly with partisanship, and sometimes, when local politics heated up, a printer felt forced to take a stand on a particular issue or else risked antagonizing both sides by his neutrality. Characteristically, however, as Stephen Botein pointed out, printers deliberately did not open their pages "wide enough to allow a full range of controversial matter into the public forum."[66] William Bradford of the *New-York Gazette* declared in 1776, "I once thought a little *Politicks* now and then thrown out among our Readers, might whet their Appetites," but on "second thoughts," he added, "we had as good let that alone."[67] The colonial press regarded itself as a free press because printers proudly remained as nonpartisan or indifferent as possible, publishing for a price whatever inoffensive articles of various opinions came their way. As Botein said, "Embedded in the prevailing colonial rhetoric concerning liberty of the press was a principle readily embraced by much of the trade—that printers should be politically neutral in the conduct of their business, and publish whatever was submitted to them. . . . A printer, in other words, should offer everyone the liberty of his press, without favoring one set of opinions over the rest."[68]

Thus, in the colonial period, at least until the 1760s, a press was "free" if persons of differing views had access to it. The colonial newspaper was like the original railroad, a road of rails on which anyone might propel his own vehicle for a price. Printers would take articles for cash from well-disposed and temperate authors, including those with complaints about public measures and men in power. Freedom to criticize the government was inseparably a part of the free-

---

[66] Botein, " 'Meer Mechanic's,' " 191. Botein's essay, cited above Chapter Two, in n. 65, is acutely perceptive and has been most helpful.

[67] *Ibid.*

[68] *Ibid.*, 177.

dom of everyone to use a newspaper's pages to express his viewpoint. Thomas Fleet, the founder of the *Boston Evening-Post*, spoke for his trade when he announced in 1733 that he was of no party and invited gentlemen "on either Side, to write anything of a political Nature, that tends to enlighten and serve the Publick . . . provided they are . . . confined within Modesty and Good Manners." Fleet himself avoided personal preferences and said he would as soon print one opinion as another if he "had a prospect of getting a Penny by it, as I have by all I print, having no other way to support my Family."[69] Compared with the London press, which bulged with partisanship and billingsgate, the press of the largest American town, Philadelphia (population 20,000 in 1760), was docile and dull. London, of course, was one of the world's great cities, the capital of a great empire, with a well-developed and somewhat centralized system of factional politics, and each faction sponsored newspapers and a pamphlet press.

After the close of the Seven Years War, Britain for the first time sought to raise a revenue in America; the Stamp Act of 1765 especially promised financial disaster for American printers. As a result, the press in America, like politics in America, underwent a sudden and radical transformation. The controversy with Britain leading to the Revolution profoundly altered press and politics. Partisanship and polemics became the vogue. Under the hydraulic pressures of the time and the inescapable polarization of opinion, an unprejudiced press became unpatriotic and unprofitable. The radical press speedily evolved into an instrument of revolutionary ideology to mobilize public opinion against Britain; a decreasing number of printers remained indifferent or backed Britain. Remaining neutral no longer helped business and became as difficult as remaining docile. Finding that they had to take sides to survive, printers became the strident and traducing voices of factions. To Americans by the 1760s, a free press could not be distinguished from a patriot press, one that reviled Parliament and the Ministry and supported the cause of liberty. Extremism in the defense of liberty emerged as a prized virtue.[70] But it

[69] *Ibid.*, 181.
[70] That seems to be the point of the strange article by Richard Buel, cited above, n. 55. Buel, who perverts what I said in *Legacy of Suppression* yet freely borrows without giving credit, does not argue that the revolutionary press was a free press or that it had a theory of press freedom broad enough to cover the rights of expression by opponents of the patriot party. He purports to show that Americans saw no inconsistency between claiming an absolute freedom for their cause while denying it to supporters of Britain. The patriots believed, said Buel, that they had to monopolize the press in order to mobilize public

was not a press that thought seriously about its own liberty. When bland and nonpartisan, it had at least constituted something of a forum for differing opinions; when the press deeply committed itself to a political position, its governing principle assumed that truth was one-sided and that freedom should be available only to believers. Liberty's opponents deserved to be silenced. Notwithstanding the fact that the events of the mid-1760s produced a watershed, neither before then nor from 1763 to 1776 did colonial America produce a broad concept of freedom of speech and press, even though English libertarian publications provided some basis for it.

---

opinion against executive power. I agree and think that Arthur Schlesinger made that point long ago in his *Prelude to Independence*—free speech existed only for the speech of freedom (independence). The difference between Buel and me or between Buel and Schlesinger is that Buel's understanding of free speech is stunted; he justifies the revolutionaries for having sacrificed their principles to the needs of a crisis. See Buel, "Freedom of the Press," p. 61. The same reasoning justifies the Sedition Act of 1798 or the Espionage and Sedition Acts of World War I or the Smith Act of the next war, and the prosecutions in all these eras of crisis. Buel's position allows no freedom of expression for the thought that we hate. Despite its title, his article shows no "evolution" and effectively ends twenty years before its announced terminal point.

CHAPTER IV

Early English Theory: From Milton to "Cato"

The philosophical principle of freedom of the mind had merely a slight influence on the expansion of freedom of speech and press, at least through the eighteenth century. Libertarian expositions were imaginative and abundant enough, but the proposition that truth could not be libelous remained an avant-garde position. In England and in America the main line of libertarian thought coincided in crucial respects with the common law. Until late in the eighteenth century freedom of political discussion had a frail history as a broad concept. Several theorists introduced significant ideas, but no one rejected the crux of the common law: traducing religion remained blasphemous libel and violating public morals obscene libel, savaging a person's public reputation in a way that tended to breach the peace was criminal libel, and ridiculing or reviling the government, its officers, or policies was seditious libel. Until libertarians repudiated the common law's principle that church, state, and morality could be criminally damaged by words alone, libertarian thought would remain stunted. Yet everyone professed to believe that freedom of thought in general, and freedom of the press in particular, was England's birthright. And in various libertarian writings intimations and suggestions may be found that were implicitly radical, pointing the way to the ultimate emergence of a new libertarianism that would undermine the doctrine of seditious libel as incompatible with free government.

   Spinoza went as far as anyone up to his time in advocating that the state should permit the utmost latitude for people to speak their minds. In his classic, *Theologico-Political Treatise* (1670), he pre-

sented as profound and sustained an analysis of freedom of thought
and speech as had been offered, climaxing his work with a concluding chapter entitled, "That In a Free State Every Man May Think
What He Likes, and Say What He Thinks." From the premise that
man is "by indefeasible natural right the master of his own thoughts"
and cannot abdicate his "freedom of judgment," Spinoza concluded
that diverse and contradictory opinions were inevitable; to compel
men "to speak only according to the dictates of supreme power"
would be disastrous to the state as well as to the individual. Believing,
however, that "authority may be as much injured by words as by
actions," he opposed an "unlimited concession" of free speech. He
recognized that the individual and social interest in freedom had to
be weighed against authority's competing claims: "we must, therefore, now inquire, how far such freedom can and ought to be conceded without danger to the peace of the state, or the power of the
rulers."[1]

Spinoza believed in the right to speak against the state, provided
that no one attempt to introduce any change in private authority and
provided that verbal opposition is grounded in reason rather than
"fraud, anger, or hatred."[2] Argument that a law is unsound and
deserves repeal should be permitted, as should any speculation concerning philosophy, religion, science, or "the liberal arts," even
though falsehoods may proceed from unworthy motives; the possibility of abuse, contended Spinoza, ought not to warrant limiting the
right.[3] That right to "freedom of speech" should be recognized by
the wise ruler so that resistance to him might be legitimatized and
lessened and "so that men may live together in harmony, however
diverse, or even openly contradictory their opinions may be."[4] The
state that punished opinions injured itself. Acts "which alone are
capable of offending," rather than the "opinions of mankind," should
be brought to trial; the rights of rulers, argued Spinoza, in secular
and sacred matters "should merely have to do with actions, but . . .
every man should think what he likes and say what he thinks."[5]

On the other hand, these libertarian notions on the scope of free
expression proceeded from a premise that was shared by Machiavelli
and Hobbes: the sovereign power, Spinoza wrote, has the "right to
treat as enemies all men whose opinions do not, on all subjects,

[1] *Theologico-Political Treatise,* in *The Chief Works of Benedict Spinoza,*
trans. R. H. M. Elwes (London, 1883), 1:258.
[2] *Ibid.,* 259.
[3] *Ibid.,* 261.
[4] *Ibid.,* 263.
[5] *Ibid.,* 265.

entirely coincide with its own"; but, he added, he was discussing the "proper" course of action for the state to follow, not its right. Properly, it should punish only politically injurious speech tantamount to a seditious act. All "opinions would be seditious . . . which by their very nature nullify the compact by which the right of free action was ceded."[6] Stirring up the people against their rulers, counseling civil disobedience, advocating the enactment of laws by unconstituted authority, teaching that contracts ought not be kept or that everyone should believe as he pleases: these were, for Spinoza, criminal libels, exceptions to his rule that overt acts, rather than mere words, were alone punishable. Thus even Spinoza, for all his tolerance, drew the line at seditious utterances.

The same may be said of an equally libertarian group, the English Levellers, "who represented the first great outburst of democratic thought in history, with John Lilburne and Richard Overton leading the way."[7] Almost any Leveller tract of the 1640s contained a passage condemning censorship and the licensing system, with an argument that freedom of speech and press were essential to the establishment of free government and personal liberty. "A Remonstrance of Many Thousand Citizens" (1646) asked Parliament to proclaim its legislative plans prior to enactment and to "heare all things that can be spoken with or against the same, and to that intent, let the imprisoned Presses at liberty, so that all mens understandings may be more conveniently informed."[8] "The Humble Petition" of 1649, Overton's work in all likelihood, argued that when men's mouths were "kept from making noise" they are robbed of their liberties, truth suppressed, and the people held in ignorance, fit only to serve the unjust ends of tyrants. A free press proved "essential unto Freedom" to prevent the nation from being placed in bondage, "for what may not be done to that people who may not speak or write, but at the pleasure of Licensers." The government must "hear all voices and judgments" by removing the "least restraint upon the Press," for the people could not enjoy liberty without "speaking, writing, printing, and publishing their minds freely."[9]

Despite such principled statements, moments came when even

[6] *Ibid.*, 260.
[7] Margaret Judson, *The Crisis of the Constitution* (Rutgers, 1949), 381.
[8] "A Remonstrance of Many Thousand Citizens," 1646, in Don M. Wolfe, ed., *Leveller Manifestoes of the Puritan Revolution* (New York, 1944), 123.
[9] "To the Right Honourable . . . The Commons of England . . . The Humble Petition . . . ," Jan. 19, 1649, in *ibid.*, 327-329. See also pp. 207 and 364; and William Haller and Godfrey Davies, eds. *The Leveller Tracts, 1647-1653* (New York, 1944), 167.

Levellers advocated a more systematic enforcement of the licensing system—so long as it was not aimed at them. Lilburne himself, after criticizing press restraints and unlawful search and seizure of unlicensed Leveller material, complained of the freedom allowed to royalist publications and "Malignant Books and Pamphlets tending to the ruine of the Kingdome . . . and freedome of People."[10] Samuel Chidley, in a pamphlet attacking Lilburne's opponents, requested Parliament "to silence such Babblers" and added: "I hold it one of the greatest abuses of the Commonwealth, that so many lying foolish Pamphlets have been, and are suffered to go abroad."[11]

William Walwyn, "the most consistently radical thinker among the Levellers,"[12] wrote a series of magnificent tracts on behalf of "the freedome of minde," liberty of conscience, and "freedome of discourse."[13] At one point he went so far as to reject the bad-tendency test by arguing that criminal deeds alone should be punishable, but not expresssion.[14] But, after defending "freedome of discourse" from the charge of tending to disturbance of the State, Walwyn added: "And as for disturbance to the State: admit any mans judgement be so misinformed, as to beleeve there is no sinne; if this man now upon this government should take away another mans goods, or commit murder or adultery; the Law is open, and he is to be punished as a malefactor, and so for all crimes that any mans judgment may mislead him unto." Thus, even Walwyn confessed, inconsistently, that words "scandalous, or dangerous to the State" had "upon good grounds" been prohibited by Parliament. He wrote, for example, in reference to "liberty of Conscience," which he thought the right of every man, that no one should be "punished or discountenanced by Authority for his Opinion, unless it be dangerous to the State," and he placed the identical restriction upon "the Presse."[15]

Several Independent tract writers went as far, but no farther, than their Leveller contemporaries in expanding the bounds of free expression. Roger Williams, for example, in his celebrated defense of toler-

---

[10] "Englands Birth-Right," 1645, in William Haller, ed., *Tracts on Liberty in the Puritan Revolution, 1638-1647* (New York, 1933), 3:269.

[11] "The Dissembling Scot . . . Or a Vindication of Lieu. Col. John Lilburne and others," 1652, quoted in William C. Clyde, *The Struggle for the Freedom of the Press from Caxton to Cromwell* (London, 1934), 219.

[12] Joseph Frank, *The Levellers* (Cambridge, Mass., 1955), 30. On Walwyn, see also W. K. Jordan, *The Development of Religious Toleration in England* (Cambridge, Mass., 1934-1940), 4:176-190.

[13] "A Helpe to the Right Understanding of a Discourse Concerning Independency," 1645, in Haller, ed., *Tracts*, 3:199, 200.

[14] *Ibid.*, 3:200.

[15] "The Compassionate Samaritane," 1644, in *ibid.*, 3:63, 67, 103-104.

ation, *The Bloudy Tenent, of Persecution, for cause of Conscience*
(1644) exempted from the civil magistrate's jurisdiction all matters
of conscience, even "scandalous" doctrines in opposition to the establishment, but he broke into his argument to note parenthetically,
". . . (I speak not of scandal against the civil state, which the civil
magistrate ought to punish)"[16] Henry Robinson, in his superb discussion, *Liberty of Conscience,* confronted the problem of free expression for Roman Catholics without betraying his principles. When he
contended that force or compulsion of any kind had no place in matters of religion and that reason and argument composed the only
allowable weapons, he expressly included "Papists, Jewes, Turkes,
Pagans, Hereticks, with all Infidels & Misbeleevers." Religious "combat" was to be "fought out upon eaven ground, on equal terms,
neither side must expect to have greater liberty of speech, writing,
Printing, or whatsoever else, then the other [*sic*]." All men without
exception were to have the "same privilege . . . to deliver their
mindes freely both in speech and writing."[17] Yet Robinson defended
an equal right of speech and press only in the context of an argument
for freedom of religion. There is no evidence that he differed from
Roger Williams or William Walwyn, no evidence, that is, that he
countenanced any expressions scandalizing the government or that
his tolerance of sectarian controversy extended to exclusively secular,
particularly state, matters.

John Milton, at least in his famous *Areopagitica,* had a secularist
approach to the problem of liberty of inquiry and expression, when
compared to Robinson, Walwyn, and Williams. Milton, of course,
receives traditional regard as a great apostle of the free mind, with
Locke, Jefferson, and Mill. Unquestionably, several passages of the
Areopagitica, which are ritualistically quoted to the exclusion of all
else, carry implications of majestic breadth, but no one who reads
him with care should refer to "Milton's dream of free speech for
everybody."[18] He might cry out, "Give *me* liberty to know, to utter,
and to argue freely according to conscience, above all liberties,"[19]

[16] *The Bloudy Tenent, of Persecution, for cause of Conscience,* ed. Samuel L.
Caldwell (1867), in *The Writings of Roger Williams,* Publications of the Narragansett Club (Providence, 1866-1874), 3:136. See also 3:96, 100, 110, 131, 147,
163, and 171.
[17] "Liberty of Conscience," 1644, in Haller, ed., *Tracts,* 3:133, 134. For a discussion of Robinson's thought, see Jordan, *Religious Toleration,* 4:140-176.
[18] See, for example, Zechariah Chafee, Jr., *Three Human Rights in the Constitution of 1787* (Lawrence, Kan., 1956), 61.
[19] *Areopagitica,* ed. William Haller, in *The Works of John Milton* (New
York, 1931-38), Frank A. Patterson, gen. ed., 4:346.

but his use of the personal pronoun is significant, for his well-advertised tolerance did not extend to the thought that he hated. Indeed, it extended only, as he specified, to "neighboring differences, or rather indifferences,"[20] which in 1644 meant Protestantism in a variety of Puritan forms. He specifically excluded from his spectrum of neighboring opinions "Popery, and open superstition" which he thought "should be extirpat," and he banned also the "impious or evil" which "no law can possibly permit."[21]

In a volume of essays littered with encomiums on Milton as the father of modern intellectual liberty, two contributions stand out as the only realistic appraisals. Salvador de Madariaga noted that as late as 1673 Milton was

> still putting forward authority, and not merely authority but Bible authority, as the standard or truth. . . . I believe that it is dangerous to listen to one who claims freedom of thought in the name of orthodoxy. . . . There is yet another standard, the willingness to grant to others that freedom of thought that you want for yourself; and from that point of view I am not certain Milton satisfies us. Indeed, I am tempted to think he did not.[22]

The Very Reverend W. R. Matthews, Dean of St. Paul's, referring to the exaggerated notion of Milton's libertarianism held by those who have not sufficiently read his book, pointed out that he "did not support freedom of religious debate for Catholics, Anglicans, Atheists or non-Christians," and concluded, "it is clear that Milton himself would have excluded not only the overwhelming majority of Christians but the greater part of the human race from the benefit of his tolerance."[23] This Anglican statement is somewhat exaggerated, since Milton later transcended his Puritanism to encompass Anglicans in a proposed united front of all Protestants against Catholics. Yet the thrust of the exaggeration moves in the right direction. Dean Matthews possibly had in mind the fact that the royalist writing that

---

[20] *Ibid.*, 4:349.
[21] *Ibid.*
[22] Quoted in Herman Ould, ed., *Freedom of Expression. A Symposium . . . to Commemorate the Tercentenary of the Publication of Milton's "Areopagitica"* (London, 1944). For a few other works extolling Milton's libertarianism, see Don M. Wolfe, *Milton in the Puritan Revolution* (New York, 1941), 136; Wilbur Elwyn Gilman, *Milton's Rhetoric: Studies in His Defense of Liberty* (Columbia, Mo., 1939), 10; Herbert Read, *A Coat of Many Colours* (New York, 1956), 336-7. For a more sensible account, see Francis Canavan, "John Milton and Freedom of Expression," *Interpretation: A Journal of Political Philosophy*, 7:50-65 (1978).
[23] Quoted in Ould, ed., *Freedom of Expression*, 78.

Milton deplored as a "court-libell against the Parlament,"[24] were Anglican in character. Milton thought they should be censored, pointing
out that if the licensing system had any justification, it would be in
the performance of the "prime service" of preventing the circulation
of such material.[25] Milton did not, in other words, even oppose the
licensing system unequivocally, despite his affirmation that free and
humane government results only from "free writing and free speaking."[26] Except for his criticism of royalist weeklies, he did not even
interest himself in one of the chief issues in the controversy over freedom of the press at the time of the *Areopagitica:* the freedom of
polemical newswriters. His silence on this issue also helps explain the
fact that in 1651 he was one of Cromwell's licensers or censors—
despite his earlier and eloquent denunciation of such officials—since
the works that came before him for his imprimatur were corontos or
newsbooks, partisan sheets of current news.[27] In all likelihood Milton
never intended that anything but the serious works of intellectuals,
chiefly scholars and Protestant divines, should be really free. A later
essay revealed the point rather explicitly when he noted that if open
expression was feared because it might "unsettle the weaker sort,"
Latin, "which the common people understand not" would be a solution for having issues "discust among the Learned only."[28]

In *A Treatise of Civil power in Ecclesiastical causes* (1659), Milton
explicitly reserved the right of "a free and lawful debate"[29] to all
Protestants, thereby allowing even Anabaptists and Socinians on the
left and Anglicans on the right to enjoy a privilege formerly the
prerogative of Puritanism only. But the "papist," whom Milton characterized as the "only heretic," remained barred from participation,[30]
though not necessarily on religious grounds. Catholicism he thought
to be less a religion than "a Roman principalitie . . . justly therefore to be suspected, not tolerated by the magistrate of another
countrey."[31] Although "just reason of state" may have been an understandable ground for restrictions on Catholic teaching and practice, at a time when the security of the government depended upon

---

[24] *Areopagitica*, in *Works*, 4:320.
[25] *Ibid.*, 4:320-321.
[26] *Ibid.*, 4:345.
[27] For Milton as a censor, see Clyde, *Struggle for Freedom of the Press*, 79-80,
172-173, and David Masson, *Life of Milton* (London, 1858-1880), 4:324-334,
432-433.
[28] *Of True Religion, Heresie, Schism, and Toleration*, 1673, in *Works*, 4:178.
[29] *Works*, 6:13.
[30] *Ibid.*, 6:14.
[31] *Ibid.*, 6:19.

maintenance of Protestant supremacy, Milton cut himself off from even this rationalization for intolerance. In 1673, in his tract on *True Religion, Heresie, Schism, and Toleration,* he wrote:

> As for tolerating the exercise of their [Catholic] Religion, supposing their State activities not to be dangerous, I answer, that Toleration is either public or private; and the exercise of their Religion, as far as it is Idolatrous, can be tolerated neither way; not publicly, without grievous and unsufferable scandal giv'n to all conscientious Beholders; not privately, without great offence to God, declar'd against all Idolatry, though secret. . . .
>
> Having shown thus, that Popery, as being Idolatrous, is not to be tolerated either in Public or in Private; it must be now thought how to remove it and hinder the growth thereof, I mean in our Natives. . . . Are we to punish them by corporal punishments, or fines in their Estates, upon account of their Religion? I suppose it stands not with the Clemency of the Gospel, more then what appertains to the security of the State: But first we must remove their Idolatry, and all the furniture thereof, whether Idols, or the Mass wherein they adore their God under Bread and Wine: for the Commandment forbids to adore. . . . If they say that by removing their Idols we violate their Consciences, we have no warrant to regard Conscience which is not grounded on Scripture.[32]

These constricted views on freedom of religion influenced Milton's thought on freedom of speech and press. Writing at a time when his party was out of power and Catholic literature was being licensed under the Restoration, he complained of having to "suffer the Idolatrous books of Papists" and recommended against a policy of open debate with them. "Shall we condescend to dispute with them," he asked, and answered emphatically, *"We are not to dispute."*[33] He appealed to all Protestants to join "on common ground against Popery," and to that end he pleaded the case of civil liberty—for Protestants only. Can one who based his religion exclusively on the Scriptures refuse with equity "to hear or read him, who demonstrates to have gained his knowledge by the same way? is it a fair course to assert truth by arrogating to himself the only freedome of speech, and stopping the mouths of others equally gifted?"[34] In context, the question demonstrates Milton's limited support of free speech. Perhaps his narrow conception of intellectual liberty stands best revealed by his own recommendation for the policy to be followed on press

[32] *Ibid.,* 6:172-173.
[33] *Ibid.,* 6:174.
[34] *Ibid.,* 6:177.

freedom. In the concluding section of the *Areopagitica* he endorsed a system of unlicensed printing, conditioned only upon the registration of all printers and authors; but he reserved the law of subsequent punishment for any abuse or licentiousness of the press: "Those which otherwise come forth, if they be found mischievous and libellous, the fire and the executioner will be the timeliest and the most effectuall remedy that mans prevention can use."[35]

To Americans of the Framers' generation, only John Locke's reputation as a libertarian rivaled Milton's. In his *Essay Concerning Human Understanding*, Locke added a new dimension to the arguments for civil liberty. His predecessors had grounded their positions on the tyranny and futility of suppression, the morality of fairness and tolerance, the self-interest of sectarianism, the dictates of the Scriptures, the needs of scholarship and of Protestantism, and the certainty that truth would best falsehood in an open encounter. Although Locke employed these arguments too, he relied mainly on the contention that the mind is so frail, its understanding so limited, that truth is inaccessible to it. All, he admonished, ought to be skeptical of the validity of their own opinions since they cannot know they are right and might very likely be in error. Opinions held with the "greatest stiffness" result more often than not from human incapacity—faulty judgment, prejudice, failure to examine one's own presuppositions, the inability to discover and use proofs, susceptibility to passion, and irrational habits of thought. Because people are forced to operate in a twilight zone of knowledge, where truth and certainty is "scanty," it would be wisest, he wrote, for all

to maintain peace and the common offices of humanity and friendship in the diversity of opinions. . . . We should do well to commiserate our mutual ignorance, and endeavor to remove it in all the gentle and fair ways of information, and not instantly treat others ill as obstinate and perverse because they will not renounce their own and receive our opinions, or at least those we would force upon them, when it is more probable that we are no less obstinate in not embracing some of theirs. For where is the man that has uncontestable evidence of the truth of all that he holds, or of the falsehood of all he condemns; or can say, that he has examined to the bottom all his own or other men's opinions? The necessity of believing without knowledge, nay, often upon very slight grounds, in this fleeting state of action and blindness we are in, should make us more busy and careful to inform ourselves than contain others.[36]

[35] *Areopagitica*, in *Works*, 4:353.
[36] *An Essay Concerning Human Understanding* (London ed. of 1879, Tegg and Co.), book IV, chap. 16, sect. 4, pp. 560-561.

98 *Emergence of a Free Press*

Despite his elaborate analysis of the formation and nature of opinion, Locke as philosopher-psychologist did no more than endorse in principle toleration for diversity of opinions. He evinced sustained interest in the problems of freedom of expression only in connection with his preoccupation for protecting liberty of conscience, the subject of his four *Letters on Toleration.* Because he addressed himself mainly to freedom for sectarian rather than secular expression, his claim of writing in behalf of "ABSOLUTE LIBERTY"[37] was overstated and even unjustifiable, considering the notable exceptions he made to principles which he supported in general. He could observe that the "opinions" of Catholics on Mass and of Jews on the New Testament, even though "false and absurd," were entitled to freedom because the business of the laws is to provide not for the truth of opinions but the safety of the Commonwealth as well as of every individual's goods and person.[38] But he also believed that "no opinions contrary to human society or to those moral rules which are necessary to the preservation of civil society, are to be tolerated by the magistrate."[39]

Advocating that the intolerant should not be tolerated, Locke proposed punishment of any who "will not own and teach the duty of tolerating all men in matters of mere religion."[40] In line with this view he framed a provision of the "Fundamental Constitutions of Carolina" outlawing reproachful or abusive language of any religion as a disturbance of the peace.[41] In an obvious reference to Roman Catholicism, he recommended prosecution of that church which taught that "faith is not to be kept with heretics." There was no inconsistency here with his thesis that the jurisdiction of the civil magistrate did not reach religious belief or practice, because he affirmed that a right ended at the point that it prejudiced others, violated their rights, or jeopardized the peace of the state.

Locke, like Spinoza, would also punish those who taught that oaths and contracts had no binding power, or that one owed no loyalty to the ruler; and like Milton he regarded the opinions of atheists and the political implications of Catholic doctrine as seditious.[42] He be-

---

[37] *A Letter concerning Toleration,* in *The Works of John Locke* (London, 1812, 11th ed.), 6:4.
[38] *Ibid.,* 6:40.
[39] *Ibid.,* 6:45.
[40] *Ibid.,* 6:46.
[41] Section 106, in "The Fundamental Constitutions of Carolina," in Francis Newton Thorpe, ed., *The Federal and State Constitutions, Colonial Charters, and Other Organic Laws* (Washington, 1909), 5:2784.
[42] *Letter concerning Toleration, Works of Locke,* 6:45-47.

lieved that the sanctions of the law should be invoked against the members of any church who arrogated to themselves the power of deposing kings or who professed doctrinal allegiance to another prince; for, he asked, did not their "doctrines signify, but that they may, and are ready upon any occasion to seize the government, and possess themselves of the estates and fortunes of their fellow-subjects; and that they only ask leave to be tolerated by the magistrates so long, until they find themselves strong enough to effect it?"[43] The statement, although an allusion to the relations between English Catholics and the Vatican, applied in principle to persons of any party that advocated, even by tenuous implication, the overthrow of the government or whose opinions could be suspected of disloyalty.

Locke, in other words, drew a line at seditious utterances. At no point did he, nor did any of his libertarian precursors among the Levellers or Independents, criticize the common law of seditious libel. Indeed, he went out of his way, in the midst of an argument for complete liberty of conscience, to declare that if any person under color of freely exercising his religion might behave "seditiously, and contrary to the public peace," he was punishable "in the same manner, and not otherwise than as if it had happened in a fair or market."[44] That Locke meant mere verbal sedition, as well as overt action, is unquestionable since he distinguished between peaceable and criminal "doctrine," and he listed slanderers, as well as the seditious, with thieves, murderers, and adulterers as deserving of being "suppressed."[45] Moreover, one provision of his "Fundamental Constitutions of Carolina" stated: "No person whatsoever shall speak anything in their religious assembly irreverently or seditiously of the government or governors, or of state matters."[46] The same constitution, incidentally, guaranteed freedom for "speculative opinions in religion" but not for political opinions. Locke would not even have permitted people to discuss public affairs. His constitution also provided that "all manner of comments and expositions on any part of these constitutions, or on any part of the common or statute laws of Carolines, are absolutely prohibited." Locke favored a variety of personal rights but not freedom of speech or press.

Locke did not even defend a general freedom of expression when he lent his enormous prestige to those who successfully opposed reenactment of the Licensing Act. In 1694 he drafted for the House of

---

[43] *Ibid.*, 6:45-46.
[44] *Ibid.*, 6:51.
[45] *Ibid.*, 6:52.
[46] Section 103, in Thorpe, ed., *Constitutions*, 5:2784.

Commons a statement of eighteen reasons for ending the system of preventive censorship, not one a principled defense of liberty of the press nor a philosophical argument for the free mind. Locke argued that the lack of free competition injured the printing trades; the Licensing Act was too vague and administratively unworkable; and it proved unnecessary because the common law adequately protected against licentiousness. On these grounds of expediency, prior restraints died in England.[47]

To suggest that Locke, or even Milton, was an enemy of the free mind would be absurd; they were undubitably the most eminent defenders of civil liberty in their time. But they were *of* their time, and one of its *a priori* premises, unthinkable for anyone to attack, was the state's incontestable right to proscribe seditious utterance, a commodious concept encompassing anything from criticism of public policy to advocacy of overthrow of the government. Neither Locke, Milton, nor their contemporaries ever indicated disagreement with the common law's spacious definition of unlawful discourse nor sought to limit its application. Subsequent generations of libertarians, with only a few persons excepted, inherited from them and passed on to the American Framers in unaltered form an unbridled passion for a bridled liberty of speech.

Charles Blount, Deist and republican, whose tracts the hangman burnt, adequately summarized seventeenth-century England's thought on the scope of permissible expression. His writings, including *Reasons Humbly Offered for Liberty of Unlicens'd Printing*,[48] aided measurably in ending preventive censorship in 1694. The following year, the introduction of a bill to reestablish that system of restraints provoked him to write *A Just Vindication of Learning and the Liberty of the Press*.[49] The thesis of the tract indicates that even radicals had a constricted understanding of freedom of the press. Despite his frenetic forebodings that a new "Inquisition" might spring from a continued requirement of imprimaturs, he complacently accepted the rigors of subsequent punishment. Unlicensed printing presented no dangers, he argued, because if a man wrote "Scandalous Reflections upon the Government, I presume he is by the present Laws of the

---

[47] See Lord King, *The Life and Letters of John Locke* (London, 1858 ed.), 202-209, for Locke's eighteen arguments. Maurice Cranston, *John Locke, A Biography* (London, 1957), states at p. 387, "Unlike Milton, who called for liberty in the name of liberty, Locke was content to ask for liberty in the name of trade; and unlike Milton, he achieved his end."

[48] (London, 1693), 32 pp.

[49] (London, 1695), 27 pp. The title page spells his name "Blunt."

Land subject to a Fine and Imprisonment."[50] He even approved of statutory restrictions against "Popish Books," although he condemned censorship as a relic of popery.[51] To Blount and the seventeenth-century libertarians, a free press meant merely the absence of prior restraints.

The century closed without any meaningful broadening in the definition of freedom of expression. Its defense had enlisted some of the most acute minds in England, but their contributions, whether polemical and sectarian or philosophically magisterial, merely established a rhetorical rationale for unfettered discourse and did nothing to break the fetters or even attack the common law. Indeed, neither the titans like Roger Williams and John Locke nor the radicals like William Walwyn and Charles Blount proposed a wider scope for unorthodox and hated opinions than had Leonard Busher, an obscure Baptist layman who preceded them. By 1700 no one had significantly advanced beyond Busher's statement of 1614.[52] "Even as the chaff before the wind cannot stand," he wrote, "so error before truth cannot abide,"[53] an expression of confidence in the open encounter of ideas to be popularized by Milton in similar words three decades later. Busher also believed that faith cannot be coerced, that the magistrate had no rightful jurisdiction over religion, and that persecution made a "shipwreck" of conscience. He proposed, accordingly, that "all sorts of Christians; yea, Jews, Turks, and pagans, so long as they are peaceable, and no malefactors," should be lawfully privileged to worship as they pleased and "to write, dispute, confer and reason, print and publish any matter touching religion, either for or against whomsoever," provided only that they quoted no church fathers as proof of any point.[54] But as Henry Burton pointed out in his introduction to a new edition of Busher in 1646, the liberty to "speak, write, print" was to be exercised under "wholesome and pertinent laws" which provided penalties "to restrain all kinds of vice or violence, all kinds of reproach, slander, or injury either by word or deed."[55]

[50] *A Just Vindication of Learning and the Liberty of the Press* (London, 1695), 23.
[51] *Ibid.*, 2, 23.
[52] *Religious Peace: or A Plea for Liberty of Conscience* (London, 1614; reprinted 1646), in Edward Bean Underhill, ed., *Tracts on Liberty of Conscience and Persecution, 1614-1661* (London, 1846), 1-81.
[53] *Ibid.*, 53.
[54] *Ibid.*, 33 and 51.
[55] *Ibid.*, 10.

Englishmen of the eighteenth century resolutely continued to ride the crest of an earlier consensus that the maintenance of established authority demanded the silencing of subversive discussion. Vivid memories of two revolutions fixed a steady course against any threat, whether real or imagined, to the good reputation of the government. Charles Davenant, the popular political economist, represented virtually a unanimous point of view when he granted in 1703 that in a free country to "restrain the tongues and pens of men" so as to prevent just public censure of the actions of private persons was not right, but censure of the government and its officers would, he thought, be intolerable. "The harmony that is to make England subsist and flourish, must have its rise from a due respect, and obedience to be paid by the whole people, to that authority with which the laws have invested the different parts that compose the government."[56] Charles Leslie, editor of the *Rehearsal*, stated a similar opinion. He praised as "wise and good" the law that prevented even true accusations against those "in post and quality. . . . For private men are not judges of their superiors. This wou'd confound all government. And the honour and dignity of our governors is to be preserv'd, without which they cou'd not govern, nor wou'd they be obey'd as they ought to be if they were render'd contemptible to their subjects; which is unavoidable if they are suffer'd to be traduced by every private person, and expos'd all over the nation."[57] He held Parliament, rather than the coffee-house or the press, to be the only and proper place for such public criticism as was permissible.

The closest approximation to a dissenting voice on this matter was Matthew Tindal's. England's leading Deist at the turn of the century, Tindal, like every writer from Busher to Blount, expressed interest in an unlicensed liberty of press from the view of one with a stake in the open airing of religious controversy. But he also claimed that everyone "has a natural Right in all matters of Learning and Knowledge" to discover what can be said by speech or press on all sides of every subject, including civil and governmental matters, even if antiministerial.[58] Tindal may have been the first to elevate freedom of speech and press to the status of a natural right, a rhetorical achievement, to be sure, but a crucial step in the creation of a theory of intellectual liberty. The process by which the phrase "freedom of

---

[56] "Essays Upon Peace at Home, and War Abroad," November 1703, Davenant's *Works*, 4:301, 302, quoted in Lawrence Hanson, *Government and the Press, 1695-1763* (Oxford, 1936), p. 1.

[57] *Rehearsal*, vol. I, no. 191, March 1707, quoted in Hanson, *Government and the Press*, 1-2.

[58] *Reasons against Restraining the Press* (London, 1704), 9-10.

speech" was transformed from a description of a privilege of parliamentarians to a personal right of citizens turned, in part, on the assimilation of freedom of speech into the natural-rights theory.

Tindal was also the first person on either side of the Atlantic to imply that citizens should have the same right to freedom of speech that legislators were guaranteed in the House of Commons. He made this important point somewhat obliquely by asking, "If the Honourable House of Commons have upon a solemn Debate thought fit to publish their proceedings to prevent being misrepresented, why should they deny those they Represent the same Liberty?"[59] In tracing the evolution of the concept of free speech, one might expect that numerous persons would have extrapolated a civil right from the parliamentary privilege, by simply arguing that if the representatives of the people enjoyed a broad customary or constitutional right to debate any issue concerning public policy and the conduct of the government, then the people, who possessed the ultimate sovereignty and to whom the representatives were responsible, should possess the same right of discussion. Tindal merely hinted at this idea which seems, surprisingly, never to have received full expression until the Sedition Act of 1798 provoked Jeffersonian thinkers to search for impregnable lines of defense. Tindal's passing thought, that the people are entitled to the same scope of freedom of expression as their deputies, potentially subverted the doctrine of seditious libel. He did not, however, understand that.

Although Tindal was one of the earliest libertarians with legal training, having been a law-fellow at All Soul's College, Oxford, he did not evaluate the common law's restrictions on expression, nor did he offer a solution for the legal problems which latitudinarian views might precipitate. His generalized opinions wove around the single theme that the reintroduction of licensing, as perennially proposed, threatened Protestantism and liberty. He never indicated disagreement with the notion that the press had become free when removed from prior restraints. His tracts defending himself, his printer, and his bookseller, upon their presentment by a grand jury for publishing an attack against the established church, rested their case on liberty of conscience and only secondarily on liberty of the press, without questioning the doctrine of subsequent punishment for the "abuse" of liberty.[60]

[59] *Ibid.*, 10.
[60] *A Letter to a Friend: Occasioned by the presentment of the grand jury for the county of Middlesex, of the author, printer and publisher of a book entitled the rights of the christian church asserted* (London, 1708). See also *A Letter*

John Asgil, politician and religious mystic, was the only contemporary of Tindal whose literary remains class him among the libertarians. Like Tindal, he was a lawyer whose books were condemned to be burned, and he himself suffered the unenviable distinction of having been expelled first from the Irish House of Commons and later from the English. With this record behind him, he wrote, in 1712, *An Essay for the Press*,[61] in which he ignored the law of seditious and blasphemous libel under which he had been censured. Although he hailed the communication of one's thoughts to others as a "natural Right of Mankind"[62] and argued, cleverly, that the abuse of this right constituted no more a reason for suppressing it than shutting church doors because hypocrites crowded in with the true worshippers, he confessed the necessity of maintaining restraints upon the press. But he drew the line against licensing and taxation. On the superficial notion that anonymous publications caused "licentiousness," he proposed to outlaw them and require all authors to identify themselves, although he published his own essay anonymously. He gave no consideration to the possibility that the danger to the press's freedom derived largely from the necessarily vague concept of licentiousness, nor to the possibility that many discussions of public value were advanced anonymously to protect their authors from subsequent punishment.

Asgil and Tindal were libertarian by contrast to most writers of the early eighteenth century. The weight of talent and reputation rested exclusively on the conservative side, as may be judged from the positions of Daniel Defoe, Jonathan Swift, Joseph Addison, and Richard Steele, as well as Charles Leslie and Charles Davenant. Whatever Defoe's virtues as a literary figure, he earned his living as a mercenary political journalist of the lowest kind, peddling his talents and shifty opinions to the highest party bidder. Pilloried, fined, and imprisoned in 1703 for a tract on religious dissent, jailed again in 1713 for his published remarks, and convicted once more in 1715, Defoe experienced his legal difficulties firm in the conviction that the law of seditious libel existed as an acceptable weapon of partisan politics, justifiably used against its critics by whatever party currently held power. "Governments will not be jested with, nor reflected upon," he warned, "nor is it fit that they should always lye at the

---

to a Member of Parliament, shewing that a restraint on the press is inconsistent with the Protestant religion, and dangerous to the liberties of the nation (London, 1698).

[61] (London, 1712), 8 pp.

[62] *Ibid.*, 4.

mercy of every pen."[63] As a political spy he fed the ministry samples of the opposition's publications which in his opinion merited prosecution for seditious libel. On one occasion, for example, he instigated the expulsion of Richard Steele from Parliament. Defoe furnished Lord Harley, the first minister of state, with allegedly seditious excerpts from Steele's journalism and warned that his recent election by the Whigs meant that the Tory cause would be "bullied in as public a manner as possible. If, my lord, the virulent writings of this man may not be voted seditious none ever may, and if thereupon he may be expelled it would discourage the party and break all their new measures."[64] Defoe also sought to destroy the principal Whig paper, *The Flying Post*, by urging that the attorney-general bring a suit against it for seditious libel.[65] In 1718 he anonymously published a tract entitled *A Vindication of the Press*,[66] in which he declaimed at length on the virtues of unlicensed liberty, but kept silent on the subject of seditious libel—perhaps because one of the press's virtues, he said, was the maintenance of the state.

Defoe's enemy, Richard Steele, essayist, playwright, and politician, also revealed fundamental infirmities as a witness for the libertarian position. His own condemnation for seditious libel, resulting in his expulsion from the House of Commons, seems only to have inspired him to revenge. When his political fortunes changed for the better and he basked in favor again, he complained in 1715 that "many libels are successfully dispersed under the notion of public News."[67] Jonathan Swift similarly engaged in the practice of singling out editors deserving, in his opinion, to be convicted as seditious libelers.[68]

The conservative position received its most bald and full exposition by an anonymous lawyer, "A Young Gentleman of the Temple," who in 1712 published a slim book elaborating the reasons for restraining the press.[69] He used the bold technique of stating systemati-

---

[63] *The Review*, vol. I, no. 46, Aug. 12, 1704, quoted in Hanson, *Government and the Press*, 1.

[64] Defoe to Harley, Feb. 19, 1714, quoted by David Harrison Stevens, *Party Politics and English Journalism, 1702-1742* (Chicago, 1916), 27, citing Portland MSS, 5:384.

[65] Stevens, *Party Politics*, 53-54, and Hanson, *Government and the Press*, 62-63.

[66] (London, 1718), 36 pp. The copy in the New York Public Library contains a bound-in letter by Prof. William P. Trent of Columbia University, expressing certainty that Defoe was the author.

[67] Quoted in Hanson, *Government and the Press*, 85, citing George A. Aitken, *The Life of Richard Steele* (London, 1889), 2:71.

[68] Stevens, *Party Politics*, 78, citing Swift's *Journal to Stella*, Oct. 9, 1711.

[69] *Arguments Relating to a Restraint upon the Press in a Letter to a Bencher, from a Young Gentleman of the Temple* (London, 1712), 52 pp.

cally the arguments that had been advanced in favor of unlicensed liberty and then one by one ridiculing and rejecting them. No religious opinion, he thought, should be printed "but under the suffrage of those, who are proper Judges of what is Evangelical Truth, or Antichristian Error," else "all Order and Discipline" would end.[70] As for the argument that such censorship would deprive men of the means of arriving at truth by learning and weighing different opinions, he answered that the Bible itself contained truth and needed no commentary.[71] He believed that appeals to the public on political issues were quite unnecessary so long as Parliament might be petitioned directly. The public had no need to be involved in political controversies, because enough had been said on all subjects and the Lords and Commons were capable of making decisions and of warding off arbitrary power. Indeed, the speakers of both houses, he recommended, ought to be among the official licensers.[72] Claims that learning would be discouraged by censorship were absurd, because only "good" books merited license, and the rest wasted time and money. That controversy would be stifled he admitted, but he preferred silence because controversy merely made trouble; people ought to examine and reject their own novel opinions instead of obtruding them on others.[73]

Far from being a natural right, "Freedom of Speech" was a high privilege belonging only to members of Parliament; whoever else assumed that privilege by arrogating to themselves "an uncontroulable Liberty, not only of Speaking, but of Writing and Publishing what they please" were guilty of a breach of the privilege.[74] Fortunately, there existed "many good Laws against the writing and publishing Seditious and Scandalous Papers," but evasion of deserved penalties remained all too common because of the undetectability of anonymous authors.[75] An even "greater mischief" attended the custom of frequenting coffee-houses where men learned the art of scandal and detraction. The existing condition of unrestrained liberty bred seditious libelers, "the very Assassins of all Government," who could no longer be endured, for a "Civil War began with Ink may end in Blood."[76] The only remedy lay in the restoration of a rigorous

[70] *Ibid.*, 8.
[71] *Ibid.*, 10.
[72] *Ibid.*, 14-16.
[73] *Ibid.*, 17.
[74] *Ibid.*, 21.
[75] *Ibid.*, 23-24.
[76] *Ibid.*, 25, 27, 33, 45.

licensing system, the details of which our anonymous lawyer worked out in a proposed statute.[77]

The moderate and more representative position was presented with considerable sophistication in another tract of 1712, ascribed uncertainly to Joseph Addison, writing under the name "Tory Author."[78] Addison, if we may assume that it was he, learnedly demonstrated that some of the most tyrranical Roman emperors, under whom libelers faced the death penalty, sometimes wisely tolerated even defamation of themselves on the theory that great people could afford to take no notice and should reply by giving as good an account of themselves as possible. Addison approved of such an attitude and even of a statement, which he quoted, from an unnamed Whig: "There never was a good Government that stood in fear of Freedom of Speech, which is the natural Liberty of Mankind; nor was ever any Administration afraid of Satyr [satire] but such as deserv'd it."[79] Private persons should have the right to criticize the government, but it would be going too far, Addison believed, to support a right for anyone to say whatever he thinks. There must be reasonable restraints, though licensing as too great a danger to liberty was not tolerable. Nor was a requirement that authors fix their names to their publications, for that would put an end to many worthwhile contributions which could only be made anonymously. Freedom of speech, as well as of press, should be confined, rather, to the limits set by truthfulness, good taste, due submission, and innocency of malice. He believed himself devoted to "Legal Liberty," the right to speak, write, or print "whatever is not against Law."

> I believe [he stated] all we mean by Restraining the Press, is to hinder the Printing of any Seditious, Schismatical, Heretical or Antimonarchical Pamphlets. We do not intend to destroy Printing itself or to abridge any one Set of Men of the Liberties of *Englishmen;* That is, of Writing and Printing what the Law allows; what may be consistent with our Loyalty to the Q———n, and our Love to the Publick Peace; what is not against Morals or Good Manners. And surely there may be a Restraint put upon such Things without striking at the Press itself.[80]

[77] *Ibid.,* 47-51.
[78] *Thoughts of A Tory Author, Concerning the Press:* With the Opinion of the *Ancients and Moderns, about Freedom of SPEECH and WRITING* (London, 1712).
[79] *Ibid.,* 13.
[80] *Ibid.,* 1-2.

Thus Addison complacently accepted the status quo, believing that freedom of expression had a broad scope and a high value when kept under the reasonable restraints of the common law without which true liberty would degenerate to licentiousness. No writer of the time more ably and accurately presented the prevailing notions on the subject than Addison, or "Tory Author."

Anthony Collins was a Deist leader with serious limitations. His *Discourse of Free Thinking* argued two propositions at great length: first, that restraints on expression resulted in cultural stagnation and ignorance; second, that every man had a right to think and express himself freely for the purpose of determining the meaning and validity of any proposition in history, science, philosophy, religion, or other realm of knowledge.[81] In another work, Collins defended the use of ridicule, jest, and raillery in all disputation; deploring restraints that made it impossible for men to "speak their Minds seriously on certain subjects," he pleaded "for freedom of debate" in any matter of "speculation."[82] However, his thought remained Miltonian in its disregard for the right to freedom of expression for any but scholars and divines. Neither the common herd nor political reporters and critics received Collins's attention. He had, moreover, a way of tacking on to a libertarian thesis a concession to orthodoxy that, innocently perhaps, bulldozed the ground out from under him. For instance, he dedicated his "Apology for free Debate and Liberty of Writing" to the following proposition: "As it is every man's natural right and duty to think, and judge for himself in matters of opinion; so he should be allow'd *freely* to *profess* his opinions, and to endeavour, when he judges proper, to *convince* others of their truth; provided those opinions do not tend to the disturbance of society."[83] Any Crown prosecutor might warmly embrace that proposition, despite its natural-rights premise, because the qualifying provision accepted in principle the law of criminal libel. Collins thought opinions punishable if they had the bad, though remote, tendency to disturb society. The dissenting position, meanwhile, had scarcely advanced beyond the "no-prior-restraints" concept. In a score of years, the libertarian chorus had been joined only the frail voices of Tindal and Asgil, despite the constant arrests for criminal libel.

[81] *A Discourse of Free Thinking* (London, 1713), 178 pp.
[82] *A Discourse Concerning Ridicule and Irony in Writing* (London, 1729), 5, 24, 75-76.
[83] Page vi of the "Apology" which appears as a preface, iii-lxii, to Collins, *A Discourse of the Grounds and Reasons of the Christian Religion* (London, 1724), 285 pp.

Then, in 1720, "Cato" burst upon the scene, bringing to his wide audience of readers a daring and well-developed theory of free speech. Others had been narrowly preoccupied with the problem of licensing, or had been unable to stomach the thought of tolerating an equal liberty for those they hated, or vigorously defended liberty of expression by declamatory statements that fell short of analyzing its functions and scope, as well as it relations to governmental forms and the laws of libel. In this respect the essays of the political journalists, John Trenchard and Thomas Gordon, collaborating under the joint pseudonym of "Cato" were unusual. Trenchard was a country gentleman of considerable wealth, excellent education, and experience as a barrister. Little is known about Gordon's life before he met Trenchard in 1719. The two collaborated on a series of articles, *The Independent Whig*, which in book form went through eight editions between 1720 and 1747. The *Independent Whig* advocated the freest exercise of religion for Protestant dissenters. The 138 essays, constituting *Cato's Letters*, first published in London newspapers between 1720 and 1723, were collected in four volumes that went through six editions between 1723 and 1755.[84] As staunch defenders of constitutional government and the rights of Englishmen, Trenchard and Gordon wrote on such subjects as "The destructive Spirit of Arbitrary Power," "The Right and Capacity of the People to Judge Government," "Liberty proved to be the unalienable Rights of All Mankind," "Civil Liberty produces all Civil Blessings," "Of the Restraints which ought to be laid upon Publick Rulers," "All Government proved to be instituted by Man," and "Of Freedom of Speech: That the same is inseparable from Public Liberty." "No one," wrote an historian familiar with the sources, "can spend any time in the newspapers, library inventories, and pamphlets of colonial America without realizing that *Cato's Letters* rather than Locke's

---

[84] [John Trenchard and Thomas Gordon], *Cato's Letters: Or, Essays on Liberty, Civil and Religious, and Other Important Subjects* (London, 1723-55). Although colonial printers and booksellers imported *Cato's Letters* for sale, there were no American editions. The first reprinting of the four-volume set since the London sixth edition of 1755 occurred in 1971 when Da Capo Press of New York, under the general editorship of Leonard W. Levy, published a facsimile copy of the sixth edition. A selection of essays from the *Independent Whig* and from *Cato's Letters* was edited with an excellent introduction by David L. Jacobson, *The English Libertarian Heritage* (Indianapolis, 1965). Caroline Robbins, *The Eighteenth Century Commonwealthman* (Cambridge, Mass., 1959), discussed Trenchard and Gordon at pp. 115-25, 392-93. See also Charles B. Realey, "The *London Journal* and Its Authors, 1720-1723," *Bulletin of the University of Kansas*, 36:1-34 (1935).

Civil Government was the most popular, quotable, esteemed source of political ideas in the colonial period."[85]

Trenchard and Gordon did not merely praise freedom of the press; they considered its values, meaning, and problems, and they also produced a rare discussion of freedom of *speech*. The essay, "Of Freedom of Speech: That the same is inseparable from Publick Liberty,"[86] received such popular acclaim in America that extensive quotation of its splendid rhetoric is justifiable:

> Without Freedom of Thought, there can be no such Thing as Wisdom; and no such Thing as publick Liberty, without Freedom of Speech: Which is the Right of every Man, as far as by it he does not hurt and controul the Right of another; and this is the only Check which it ought to suffer, the only Bounds which it ought to know.
>
> This sacred Privilege is so essential to free Government, that the Security of Property, and the Freedom of Speech, always go together; and in those wretched Countries where a Man cannot call his Tongue his own, he can scarce call any Thing else his own. Whoever would overthrow the Liberty of a Nation must begin by subduing the Freedom of Speech; a Thing terrible to publick Traytors. . . .
>
> That Men ought to speak well of their Governors, is true, while their Governors deserve to be well spoken of; but to do publick Mischief, without hearing of it, is only the Prerogative and Felicity of Tyranny; A free People will be shewing that they are so, by their Freedom of Speech.
>
> The Administration of Government is nothing else, but the Attendance of the Trustees of the People upon the Interest and Affairs of the People. And as it is the Part and Business of the People, for whose Sake alone all publick Matters are, or ought to be, transacted; so it is the Interest, and ought to be the Ambition, of all honest magistrates, to have their Deeds openly examined, and publickly scanned: Only the wicked Governors of Men dread what is said of them. . . .
>
> Misrepresentation of publick Measures is easily overthrown, by representing publick Measures truly: when they are honest, they ought to be publickly known, that they may be publickly commended; but if they be knavish or pernicious, they ought to be publickly detested. . . . Freedom of Speech is the great Bulwark of Liberty; they prosper and die together: And it is the Terror of Traytors and Oppressors, and a Barrier against them. It produces excellent Writers, and encourages Men of fine Genius. . . .

[85] Clinton Rossiter, *Seedtime of the Republic* (New York, 1953), 141.
[86] No. 15, Feb. 4, 1720, in *Cato's Letters* (6th ed., 1755), 1:96-103.

All Ministers, therefore, who were Oppressors, or intended to be Oppressors, have been loud in their Complaints against Freedom of Speech, and the License of the Press; and always restrained, or endeavoured to restrain, both. In consequence of this, they have browbeaten Writers, punished them violently, and against Law, and burnt their Works. By all which they shewed how much Truth alarmed them, and how much they were at Enmity with Truth. . . .

Freedom of Speech, therefore, being of such infinite Importance to the Preservation of Liberty, every one who loves Liberty ought to encourage Freedom of Speech.

In subsequent essays on the subject of libels, Cato continued his discussion. He ridiculed government officials who called "every Opposition . . . and every Attempt to preserve the People's Rights, by the odious Names of Sedition and Faction."[87] Libels, he declared, rarely fomented causeless discontent against the government; the benefits from what the law denominated libels, by keeping great men in awe and checking their behavior, outweighed their mischiefs. Libels inevitably resulted from a free press, "an Evil arising out of a much greater Good."[88] Without freedom of speech and press, there could be "neither Liberty, Property, true Religion, Arts, Sciences, Learning, or Knowledge."[89] Admittedly, a risk arose in allowing liberty of expression. Let men talk freely about philosophy, religion, or government, and they may reason wrongly, irreligiously, or seditiously; but to restrain their opinions would simply result in "Injustice, Tyranny, and the most stupid Ignorance. They will know nothing of the Nature of Government beyond a Servile Submission to Power."[90]

Cato did not wish to be misunderstood as arguing for the uncontrolled liberty of men to calumniate each other or the government. "Libels against the Government . . . are always base and unlawful,"[91] especially when untrue, and should be punished as an abuse of liberty so long as England's "very good laws" were "prudently and honestly executed, which I really believe they have for the most part been since the Revolution."[92] In a related essay, Cato reinforced the thought by saying, "I do agree, when the natural and genuine Meaning and Purpose of Words and Expressions in libellous Writings carry a criminal Intention, that the Writer ought not to escape Pun-

---

[87] "Discourse upon Libels," No. 100, Oct. 27, 1722, *ibid.*, 3:293.
[88] "Reflections upon Libelling," No. 32, June 10, 1721, *ibid.*, 1:252.
[89] "Discourse upon Libels," 3:295.
[90] *Ibid.*, 3:296-97.
[91] "Reflections upon Libelling," 1:250.
[92] "Discourse upon Libels," 3:299.

ishment by Subterfuge or Evasion."[93] Notwithstanding these genuflec-
tions toward the law, keeping Cato on its safe side, he thought the
law of criminal libel was neither good nor prudently executed, indeed, that it proved quite dangerous to public liberty and good
government. He disapproved of prosecutions for libel except in extreme cases and even then only under a law which did not penalize
criticism whose validity was demonstrable.

On ground that the public had an interest in the truth about public
measures and men, Cato argued that truth should be admitted as a
defense against a criminal libel charge, in other words, that a defendant who could prove the accuracy of his allegedly seditious utterance should be acquitted. The doctrine that a libel "is not the less a
Libel for being true," Cato declared, should apply only in private
suits for defamation of character, but "it is quite otherwise when the
Crimes of Men come to affect the Publick. . . . The exposing therefore of publick Wickedness, as it is a duty which every Man owes to
Truth and his Country, can never be a Libel in the Nature of
Things."[94] "Tory Author" in 1712 had fleetingly suggested the same
point.[95] Cato developed and popularized this idea, which has usually
been attributed to Andrew Hamilton in his defense of Peter Zenger
in 1735. In England, Solon Emlyn, the editor of the 1730 edition of
State Trials, remarked in his preface: "Thus in the Case of defamatory Libels, or of Scandalum Magnatum, when the word *falso* is inserted, the Defendant ought not be found guilty, if the assertion be
true. Whether it be necessary to insert the word *falso*, is another
question, (tho' I believe it would be difficult to maintain an Indictment without it) yet certainly where the Indictment charges a man
with falsely writing a Libel, he cannot justly be found guilty of that
Indictment so laid, if the words be true."[96] The idea of truth as a
defense was not accepted in English law until Lord Campbell's Act
of 1843. Cato also opposed the practice of the courts in attributing
a criminal or seditious intention to defendants whose words in their
"literal and natural Meaning, import nothing that is criminal; then to
strain their genuine Signification to make them intend Sedition
(which possibly the Author might intend too) is such a Stretch of
discretionary Power as must subvert all the Principles of free Government, and overturn every Species of Liberty."[97]

[93] "Second Discourse upon Libels," 3:302-03.
[94] "Reflections upon Libelling," 1:246-47.
[95] *Thoughts of a Tory Author*, 25-26.
[96] Thomas B. Howell, ed., *Cobbett's Complete Collection of State Trials*
(London, 1809), 1: Prefaces, xxxi.
[97] "Second Discourse upon Libels," no. 101, Nov. 3, 1722, in *Cato's Letters*,
3:303.

The best way to treat undeserved libels, thought Cato, was to "laugh at them, and despise them," rather than prosecute them.[98] He reasoned that in a free country, to punish libels by a general law, however much they deserved punishment, seemed improper because "such a Law, consisting of so many Branches, and being of such vast Latitude, would make all Writing whatsoever, how innocent so ever, and even all Speaking, unsafe. . . . As long as there are such Things as Printing and Writing, there will be Libels: It is an Evil arising out of a much greater Good. . . . I must own, that I would rather many Libels should escape, than the Liberty of the Press should be infringed; yet no Man in *England* thinks worse of Libels than I do; especially of such as bid open Defiance to the present Protestant Establishment."[99] Clearly, Cato was the rare man who, recognizing the social utility of freedom of expression and its relationship to free government, could tolerate the thought that he hated. Others probably shared Cato's views, but did not leave a record of their argument that would influence Englishmen in the colonies.

Cato's Letters was quoted "in every colonial newspaper from Boston to Savannah,"[100] and "the most famous"[101] of his letters was the one on "Freedom of Speech." Young Ben Franklin first reprinted this essay in America after the Massachusetts legislature imprisoned his brother; the *New-England Courant* also reprinted Cato's "Reflections upon Libelling," an essay often referred to in American newspapers as "Of the Liberty of the Press."[102] Zenger's *New-York Weekly Journal* twice published Cato on free speech as well as his "Reflections upon Libelling," his "Discourse on Libels," and numerous other essays from *Cato's Letters*.[103] *Cato's Letters* also provided columns for readers of the *South Carolina Gazette*.[104] The *Boston Gazette* reprinted the essay on free speech at least seven times[105] and "Of the

[98] "Discourse upon Libels," 3:297-98.
[99] "Reflections upon Libelling," 1:252-53.
[100] Elizabeth Christine Cook, *Literary Influences in Colonial Newspapers* (New York, 1912), 81.
[101] Rossiter, *Seedtime*, 299.
[102] *New-England Courant*, July 9, and Sept. 21, 1721. The same paper copied from the *London Journal* at least five other essays from Cato within less than a year and occasionally printed others. See Oct. 9, 16, 23, 30, 1721; July 16, 1722; May 3 and 10, 1725.
[103] Feb. 18 and Nov. 11, 1734; Feb. 25, March 4, Dec. 9, 1734, all reprinted in Leonard W. Levy, ed., *Freedom of the Press from Zenger to Jefferson* (Indianapolis, 1966), 11-24. See also Nov. 19, Dec. 10, Dec. 31, 1733; Jan. 28, Feb. 4, Feb. 11, March 11, April 15, May 27, Dec. 30, 1734; Feb. 17, July 14, July 21, Sept. 1, 15, 23, 1735.
[104] June 12, 1736; July 16 and 29, August 8, 1748; March 20, 1749; Oct. 17, 1754, *South-Carolina Gazette*.
[105] April 21, May 12, and 19, June 23, 1755; Nov. 9, 1767; May 6, 1771; Aug. 14, 1780.

Liberty of the Press" at least four times.[106] Between 1768 and 1787 the *Maryland Gazette* reprinted seven of Cato's letters, including the one on the press.[107] The *Massachusetts Spy* reprinted the essay on free speech twice in 1771 as well as the essay on the press,[108] plus at least ten other essays by Cato in 1771 and 1772. Isaiah Thomas, the printer of the *Spy*, wrote, "Cato's Letters are now busily parceling out in every essay with which of late we are pretty plentifully served up."[109] The *Boston Post-Boy* reprinted the essay on the press as late at 1773.[110]

John Dickinson, John Adams, and Thomas Jefferson quoted Cato; Jefferson had a copy of *Cato's Letters* in his personal library.[111] Many private libraries, college libraries, and bookstores had copies of *Cato's Letters*.[112] Benjamin Franklin recommended that students read *Cato's Letters*.[113] Josiah Quincy bequeathed to his son the works of Algernon Sydney, John Locke, and Trenchard and Gordon, and declared, "May the spirit of liberty rest upon him."[114] Chief Justice William Cushing of Massachusetts in 1789 inquired of John Adams whether Cato was right in advocating that truth could not be a libel in matters involving government, religion, and society.[115] David Ramsay in his near contemporary history of the Revolution, commenting on the popularity of "fashionable authors, who have defended the cause of liberty," wrote: "*Cato's Letters*, the *Independent Whig*, and such productions were common."[116] Old John Adams, reminiscing about the coming of the American Revolution, began his list of "fashionable reading" among Americans of the late colonial period with *Cato's Letters*.[117] In the history of political liberty as well as of freedom of speech and press, no eighteenth century work exerted more influence than *Cato's Letters*.

[106] May 26, 1755, June 2, 1755, March 8, 1756, May 6, 1771.
[107] No. 32 appeared in the *Maryland Gazette* on April 19, 1770.
[108] March 7 and 28, April 25, 1771.
[109] *Spy*, May 2, 1771.
[110] Sept. 27, 1773.
[111] Paul Leicester Ford, ed., *The Writings of John Dickinson* (Philadelphia, 1895), vol. 14 of Memoirs of the Historical Society of Pennsylvania, p. 343 of Letters of a Farmer, no. 7, E. Millicent Sowerby, *Catalogue of the Library of Thomas Jefferson* (Washington, 1952), 3:133.
[112] H. Trevor Colbourn, *The Lamp of Experience: Whig History and the Intellectual Origins of the American Revolution* (Chapel Hill, 1965), 200-230 passim.
[113] Leonard W. Labaree, ed., *Franklin Papers*, 3:406.
[114] Josiah Quincy, *Memoir of the Life of Josiah Quincy* (Boston, 1825), 350.
[115] Discussed below, pp. 198-203.
[116] Ramsay, *History of the American Revolution* (Dublin, 1793), 1:26-27.
[117] Charles Francis Adams, ed., *Works; with a Life of the Author of John Adams* (Boston, 1850-56), 10:202, letter to Jedidiah Morse, Jan. 5, 1816.

Cato did not, however, initiate a break-through in libertarian thought. He was a flashing star in an orthodox sky that exponents of intellectual and political liberty occasionally but dimly lit. The Deist leaders of his time who might have been expected to share his avant-garde views on the scope of free speech were themselves only slightly enlightened. John Toland, for example, a significant figure in the history of rationalism, while a pluperfect liberal on the right to advance any opinions concerning religion, followed Roger Williams in drawing limits on political criticism. Though professing publicly to champion liberty of the press, Toland deplored the circulation of seditious innuendoes and the licentious abuse of government ministers. He recommended that the government defend itself by extending the stamp tax on newspapers and even by prohibiting certain journals.[118]

Conventional thought received legal expression in 1729 by the anonymous author of *State Law: Or, the Doctrine of Libels, Discussed and Examined*, purportedly another defense of libertarianism.[119] The author intended that his book should "serve as an Argument for the Liberty of the Press, as it now stands, since it shews the little necessity of any farther Restraint upon it, by demonstrating, that every one who prints any thing with a mischievous Intent, does it at his own Peril. . . ."[120] Glowing rhetoric suffered vitiation by the standpatter's conviction that Englishmen already enjoyed genuine freedom of opinion under a body of law that had but one defect: a few loopholes made is possible for cunning writers to evade the deserved penalties for Crown libels and other licentious statements.[121]

Henry St. John, Viscount Bolingbroke, who achieved minor eminence as a political philosopher, about this time became the principal founder of, and a contributor to, the *Craftsman*, the organ of opposition to Walpole's administration. Bolingbroke represented himself as a zealous advocate of liberty of the press, sustaining in particular the right to animadvert on public men and measures. His conversion to libertarianism may have been more tactical than principled, because Bolingbroke in power had been suppressive, but out-of-power he felt forced to take cover in the liberty of political criticism. In 1712, when secretary of state, he had been of the opinion that, "It is a melancholy consideration that the laws of our country are too weak

---

[118] Frederick S. Siebert, *Freedom of the Press in England, 1476-1776* (Urbana, 1952), citing British Museum Additional *MS* 429, folios 49, 50.

[119] (London, n.d., [1729], 2nd ed.), 136 pp.

[120] *Ibid.*, Preface. The identical statement appears in *A Digest of the Law Concerning Libels* (London, 1778), p. xiii, a book attributed to John Raynor, who obviously plagiarized heavily from the earlier author of *State Law*.

[121] *State Law*, 135.

to punish effectually those factious scribblers who presume to blacken the brightest characters and to give even scurrilous language to those who are in the first degree of honour. This, my Lord, among others, is a symptom of the decayed condition of our government, and serves to show how fatally we mistake licentiousness for liberty."[122] Bolingbroke had also initiated stamp taxes upon printed matter, with the intention of driving out Whig journals, and he had masterminded an intensive campaign to crush allegedly seditious writings. When he turned to the cause of a free press, an anonymous Whig, undoubtedly with Walpole's aid, published a documentary record of Bolingbroke's former suppressions, exposing his hypocrisy and discrediting his self-interested support of open debate.[123]

Whatever his past, Bolingbroke supported *Craftsman's* energetic denunciations of the government for prosecuting Tory opinions as seditious libel. When Richard Francklin, the *Craftsman's* publisher, was indicted, one of the Bolingbroke-Francklin faction anonymously wrote a tract, in 1731, starting with the increasingly familiar generalization that in a free government, "every Man has a right to speak his Sentiments," on state matters as well as others.[124] But he did not, like most of his precursors, conclude his case with bombastic endorsements of free speech and press as if dealing with self-evident truth. His tract was distinguished by his reasoned consideration of the repressive practice of Crown prosecutors and judges in wresting a seditious construction from the least innuendo of a writer who has been forced, by the penalty for outright utterance, to resort to historical analogies and circumlocution to make his point. "If this Method of Construction be allowed," demanded the *Craftsman's* defender, "what Writer can be safe? It will soon be found as effectual a Way to destroy the Liberty of the Press, and in that the Liberties of the Subject, as the appointing a Licenser previously to peruse and approve all Books, before they are admitted to be printed."[125] Thus, without at any time repudiating the concept of seditious libel, the author reprehended its conventional application, which is more than anyone excepting Cato had done.

No English libertarian protested the fact that the law punished words against the state, religion, or morality, although a few liber-

[122] Hanson, *Government and the Press*, 63, quoting *Letters and Correspondence of . . . Henry St. John, Lord Viscount Bolingbroke*, ed. Gilbert Parke (London, 1798), 2:486.
[123] *The Craftsman's Doctrine and Practice of the Liberty of the Press* (London, 1732), 61 pp.
[124] *The Doctrine of Innuendo's Discuss'd; Or The Liberty of the Press Maintain'd* (London, 1731), 26 pp.
[125] *Ibid.*, 11.

tarians protested the application of the law, and a few advanced ideas that in time would fashion a new theory of intellectual liberty and freedom of political expression. Tindal, Asgil, and Collins deserve credit for describing free speech and even freedom of the press as natural rights, that is, as rights belonging to humanity in a state of nature before people contracted for government to preserve law and order. In half a century Americans would be the first people in the history of the world to give written constitutional recognition to natural rights, on the theory that the people reserved those rights to themselves and instituted governments to protect them. The theory of free political expression as a natural right and the concept of seditious libel could not forever coexist.

Other ideas that were destined to come into conflict with the concept of seditious libel emerged in early English libertarian thought. One considered a free press as a check on government, another as the indispensible matrix of political liberty and the maintenance of a free state. *Cato's Letters* best expressed these ideas. "What are usually called Libels," Cato wrote, "undoubtedly keep Great Men in Awe, and are some *Check* upon their Behavior, by shewing them the Deformity of their Actions as well as warning other People to be upon their Guard against Oppression."[126] The obligation as well as right of the press to engage in political criticism, condemn public measures injurious to the people, and expose corruption in high office led, ultimately, to a theory of the press as the "fourth estate," a watchdog of government on behalf of the people. In this connection Cato at one point turned the law of seditious libel upside down by discussing "libels against the people" perpetrated by the government. The people often "judge better" than their governors, he said, despite the habit of their governors to rail at or distrust them. "Let it be remembered," he added, "for whose sake Government is, or could be appointed, and then let it be considered, who are more to be regarded, the Governours, or the governed."[127]

An allied idea, although not then perceived as such, was Tindal's radical proposition that the people should enjoy the same freedom of speech as their representatives, who were not responsible to the law for anything said in Parliament concerning public matters. Moreover, Cato, as well as Addison (or Tory Author), had suggested that truth cannot be a criminal libel. That proposition contradicted the common law and if adopted would broaden the scope of political expression.

Should ever a time come when the public accepted these maverick

---

[126] "Discourse upon Libels," 3:297, emphasis added.
[127] "Reflections upon Libelling," 1:248-49.

ideas, that all liberty including the existence of a free state depended on freedom of speech and press, that truth could not be a libel, that the press had to be free to serve as a check upon government, and that the right of political expression was an inalienable natural right unabridgeable by the state, then the common law's restraints upon freedom of the press as well as on oral or written utterances inevitably faced erosion. On the other hand, to read too much into some novel suggestions advanced by a few writers would be mistaken, because even those few did not integrate these suggestions into a grand theory; indeed for the most part, excepting perhaps only Cato, they did not even understand the implications of their fleeting suggestions, let alone try to reconcile them with their unanimous acquiescence—and that includes Cato—in the basic principle of the law on political discourse: opinions that hurt government were criminal.

CHAPTER V

The Free Press Theory of the Zenger Generation

The American contribution to libertarian theory of freedom of speech and press, so strikingly absent prior to the Zenger case of 1735, remained almost as inconspicuous for long after. Even in that celebrated case America produced no broad concept of freedom of expression, none that rejected the suppressive idea of the common law that government, religion, or morality can be criminally attacked just by bad opinions. That did not come until late in the eighteenth century. In pre-Zenger America, no one had ever published an essay on the subject, let alone repudiated the concept of seditious libel or condemned its conventional application by the common-law courts or by parliamentary punishment for breach of privilege. To be sure, Englishmen in America admiringly read and quoted Cato, particularly if his eloquence suited some special purpose. But the colonists gave little independent thought and even less expression to a theory of unfettered political debate.

Benjamin Franklin, a towering figure among colonial printers and thinkers, best illustrates the point. In 1722, when only a youth, he reprinted at length Cato's essay on "Freedom of Speech," in the *New-England Courant* after his brother, James Franklin, had been imprisoned for an article that offended the Massachusetts legislature.[1] Then, in 1731, when in England *Craftsman*'s supporter was detailing an indictment of the repressive application of the law of seditious libel, Franklin's "most influential statement on freedom of the press" appeared in his *Pennslyvania Gazette*, a statement which an expert

---

[1] *New-England Courant,* July 9, 1721; see also *ibid.,* Sept. 21, 1721.

on the colonial press deemed "worth quoting at length, for it is an accurate representation of the principles of a free press which governed popular thinking in eighteenth-century America."[2] Yet Franklin simply argued that printing had to do with promoting and opposing the various opinions of men, that all opinions ought to be heard, that truth would "overmatch" error, and that vice and immorality ought not to be countenanced.[3]

Benjamin Franklin had no interest in abstract theory about the press. He confronted a practical problem: something he had printed offended certain clergymen and their supporters, with the result that he stood to loose money by losing readers and advertisers. Accordingly, he argued, printers could not avoid giving offense; they dealt in opinions. But he thought that they should not be blamed; they no more intended offense than any other tradesman or merchant who sold wares to all comers. Printers, Franklin wrote, served "all contending Writers that pay them well, without regarding on which side they are of the Question in Dispute." Having no stake in the rightness or wrongness of the opinions submitted to them, printers impartially published whatever made them money, excepting "bad things" or harm to private parties. Therefore, censuring printers for what appeared in their pages misconceived their function.

As Stephen Botein said of this view espoused by Franklin and so many other colonial printers, most "had an economic stake in maintaining the liberty of their presses. Although 'liberty of the press' was a noble concept . . . colonial printers were not inclined to dwell on such elevated matters. More commonly . . . they would disclaim all interest whatsoever in the political or intellectual functions of their craft, and explain their preference for impartiality merely as a business instinct to serve all customers. . . . What is apparent, however, is that their ideal of a 'free press' conducted by a politically indifferent craftsman made good sense to them as a business strategy."[4]

Franklin undoubtedly practiced freedom of the press, but his celebrated "Apology for Printers" hardly presented a definition or a phi-

---

[2] Clinton Rossiter, *Seedtime of the Republic* (New York, 1953), 300. Similarly Stephen Botein wrote, "By far the most sustained and best-known colonial argument for an impartial press was Franklin's 'Apology for Printers,' in Botein, " 'Meer Mechanics' and an Open Press: the Business and Political Strategies of Colonial American Printers," in Donald Fleming and Bernard Bailyn, eds., *Perspectives in American History* 9 (1975):182.

[3] "An Apology for Printers," *Philadelphia Gazette*, June 10, 1731, reprinted in Leonard W. Labaree, ed., *The Papers of Benjamin Franklin* (New Haven, 1959), 1:194-199; reprinted also in Leonard W. Levy, ed., *Freedom of the Press from Zenger to Jefferson* (Indianapolis, 1966), 3-10.

[4] " 'Meer Mechanics'," 179-80, 183.

losophy of a free press. He wrote as if such things as the imprisonment of his brother had never happened. He did not, in other words, face any of the problems connected with freedom of the press. If his statement was as influential and representative as it has been reputed, it simply shows the superficiality of American thinking on this subject.

If, indeed, we do not dignify as a definition of a robust freedom of the press, or of speech, the right to disagree with public policy or to say anything that the community or the law is indifferent to, finding a broad libertarian theory in America before the American Revolution—or even before the First Amendment—proves difficult. Indeed, none was possible until Americans understood the incompatibility between seditious libel and free government. Remarkably few even advocated that true statements should not be criminal, although the principle of truth as a defense to the charge of libel constituted the foremost American accomplishment toward the concept of a free press. Englishmen invented that principle; Americans applied it. The law, however, continued to regard truth as libelous, even as aggravating the crime, but truth as a defense gradually altered the American understanding of press freedom. Americans, printers especially, rarely thought in theoretical terms. Printers, having their businesses to operate, simply practiced freedom of the press as they understood it, by publishing whatever they pleased that they believed inoffensive. A writer in Andrew Bradford's *American Weekly Mercury* of Philadelphia commented in 1732 that wherever liberty reigned, "every man has a privilege of declaring his sentiments with the utmost freedom; provided he does it with a proper decency and a just regard to the laws."[5]

Americans, nevertheless, had a greater interest in going as far as they could, without getting into trouble, than they had in devising coherent theories about freedom of the press. Unless a printer received heavy business from his provincial government, he had no economic incentive to curry its favor or promote just its side. Having no ideological or political stake in the opinions that appeared in his columns, the colonial printer published whatever turned a profit and did not seem unlawful. Government officials acting in their public capacities made good targets for critical comment, although the colonial press, Zenger's excepted, was mild, if not timid, compared with London's press of the same period. The fact that the law posed a threat to a printer's freedom inhibited him far less than his own sense

[5] April 6, 1732.

of self-restraint. Actual prosecutions even for breach of parliamentary privilege never suppressed the press, because the prosecutions tended to be sporadic, exemplary, and personally or politically motivated, rather than systematic. The threat of prosecution, however, had a prudential if not intimidating effect, keeping printers aware of what might be unwise or risky to publish. Self-censorship, far more than prosecutions, restrained printers. Although few printers troubled to analyze freedom of the press, many briefly declaimed its virtues in standardized clichés, that it was, for example, the palladium of liberties or the jewel of freedom.

A broad-*sounding* statement on freedom of the press appeared in the first issue of Lewis Timothy's *South Carolina Gazette* in early 1734. He borrowed from *Cato's Letters* the ideas that a free press was "absolutely necessary to the Liberty of Great Britain" and served as a check on government. The latter idea he expressed in these words: "The *Liberty of the Press*, is the most unlucky Scourge that can hang over the Heads of a *corrupt* and *wicked* Ministry; and when this essential branch of our Liberties is either *attack'd*, *abridged*, or *taken away* from us, every Man . . . may certainly predict *Slavery* and *Ruin* to his Fellow-Citizens." Sandwiched between these thoughts was a crucial qualification that can easily be misunderstood. "Neither do I see," Timothy wrote, "how any *Restraint* can be put upon the *Press*, in a Nation that pretends to *Liberty*, but what just sufficient to prevent men from writing either *Blasphemy* or *Treason*."[6]

Blasphemy was purely a verbal crime—rejecting, reviling, or ridiculing Christianity, God, Jesus, or the Bible.[7] Treason, however, was not a verbal crime in English law; it could not be committed by mere words. Timothy nevertheless referred to treason committed by the press. What he meant, according to English law, was the cognate crime of treasonous words known as "constructive treason." Treason meant killing the king or attempting to kill him; committing any overt act toward that end; levying war against him; or adhering to his enemies. Constructive treason meant words or acts that could be

---

[6] *South Carolina Gazette*, Feb. 2, 1734, copy supplied by Jeffery A. Smith. Both Smith, in his "Impartiality and Revolutionary Ideology: Editorial Policies of the *South Carolina Gazette*, 1732-1755," *Journal of Southern History*, prepublication typescript, p. 7, and Lawrence H. Leder, *Liberty and Authority: Early American Political Ideology, 1689-1763* (Chicago, 1968), 25, misconstrue Timothy's article as a very broad libertarian statement. See my review of Leder's book in *Pennsylvania Magazine of History and Biography* 93 (1969):115-17. The *New-York Weekly Journal*, March 4, 1734, and the *American Weekly Mercury* (Philadelphia), March 12, 1734, reprinted Timothy's essay.

[7] See Leonard W. Levy, *Treason against God: the Offense of Blasphemy* (New York, 1981).

construed as a step, however remote, toward treason, such as imagining the death of the king, calling him a tyrant or usurper, advocating his deposition, or sympathetically corresponding with his enemies. In effect then, treason as a verbal crime, unconnected with any overt act, bore similarity to the crime of seditious libel. Words tending to the subversion of the constitution of the realm could be either constructive treason, severely punished, or seditious libel, less severely punished. Well before Timothy referred to treason committed by the press, the common law had absorbed within the concept of seditious libel the crime that had been constructive treason; by the end of the eighteenth century, however, when revolutionary France threatened England's security, Parliament revived constructive treason as a statutory crime after juries acquitted defendants charged with that crime under the common law for having advocated annual Parliaments and universal suffrage.[8]

The point, of course, is that when Timothy acquiesced in the propriety of punishing blasphemy and treason committed by the press, he accepted the common law of criminal libels, which punished words against religion and the government. In effect Timothy differed not at all from the writer in the *American Weekly Mercury* who advocated the utmost freedom of the press subject to a just regard for the laws.

In 1734 William Bradford's *New York Gazette* made the same point as Timothy in a conventional way. Punishing "the licentiousness of the press" did not diminish its freedom because, "'Tis the abuse not the use of the press that is criminal and ought to be punished."[9] "I must own," said the *Gazette* later that year "that no restraint ought to be put upon the press but what is sufficient to prevent the grossest abuses of it, abuses that dissolve society and sap the very foundation of government . . . but with regard to abuses of a less flagrant nature, I had rather see such permitted than the liberty itself ignored." Again, therefore, the common principle prevailed: the utmost freedom of the press under the law.[10] The *American Weekly Mercury*, which had advanced that principle in 1732, published an elaboration in 1734. The writer attempted a well-reasoned distinction between liberty and licentiousness. By liberty, he explained, he did not mean animadversions on the Crown, the constitution, or the fundamentals

---

[8] James Fitzjames Stephen, *A History of the Criminal Law of England* (London, 1883, 3 vols.), 2:243-81, and William S. Holdsworth, *A History of the English Law* (London, 1938-66, 16 vols.), 8:307-18.

[9] *New York Gazette*, Feb. 4, 1734.

[10] *Ibid.*, Oct. 28, 1734.

of religion and morality. Nor did he mean "Traducing the Conduct, of those Gentlemen who are appointed our Lawful Governors," although he conceded that when they misbehaved, "their Measures are to be remonstrated against in Terms of *Decency*."

> But, by the Freedom of the Press [the author declared], I mean a Liberty, within the Bounds of Law, for any Man to communicate to the Public, his Sentiments on the Important Points of Religion and Government; of proposing any Laws, which he apprehends may be for the Good of his Countrey, and of applying for the Repeal of such, as he Judges pernicious. I mean a Liberty of detecting the wicked and destructive Measures of certain Politicians; of dragging Villanny out of its obscure lurking Holes, and exposing it in its full Deformity to open Day; of attacking Wickedness in high Places, of disintangling the intricate Folds of a wicked and corrupt Administration, and pleading freely for Redress of Grievances: I mean a Liberty of examining the great Articles of our Faith, by the Lights of Scripture and Reason, a Privilege derived to us in its fullest Latitude, from our most excellent Charter. This is the Liberty of the Press, the greatest Palladium of all our other Liberties.[11]

This handsome statement was predicated on a catch-clause appearing in the first line, "a Liberty, within the Bounds of Law . . . ," indicating the standard concurrence with the restraints of the common law. In his prefatory remarks the author had defined licentiousness as subverting religion or traducing the conduct of the government. Since "traduce" means to speak evil of or defame, he might as well have said pithily that he favored a liberty of the press as defined by the royal judges.

The work of another American during the same decade deserves the utmost attention. He was James Alexander, Cato's principal disciple in the colonies, the mastermind of the Zenger defense. Alexander's name has been obscured by the attention lavished upon his famed printer and client, John Peter Zenger, and upon his fellow attorney, Andrew Hamilton. A man of versatile talents, Alexander was a founder of the American Philosophical Society, surveyor-general of both New Jersey and New York, a member of the Council of both those colonies, a legal reformer, attorney-general of New Jersey, and editor of Zenger's *New York Weekly Journal*, the first politically

---

[11] *American Weekly Mercury* (Philadelphia), April 25, 1734, reprinted in Levy, ed. *Freedom of the Press from Zenger to Jefferson* (Indianapolis, 1966), 37-43. Anna Janney DeArmond, *Andrew Bradford, Colonial Journalist* (Newark, Del., 1949), is good on William Bradford's son.

independent newspaper in America. When Zenger, the printer and publisher, came under indictment in 1735 for seditious libel, Alexander, who should have been in the prisoner's dock instead, served as his counsel. It was Alexander who wrote the allegedly seditious articles in Zenger's paper about Governor William Cosby. It was Alexander who reprinted in Zenger's paper the essays from *Cato's Letters* on freedom of speech and press and on libels. It was Alexander who, when summarily disbarred in the pretrial stage of the case for accusing the presiding judge of bias, brought in Andrew Hamilton to argue the cause and provided him with a detailed brief of the argument that proved victorious. It was also Alexander who edited the famous account of the case that was reprinted so often and perpetuated the reputations of Zenger and Hamilton as heroes in the cause of freedom of the press. Finally it was Alexander who was the first colonial figure to develop a philosophy of freedom of speech-and-press.[12]

In his initial essay, published in two parts in the second and third issues of Zenger's paper, Alexander contrasted the state of the press in an absolute monarchy and a limited one. In an absolute monarchy, he observed, a freedom of the press to complain of grievances would be inconsistent with the constitution of the state, because the will of the prince being law, to protest would subvert his rule. In the limited monarchy of Britain, however, the people knew in advance the laws that bound both them and the government, "and therefore an Offense against the Laws is such an Offense against the Constitution as ought to receive proper adequate punishment. . . ." Freedom of the press, however, Alexander wrote, was "incorporated and interwoven with our very Constitution." That constituted an original and significant idea, from which he concluded that the press should enjoy freedom from restraint.[13]

Alexander acknowledged that the press sometimes traduced the character of good officials, but he asserted that the benefits of an unrestrained press outweighed its disadvantages. Calumnies, he reasoned, could not really damage just governors, whereas the truth could curb bad ones. Although he contended that a person who pleaded "for any

[12] On Alexander and his relationship to the Zenger case, see *Dictionary of American Biography* and Vincent Buranelli, "Peter Zenger's Editor," *American Quarterly* 7 (Summer 1955):174-181; Buranelli, *The Trial of Peter Zenger* (New York, 1957), iii, 24-25, 30-32, 68-70. Levy, ed. *Freedom of the Press*, 10-24, reprints Cato's essays as they appeared in Zenger's *New-York Weekly Journal*.
[13] *New-York Weekly Journal*, Nov. 12, 1733.

Restraint upon the Press" was an enemy of the country and its constitution, he did not explain what he meant by "restraint."[14]

A subsequent essay showed that he did not mean only prior restraint. He asserted, most conservatively, that anyone who spoke "irreverently and disrespectfully of Magistrates . . . was and is, always
will be, criminal." But the magistrate who abused power, he added,
deserved no respect. Some people favored prosecuting libels against
the government, even though such libels, in Alexander's opinion, defied definition. He did not say whether in his opinion a libel could
exist, but he had already affirmed the criminality of speaking disrespectfully. He probably meant that speaking disrespectfully of a good
or just magistrate constituted a libel against government. He emphasized, however, the overloose usage of the concept of libel. People
called "any Paper they don't like, that treats of Governours or Magistrates, a Libel against Government." They called passages in Zenger's
paper "an aggravated Libel," a term that made no sense to Alexander.
Sergeant William Hawkins, the great authority on Crown libels, provided such people with their definitions; Alexander rejected Hawkins,
preferring the judgment of a jury. Although he conceded that the
abuse of the press was "blameable," he thought his readers could judge
better than the government as to what constituted an abuse.[15]

In another essay Alexander followed Cato in declaring, "the Liberty
of the Press is a liberty for every man to communicate his sentiments
freely to the public, upon political or religious points; it is either this
or nothing." Alexander did not, however, follow a consistent line on
the freedom of the press. Some printers, he said, continued to abuse
the press with impunity. "I cannot conceive how any man can see a
liberty, and an essential liberty of a constitution, abused with impunity, and see that abuse with great satisfaction, too, except himself
be an abuser, or some of his friends." Although he insisted that the
liberty to communicate one's sentiments freely meant "without the
Fear of Danger of being punished," he conceded that "Abuses that
dissolve society and sap the Foundation of Government are not to be
sheltered under the Umbrage of the Liberty of the Press." That statement denied his Catonian proposition that truth could not be a libel.
However contradictory Alexander's thought, he had a libertarian
point to make. The government was then attempting to initiate a
prosecution against Zenger. Alexander informed his readers that the

[14] *Ibid.*, Nov. 19, 1733. Levy, ed., *Freedom of the Press*, 27-32, reprints the
two-part essay.
[15] *Ibid.*, Feb. 11 and 18, 1734, reprinted in Levy, ed., *Freedom of the Press*,
32-35.

government could not be trusted to decide which abuses of the press deserved punishment. Authors and printers had good reason to fear the government. Talking of freedom of the press seemed farcical, he stated, when in fact the press did not enjoy impunity for its opinions. "We may write what we please," he sarcastically declared, "but then we must take Care that what pleases us pleases our Masters too. . . . if we do not write as they think fit, they'll make us smart for it." These early essays by Alexander, lacking coherency and consistency, were no more libertarian than Bradford's essays. Alexander simply had not yet developed his philosophy of freedom of the press. Zenger's trial, Alexander's brief for Zenger, Hamilton's argument, and Alexander's report of it sharpened his thinking.[16]

The Hamilton-Alexander trial argument, despite its fame as a broad libertarian statement, was only slightly conceptual in character. The few passages constructing a rationale for freedom of the press, though not lacking in trenchancy and eloquence, were limited to the sole theme that villainy in government deserves exposure, even if the remonstrance against abuses of power be put in truth's strongest terms. In a free government, urged Hamilton, the people's mouths should not be stopped when they feel themselves oppressed. He confessed, however, that "nothing ought to excuse a man who raises a false charge or accusation, even against a private person, and that no manner of allowance ought to be made to him who does so against a public magistrate."[17] He never conducted a frontal assault on the concept of seditious libel. He never argued that publications tending to damage the reputation of the government in the minds of the people should be free from criminal prosecution. He extolled criticism of a "bad administration" or an "arbitrary government" (Cosby's of course) but he did not justify criticism of any government that he might think to be good or just.

At the same time, he must be credited with having conducted the first sustained assault, even if only indirect, upon the common law of criminal utterance. "*Truth*," he insisted, "ought to govern the whole affair of libels."[18] This proposition would have altered the substance of the common-law rule that the truth of a charge worsened the libel. The rule rested on the theory that truth would more likely provoke the impugned party to an act of revenge, breaching the

---

[16] *Ibid.*, Nov. 4, 1734, in Levy, ed., *Freedom of the Press*, 35-37.
[17] James Alexander, *A Brief Narrative of the Case and Tryal of John Peter Zenger Printer of the New-York Weekly Journal*, ed. by Stanley Nider Katz (Cambridge, Mass., 1972, 2nd ed.), 84.
[18] *Ibid.*

peace, than a falsehood which he might contemptuously ignore. Hamilton ridiculed the rule, declaring it to be a "Star Chamber" inheritance that left truth a greater sin than falsehood. The main point of his argument was that the truth of a defendant's allegedly libelous statement should render him immune to punishment.[19] When the court rejected this proposition, Hamilton retreated to the position that the jury should decide the law as well as the facts in a criminal-libel case, instead of their returning a special verdict on the question whether the defendant had as a matter of fact made the statement charged and leaving the court to rule, as a matter of law, whether the words were criminal per se.

The propositions that truth should constitute an adequate defense and that the jury should decide the whole question of libel were to become the heavy cannon of the embattled libertarians of the eighteenth century. Yet, when they finally won, after many decades of contention, they might have exclaimed with Pyrrhus, "Another such victory and we are lost!" At a time when judges were dependent instruments of the Crown, a jury of one's peers and neighbors proved to be a promising bulwark against the tyrannous enforcement of the law of seditious libel by the administration and its judges. That the jury, as a popular institution, would protect political critics was an accepted article of faith. Juries had acquitted William Bradford, Thomas Maule, and Peter Zenger. But juries, with the power of ruling on the guilt or innocence of alleged libels, proved to be as susceptible to prevailing prejudices as judges when they decided the fate of defendants who had expressed unpopular sentiments in times of crisis. Only one verdict of "not guilty" was returned in the numerous prosecutions under the Sedition Act of 1798.[20] In England, where Fox's Libel Act of 1792 secured the power of juries in libel cases, the most repressive prosecutions succeeded with very few exceptions.[21] Jurors in America and England acted in a manner not noticeably different from Scroggs, Jeffreys, or Chase. They could be relied upon to support freedom of speech-and-press, as in the Zenger case, if public opinion opposed the administration or the prosecution. An unpopular administration might hesitate to prosecute if it had to pass the gauntlet of a jury as in all other criminal cases.

Yet the power of the jury in seditious libel cases was a procedural

[19] Alexander, *Brief Narrative*, Katz, ed., 62, 69-72, 75, 84, 87.

[20] James Morton Smith, *Freedom's Fetters: The Alien and Sedition Laws and American Civil Liberties* (Ithaca, 1956), 185.

[21] Thomas Erskine May, *The Constitutional History of England Since the Accession of George III, 1760-1860* (London, 1880), 2:142-50.

safeguard that did not alter the substantive law. And even as a procedural safeguard, it proved capable of creating procedural traps to the defendant's disadvantage. He could have no basis for appealing a conviction by a jury that decided the law for itself, because the law incorporated by a jury in its general verdict of "guilty" is formally unknowable even if it should have been incorrect. Fair procedure can be afforded only if the presumption can obtain that the jury took its law, though incorrectly, from the court. Moreover, the meaning and application of the law when decided by a jury can fluctuate from case to case, in effect annulling the security to which every citizen is entitled by a uniform administration of justice.[22] Nevertheless, allowing a jury to return a general verdict would have prevented a biased court from deciding whether the words charged constituted a crime as a matter of law.

More sound was the proposition that a defendant who could prove the truth of his charges should be freed. Here was a safeguard, concerning the conduct of the defense, which would have modified the substance of the law by extending the scope of permissible expression—but not by much. Where before, revelation of corruption, injustice, or incompetence in government, however documented or accurate, might be punished on the theory that truth aggravated the libel, men might, under the Cato-Hamilton-Alexander proposal, exercise the right to denounce and expose "in the strongest terms" if only they hewed to the truth. On this the Zenger defense reached bedrock: truth could not be a libel; truth fixed the bounds of the right to speak, write, and publish opinions on the conduct of men in power. But to define liberty of expression as "speaking and writing truth" rooted it in shallow soil, for the very criticism that Hamilton directed at the concept of libel—that there was a "great diversity of opinions" and an even "greater uncertainty" concerning what words were or were not defamatory—applied analogously to the concept of "truth." That one man's truth is another's falsehood, or that the truth of opinions is not susceptible of proof, Hamilton did not consider. Eighteenth-century libertarians belatedly discovered that they had mistaken for brick a prop of straw. Truth as a defense could prove to be of real value, and in fact proved to be so, if the defendant's statement lent itself to verification as a matter of fact.

Because criminal juries decide guilt or innocence but do not, like

---

[22] See Mark DeWolfe Howe, "Juries as Judges of Criminal Law," *Harvard Law Review* 52 (February 1939):582-616, a general discussion of the subject. I have stated my own views more fully in *The Law of the Commonwealth and Chief Justice Shaw* (Cambridge, Mass., 1957), 290-293.

appellate courts and legislatures, make law, the Zenger verdict created no "precedent" in any legal sense. But it raised a standard that some American legislatures chose to follow in their own judicial proceedings, in cases involving breach of parliamentary privilege in which the accused could be put to proof. In the 1740s Fleet in Massachusetts and Parks in Virginia could produce evidence to support the charges that got them into trouble. Fleet could prove that a naval officer gave him certain information; Parks could prove that a burgess had a criminal record. Similarly, a decade later, Bodley in North Carolina could prove that a certain person had lied. In none of these cases was the validity of a political opinion at issue. William Smith in Pennsylvania and Alexander McDougall in New York, if given the privilege of truth as a defense, could not have demonstrated the inerrancy of their subjective remarks.

Regardless of the possible limitations of Hamilton's argument as a libertarian defense of freedom of the press, it was an argument which, judging from its impact on the bench, was like the stagecoach ticket inscribed, "Good for this day only." The Zenger jury, responding to the magnificent forensics of a great lawyer engaged in a popular cause, returned a verdict of "not guilty," but the common law remained unchanged. As late as 1804, Chief Justice Morgan Lewis of New York, a Jeffersonian no less, voiced the opinion that truth did not constitute a defense against a charge of seditious libel.[23] Not until 1805 did New York, the home of Zenger, make truth a defense, if published "with good motives for justifiable ends."[24]

Alexander's *A Brief Narrative of the Case and Tryal of John Peter Zenger*, published by Zenger in 1736, was, with the possible exception of *Cato's Letters*, the most widely known source of libertarian thought in England and America during the eighteenth century.[25] But scant fame attended his excellent 1737 essay on freedom of speech, which he wrote in reply to attacks upon the ideas he had advanced, via Hamilton, at the trial. In 1737 two West Indian lawyers, one of whom was probably Jonathan Blenman, the king's attorney in Barbados, published severe strictures of a technical character against the Zenger defense, purporting to disprove on legal grounds the contention that truth was a defense against a libel charge; both "Anglo-Americanus" and "Indus-Britannicus" held to the thesis that truth

---

[23] *People v. Croswell*, 3 Johnson's (N.Y.) Cases 336, 363-394 (1804).
[24] *Ibid.*, 411-13.
[25] For a bibliography of the various editions of Zenger's trial, see Rutherfurd, *John Peter Zenger, His Press, His Trial and a Bibliography of Zenger Imprints. Also a Reprint of the Edition of the Trial* (New York, 1904), pp. 249-255.

not only could be libelous but necessarily exacerbated the libel.[26] Andrew Bradford, the Philadelphia printer and long-time enemy of Andrew Hamilton, speedily republished their "Remarks on the Trial of John Peter Zenger."[27] Alexander replied in a four-part essay which was first published, appropriately, in the paper of Bradford's competitor, Franklin's *Pennsylvania Gazette* and reprinted in Zenger's paper.[28]

Alexander, who used to copy selections from *Cato's Letters* for his personal edification as well as for Zenger's paper,[29] met his critics in the grand manner by sketching a history and theory of freedom of speech. Because only one other American, William Bollan, attempted the same task before the very last years of the century,[30] Alexander's essay deserves the fullest consideration. He began with first principles: "Freedom of speech is a *principal Pillar* in a free Government: when this Support is taken away, the Constitution is dissolved, and Tyranny is erected on its ruins. Republics and limited monarchies derive their strength and vigour from a *Popular Examination* into the Actions of the Magistrates."[31] Acknowledging the risks inherent in a policy of free speech, he argued that licentious expression was the price that society had to pay in return for the benefits received. "These abuses of Freedom of Speech are the excrescences of Liberty. They ought to be suppressed; but to whom dare we commit the care of doing it? An evil Magistrate, entrusted with a *power* to punish Words, is armed with a Weapon the most destructive and terrible. Under the pretense of pruning off the exuberant branches, he frequently destroys the tree."[32] What about the fair magistrate obligated by his duty to apply the law of seditious libel? Alexander did not consider that question nor the distinction between true facts and opinions that might be false.

[26] "Remarks on the Trial of John Peter Zenger," signed by "Anglo-Americanus," first appeared in *Keimer's Barbadoes Gazette* between June 25 and July 23, 1737, to which "Indus-Britannicus" added a supplemental essay, with the same title, on Aug. 10, 1737. The "Remarks" of both writers were reprinted in *Caribbeana* (London, 1741), 2:198-241, in Thomas Bayly Howell, comp., *A Complete Collection of State Trials to 1783*, continued by T. J. Howell to 1820 (London, 1816-28), 21:726-764, and in Katz's edition of Alexander's *Brief Narrative*, 152-80.

[27] DeArmond, *Andrew Bradford*, 107.

[28] Nov. 17-Dec. 8, 1737, Numbers 466-469, reprinted also in Levy, ed., *Freedom of the Press*, 61-74.

[29] Buranelli, "Zenger's Editor," *American Quarterly* 7:179.

[30] [William Bollan], *The Freedom of Speech and Writing upon Public Affairs, Considered, with an Historical View* (London, 1766), 160 pp.

[31] *Philadelphia Gazette*, Nov. 17, 1737.

[32] *Ibid.*

Then followed a history of prosecutions for libel, with every line radiating hatred of restraints on expression. He pictured a tyranny under the Roman Empire so great that "no man could write or open his Mouth, without being in danger of forfeiting his Head." Turning his wrath against the Tudors and Stuarts, he tersely demonstrated how each monarch aiming at despotic power had been "absolutely determined to suppress all Freedom of Speech." Quickly, and effectively, he told of the martyrdoms of Sir John Elliot, William Prynn, Henry Burton, John Bastwick, and Algernon Sydney, among others, whose rightful exercise for free speech had resulted in their punishment as "disturbers of the GOVERNMENT." These tragic events Alexander ascribed to the "Star-chamber doctrine" of libel. His historical review, he explained, endeavored to prove "the fatal dangers that necessarily attend a Restraint on freedom of speech and the liberty of the press: upon which the following Reflection naturally occurs, viz. THAT WHOEVER ATTEMPTS TO SUPPRESS EITHER OF THOSE, *OUR NATURAL RIGHTS,* OUGHT TO BE REGARDED AS AN *ENEMY* TO LIBERTY AND THE CONSTITUTION."[33] In the end, however, the only concrete suggestion that he offered as a means of protecting these rights was truth-as-a-defense, a liberalization of the common law, certainly, but an Achilles heel nevertheless. For nonmalicious falsehoods or mistakes, even unprovable truths, indeed, even mere opinions or conclusions from facts, might still be punishable as seditious libel. Alexander himself confessed, as had Hamilton in the Zenger defense, that "to infuse into the minds of the people an ill opinion of a just administration, is a crime that deserves no mercy."[34] The law of evidence, he failed to consider, would hardly help in any effort to prove that an administration was just or not. Opinion, derived from invisible moral standards and from seamy considerations as to whether one's ox was being gored, would be more to the point than legal proof.

Alexander's comment on the conduct of Zenger's defense candidly admitted that it rested in part on an appeal to popular feelings:

> But when the defendant is innocent and unjustly prosecuted, his Counsel may, nay ought to take all advantages and use every Strategem that his skill, art and learning can furnish him with. This last was the case of *Zenger* at *New-York*, as appears by the printed Trial and the VERDICT of the Jury. It was a popular cause. The LIBERTY OF THE PRESS in that Province depended on it. On

---

[33] *Ibid.,* Dec. 1, 1737.
[34] *Ibid.;* Katz, ed., *Brief Narrative,* 190, or Levy, ed., *Freedom of the Press,* 66.

such occasions the dry Rules of strict pleading are never observed. The Counsel for the Defendant sometimes argues from the known principles of Law, then raises doubts and difficulties to confound his Antagonist, now applies himself to the affections, and chiefly endeavors to raise the passions. *Zenger's* Defense is to be considered in all those different lights. Yet a Gentleman of *Barbadoes* assures us that it was published as a Solemn argument in the Law, and therefore writes a very elaborate confutation of it.[35]

The passions upon which Alexander counted could boomerang. In Zenger's case, the grand jury, the city aldermen, and the provincial Assembly, as well as a powerful political faction, opposed the prosecution and supported the defendant. In other times and places, in the United States in 1798, for example, passion ran against the Sedition Act defendants who were as worthy and innocent as Zenger.

The crux of Alexander's position, however, drew strength from an impregnable principle: "But a free constitution and freedom of speech have such a reciprocal dependence on each other that they cannot subsist without consisting together."[36] Unfortunately he failed to propose a test that would protect opinions neither true nor false. He claimed that the "abuses of free speech" were "excrescences of Liberty," allowing opponents to perpetuate a distinction between the proper use of liberty and its licentious abuse. Abuses, Alexander declared, "ought to be suppressed," but when considering who should judge the propriety of a suppression, he too easily dismissed the "evil" magistrate without considering the just one.

Alexander's position had a fatal defect: his acceptance of the principle that words giving an "ill opinion" of the government, even a "just" one, should be punished. This was the core of the concept of seditious libel, and until the libertarians attacked the core, their defense of freedom of speech or press was restricted conceptually and vulnerable to many of the very criticisms with which they lashed their opponents.

An historian who rediscovered Alexander's essay claims, "It presents him as the most important theorist of freedom of the press this country has ever produced."[37] He doubtless deserves the accolade as our first and greatest *colonial* theorist of the rights of free expression, for with the sole exception of William Bollan, who published in 1766, Alexander had no rivals. Other colonials may have shared his prin-

---

[35] *Philadelphia Gazette*, Dec. 9, 1737, quoted in Levy, ed., *Freedom of the Press*, 69.
[36] *Ibid.*, Dec. 8, 1737, quoted in Levy, 74.
[37] Buranelli, *The Trial of Peter Zenger*, 141.

ciples, which were Cato's, but did not develop them in print. Many Americans expounded on freedom of conscience, trial by jury, the natural-rights theory, and popular sovereignty, but it would be an exaggeration to conclude from Alexander's almost unique essay, which was apparently forgotten shortly after its newspaper appearance,[38] that America produced a broad definition or a philosophy of freedom of speech or press.

Alexander's account of the trial went through four or five editions in England in 1738, the same year in which a journal that had joined *Craftsman* as a voice of opposition to the Whig government of Walpole published *Common Sense*, two unsigned essays which showed an attentive reading of Cato.[39] Both authors felt provoked to express themselves on the subject of free political discussion because of recent punishments for seditious libel and the clamor of the administration press for additional checks against Tory licentiousness. Both, like Cato and Alexander, ably discoursed on the indispensability of open political debate to the maintenance of free government, evincing thereby a well-conceived theory of libertarianism.

They stressed the necessity and right of the people to be informed of their governors' conduct so as to shape their own judgments on "Publick Matters" and be qualified to choose their representatives wisely. No one before had related the electoral process to freedom of expression—a significant advance in political and libertarian theory. The first essayist, in depicting the wholesome influence of liberty of the press upon the formation of public opinion, also propounded the novel thesis that the "Bulk of Mankind" were quite capable of governing themselves; the opinion that they could not understand and decide public issues he condemned as "the Off-spring only of Priestcraft and Tyranny, for they alone would have the People ignorant whose desire is to deceive them."[40] Warning that a zest for punishing libels might uproot the wheat for the sake of a few tares, the author also recommended a policy of tolerating most falsehoods and licentiousness as "trivial inconveniences" arising from the liberty of the press. The second essayist, in championing the "salutary effects" of "Freedom of Debate," wisely suggested that the public should be exposed to every kind of controversy, in philosophy, history, science, religion, and literature, as well as in politics, because in the course of

[38] The essay was reprinted by Zenger's *New York Weekly Journal*, Dec. 19, 1737-Jan. 17, 1737/38; by the *Barbadoes Gazette*, Jan. 21, 1737/38; and in *Caribbeana* (London, 1741), 2:264-271.

[39] *Common Sense: or, the Englishman's Journal* (London, 1738), 331-341 and 349-354.

[40] *Ibid.,* 336.

"examining, comparing, forming opinions, defending them, and sometimes recanting them," the public would acquire a "Readiness of Judgment and Passion for Truth."[41]

Despite their genuine understanding of the need for a broad policy of political and intellectual liberty, both writers strikingly failed to criticize the substantive law of criminal libel. "Let Calumny and Detraction be punished as they ought to be, in a legal manner," wrote one, while the other supported "that Freedom of Inquiry we at present enjoy . . . unrestrained but by equitable Laws, which constitute the very essence of our Civil Liberty."[42] The first writer, like Cato, may have been somewhat disingenuous by giving the appearance of accepting conventional premises, but the second embraced them. The evidence does not warrant the belief that either would have exempted all verbal attacks on the government from subsequent punishment. Their position, in brief, was that utterances they did not consider subversive should be criminally immune. But their party was not in power at the time. Being in power alters one's vision. Harmless utterances directed by an opposing faction sometimes turn the color of seditious libel.

Both writers, however, contributed more to libertarian theory than the eminent philosopher, David Hume. He defended the general principle of a free press as he understood it without considering the law on the subject. He concerned himself with the philosophy of the matter, not the existence and enforcement of the law of seditious libel, nor the power of Parliament to punish aspersive speech and publications as a breach of privilege. How else could he write about "the extreme liberty, which we enjoy in this country, of communicating whatever we please to the public, and of openly censuring every measure, entered into by the king or his ministers"?[43] The first sixteen editions of his essay, from 1742 to 1768, carried a passage minimizing the dangers that might result from abuse of the press and claiming "this liberty . . . as the common right of mankind." But the 1770 edition omitted the passage, and the final revised edition added a concluding line characterizing the "unbounded liberty of the press" as "one of the evils" attending mixed form of government. By then, Hume, with a growing desire to publish *Dialogues Concerning Natural Religion*, and fearful that friends and enemies would stymie his failing wishes for its release, may have curried favor with the govern-

---

[41] *Ibid.*, 350.
[42] *Ibid.*, 338 and 350.
[43] "Of the Liberty of the Press," in *Essays, Moral, Political, and Literary*, eds. T. H. Green and T. H. Grose (London, 1898), 1:94.

ment. But any edition of Hume gave the impression that the press was as free as it ought to be.

Still, the important Hume on this issue of the freedom of the press was the Hume that the American colonists read in their newspapers, and what they read was "the celebrated Mr. Hume's Observations on the Liberty of the Press," an unrevised version of the original, widely reprinted in the colonial newspapers. In that article Hume observed that the quiet reading of a newspaper could not galvanize anyone into action. Therefore liberty of the press, "however abused, can scarce ever excite popular tumults or rebellion." In effect, he denied that a libel regarded as seditious could breach the peace, a repudiation of the rationale for the law's suppressive doctrine. He also declared that the law of seditious libel had gone about as far as it could and that if courts exercised any further discretion, the result would be a "barefaced violation of liberty of the press" by letting judges punish whatever displeased them. Most editions of Hume's works printed a revision of the essay that deleted the most libertarian passages.[44]

In 1747 Henry Fielding, novelist and political journalist, revealed his sentiments more bluntly. When the Tories returned to power, after the fall of the Walpole ministry, he edited a pro-administration journal which took a dim view of Whig criticism. "In a free country," he confessed, "the people have a right to complain of any grievance which affects them, and this is the privilege of an Englishman; but surely to canvass those high and nice points, which move the finest wheels of state, matters merely belonging to the royal prerogative, in print, is in the highest degree indecent, and a gross abuse of the liberty of the press."[45]

Across the Atlantic, notwithstanding the Zenger case and Alexander's magnificent efforts, no progress was being made in libertarian thought. Indeed, there was hardly any American libertarian thought between Alexander in 1737 and Bollan in 1766—and not much after, not until 1798. Charles Chauncy, "undoubtedly the most influential clergyman of his time in Boston," and "acknowledged leader of the liberals of his generation,"[46] wrote a great sermon in 1739 on liberty of conscience, but hewed to orthodoxy in banning undefined abuses

[44] I am indebted to Jeffery A. Smith of the University of Iowa for calling my attention to the appearance of the Hume article in the colonial press. The most readable copy he sent me was in the *South Carolina Gazette*, Dec. 31, 1765.

[45] *Jacobite's Journal*, no. 26, May 28, 1747, quoted in Lawrence Hanson, *Government and the Press, 1695-1763* (Oxford, 1936), 2.

[46] *Dictionary of American Biography.*

of liberty or "Licentiousness."[47] One historian has alleged that Thomas Fleet, the printer of the *Boston Evening Post*, published several "personal statements," in 1740 and 1741, "on freedom of the press that rivalled anything written by Cato or other libertarians." Fleet's statements do not deserve notice and reflect no libertarianism.[48] A tract of 1744, ascribed to Elisha Williams, speaker of the Connecticut House, formerly president of Yale and a judge, brilliantly pleaded for the right of private judgment without any control from civil authority, not only as to affairs of conscience but on all issues. Williams generously supported *"the Right that every one has to speak his Sentiments openly concerning such Matters as affect the good of the whole."*[49] But "every one" meant only Protestants, because Williams expressly excluded "Papists." Moreover, he neglected to confront any of the problems of libel law.

In the same year, 1744, Jeremiah Gridley also failed to confront legal issues in his essay on liberty, despite the fact that he was one of the leading lawyers of Massachusetts. His essay deserves attention because he regarded the liberty of speaking or writing one's sentiments on any matter concerning the public as a natural right. Yet he did nothing with that thought, and when he tried to defend the right to criticize the government, he resorted to a nautical metaphor. A passenger had a right to give notice when the vessel was in danger, but the captain, even if refusing to take notice, had no right to punish the well-meant information. Gridley, the lawyer, apparently felt too restrained to make his point directly and to cope with any of the real problems that his mistress, the common law, posed for freedom of political expression.[50] Four years later a writer in the Boston *Independent Advertiser* proved to be equally evasive in the course of an article defending the right to "remonstrate his grievances" under a "good legal constitution."[51] Jonathan Mayhew, however, understood

---

[47] *The only Compulsion proper to be made Use of in the Affairs of Conscience and Religion* (Boston, 1739), 15.

[48] Mary Ann Yodelis, "Boston's First Major Newspaper War: A 'Great Awakening' of Freedom," *Journalism Quarterly* 51 (1974):209-10. Fleet, a merely tolerant and independent man, cannot be compared with Andrew Bradford, let alone Cato or Alexander. He merely insisted on his right to manage his own newspaper, claimed to be of no party, would as soon serve one side and as another, and refused to quarrel with someone who did not think as he did.

[49] *A Seasonable Plea for the Liberty of Conscience, and the Right of private Judgment, in Matters of Religion, without any Controul from human Authority*, By a Lover of Truth and Liberty [signing himself "Philalethes"] (Boston, 1744), 6, 40.

[50] *American Magazine and Historical Chronicle* (Boston), 1:556-57.

[51] August 8, 1748.

practical considerations. A radical agitator, regarded as a prophet of
the American Revolution by Otis and the Adamses, this great liberal
minister, in the midst of his famous sermon of 1750 on the right of
revolution and civil disobedience against wicked laws, took occasion
to condemn the querulous and contemptible men in every state, "men
of factious, turbulent and carping dispositions" who took hold of
every trifle to justify and legitimate "seditious practices" against their
rulers.[52] This superb example of unconscious irony indicated little
sympathy on Mayhew's part for words *he* considered to be seditious.

In 1753 the colonial understanding of the scope of free expression
was further revealed by an editorial in *The Independent Reflector*,
the voice of the New York "Triumvirate," William Livingston, John
Morin Scott, and William Smith, young lawyers with republican
ideas and a passion to be heard. William Livingston learned law in
the office of James Alexander but absorbed little of Alexander's libertarianism. In 1752 Livingston and his friends founded *The Independent Reflector*, a weekly magazine "to oppose superstition, bigotry,
priestcraft, tyranny, servitude, public mismanagement and dishonesty
in office," and to advocate "the inestimable value of liberty." The
essay, entitled "Of the Use, Abuse, and Liberty of the Press," reputedly reflected mid-century American libertarian theory at its best,
but it was in fact reactionary if not vicious. The author, Livingston,
subsequently became a spirited opponent of parliamentary interfer-
ence in provincial affairs, served as a delegate to the First and Second
Continental Congresses, became the first governor of the state of New
Jersey, and represented that state at the Philadelphia Constitutional
Convention in 1787. That a Framer could ever have held such views
surprises. The leading essays in *The Independent Reflector* have recently been republished. Their editor, Milton M. Klein, defending
the essay on the press against attempts to minimize its libertarian character, argued: "The distinction he [Livingston] drew in this issue was
not between a legitimate use of the press against executive prerogative and its abuse when employed against legislatures but rather between a press employed to promote liberty and one used to advance
what he regarded as 'superstition and thralldom'."

Only Livingston's own words, in context, can serve to reveal his
thought. He wrote:

No Nation in *Europe*, is more jealous of the *Liberty of the Press*
than the *English*, nor is there a People, among whom it is so grossly

---

[52] "A Discourse Concerning Unlimited Submission," in Perry Miller and
Thomas H. Johnson, eds., *The Puritans* (New York, 1938), 279-280.

abused. With us, the most unbounded Licentiousness prevails. We are so besotted with the Love of Liberty, that running into Extreams, we even tolerate those Things which naturally tend to its Subversion. And what is still more surprizing, an Author justly chargeable with Principle destructive of our Constitution, with Doctrines the most abject and slavish, may proceed even with inveterate Malice, to vilify, burlesque and deny our greatest Immunities and Privileges, and shall yet be suffered to justify himself under the unrestrainable Rights of the Press. An Absurdity grossly stupid and mischievous.

Livingston further declared "that when the Press is prejudicial to the public Weal, it is abused." Any broader foundation for the press, he believed, would destroy public peace. The true liberty of the press promoted the good of society and published nothing against it.

Continuing in this vein, Livingston stated his credo on the freedom of the press, inspired by the refusal of a New York printer to publish an article of his composition:

A Printer ought not to publish every Thing that is offered to him; but what is conducive of general Utility, he should not refuse, be the Author a Christian, Jew, Turk or Infidel. Such refusal is an immediate abridgement of the Freedom of the Press. When on the other Hand, he prostitutes his Art by the Publication of any Thing injurious to his Country, it is criminal. . . . It is high Treason against the State. The usual Alarm rung in such Cases, the common Cry of an Attack upon the LIBERTY OF THE PRESS, is groundless and trifling. The Press neither has, nor can have such a Liberty, and whenever it is assumed, the Printer should be punished.[53]

The most willing tool of the Crown could have applauded this definition of a free press by the republican patriots from the colony identified with Zenger and Alexander. On the other hand there could be no greater danger to open political debate than the vague crime of constructive treason, particularly if it could be committed by mere words. Even a Crown lawyer knew that the law tended to rule out treason in any case where words against the government lacked a connection with some treasonous project for carrying them out; such words entailed criminal punishment as seditious libel, a distinction of

[53] *The Independent Reflector* (New York City), Aug. 30, 1753, reprinted in William Livingston and Others, *The Independent Reflector*, ed. by Milton M. Klein (Cambridge, Mass., 1963), 336-44, and in Levy, ed. *Freedom of the Press*, 74-82, quotations at 78 and 81. Klein's warped statement is in his edition at 343-44 note.

importance since the latter was a mere misdemeanor, while treason was a capital crime. That fact reveals the severity of the remarks by the New York lawyers.

A year later a writer in the *New-York Mercury* made a good point about the supposed licentiousness of the press, but he left it hanging. Noting that many people complained that "the press may be abused," he commented that anything might be abused, even the Bible, the laws, and the constitution, "yet we have a birthright in them all, and we should be miserable if they were taken from us." It was a flabby thought, providing no analysis whatever of licentiousness. If someone reviled the Bible, the laws, and the constitution, the article in the *Mercury* provided no guidance for the public or for prosecutors.[54]

In 1755 another article in the same newspaper cogently revived the Zengerian principle that truth should be a defense to a charge of criminal libel. "It is true," the author said, that

> by a variety of adjudged cases, in our law-books, the publication of any writing which charges a person in office, with the commission of a crime, or exposes him to popular odium and reflection, is not the less libellous for being true. Which piece of law is founded upon this reason, that tho a libel be true, yet it may tend to stir up sedition, or cause a breach of the peace; and therefore the law relating to libels, may sometimes be wholesome. But as every general rule admits of some exceptions, so in particular cases, a state may be ruined by the persons to whom the management is committed, for want of timely notice to those whose interest, were they apprized of the danger, would urge them to the utmost exertion of their abilities in its support. And if a people can be presumed to have a right in any instance to oppose the undue measures of an arbitrary ruler, when they strike at the very vitals of the constitution, they are certainly justifiable in opposing them not only with the pen, but even with the sword. And then, what becomes of the reason upon which the above law, relating to libels, is founded?[55]

The author contributed nothing new to libertarian thought, but he joined the few who perpetuated the general principle that truth can be no libel, a modification of the common law.

The *Connecticut Gazette* in 1756 published an article on freedom of the press in which the author in flowery language conceded that the press sometimes abused its freedom. He contended, however, in

[54] Dec. 9, 1754.
[55] *New York Mercury*, Jan. 27, 1755; copied in the *Virginia Gazette*, March 7, 1755.

the spirit of Cato, that "It has been tho't safer to suffer it to go beyond the bounds that might strictly be justified by reason," because to restrain it jeopardized its essential functions. "And this the rather because a stretch of liberty in the press, cannot be attended with any very consequences, as the restraint of it may." The best way to cope with extravagances of the press, the author believed, was to allow the same liberty impartially to everyone so that objections could be raised by those who disagreed.[56] Essentially, the author presented the Miltonic principle that truth will best error in a fair encounter. His discussion, however, like so many others, rose above the practical problems presented by the law's insistence on holding the press responsible for statements damaging to the government, religion, or public morality, as well as for statements that supposedly tended to a breach of the public peace. Even elevated discussions about freedom of the press were rare. This one had a clearly libertarian but excessively transcendental tone. The *Boston Gazette* in the same year also ran a piece urging leniency for alleged licentiousness, undefined, on ground that any liberty could be abused. The logic of imposing restraints on punishment for abuse, the author declared, led to the enslavement of the people to prevent their abuse of their freedom.[57] The author was more evasive than clever, because he ignored the problem of someone claiming that Christ was a fraud, or that the king was a pretender, or that the Assembly tyrannically exploited the people.

A few years after Livingston had published the *Independent Reflector*'s credo on liberty of the press, James Parker, who had been their printer and editor, wrote a broadside opposing a proposed stamp tax on newspapers being considered by the New York Assembly. Parker announced that in countries "where Liberty truly reigns, every one hath a Privilege of declaring his Sentiments upon all Topicks with the utmost Freedom, provided he does it with proper Decency and a just Regard to the Laws."[58] It was a neat but trite way to say that all sentiments short of seditious libel were free, an epitome of the American view of the matter.

By comparison, English libertarian thought showed progress. During the decade of the 1750s, only Thomas Hayter, the bishop of London, essayed an explanation of the meaning and compass of allowable

---

[56] Feb. 7, 1756.
[57] April 26, 1756.
[58] Nov. 1759, quoted in Beverly McAnear, ed., "James Parker *versus* New York Province," *New York History* 32 (July 1941):322.

discourse.⁵⁹ Although Hayter was most concerned with the sinfulness
of personal slander, as befitted a clergyman, he generalized on secular
principles in an original and startlingly libertarian manner. Freedom
of speech in his mind stood atop a hierarchy of nonreligious values, a
right belonging and essential to the liberty of the subject. Printing
being "only a more extensive and improved kind of speech," freedom
of the press deserved to be cherished because it "derived from the
Natural Right and Faculty of Speech."⁶⁰ Earlier writers had also
elevated free speech to the status of a right reserved to persons in the
formation of the social contract, but Hayter was the first to elaborate
this notion and give it the appearance of legitimacy by association
with the talismanic symbol of English freedom, Magna Carta. He
argued, at the same time, that "Liberty of Speech" was "antecedent
to that great Charter of British Liberties," and concluded with the
seminal proposition that speech and press were "constitutional" rights
because they were "natural" rights.⁶¹ No one, not even Cato, had
hallowed freedom of speech more than Hayter, and if his declaration
of faith was historically and legally groundless, it had the quality of
mythmaking which characteristically transcends the grubbiness of
fact.

Genuinely committed to natural and constitutional rights, Hayter
would have permitted them a generous scope of operation. Voltaire's
apocryphal aphorism, that he wholly disapproved of what Helvetius
said, but would defend to the death his right to say it, described
Hayter's views. He vehemently despised the opinions of Bolingbroke
and of an unnamed writer for the *London Evening Post*, denouncing
them uncharitably for their "pestilential" and "atrocious" abuses of
the press and specifically charging them with "Libel against the Public."⁶² Yet he would not punish such opinions, however noxious, for
fear of abridging "the Right of Communicating our Thoughts," unless the words expressed fell into one of three categories of licentious
offenses against the whole community: blasphemy, perjury, and treason. These, he thought, composed the only offenses of speech and
press over which the government had cognizance.⁶³ Since the first

⁵⁹ *An Essay on the Liberty of the Press, Chiefly as It Respects Personal
Slander* (London, n.d.), 47 pp. From internal evidence this tract seems to have
been published in the late 1750s. See, for example, at pp. 19-20, the reference
to the recent posthumous publication of Bolingbroke's *Works* which appeared
in 1754.
⁶⁰ *Ibid.*, 6, 8.
⁶¹ *Ibid.*, 8, 18.
⁶² *Ibid.*, 20, 22, 29.
⁶³ *Ibid.*, 9.

two were crimes against God, the good bishop's intolerance of them is understandable; his proscription of treasonable words, which he failed to define, did not, however, conform with his overall position. By treasonable words Hayter, who had no skill in the law, probably meant seditious libel, which no one in history had yet included within the range of legally permissible utterance. Yet Hayter must be ranked with Cato, not for the perspicacity of his analysis but as a rare representative of ultra libertarianism; for, despite the limitations he would have imposed upon speech, he genuinely cautioned against prosecution. He powerfully emphasized the conviction that the benefits of free expression outweighed its mischiefs and should not be sacrificed merely to ward off dangers to peace and security which were usually imaginary.[64] This view proved particularly telling in a decade that had witnessed the jailing of one man for criticizing a Revolutionary settlement of nearly seven decades earlier, and the imprisonment of another for his acid remarks about a dead monarch.[65]

[64] *Ibid.*, 1, 36.

[65] The reference here is to the trials of Richard Nutt in 1754 and of John Shebbeare in 1758, both unreported cases. See James Paterson, *The Liberty of the Press, Speech, and Public Worship* (London, 1880), 97. Chief Justice Mansfield cited Nutt's case in *Rex* v. *Dean* of St. Asaph, Howell, *State Trials*, 21: 1038 (1783).

CHAPTER VI

On the Eve of the American Revolution

Beginning in the 1760s a desultory public discussion of freedom of the press erupted into an intense debate that maintained a quick tempo throughout the remainder of the century. The celebrated Wilkes case triggered the change, but it probably would have occurred anyway because of the burgeoning of the English press and the growth of the party system. London alone, at the beginning of George III's reign, had almost ninety newspapers and innumerable presses churning out pamphlets. Every political faction had its literary hacks who practiced their invective and scorn on men in power and those aspiring to it. A faction esteemed a good writer as much or more than a placeman in the House of Commons, because the press had become a new force in English politics. Horace Walpole called the press "a third House of Parliament."[1] The press, once the object of censorship, placed the government under its censureship. Printers, booksellers, and publishers, all of whom sought profits, sold information peppered with prejudice, partisanship, and politics to serve the factions. The Ministry manipulated the press, subsidized it, and prosecuted it, but could not control it. Prosecutions for breach of parliamentary privilege or for seditious libels chastened some writers and publishers, but it did not stop them; there were simply too many and the incentives for scandal and scurrility too irresistible. One administration after another showed more fear of the press then it could instill in the press. Power and profits outweighed considerations of prudence. As Robert R. Rea has written, "The union of interest be-

[1] Helen W. Toynbee, ed., *The Letters of Horace Walpole, Fourth Earl of Oxford* (Oxford, 1903-05, 16 vols.), 4:446.

tween the publisher and head of faction was many-sided. Tracts and papers were the bread and butter of the publisher, the lifeblood of the politician. Without them both would fade into oblivion or suffer heavily in purse or popularity."[2]

Unpopular policies under George III, who meant to rule as well as reign, provoked a rash of press criticism that the king and his equally thin-skinned ministers fiercely resented. The studied insult of the king's speech of 1763 by John Wilkes in the forty-fifth issue of his journal, the *North Briton*, proved unendurable. Upon an information for libel filed by the attorney-general, one of the secretaries of state issued general search warrants leading to the arrest of no less than forty-nine persons, including Wilkes, his printer, and his publisher. Within a short time, about two hundred informations were filed, more than the number of prosecutions in the whole reign of George II, lasting thirty-three years.[3] The vast majority of cases never came to the trial stage, but the mass arrests, harassments, and imposition of costs upon the persons concerned stimulated a widespread and growing suspicion that the government's administration of the law in Crown-libel cases fell short of minimum standards of justice. By its tactics the government probably hoped to subdue the press at least by inspiring self-censorship.

In the treatment and prosecution of Wilkes himself, however, the government found that it had mounted a tiger. No one since the days of John Lilburne, more than a century earlier, proved to be such a resourceful and pugnacious antagonist against the combined forces of all branches of the government. Capitalizing on the stupid and relentless persecution against him, Wilkes made his cause the symbol of constitutional liberty. The government had ransacked his private study on a general warrant and seized all his papers in a search for incriminating evidence; the House of Commons voted his *North Briton* No. 45 to be a seditious libel, ordered it to be burned, and expelled Wilkes from its membership. He fled across the Channel to escape street gangs and certain conviction in the courts. Convicted in absentia of seditious libel and of obscene libel, as well, for an unpublished manuscript obtained by the government through bribery, Wilkes was outlawed when he failed to appear for sentencing. His letters and tracts from Paris won him so sympathetic a response at

---

[2] Rea, *The English Press in Politics, 1760-1774* (Lincoln, Neb., 1963), 91. See also A. Aspinwall, "Statistical Accounts of the London Newspapers in the Eighteenth Century," *English Historical Review* 63 (1948):208-28.
[3] Thomas Erskine May, *The Constitutional History of England* (New York, 1880), 1:112 n. 2, relying on the *Memoirs of Horace Walpole*.

home that he returned to clear his name. Lord Chief Justice Mansfield reversed the sentence of outlawry on a technicality, but the popular idol stayed jailed for twenty-two months to serve his conviction for criminal libels. His fine of one thousand pounds was raised twenty times over by public subscription under the auspices of the newly formed and well-organized "Society for Supporting the Bill of Rights," which was also instrumental in his being thrice elected to Commons while still in prison. He emerged as the most popular political figure in England and served constructively in Parliament where, it is not irrelevant to add, he ably defended the American cause, justifying his inflated reputation among the colonists, to whom the name Wilkes personified liberty.[4] They associated Wilkes with freedom of press with the same fervor as they did Zenger.[5]

Ironically, Wilkes himself held rather orthodox opinions on the subject of freedom of the press. He was, to be sure, one of its most staunch practitioners, but he gave little thought to the subject despite his grueling experiences with the law of criminal libel. The famous *North Briton* papers ignored all theory about freedom of the press, with the slight exception of No. 1, which fleetingly hailed a free press as an Englishman's birthright and "the firmest bulwark of the liberties of the country." A free press, said Wilkes, was the means of terrorizing evil ministers by exposing their designs and duplicity.[6] In the course of Wilkes's intensive defense of himself over a four-year period, nothing in his private correspondence, public letters, speeches, or pamphlets indicates disagreement with the substantive law of seditious libel.[7] At one point he asserted that truth could not constitute a libel, but his principal defense was a flat denial that his words were libelous, a defense that somehow implied a criticism of the existing law.[8] He admitted, however, that the expression of opinion should not give "any open public offense" to any establishment or individual. "The crime," declared Wilkes, "commences from thence, and the magistrate has a right to interpose and even to punish outrageous and indecent attacks on what any community has de-

[4] My summary of the Wilkes case is based chiefly on Raymond Postgate, *That Devil Wilkes* (New York, 1929); George Nobbe, *The North Briton* (New York, 1939), particularly chap. 16; Rea, *The English Press;* and George Rude, *Wilkes and Liberty* (Oxford, 1962).

[5] Clinton Rossiter, *Seedtime of the Republic* (New York, 1953) n. 158.

[6] *The North Briton* (Dublin, 1766), 1:1, June 5, 1762.

[7] See [John Wilkes], *English Liberty . . . containing the Private Correspondence, Public Letters, Speeches, and Addresses, of John Wilkes* (London, n.d. [1769]), 391 pp.

[8] *Ibid.*, 128.

creed to be sacred; not only the rules of good breeding, but the laws of society are then infringed."[9] This was a good formulation of the conservative position which no libertarian could possibly endorse. When Wilkes defined the "two important questions of public Liberty" that were involved in his case, he did not even mention freedom of the press; only the danger of general warrants and of the seizure of private papers interested him, and when he added a third question of public liberty it dealt with outlawry.[10]

In addition to Wilkes, the government also convicted one of his booksellers, John Williams, who distributed the *North Briton*. His lawyer, John Glynn, who had also defended Wilkes, tried to reenact the role of Andrew Hamilton in Zenger's case by appealing over the head of the court to the jury, but Chief Justice Mansfield (William Murray) shut Glynn up. The jury returned a guilty verdict, and Mansfield sentenced Williams to the pillory, heavily fined him, and imprisoned him for six months.[11]

Although Wilkes himself did nothing whatever to advance freedom of the press, his case stirred up an unflagging controversy about it. Outraged conservatives, who repeated their stale views in support of the government, united behind the conviction that the Wilkes case demonstrated that there were instances "in which the Hangman may be properly employed to correct the political Errata of the Press, without injuring its Liberty."[12] "Candor," who identified himself only as a Gray's Inn lawyer, wrote the ablest conservative tract; it went through three editions between 1764 and 1770.[13] Although he excoriated the government for its "inquisitorial" policies of search and seizure in the hope of ferreting out evidence of seditious libel,[14] Candor confessed his admiration of the law as laid down by Lord Mansfield in Wilkes's case. Liberty of the press meant simply freedom from prior restraint, subject to the penalties of the common law for abuse of that liberty. The truth, far from being a defense, aggravated a libel. The function of the jury was limited to deciding whether the defendant had in fact made the statement charged,

[9] *Ibid.*, 132.
[10] *Ibid.*, 156, 192.
[11] Rea, *The English Press*, 82-85, 244 n. 31.
[12] Anon., *The Liberty of the Press* (London, n.d., [*ca.* 1763]). See also John Brown [Vicar of Newcastle], *Thoughts on Civil Liberty, on Licentiousness, and Faction* (London, 1765), 153-55.
[13] *A Letter from Candor to the Public Advertiser* (London, 1764). I have used the third edition, of 1770, available in *A Collection of Interesting Political Tracts*, edited, probably, by J. Almon (London, 1773), 1:1-40.
[14] *Ibid.*, 22-23.

while the court reserved exclusively to itself as a matter of law the question whether the statement was criminally libelous. The law was clear and just to Candor, and he wrote in the hope that

> unlearned men will acquiesce in the respectable authorities which I have quoted, and cease to reflect upon government, or the ways of administration and public justice. In God's name, what business have private men to write or to speak about public matters? Such kind of liberty leads to all sorts of license and obloquy, the very reverse of politeness; and the greatest man, be he ever so cautious, if such things are endured, may be traduced. . . .
> The advantage of inoffensive speech or writing, and absolute submission to government is so great, that I am sure every man ought to rejoice in such wholesome regulations. . . . It seems to me to be really an excellent device for keeping the scribbling race from meddling with political questions, at least from ever drawing their pens a second time upon such subjects.[15]

The reply to Candor came in a small book which went through seven editions between 1764 and 1771.[16] The author, identifying himself only as "Father of Candor," was, from internal evidence, an eminent public figure with a legal background. Whatever his identity, he was the first in England since Cato, Craftsman, and *Common Sense*'s author in the 1730s and Hayter in the 1750s to assail, even indirectly, the common law of seditious libel. He did so in the same manner as had James Alexander and Andrew Hamilton in the Zenger case, twenty-nine years earlier, speaking thunderously, making crucial points, but sometimes thrashing about with a frail stick. "The whole doctrine of libels," he proclaimed, "and the criminal mode of prosecuting them by information, grew with that accursed court the star-chamber" which had relied upon "that slavish imperial law, usually

---

[15] *Ibid.*, 8, 9-10. Rea, *The English Press*, presented Candor as a libertarian ironist and, bizarrely, as the same person as Father of Candor, whom Rea identified as either John Dunning, the solicitor-general and future Lord Ashburton, or Lord Chief Justice Camden (Charles Pratt).

[16] The first edition bears the title *An Enquiry into the Doctrine, Lately Propagated, concerning Libels, Warrants, and the Seizure of Papers . . . in a Letter to Mr. Almon from the Father of Candor* (London, 1764), 135 pp. Although I used the then-rare first edition, my citations are to the more easily obtainable seventh edition, which was reprinted in volume I of the same *Collection of Interesting Political Tracts* in which Candor's essay appeared. The seventh edition of Father of Candor bears the title, *A Letter Concerning Libels, Warrants, the Seizure of Papers, and Sureties for the Peace of Behaviour . . . With the Postscript and Appendix* (London, 1771), 164 pp. In 1970 Da Capo Press of New York reprinted, under my general editorship, a facsimile copy of the first edition of 1764.

denominated the civil law. You will find nothing of it in our books higher than the time of Q. Elizabeth and Sir Edward Coke."[17] None could guess what might or might not be considered a seditious libel by some judge or attorney-general. The crime dangerously lacked definition, the name libel an "arbitrary brand."[18] The public had a vital stake in continuance of so-called "libels." Had it not been for such speeches and writings that had been prosecuted as libels, declared Father of Candor, there never would have been a Glorious Revolution nor would England be enjoying either a Protestant religion "or one jot of civil liberty."[19] The liberty of "exposing and opposing a bad Administration" he thought was a necessary right of a free people and the foremost benefit that could be derived from an unrestrained press. He did not discuss the liberty of opposing a good administration.

Should a critic be charged with crime, however, he had a right to be tried by a jury of his peers, not by a royally appointed judge. There was a "constitutional reason of infinite moment to a free people" why jurors should always decide whether an accused's words were libelous: ninety-nine times out of a hundred, prosecutions for public libels derived from a dispute between the ministers and the people. If the jury could not decide the question of libel, England, he warned, would lose not only the liberty of the press but every other liberty besides. No one who disapproved of the measures of a court would venture to discuss their propriety. No one would dare utter a syllable in print against any power of office, much less against any royal prerogative, however illegally usurped. He would be sure to be charged with a libel by the attorney-general and end in prison.[20] "I will venture to prophecy," wrote Father of Candor, "that if the reigning notions concerning libels be pushed a little farther, no man will dare to open his mouth, much less to use his pen, against the worst administration that can take place, however much it may behoove the people to be apprised of the condition they are likely to be in. In short, I do not see what can be the issue of such law, but a universal acquiescence to any man or measures, that is, a downright passive obedience."[21]

The saving way lay in an encouragement of animadversions upon the conduct of ministers to check their bad actions and give them in-

---

[17] *Ibid.*, 23.
[18] *Ibid.*, 40-41.
[19] *Ibid.*, 49.
[20] *Ibid.*, 17.
[21] *Ibid.*, 46.

centive for doing what is praiseworthy. But if criticism was deemed libelous whether true or false, if truth could be a libel, then England was a short step from "complete despotism" which would be reached when the same doctrine was applied to oral utterances. "And then what a blessed condition should we all be in! when neither the liberty of free writing or free speech, about every body's concern, about the management of public money, public law and public affairs was permitted; and every body was afraid to utter what every body however could not help thinking."[22] The only remedy that would avert the evil was to make truth, as judged by a jury, "an absolute defence" in the case of state libels.[23] Of course, granted Father of Candor, a "wilfully false" publication was certainly damnable and seditious, but the question of willfulness or malicious intent should also be left to the jury.[24]

The reforms suggested by Father of Candor, although considerably widening the threshold of permissible discussion, would have made jurors the virtual *ex post facto* censors of publications. But in theory at least, the threshold would have been widened even more than proposed by the Zenger defense, if, as a condition of being judged seditious, a falsehood had to be wilfully or maliciously made. Assuming that a jury could accurately judge an accused's state of mind at the time of his composition, his publication, however wrong or false, if not maliciously inspired, would not be criminal unless tending in the opinion of the jury to breach the peace or cause crime. On the other hand the notion that mere words deserved punishment because of their bad tendency held repressive implications; and malice or criminal intent, which had always been held an essential element of the crime of seditious libel,[25] was usually presumed from the publication's bad tendency, which was itself a presumption. Were truth an "absolute defence" as Father of Candor demanded, malice and bad tendency would be irrelevant considerations. They would be highly relevant, however, if the defendant could not prove

---

[22] *Ibid.,* 47.

[23] The same position was adopted by Joseph Towers in his tract, which also appeared in 1764, *An Enquiry into the Question, Whether Juries are, or are not, Judges of Law, as well as of Fact; With a particular Reference to the case of Libels* (London, 1764), 31 pp.

[24] Father of Candor, *An Enquiry,* 48 and 160.

[25] Sir James F. Stephen argued, however, that a criminal intention in the writer was either not part of the common-law definition or else mere surplusage which need not be proved, since the crime itself was simply the publication of censure, the intention therefore being only the intention to publish censure and not the intention to produce by the publication some evil effect. Stephen, *A History of the Criminal Law of England* (London, 1883), 2:344, 350-53.

the truth of his statements, which would be the case if they were in fact false, or if they were opinions neither true nor false, or if they were factually correct but unprovably so. In either of these three instances, none of which Father of Candor considered, truth as a defense, his main prop, was useless; it was also irrelevant because the defendant's fate would then depend on whether or not the jury found his intent to be malicious, a judgment which they would form from their subjective evaluation of the harmless or harmful tendency of his words, an evaluation which later practice showed to be dependent upon their approval of his character and opinions. The history of sedition trials in the United States, under the federal sedition acts of 1798, 1918, and 1940, demonstrates that a requirement that criminal intent be proved to a jury's satisfaction is a *pro forma* one, an empty protection of the accused.

Father of Candor intended, however, that jurors be guided by the general principle that the bad tendency of words should not warrant their punishment. This constituted his most significant contribution by far to libertarian theory, for with the exception of the idea that words per se should not be deemed criminal, Father of Candor's repudiation of the bad-tendency test promised the most far-reaching protection for freedom of discourse and criticism. At one point, it seemed as if he might go all the way by endorsing the principle that only overt acts should be subject to the criminal law, for he declared that "sedition cannot be committed by words, but by public and violent action."[26] The notion was an aberration, however, since he regarded willfully false publications against a just administration to be seditious. Although his repudiation of the bad-tendency test cannot be taken at face value, the principle that he laid down, being of far greater importance than his own exceptions to it, implied a tremendous expansion in the scope of allowable expression. He grounded his position on the premise that libel was not an "actual breach of the peace."[27] That crime, he declared, "seems to express, *ex vi termini*, some positive bodily injury, or some immediate dread thereof at least; and that, whatever a challenge, in writing, to any particular might be, a general libel upon public measures, could never be construed to be so."[28] This, he claimed, was a point of the utmost importance because libels were held to be criminal because of their tendency to breach of the peace. But, he argued, "what only tends to, cannot be itself, a breach of the peace, as the thing tending to can-

[26] Father of Candor, *An Enquiry*, 34.
[27] *Ibid.*, 71.
[28] *Ibid.*, 20.

not be one and the same with the thing tended to; and consequently such tendency cannot by any possibility be an *actual* breach of the peace."[29]

Only four theorists had ventured as far as Father of Candor in explicitly suggesting as much free play for the expression of opinion, and all, like Father of Candor, inconsistently qualified their presentations so as to acknowledge the criminality of utterances which they considered malicious, scandalous, seditious, or dangerous to the state. As early as 1644 Roger Williams had vaguely implied that opinions should be exempt from punishment unless directly causing the commission of some criminal deed,[30] but he referred only to the realm of religion. He not only supported punishment of scandal against the state; he believed that if anyone under color of conscience "should preach or write that there ought to be no commanders or officers, because all are equal in Christ, therefore no masters nor officers, no laws nor orders, nor corrections nor punishments;—I say, I never denied, but in such cases, whatever is pretended, the commander or commanders may judge, resist, compel and punish such transgressors."[31] William Walwyn, in 1645, more clearly proposed an overt-acts test. In the course of rebutting an antagonist's charge that "freedom of discourse" would "tend to the encreasing of erronious [sic] opinions, and disturbance to the State," he concluded: "And as for disturbance to the State; admit any mans judgment be so misinformed, as to beleeve there is no sinne; if this man now upon this government should take away another mans goods, or commit murder or adultery; the Law is open, and he is to be punished as a malefactor, and so for all crimes that any mans judgment may mislead him unto [sic]."[32] Spinoza was the next to advocate that "only the acts which alone are capable of offending" should be punished, but that every man should think what he likes and say what he thinks.[33]

[29] *Ibid.*, 161.

[30] "Secondly a false religion and worship will not hurt the civil state in case the worshipper breaks no civil law. . . . The civil laws not being broken, the civil peace is not broken: and this only is the point in question." *The Bloudy Tenent, of Persecution, for cause of Conscience*, in *The Writings of Roger Williams*, Publications of the Narragansett Club (Providence, 1866-74), 3:198. See also at 78-79, 96, 100, 147, 163, 171.

[31] "To the Town of Providence," January 1654/55, in *Letters of Roger Williams*, ed. John Russell Bartlett (vol. 6 of *Writings on Williams*), 279.

[32] "A Helpe to the Right Understanding of a Discourse Concerning Independency," 1645, in William Haller, ed., *Tracts on Liberty in the Puritan Revolution 1638-1647* (New York, 1933), 3:200. See the discussion of Walwyn, above, p. 92.

[33] *Theologico-Political Treatise*, 1670, in *The Chief Works of Benedict de Spinoza*, trans. R. H. M. Elwes (London, 1883), 1:265. See the discussion of Spinoza above, 89-91.

Yet Spinoza and Walwyn both accepted the validity of punishing seditious libel.

Baron Montesquieu in 1748, in his *Esprit des Lois*, had also broached the overt-acts test. At one point he told the story of the execution of Marsyas for having dreamed of murdering Dionysius. Dionysius's retaliation was tyrannical, declared Montesquieu, for though murder had been the subject of Marsyas's thought, "yet he had made no attempt towards it. The laws do not take upon them to punish any other than overt acts." In a footnote he added, "The Thought must be joined with some sort of action."[34] Discussing unlawful speech, Montesquieu observed that malicious words deserved punishment as did certain words whose specific nature had been defined and outlawed, but words generally "do not constitute an overt act; they remain only an idea." Carried into action, however, they assumed the nature of that action. He gave, as an example, the case of a man who went into the marketplace with the intention of inciting the subjects to revolt. His words became treasonous when "annexed to a criminal action."[35] But for Walwyn, Spinoza, Montesquieu, and possibly Williams, no one before Father of Candor had proposed, however inconsistently, a repudiation of the bad-tendency test or an acceptance of the test of overt acts.[36] Until someone worked out a formulation of this position, supported by a consistent body of thought analyzing the tough problems that it presented and suggesting workable guidelines of application, libertarian discussion on the meaning and scope

---

[34] Book XII, "Of Thoughts," sect. 11, var. eds.

[35] Book XII, "Of Indiscreet Speeches," sect. 12.

[36] In Theodore Schroeder's little-known, extremely useful, and often unreliable book, *Constitutional Free Speech Defined and Defended in an Unfinished Argument in a Case of Blasphemy* (New York, 1919), there is a long chapter, "Overt Act and Actual Injury *versus* Evil Psychological Tendency," pp. 391–427, that purports to be a history of the overt-acts test to 1800. Schroeder ignores Walwyn, Williams, and Spinoza, but does include Montesquieu in his discussion of the precedents prior to Father of Candor's book. In his eagerness to adduce precedents, Schroeder includes the writings of Martin Luther, John Milton, Jeremy Taylor, Edward Bagshaw, John Owen, John Locke, Thomas Delaune, Hubert Languet, [Edward?] Hitchin, Joshua Toulmin, John Hoadley, John Wickliffe, John Jones, and Anthony Ellys. I have examined their writings, which Schroeder cites to prove their endorsement of the overt-acts test, and can state that neither those writings nor the extracts from them reproduced by Schroeder warrant his inclusion of any of the named individuals as supporters of that test. In many cases Schroeder's own evidence disproves his point. His chapter is a combination of prodigious research and wishful thinking. Endowed with a vivid imagination, he read into most passages meanings which they simply do not have and often contradict. I am nevertheless indebted to Schroeder's book and in particular to his *A Free Speech Bibliography* (New York, 1922), an invaluable guide to the sources that historians of the First Amendment freedoms have grossly neglected.

of free speech would be surrounded by a haze of rhetoric that obscured inchoate, contradictory, and illusory principles.

In 1766 the *Pennsylvania Journal* published one of those short panegyrics on the liberty of the press that so commonly appeared in the colonial period, full of overarching rhetoric and not to be taken seriously, at least not literally. The author announced: "To the freedom of the press in America, we may in great measure attribute the continuance of those inherent and constitutional privileges, which we yet enjoy. . . . We cannot therefore doubt, but that the happiness which now reigns through all the British plantations, will inspire every friend of his country with an honest and generous indignation against the wretch that would attempt to enslave his countrymen by restraints on the press."[37] The passage would not be worth quoting but for the final clause. Because no one proposed to reimpose a system of censorship in advance of publication, the final clause had to refer to subsequent restraints. Taken literally it can be stretched into a repudiation of the entire law of criminal libels. What the author actually had in mind or expected his readers to understand is impossible to guess. In view of the fact that no one on either side of the Atlantic had advocated the abolition of laws against obscenity, blasphemy, or seditious libel, the likelihood is slight that the author of the passage implicitly intended a sudden and radical break with the past. The complacency of the passage accords, rather, with an acceptance of the status quo.

William Bollan, once the agent in England for the Massachusetts upper house, formerly advocate-general of the colony, published in 1766 the most learned work in English on the subject of free speech. *The Freedom of Speech and Writing upon Public Affairs, Considered, with an Historical View*,[38] while a first-rate, elaborately detailed legal history of the subject from the time of the ancients, essentially restated the ideas earlier presented by Cato and Alexander. Yet it is significant as being the only work by an American besides Alexander's until the very close of the century; indeed, it was the last restatement in English of the theory and function of free expression until 1793 when the Reverend Robert Hall of England published his address on the subject.[39] The many tracts that appeared in England between Bollan's work and Hall's passed lightly over or ig-

[37] Quoted in Clyde Augustus Duniway, *The Development of Freedom of the Press in Massachusetts* (New York, 1906), 128 n. 1.

[38] (London, 1766). The volume is 160 folio-sized pages of small print. Reprinted in 1970 by Da Capo Press of New York under the general editorship of Leonard W. Levy.

[39] See below, pp. 287-88, for a discussion of Hall.

nored the relation of free speech to responsible government, the preservation of personal liberty, the formation of enlightened public opinion, the discovery of new knowledge, and, generally, the advancement of the public welfare. Bollan embedded his explanation of the rationale for a policy of broad freedom in an interminable rehearsal of tyranny under the Stuarts, with the Court of Star Chamber cast as the villainous body responsible for having introduced unconstitutional doctrines of criminal libel. Although an Anglican himself, Bollan movingly related the stories of Prynn, Leighton, Lilburne, and other Puritans persecuted for their political and religious opinions; in the course of his narrative he sought to demonstrate how the repression of "free inquiry" led to arbitrary searches and seizures, cruel punishments, compulsory self-incrimination, and trial by judge instead of by jury.

But Bollan's recommendations lacked originality and breadth, for the theme of the book derived from Zenger's case: the accused in a criminal libel case should have the right to plead truth as a defense, and the jury should have the power of deciding questions of falsity and malice. But for these reforms, which were partly procedural in character, he left the substance of the law of seditious libel uncriticized, no doubt because he thought the power of the press so great that it might be used by the wrong people to "divide and destroy us." Lamenting abuses of freedom, he cautioned that railing was not reasoning; moreover, recriminations might injure and inflame but never inform or reform. There must be "just and proper bounds," he observed;[40] and Sir William Blackstone, in his fourth volume of *Commentaries on the Laws of England*, concurred.[41]

So did "Freeborn American," a contributor to the *Boston Gazette*, published by those "trumpeteers of sedition," Benjamin Edes and John Gill, whom Chief Justice Thomas Hutchinson vainly sought to indict for "threatening the Subversion of all Rule among us." As a fiercely polemical opponent of the British and the royal governor, the *Boston Gazette* might have been expected to develop a libertarian theory of political discourse. It did not, despite the fact that it frequently quoted *Cato's Letters* and no less than four times had reprinted the essay on "Freedom of Speech." The *Gazette* specialized, rather, in bombastic endorsements of freedom of speech and press, as if the terms defined themselves. That they did not is clear from the article by "Freeborn American." Without saying so, he meant that only those who supported the American cause against England had a

[40] Bollan, *Freedom of Speech and Writing*, 137.
[41] Vol. 4, chap. 11, sect. 12, pp. 150-53.

right to freedom of speech and press. He said, however, that a country whose laws "least restrain the words and actions of its members, is most free" and that in no country was free speech "more extensive" than among the English. Rulers should exercise power only for the good of the people, who had an obligation to oppose every encroachment on their rights. The press acted as a check on government. "Without this check, we should be liable to oppression, whenever a tyrant was in power." The tyrant would always stigmatize as licentious every opposition to his injurious schemes.

An extraordinary passage prefaced all this Whig rhetoric:

> Man, in a state of nature, has undoubtedly a right to speak and act without controul. In a state of civil society, that right is limited by law. Political liberty consists in freedom of speech and action, so far as the laws of a community will permit, and no further: all beyond is criminal, and tends to the destruction of Liberty itself.

Hawkins, Mansfield, and Hutchinson could not have disagreed, and Blackstone effectively codified the point two years later in 1769.[42]

In that year, when crowds still clustered about the gates of John Wilkes's London prison, shouting huzzas in his honor, the government had cause to prove that the "proper bounds" of a free press prevented criticism of the king. A letter under the pseudonym of "Junius," first appearing in the *London Evening Post* and republished in most of the city's newspapers, blamed George III for a series of stupid blunders, advised a change of policy, and demanded a new ministry. It was a daring performance, sarcastically castigating the government and cautioning the king to bear in mind the fate of the Stuart despots. Efforts to discover the identity of "Junius" failing, the government turned its wrath upon the many publishers of the notorious letter, which had become a best-seller when reprinted in *The London Museum*, a monthly journal published and distributed by John Almon. Almon already enjoyed a reputation among government officials as a sedition-monger; not the least of his infamy was his publication of Father of Candor in 1764, followed the next year by a new edition of the Zenger trial. The most logical scapegoat, Almon suffered prosecution and conviction for seditious libel, Lord Chief Justice Mansfield himself deciding that the accused's publication and sale of the "Junius" letter constituted the crime charged.[43]

[42] *Boston Gazette*, March 9, 1767, reprinted in Levy, ed., *Freedom of the Press*, 95-97.

[43] *Rex v. Almon*, Thomas Bayly Howell, comp., *A Complete Collection of State Trials to 1783*. Continued by T. J. Howell to 1820 (London, 1816-28), 20:803 (1770).

In the next trial, that of Henry Woodfall, in whose paper the "Junius" letter first appeared, the jury balked by returning a verdict of guilty of publishing "only," suggesting that they did not believe the accused to be a seditious libeler.[44] Mansfield took the uncertain verdict under advisement and finally ruled on the necessity of a new trial. The government grimly proceeded with the prosecutions of two more of Junius's publishers, despite the mounting criticism in the London press against Mansfield's exposition of trial procedure in state libels.

In two new trials, staged the same day, the juries stunningly returned general verdicts of not guilty, in spite of Mansfield's instructions that they possessed no power to do so unless convinced that the defendants had not in fact published the Junius letter, which they positively had.[45] Mansfield had done all that he could to avert another Woodfall verdict, yet ended by getting a Zenger verdict. In another Junius trial a member of the jury interrupted the judge's charge by shouting, "You need not say any more, for I am determined to acquit them." Confronted by popular acclamation of the acquittals, the government quietly dropped the prosecutions of the other publishers against whom informations had been filed. When Woodfall came to trial again, the attorney-general had "lost" the original newspaper which alone proved the fact of publication, and he dropped the case. Almon, the only one of six Junius publishers to be convicted, appeared for sentencing after the government had been defeated. The court merely assessed a moderate fine and made Almon put up a stiff surety for good behavior; that was a light punishment for one said to have earned 10,000 pounds for "selling libels."[46] Despite the government's losses, it could not quash the public alarm that Crown-libel doctrines menaced the Englishman's beloved institution, trial by one's peers. In effect public opinion expressed in the verdicts of jurors crippled the effectiveness of the doctrine of seditious libel and validated the argument of Almon's counsel who declared, "The freedom of political discussion is of the utmost consequence to all our liberty, and . . . the actions of this government may be canvassed freely."[47]

The public alarm, spreading to Parliament, provoked a debate on the legitimacy of Mansfield's rulings. Lords Camden and Chatham, the elder Pitt, led Mansfield's censurers, but in the end the House of

---

[44] *Rex* v. *Woodfall*, Howell, *State Trials*, 20:895 (1770).

[45] *Rex* v. *Miller*, Howell, *State Trials*, 20:870 (1770). See Rea, *The English Press*, chap. 10, for an excellent discussion of the Junius trials.

[46] Rea, *The English Press*, 181.

[47] *Ibid.*, 178.

158

Emergence of a Free Press

Lords inconclusively dropped the subject. In the Commons, Edmund Burke and John Glynn, the sergeant-at-law who had represented the Junius defendants, also assailed the doctrine that the criminality of an alleged libel did not fall within the cognizance of a jury; but the Commons failed to pass a bill supporting jury powers. Thus Parliament implicitly endorsed Mansfield's interpretation of the law of the land in cases of seditious libel.[48] Most significantly of all, not even his critics had questioned his narrow definition of a free press. In Woodfall's case, he had declared: "As for the freedom of the press, I will tell you what it is; the liberty of the press is, that a man may print what he pleases without license; as long as it remains so, the liberty of the press is not restrained."[49]

Their efforts unavailing in Parliament, the reformers appealed to the court of public opinion. A succession of letters, tracts, and books appeared in the next several years, purporting, in the words of one subtitle, to be *A Full Refutation of Lord Mansfield's lawless opinion in Crown Libels.*[50] What turned out to be "lawless," however, was Mansfield's supposed subversion of the rights of jurors and the related right of the accused to be tried by his peers when charged with a crime. Most of the writers expressed much more concern with criminal procedure in libel trials than with the substantive problem of libels or freedom of the press. Robert Morris, a barrister and secretary of the Society for Supporters of the Bill of Rights, might blast Mansfield's "Star-Chamber law" of libels as "the most pernicious and abominable doctrine," but he spoke about the denial of the jury's right to accept truth as a defense and judge for themselves whether the words charged were libelous. He did not reject the doctrine of seditious libel, although he did angrily deny that a publication praised by the nation could be libelous, and he questioned how printing and publishing, once useful trades, could "become of a sudden criminal."[51]

Henry Woodfall, himself a publisher and a defendant in the Junius trials, writing as "Phileleutherus Anglicanus," admitted that false or malicious vilification of the government was criminal. He simply wanted an accused's intent to be judged by a jury. That he cared about freedom of the press is unquestionable, but he did not direct his attack at Mansfield's definition of it. Although he ran on about the "gag" imposed by the "inquisition" of the judges, whom he com-

[48] May, *Constitutional History of England,* 2:116-18.
[49] Howell, *State Trials,* 20:903 (1770).
[50] *The Juryman's Touchstone; or, A Full Refutation. . . .* By The Censor General (London, 1771), 93 pp.
[51] *A Letter to Sir Richard Aston . . . Containing . . . some Thoughts on the Modern Doctrine of Libels* (London, 1770), 20, 38-39.

pared with Jeffreys and Scroggs, he confidently relied on juries to secure for the press its proper freedom.[52] Mansfield refused to prosecute. Woodfall went too far, however, when he published a letter signed "A South Briton." A jury convicted him of seditious libel, and the court sentenced him to imprisonment and a fine.[53] So, too, the anonymous author who viewed "with pleasure" the recent prosecutions of those who had circulated "such dangerous productions" as the Junius letter,[54] yet could characterize the law of Crown libels as "the great canker-worm of the state."[55] It was the minimizing of the jury's function that galled him. Although he thought an attack on the constitution or government to be criminal, he could tolerate public censure of ministers if a jury judged a writer's intent as not malicious. Junius himself roasted Mansfield in the press, declaring: "Your charge to the jury, in the prosecution against Almon and Woodfall, contradicts . . . the plainest dictates of reason. . . . When you invade the province of the jury in matter of libel, you . . . attack the liberty of the press, and, with a single stroke, wound two of your enemies."[56]

Another anonymous author believed England to be menaced by a "Rebellion of the Press . . . which has made the pen of prostituted scribblers more destructive than the sword." He asked Parliament to legislate additional restrictions on "intellectual licentiousness" by making truth and temperance of criticism an adequate defense against a charge of libel.[57] But that was the old view. "Censor General's" condemnation of the government's practice of prosecuting by information in cases of seditious libel and thereby evading the necessity of securing a grand jury's assent[58] represented a widespread sentiment composing part of the concentrated concern for securing accused libelers a trial by their peers similar in every respect to trials for other

[52] *A Summary of the Law of Libel. In Four Letters* (1770), reprinted in *A Collection of Scarce and Interesting Tracts* (London, 1788, editor unnamed), 4:197-221.
[53] Rea, *The English Press*, 220-21. For the history of seditious libel in England during this period, see Stephen, *History of the Criminal Law*, 2:317-66, and Sir William S. Holdsworth, *A History of English Law*, 6th ed. rev. (Boston, 1938-66), 10:672-96.
[54] *Another Letter to Mr. Almon, in Matter of Libel* (1770), reprinted in *A Collection of Scarce and Interesting Tracts*, 4:7. The *Letter* covers pp. 5-157.
[55] *A Second Postscript to a Late Pamphlet, Entitled, A Letter to Mr. Almon, in Matter of Libel*, in *A Collection of Scarce and Interesting Tracts*, 4:196. The *Second Postscript* is at pp. 158-196.
[56] Rea, *The English Press*, 190.
[57] *Literary Liberty Considered; in a Letter to Henry Sampson Woodfall* (London, 1774), 6-7, 12, 16, 22.
[58] *The Juryman's Touchstone*, 85-86.

crimes. Francis Maseres best summarized this newer view, as the American Revolution foreclosed the debate for a time. A leader of the Middle Temple, former attorney-general of Quebec, and a baron of the exchequer, Maseres was a legal luminary whose opinions merited respect. He noted that prosecutions for seditious libel were attended with so much danger to "the right of animadverting freely and publicly (but with a strict adherence to truth) on the pernicious tendency of public measures, that one would wish them entirely under the controul of the people themselves."[59] Maseres contended for Zengerian principles, not the scrapping of the legal concept of seditious libel.

Judge William Smith of New York also championed the principles of the Zenger case. His father of the same name had closely associated with James Alexander as co-counsel to Zenger. The son sat on the highest court of New York and in the governor's Council in 1770 when he published his essay in the *New-York Weekly Post-Boy*. The indictment of Alexander McDougall for seditious libel occasioned that essay, which Smith published anonymously. He addressed himself to "the Law concerning Libels." A true libertarian, Smith asserted, "The general Course of Proceedings in England, with respect to defamatory publications, is conducted according to Resolutions absurd in themselves and subversive of a free state." He did not mean that seditious libel should be exempt from prosecution and at one point acknowledged that McDougall belonged in jail if a jury found him guilty of writing a seditious manifesto. Smith professed astonishment, however, that England's legal luminaries had followed the "pernicious doctrines of despotic times."

> But the Malignancy of the Crown Law, in the Decisions relative to Libels, respect the Mode and Power of bringing a Man to Trial, for what he writes or prints or publishes, and at the arbitrary Pleasure of an Attorney General, a dependent Will and Pleasure Officer, and the Practice of the Courts, first in over-ruling all Proof of the Truth of the Publication, then labouring to get the Jury to confine themselves merely to declare the Point of Fact by special Verdict, that the Defendant wrote or published the Paper; and last

[59] *An Enquiry Into the Extent of the Power of Juries, on Trials of Indictments or Informations, for Publishing Seditious, or other Criminal Writings, or Libels. Extracted from a Miscellaneous Collection of Papers that were Published in 1776, Intitled, Additional Papers Concerning the Province of Quebec* (Dublin, 1792), 4. See also William Bollan, *Essay on the Right of Every Man in a free State to Speak and Write Freely* (London, 1772), an abridgment of Bollan's large book of 1766; and [James Burgh], *Political Disquisitions: Or, An Enquiry into Public Errors, Defects and Abuses* (London, 1775), 3:246-47.

of all in pronouncing the horrid Judgment that the Truth of the Facts rather aggravates than mitigates the Offence.

The abolition of the Court of Star Chamber in 1642, Smith noted, resulted in the common law courts having inherited its jurisdiction and its doctrines. Because the common-law courts could not convict without the verdict of a jury, judges attempted to persuade juries to reach verdicts that the judges wanted. They did this by refusing to let juries hear proof of the truth of the libel, "forseeing the extreme Difficulty of persuading Twelve honest Men of common sense, to bring in a Verdict against a defendant, for publishing what is proper for the Country to be informed of, and what he clearly made out in Proof." Every juror, Smith believed, should concern himself with the truth of the charge, and if he believed the alleged libel to be true, he should return a verdict of guilty, even with "a *Jeffries* on the Bench."

Smith's blunt, hard-hitting essay did not reject the concept of seditious libel, any more than had James Alexander and Andrew Hamilton. The libertarians wanted two modifications of the law: allowing truth as a defense and affirming the power of a jury to return a general verdict based on its understanding of the law as well as the facts. Judge Smith did not want judges to reserve to themselves as a matter of law the decision whether the publication was seditious.[60]

Within a month the same newspaper published another anonymous article in which the author examined the treatise of Sergeant Hawkins, "the greatest Authority among Crown Lawyers," and found his chapter on libels "utterly subversive of the Liberty of the Press." Following an objective summary of Hawkins, the essayist blasted "this Star Chamber Trumpery" with its "horrid" doctrines that could make any writer guilty, against all reason and common sense. He closed with that thought, not bothering to propose any specific changes in the common law and without even referring to seditious libel in particular.[61]

A far more libertarian position appeared in the pages of Isaiah Thomas's *Massachusetts Spy* in late 1771 during the controversy over the *Spy's* "Mucius Scaevola" article. That article, calling the royal governor of Massachusetts a "usurper" and his lieutenant governor "a perjured traitor," met any standard for measuring seditious libel, and "Centinel," writing a series for the *Spy*, supplied the tough-

[60] *New-York Weekly Post-Boy,* March 19, 1770, reprinted in Levy, ed., *Freedom of the Press,* 106-14.
[61] *New-York Weekly Post-Boy,* April 9, 1770, reprinted in Levy, ed., *Freedom of the Press,* 114-17.

est standard. Significantly he did not reject the concept of seditious libel, even though he construed it to be a crime that no patriot could commit. Centinel, believing that Scaevola had merely stated incontrovertable truths in "a *decent*, manly way," demanded evidence proving that the writer sought only to stir sedition and had falsely attacked the constitution, stated criminal notions of government, and wrote maliciously.[62] For all that Centinel assumed that the wrong words could libel the government. He opposed prosecution based on information rather than indictment by grand jury, asserting that no grand jury would "see government insulted and a worthy ruler infamously traduced." After slamming the Star Chamber doctrine that truth is a libel, he insisted that he favored the prosecution of anyone who "maliciously and seditiously" blackened a good administration. He accepted all Zengerian principles.[63]

One tantalizingly brief passage in Centinel seems stunningly precocious to the point of being a nearly impossible anachronism that suited 1800, not 1771. He did not even pass on his own opinion, because the words he attributed to an unnamed "celebrated" lawyer conflicted with his own acceptance of the concept of seditious libel. The lawyer seems to have believed that at some remote time in the past the law recognized only a civil remedy for libel and only a libel against a particular person. He blamed the Star Chamber for having invented the whole doctrine of criminal libels, especially libels against government. Thinking of the good old days when the law knew only the private suit for damages, the lawyer informed Centinel that "the method itself, of pursuing a libel *criminally*, is unknown to our law, and the reason seems to be founded on the maxims of free government. It supposes that the rulers are servants to the people, and that people for whom they were created, had a right to call them to account."[64] No one on either side of the Atlantic had said anything remotely as radical. The unnamed lawyer had grasped the crux of a libertarian theory whose expression belonged to the next generation. Centinel's generation, like Centinel himself, thought and behaved as if the lawyer never existed. He left not even a smidgen of influence, probably because his thought was so unorthodox. Americans should have loved and emulated him. They ignored him.

In England at about this time, when many people cared about preserving trial by jury as a means of securing the freedom of the press, a dissenting minister, preoccupied with the rights of conscience, car-

[62] *Massachusetts Spy*, Jan. 2, 1772.
[63] *Ibid.*, Dec. 5, 12, 19, and 26, 1771.
[64] *Ibid.*, Dec. 5, 1771.

ried libertarian theory almost as far as it could go. He was the Reverend Philip Furneaux, a nonconformist leader, who in 1770 published a volume criticizing Blackstone's exposition of the laws of toleration.[65] In the course of a masterful analysis, Furneaux challenged the common law's imposition of restraints on the expression of religious and irreligious opinions. He upheld as not criminally libelous the profession of atheistic beliefs, denial of God or the Trinity, railing against the ordinances of the established church, exposing the Scriptures to contempt, and in general any opinion allegedly tending to produce in the minds of the people a bad opinion of religion. Furneaux rejected the concept of blasphemous libel, which was analogous to that of seditious libel, the main difference being that the sanctions of the law presumably protected the good reputation of God or religion instead of the government. Although Furneaux never addressed himself to the problem of political speech, the principles that he supported logically applied to the law of seditious libel as to libels on religion. Furneaux, however, limited himself to the ultralibertarian thesis that the expression of opinions on religion should be entirely free. He flatly rejected the bad-tendency test of words, proposing in its place punishment of overt acts only.

Furneaux was not the first to advocate this view. His predecessors, as noted earlier, had been Walwyn, Spinoza, Montesquieu, and Father of Candor. In their cases, however, the principle of punishing deeds instead of words had been incidentally mentioned in the midst of a text to which it was foreign. They had acknowledged the principle, to their vast credit, but left it unused as if it were a round hole into which the square pegs of their thought would not fit. By contrast, Furneaux built his whole structure around that principle, thereby avoiding the inconsistencies and exceptions to it that his precursors had made foundational. Furneaux alone smashed through the heavy crust of conventional limitations on expression which other libertarians had accepted. Whether out of innocence or an imperious scorn for the unimportant, he ignored the controversial issues of trial procedure, jurors' rights, malice, and truth versus falsity which had so gripped their attention. Where they bowed before the concept of licentiousness as a bound, and with it, the rightfulness of punishing supposed abuses of the liberty of expression, he condemned that concept as worthless on the ground that licentiousness could have only a personal definition. Where they sanctioned the punishment of hate-

---

[65] *Letters to the Honourable Mr. Justice Blackstone, Concerning His Exposition of the Act of Toleration . . . in His Celebrated Commentaries on the Laws of England* (London, 1770; 2nd ed., 1771).

ful sentiment whose tendency they or a jury might admit to be dangerous or subversive, he utterly cast aside the bad-tendency test as a subjective rationale for repression. For these reasons and because his work was republished in at least two editions in America on the eve of the Revolution,[66] extracts from his elaborate formulation are warranted, even though he focused almost exclusively on freedom of religious speech.

"Are we," he asked, "to leave every man at liberty to propagate what sentiments he pleases?" His affirmative answer was categorical, based on the premise that the laws of society should have nothing to do with mere principles, opinions, or sentiments, "but only with those overt acts arising from them, which are contrary to the peace and good order of society."[67] Some might object that this policy would give free rein to even views "which have a *tendency* to introduce immorality and licentiousness," which the magistrates ought to check. But, Furneaux rejoined, the magistrate had no business checking any religious opinions:

> For if the magistrate be possessed of a power to restrain and punish any principles relating to religion because of their tendency, as he be the judge of that tendency; as he must be, if he be vested with authority to punish on that account; religious liberty is entirely at an end; or, which is the same thing, is under the controul, and at the mercy of the magistrate, according as he shall think the tenets in question affect the foundation of moral obligation, or are favourable to religion and morality. But, if the line be drawn between mere religious principle and the tendency of it, on the one hand; and those overt acts which affect the publick peace and order, on the other; and if the latter alone be assigned to the jurisdiction of the magistrate, as being guardian of the peace of society . . . the boundaries between civil power and liberty, in religious matters, are clearly marked and determined; and the latter will not be wider or narrower, or just nothing at all, according to the magistrate's opinion of the good or bad tendency of principles.
> If it be objected, that when the tendency of principles is unfavourable to the peace and good order of society, as it may be, it is the magistrate's duty then, and for that reason to restrain them

---

[66] *An interesting appendix to Sir William Blackstone's Commentaries on the laws of England* (Philadelphia, 1773); and *The Palladium of Conscience* (Philadelphia, 1773). Both American editions were reprintings of the second English edition of Furneaux, published in London, 1771. My citations are to the latter edition; see the preceding note. Da Capo Press of New York reprinted *The Palladium of Conscience* in 1970 under the general editorship of Leonard W. Levy.

[67] *Ibid.*, 59.

by penal laws: I reply, that the tendency of principles, tho' it be *unfavourable*, is not *prejudicial* to society, till it issues in some overt act against the public peace and order; and when it does, *then* the magistrate's authority to punish commences; that is, he may punish the *overt acts*, but not the *tendency*, which is not actually hurtful; and therefore his penal laws should be directed against *overt acts only*, which are detrimental to the peace and good order of society, let them spring from what principles they will; and not against *principles*, or the *tendency* of principles.

The distinction between the tendency of principles, and the overt acts arising from them is, and cannot but be, observed in many cases of a civil nature, in order to determine the bounds of the magistrate's power, or at least to limit the exercise of it, in such cases. It would not be difficult to mention customs and manners, as well as principles, which have a tendency unfavourable to society; and which, nevertheless, cannot be restrained by penal laws, except with the total destruction of civil liberty. And here the magistrate must be contented with pointing his penal laws against the overt acts resulting from them. In the same manner he should act in regard to mens professing, or rejecting, religious principles or systems. Punishing a man for the tendency of his principles is punishing him *before* he is guilty, for fear he *should* be guilty.[68]

Furneaux had proposed the ultimate freedom for words, at least for words about religion. His reference to civil as distinguished from religious cases, in the quotation above, and his thesis that "religious and *civil* liberty have a reciprocal influence in producing and supporting one another,"[69] indicate, although uncertainly, that his overt-acts test of criminality may have been intended to refer to words of any nature, political as well as religious. His test was as applicable to the one as to the other, with the common law basically the same for both. In either case, Furneaux may have gone too far, for he would have left society defenseless against verbal crimes of any nature, be they public obscenities, solicitations to crime, or direct incitements to crime. Punish "the overt acts," he wrote, "not the tendency . . . penal laws should be directed at *overt acts only*." Montesquieu's case of the man who goes into the marketplace with the intention of provoking the subjects to revolt cannot be ignored. If the speaker actually incited others to violence, he deserved punishment. Should he fail, there might still be a justification for locking him up if he had knowingly and expressly counseled the commission of some crime. The authorities might even be warranted in taking

[68] *Ibid.*, 61-63.
[69] *Ibid.*, 202.

steps to silence him in the midst of his speech, if, in the phrase of Father of Candor, they had "some immediate dread" of an actual breach of peace.[70] A test of criminality that weighs the danger of a criminal deed being immediately provoked is particularly relevant in the case of a publication, when the writer, unlike the speaker, cannot be interrupted.

To his credit, Furneaux erred on the side of freedom, but his margin of error was so great as to render his formulation intolerable even to a society that conscientiously strives to maintain the uttermost freedom of discussion consonant with its own safety. Repudiation of the bad-tendency test, on the ground that it condemns words that might theoretically at some future time cause some imaginary harm, does not require that the overt-acts test of criminality must be embraced as the only valid libertarian position. If political change of a radical character is possible by peaceable means through representative institutions that are responsive to public opinion, there is little reason to extend the protection of the laws to utterances that directly and intentionally incite to imminent overt acts that Furneaux himself would punish.

The idea that he had thrown into the debate on the scope of permissible expression took only shallow root. A century earlier, freedom of speech and press had been championed primarily by those who sought an open debate on religion; so, too, the new and ultralibertarian view seemed at first to appeal chiefly to the dissenters and others devoted to the cause of liberty of conscience. One of Furneaux's followers, the Reverend Ebenezer Ratcliffe, regarded the risk of danger from opinions as "no great price to pay for truth and the privilege of expressing our sentiments without controul."[71] Though Ratcliffe distinguished deeds, which were punishable, from words, which were not, he formulated the principle, perhaps innocently, in a way that properly acknowledged a power in the government to reach the utterance as well as the criminal conduct which it inspired; for he contended "that the magistracy has no right to take cognizance of sentiments and opinions, till they have produced criminal overt acts, evidently injurious to society."[72]

In the same year, 1773, the Reverend Andrew Kippis, another nonconformist minister, restated the Furneaux thesis in its pristine purity. Observing that penal statutes extended only to such offenses

---

[70] *A Letter Concerning Libels*, in *A Collection of Interesting Political Tracts*, 1:20.
[71] *Two Letters Addressed to the Right Rev. Prelates* (London, 1773), 50.
[72] *Ibid.*, 100.

as endangered the safety of the state or inflicted injury to persons and property, Kippis concluded that the law should punish only overt acts. "The true and proper notion of an overt act," he contended, "is an act done with malicious intention, an act criminally injurious to the public, and which can be proved to be such by just and legal evidence."[73] Neither preaching nor publication could constitute an overt act, according to Kippis, because he insisted that physical injury alone could override the claims of conscience. If the state interfered at any point before the actual injury occurred, under the pretext of the evil tendency of the words, "it will be impossible to know where to stop. Speculations and fancies about the tendencies of opinions may be carried on to the entire destruction of liberty."[74]

Among secular writers, Francis Maseres, in 1776, came close to the Furneaux-Kippis position, but he more realistically understood the potential criminality of some words. He insisted that the "dangerous tendency" must be proved "real and manifest" to the jury's satisfaction; at one point, Maseres seemed to adopt the view that unless witnesses testified that the supposedly seditious statement "actually occasioned that disturbance which it seemed to be intended to create," its tendency would not warrant a verdict of guilty. Like Father of Candor he worried about the immediate dread of a breach of the peace. Maseres really favored a direct incitement test of the criminality of verbal expressions. The overt-acts test, by exempting words and punishing only actual breaches or criminal deeds, went too far. Maseres's test provided the most practical and broad protection for speech and press, comparable to the clear and present danger test of our time. He also advocated truth as a defense.[75]

The only other secularist to adopt an ultralibertarian position before Jefferson did so was the great Jeremy Bentham, in 1776. In a critique of Blackstone's ideas on government, Bentham blithely declared without any explanation that the existence of a free government depended in part upon the freedom with which "malcontents may communicate their sentiments, concert their plans, and practice every mode of opposition short of actual revolt, before the executive power can be legally justified in disturbing them."[76] This was the broadest statement on the scope of *political* expression that anyone had ever or could ever make. Perhaps Bentham did not intend his

[73] *A Vindication of the Protestant Dissenting Ministers* (London, 1773), 98.
[74] *Ibid.*, 99.
[75] Maseres, *An Enquiry Into the Extent of the Power of Juries*, 6, 24; see also 13, 18, 22, 28.
[76] *A Fragment on Government* (London, 1776), chap. IV, sect. xxiv, at p. 154 of the 1st edition.

undeveloped thought to be taken literally or did not understand that it condoned seditious conspiracy and successful incitement to breach of the peace, riot, and other crimes short of actual revolt. Not even the Jeffersonians at the height of their libertarian theorizing, between 1798 and 1801, went that far.

The history of Anglo-American thought on freedom of speech and press from the early seventeenth century to the American Revolution had been remarkably uniform until the eve of the Revolution when a few aberrant writers broke away from a fixed pattern. No one had ever explicitly disavowed the concept of seditious libel even to the point of supporting a right to advocate the peaceable abolition of the monarchy, the House of Lords, or the constitution. Bentham to be sure clearly implied as much, but only in passing, and his fugitive thought had no support whatever from earlier writers, not even the most radical of them. Excepting the few who endorsed the overt acts test, all, expressly or by clear and necessary implication, had accepted in principle the notion that the state might be criminally assaulted merely by words, even by words which had no consequence other than producing contempt for the government in the minds of the people. Some of them insisted on a showing of good evidence that such was the effect of the words; many demanded that the speaker's words be maliciously intended to have that effect and/or be false. Others would invoke the sanctions of the law against mere words in extreme cases only, a formula usually covering liars in the opposing party rather than the purveyors of crafty innuendo or unvarnished truth on their own side. Thus their explicit criticism aimed at a promiscuous or wrong application of the law of seditious libel rather than at the substance of that law.

On the other hand, they raised libertarian standards by advocating freedom for utterances and publications deemed seditious by the government. They rejected the remote bad-tendency test and proposed in its place new tests that would have emancipated speech and press. The overt-acts test, exactly because it was extreme, could not be reconciled with the concept of seditious libel. Maseres proposed the test of direct and immediate incitement to crime as a yardstick to measure the criminality of words, allowing the greatest degree of latitude possible for verbal expression. His test, too, implicitly conflicted with the doctrine of seditious libel and other criminal libels that did not actually breach the peace. Regardless of the failure of the libertarians to effect a change in the law, the fact that the government's prosecutions faced increasing popular disapproval showed that libertarians exerted a real influence on public opinion, especially in the wake of the Wilkes and Junius affairs.

Libertarians also placed an extraordinary stress on the functions of juries in libel prosecutions. However, if a jury, having judged the whole of the law and fact, returned a verdict of guilty upon an indictment for utterances tending toward sedition, no secularist libertarian, again excepting Bentham, could or would protest. Perhaps the Reverend Messrs. Furneaux, Ratcliffe, and Kippis, advocates of the overt-acts test, could have joined Bentham's protest, but none of them had taken a stand on the problem of seditious libel. They had defended religious rather than political speech. Libertarian thought over the course of a century and a half conformed to the belief that seditious libel, as well as seditious acts, was a crime. It conformed also, and unquestioningly, to Parliament's power to punish criminal utterances as a breach of privilege. Not one of the libertarians, whether for want of courage or want of disagreement, even ventured to discuss the subject. Yet freedom of expression was every bit as severely restrained by Parliament as by the legal officers of the Crown in the cabinet and in the courts.

An elaborate rationale for a broad policy of free speech and press had been worked out, a significant achievement that also showed genuine progress. But from Milton to Maseres, libertarian theorists balked at applying the principle of their own arguments. They either retreated to vitiating exceptions or stopped short of following the principle to its logical conclusion. Despite all their grand reasoning that should have brought them to an outright rejection of the concept of seditious libel, they either failed to confront it or acquiesced in it, and acquiesced also in the law's definition of the scope of permissible political expression. Milton, Roger Williams, Locke, and the seventeenth-century writers could conceive of no freedom for political expression greater than that existing in the absence of prior restraints. The utmost of their demands was the end of the licensing system of previous censorship. By 1776 the libertarians had progressed considerably farther. They had named as a legitimate object of animadversion all public men, measures, and institutions, and they had enlarged on the benefits to be derived from the most critical and candid discussions. They supported truth as a defense, the power of a jury to return a general verdict in libel prosecutions, and even the need to prove rather than presume the writer's malicious intention. They also showed the relationship of freedom of political discourse to the electoral process and the maintenance of a free state. And the most advanced libertarians, a precious few that included Bentham, who did not render a reasoned or extended judgment, Maseres, and perhaps Furneaux and his followers, undermined the common law of criminal libels, at least by implication.

If, however, they confronted the law of criminal libels, directly, most libertarians tended to condition the exercise of free speech and press on subservience to the laws of the land, like Father of Candor. A patriot newspaper in Boston put the thought concisely in 1767 when declaring that "Man, in a state of nature, has undoubtedly the right to speak and act without controul. In a state of civil society, that right is limited by the law—Political liberty consists in a freedom of speech and action, so far as the laws of a community will permit, and no farther; all beyond is criminal, and tends to the destruction of Liberty itself."[77] The nearly universal acceptance of this theory resulted in an acceptance, too, of a definition of freedom of the press as a freedom from prior restraints, or, what amounts to the same thing, a freedom circumscribed by the penalties for criminal libel. On this definition the seventeenth-century libertarians from Busher to Blount had made their stand, and the eighteenth-century libertarians—Cato, Alexander, Bishop, Hayter, Father of Candor, Bollan, and Maseres—concurred, and by concurring they accepted in substance the Blackstone-Mansfield definition: freedom, under law, from prior restraint. But if they did not reject the principle of subsequent punishment, they vehemently disagreed with the prevailing application of the law.

Speech, of course, unlike publications, had never and could not have been subject to the licensing system, there having been no requirements for permits for speakers, excepting preachers. Therefore, the "no prior restraints" definition was, technically, not relevant to oral utterances. What is important, however, is that the barricade against criminal utterances always limited freedom of speech. When the press secured its freedom from prior restraints it simply became directly amenable to the law of criminal defamation as speech had always been. Thus, libertarians rarely distinguished freedom of speech and freedom of the press, because the law subjected both to the same restraints of subsequent punishment. Most writers, including Addison, Cato, and Alexander, who employed the term "freedom of speech" with great frequency, used it synonymously with freedom of the press. Even in the seventeenth century when the licensing system was still operative, Walwyn, Robinson, and Milton used

[77] *Boston Gazette*, March 9, 1767.

"freedome of speech," "liberty of speaking," or some such reference to oral statement when they were inveighing against prior restraints and therefore must have meant freedom of the press. Father of Candor and William Bollan were the only authors who did not refer to the two rights interchangeably, for both noted that speech was free so long as it was truthful, while truth was not a lawfully acceptable defense to a charge of libelous publication. In this respect, speech was freer than the press, but not by much, for truth, as has been pointed out, had its limitations as a defense, particularly when opinion was prosecuted. At best, most libertarians dissented from Blackstone and Mansfield when defining the outermost bounds of the press only by claiming that a true publication could not be libelous. But for this difference Father of Candor and Bollan were at one with Blackstone and Mansfield in agreeing on the criminality of utterances, spoken or printed, that defamed the government. They would not likely have agreed, though, on whether an utterance defamed the government.

Those who were dissatisfied with the common law aimed their strictures at prosecutions by information, at the doctrine that truth aggravated a libel, and at the limited function of juries. But most critics failed to suggest that the prosecutions against alleged seditious libelers should never have been instituted in the first place. They failed, that is, to repudiate the concept of seditious libel. Bentham, had he descended from Olympus and dealt with real problems, might have done so; Furneaux and his followers among the religious libertarians might have done so also, had they addressed themselves to secular problems like the Junius prosecutions. As for the civil libertarians, however, their flaming bolts of denunciation against the "Star Chamber law of libel" fizzled out when they could agree with their martyred leader, John Wilkes, that no one who publicly offended a community by outrageous attacks on whatever it had deemed "sacred" should be tolerated. Wilkes was pure of heart, as he was the first to affirm, but genuine malefactors would do well to beware the penalties awaiting them for verbal disobedience to a just government whose proscription against seditious discourse suffered only from certain remedial defects not affecting the fundamental soundness of the law.

Commitment to this view of the matter, side by side with a rhetorical tradition that should have implied the contrary but addressed itself only to transcendent propositions uncontaminated by reality, constituted the main American inheritance from libertarian thought. It was not, however, the only inheritance the colonists knew. The

English experience, like the experience of Massachusetts, proved that the law of Crown libels could become a prosecutor's necropolis when he confronted an obdurate grand jury or an independent trial jury. Americans learned that Zengerian principles could have the practical effect of subverting the law without attacking it directly. The Junius prosecutions taught a similar lesson in England. In 1771 Edmund Burke, no friend of the Junius prosecutions, thundered in Parliament, "Libels have conquered the law. The liberty of the press has run into licentiousness . . . too strong for the government. The law is beaten down, and tramped upon."[78] Chief Justice Hutchinson had already understood that, even though the law in the books remained intact and no American printer or theorist had bothered to repudiate it. If, with the exceptions of Alexander, Bollan, and William Smith, Americans inherited an English rather than American libertarian theory, though the two can scarcely be distinguished, that only revealed the comparatively impoverished condition of American thinking on the subject of the theory of the freedom of the press. The one word best summarizing that thinking was acquiescence, acquiescence in the concept that seditious libel criminally assaulted government. Americans believed, however, that experience counted more effectively as a teacher than theory. The government could have its law, and philosophers could have their theories, if printers could have truth on their side, the support of public opinion, a jury trial, and a good lawyer.

[78] Rea, *The English Press*, 192.

CHAPTER VII

From the Revolution to the First Amendment

The conduct of the American revolutionists usually conformed with the maxim *inter arma silent leges* (in time of war the laws are silent). The benefits of another maxim, more congenial to the spirit of liberty, *fiat justicia ruat coelum* (let justice be done though heaven fall), did not extend to citizens suspected of Tory thoughts and sympathies. Speech and press, therefore, were not free during the Revolution. A long war for independence hardly provides a propitious time for respecting, let alone nurturing, freedom of political expression or any civil liberties. The imperatives of political survival and victory superseded the moral values that normally claimed the devotion of humane libertarian leaders. They did not believe that they could risk tolerating profoundly serious differences of political opinion on the issue of independence; they accepted no alternative to complete submission to the patriot cause. Everywhere unlimited liberty existed to praise the American cause; criticism of it brought the zealots of patriotism with tar and feathers. Even on the rare occasion when some revolutionist might ritualistically reaffirm devotion to freedom of expression, he shared with others a tacit understanding that "liberty of speech," as Arthur M. Schlesinger so aptly said, "belonged solely to those who spoke the speech of liberty."[1]

The Continental Congress offered an illuminating example. In presenting its case before the inhabitants of Quebec, Congress on the eve of the Revolution had made a great statement on the functions of a free press:

[1] *Prelude to Independence* (New York, 1958), 189.

The last right we shall mention regards the freedom of the press. The importance of this consists, besides the advancement of truth, science, morality and arts in general, in its diffusion of liberal sentiments on the administration of government, its ready communication of thoughts between subjects, and its consequential promotion of union among them, whereby oppressive officials are shamed or intimidated into more honorable and just modes of conducting affairs.[2]

This was one of the rare American declarations that comprehended so broad a concept of the public affairs which might be openly discussed. Comparable statements usually referred only to matters of government and perhaps religion; Congress, by contrast, included "truth, science, morality and arts." But the noble libertarianism of the Quebec declaration of 1774 was not for home consumption, because its most significant phrase stressed the diffusion of "liberal sentiments." The American revolutionists simply suppressed illiberal, that is, Loyalist, sentiments.

The Committee of Inspection for Newport, Rhode Island, which included the censorship and intimidation of printers among its duties, showed the American understanding of Congress's Quebec declaration by invoking it as justification for boycotting a Tory publisher, James Rivington. Following the old common-law distinction between liberty and licentiousness, the Newport Committee argued that freedom of the press meant diffusion of "liberal sentiments" but not "wrong sentiments respecting the measures now carrying on for the recovery and establishment of our rights."[3] Late in 1775 a band of armed men led by America's Wilkes—Alexander McDougall—and Issac Sears, one of his most steadfast supporters back in those trying days of 1770 when McDougall had been martyred for the liberty of the press, smashed Rivington's press.[4]

Patriot committees closely supervised all printers, including Daniel Fowle, who had fled to New Hampshire after his imprisonment in Massachusetts back in 1754. When his *New Hampshire Gazette* pub-

[2] "To the Inhabitants of the Province of Quebec," Oct. 24, 1774, in Worthington Chauncey Ford, *et al.*, eds., *Journals of the Continental Congress, 1774-1789* (Washington, 1904-37), 1:108.

[3] Peter Force, ed., *American Archives: Consisting of a Collection of Authentic Records* (Washington, 1837 ff.), 4th ser., 2:12-13.

[4] The Rivington story is related in Thomas Jones, *History of New York During the Revolutionary War*, ed. E. F. deLancey (New York, 1879), 1:65-66 and 561-68, 2:341; Arthur M. Schlesinger, *Prelude to Independence: The Newspaper War on Britain, 1764-76* (New York, 1958), 240; and Sidney I. Pomerantz, "The Patriot Newspaper and the American Revolution," in Richard B. Morris, ed., *The Era of the American Revolution* (New York, 1939), 316-18.

lished a piece in January of 1776 against the trend toward independence, he was reported to the provincial Assembly, summoned before its bar, and censured for statements "Derogatory to the Honour of this Assembly, as well as of the Honble Continental Congress and Injurious to the cause of Liberty Now Contending for." Fowle took a sharp warning to heart and promptly suspended his paper.[5]

Four months before Congress declared independence, Samuel Loudon, patriot editor of the *New York Packet*, permitted remuneration rather than republicanism to influence his judgment when he accepted the job of printing a loyalist reply to Tom Paine's *Common Sense*. His dedication to the principle that both sides should have a hearing impelled him to advertise the forthcoming pamphlet. For Loudon's pains, McDougall, John Morin Scott, Sears, and Lamb, at the head of a gang of vigilantes, broke down the door of his house, hauled him from bed, and forced him to lead them to the plates of the loyalist tract. They destroyed the plates and burned 1,500 impressions along with the manuscript. The next day revolutionists boasted about the preceding night's events as acts of patriotism and liberty, and every printer in New York City read a copy of the following communique: "Sir, if you print, or suffer to be printed in your press anything against the rights and liberties of America, or in favor of our inveterate foes, the King, Ministry, and Parliament of Great Britain, death and destruction, ruin and perdition, shall be your portion. Signed, by order of the Committee of tarring and feathering. Legion." Thereafter no Loyalist publication was printed in New York while it remained in American control.[6]

John Adams's writings suggest the manner in which the patriots manipulated the common law of seditious libel. Back in 1765, when the British were in control, Adams had written an essay for the *Boston Gazette* in which he addressed his publishers, Edes and Gill, in the following brave words:

> The stale, impudent insinuations of slander and sedition, with which the gormandizers of power have endeavored to discredit your paper, are so much the more to your honor; for the jaws of power are always stretched out, if possible, to destroy the freedom of thinking, speaking, and writing. . . . Be not intimidated, there-

---

[5] Philip Davidson, *Propaganda and the American Revolution, 1763-1783* (Chapel Hill, N.C., 1941), 172.

[6] Thomas Jones, *History of New York During the Revolutionary War*, ed. E. F. deLancey (New York, 1879), 1:63-64, 566-67. See also *American Archives*, 4th ser., 5:439-440, 1389, 1441-1442, and the sketch of Loudon in the *Dictionary of American Biography*.

fore, by any terrors, from publishing with the utmost freedom *whatever* can be warranted by the laws of your country.[7]

By 1774, when the "jaws of power" were beginning to grow American incisors, Adams began to sound still more like Chief Justice Hutchinson, who agreed that the law limited the right to publish. In his most widely circulated contribution to the literature of the Revolution, the "Novanglus" letters, Adams censured "the scandalous license of the tory presses."[8] Hutchinson had naturally regarded defiance of Crown authority as scandalous license, but he and Adams were in agreement on the fundamental principle that abuse of the press, as each understood it, was a thing apart from the true liberty of the press. By early 1776 Adams evinced the spirit of the Newport Committee of Inspection when he proposed that making adherence to the independence movement the legal test of loyalty would have the beneficial result of stopping "unfriendly" papers. Then, "the presses will produce no more seditious or traitorous speculations. Slanders upon public men and measures will be lessened."[9]

Francis Hopkinson of the Continental Congress, a signer of the Declaration of Independence, expressed similar views that same year. The liberty of the press, he declared, ranked as one of the most important privileges in a free government. Indeed, no man held that privilege in more sacred esteem than he. The channels of information must be kept open and uncorrupted. "But when this privilege is manifestly abused, and the press becomes an engine for sowing the most dangerous dissensions, for spreading false alarms, and undermining the very foundations of government, ought not that government, upon the plain principles of self-preservation, to silence by its own authority, such a daring violator of its peace, and tear from its bosom the serpent that would sting it to death?" He concluded that the council of safety would be justified in "silencing a press, whose weekly productions insult the feelings of the people, and are so openly inimical to the American cause."[10] Clearly, when the passage of power to the Americans presented the opportunity of legal repres-

[7] "A Dissertation on the Canon and Feudal Law," in John Adams, *Works; with a Life of the Author*, ed. Charles Francis Adams (Boston, 1850-56), 3:457.
[8] *Works*, 4:32.
[9] Letter to John Winthrop, June 23, 1776, in *ibid.*, 9:409.
[10] The first lines quoted are from Schlesinger, *Prelude to Independence*, 298, citing Hopkinson's article in the *Pennsylvania Evening Post*, Nov. 16, 1776. The last line quoted is from the same article, slightly revised, in *The Miscellaneous Essays and Occasional Writings of Francis Hopkinson* (Philadelphia, 1792), 1:136.

sion by the newly constituted state governments, "the ghost of John Peter Zenger quietly sank back into its grave."[11] That was true, in one sense, only of people with Tory opinions. In another sense it was true of everyone, because no state, despite its new freedom, adopted Zengerian reforms during the era of the American Revolution.

In 1776 Congress urged the states to enact legislation to prevent people from being "deceived and drawn into erroneous opinion."[12] Connecticut anticipated this recommendation by its statute of 1775 providing for the prosecution of any person who wrote or spoke a libel against Congress or the acts of the state legislature.[13] By 1778 all the states had acted.[14] The mass of legislation, which included loyalty oaths for all male citizens, went far beyond the needs of military security. Punishment for revealing troop movements or discouraging enlistments was necessary; punishment for derogatory comments about the Continental curency or misconduct of the war effort passed the abyss between legitimate war measures and tyrannous repression. Open denunciation of the patriot cause was in several states a crime even worse than sedition. As Willard Hurst said in his study of "Treason in the United States," during the Revolution the concept of treasonable adherence to the enemy "was certainly given an extremely sweeping application in the legislation which imposed penalties ranging from heavy fines or jail sentences to the death sentence and complete forfeiture of property *for the mere utterance of opinions* denying the independent authority of the new states and asserting the continued sovereignty of the King."[15]

Virginia's history illuminates the point. In 1776 its legislature passed an act against "crimes injurious to the Independence of America, but less than treason." It was, in part, a loosely drawn interdict against freedom of political expression to punish seditious conduct, such as obstructing the execution of war measures, or even to proscribe direct and immediate incitements to seditious conduct. But the line between defensible war measures and deliberate repression of "erroneous" opinion has been passed when the crime is also defined as "any word," or attempt to "persuade," in behalf of the authority of the king or

[11] The phrase is Schlesinger's, *Prelude to Independence*, 189.
[12] *Journals of Continental Congress*, 4:18, Jan. 2, 1776.
[13] Claude H. Van Tyne, *The Loyalists in the American Revolution* (New York, 1902), 199.
[14] See Van Tyne, *Loyalists*, Appendix C, 327-329, for a state-by-state list of "Laws Against Freedom of Speech and Action."
[15] Willard Hurst, "Treason in the United States," *Harvard Law Review* 58 (1944):266. Italics added.

Parliament. For these traitorous but not treasonable words and activities, the statute fixed a maximum sentence of five years' imprisonment and a fine of 20,000 pounds.[16]

The legislature revised and expanded this statute in 1780 to include new verbal crimes "inferior in malignity to treason" but injurious to independence. A maximum fine of one hundred thousand pounds' weight of crop tobacco and five years' imprisonment was the punishment for any person who "by writing or by printing, or by open preaching, or by express words" should maintain that the United States or any part of it was dependent upon the British Crown or Parliament, or should acknowledge the king to be sovereign or himself a subject of the king, or should attribute to Great Britain any authority over the United States, or should wish health, prosperity, or success to the king, or should induce anyone to express any of the prohibited sentiments.[17] A spirit of forgiveness tempered the actual enforcement of the act, because persons imprisoned for their criminal opinions received pardons if they would take the oath of loyalty to the Commonwealth.[18] The statute served as a useful dragnet against persons who could not be convicted for the greater crime of treason. Governor Jefferson, for example, ordered the imprisonment of all persons in besieged Gloucester and York counties against whom "legal evidence cannot be obtained" despite "Suspicion that they have been guilty of the offences of treason or Misprison of Treason, or . . . are disaffected to the Independence of the United States, and will, when Occasion serves, aid or advise the Operations of the Enemy." Persons imprisoned on mere suspicion that they had or *might* aid the enemy during military emergency awaited the governor's pleasure on the disposition of their cases.[19]

The loyalty oath, passed at the May 1777 session of the Virginia legislature, constituted an unreasoned effort to enforce true patriotism despite the claims of conscience. The chief purposes of the oath were to coerce loyalty and to identify for purposes of punishment every person who, in Jefferson's ugly phrase, was "a traitor in thought, but not in deed."[20] The punishment was severe. Nonjurors lost their civil

---

[16] William Waller Hening, ed., *The Statutes at Large, Being a Collection of All the Laws of Virginia, 1619-1792* (Richmond, 1809-23, 13 vols.), 9:170-71 (Oct. 1776 sess., chap. V, "An Act for the Punishment of Certain Offenses").

[17] *Ibid.*, 10:268-70 (May 1780 sess., chap. XIX, "An Act affixing Penalties to Certain Crimes"); *The Papers of Thomas Jefferson*, ed. Julian P. Boyd (Princeton, 1950-   ), 3:493.

[18] H. J. Eckenrode, *The Revolution in Virginia* (Boston, 1916), 242.

[19] Jefferson to James Innes, May 2, 1781, *Papers of Jefferson*, 5:593.

[20] "A Tory has been properly defined to be a traitor in thought, but not in deed. The only description, by which the laws have endeavoured to come at

rights and had to pay additional taxes; they also faced public opprobrium and possible internment. Jefferson and Washington agreed that only those who swore loyalty to American Independence should enjoy the rights of citizenship and that all others were "secret enemies."[21] All states by 1778 had adopted loyalty or test oaths, "weapons of savage coercion" that failed to distinguish between loyalty itself and the ritual of swearing it.[22]

The Virginia statute required all free males above the age of sixteen to renounce the British Crown and swear allegiance to Virginia "as a free and independent state," and to inform on "all treasons or traitorous conspiracies which . . . now or hereafter shall . . . be formed against this or any of the United States of America." Nonjurors were disarmed and lost all rights to vote, hold public office, serve on juries, sue for debts, or buy property.[23] By a supplementary act of the next session, nonjurors were also subject to double taxation.[24] Jefferson had a hand in drafting a statute in 1778 which subjected all nonjurors or recusants to triple taxation.[25] He also drafted a revised form of the oath for "every person, by law required to give assurance of fidelity," but did not alter its substance.[26]

Jefferson also supported a statute that legalized the Age of Enlightenment's rudimentary precursor of modern internment camps for political suspects. The statute had its origin in a war measure of the state's Committee of Safety. On April 10, 1776, the Committee of Safety ordered all persons in Norfolk and Princess Anne counties who supported Lord Dunmore to move into the interior at least thirty miles from the enemy. This measure, however rulthless, was

---

them, was that of non-jurors, or persons refusing to take the oath of fidelity to the state." Thomas Jefferson, *Notes on the State of Virginia*, ed. William Peden (Chapel Hill, N.C., 1955), Query XVI, 155.

[21] Quoted in Harold M. Hyman, *To Try Men's Souls: Loyalty Tests in American History* (Berkeley, Cal., 1959), 85, citing an undated manuscript fragment from the Jefferson Papers, no. 1003, Library of Congress. Professor Hyman generously provided me with a true copy of the fragment, which does not appear in the Boyd collection. The fragment included the remark "General Washington's work against Tories best. Uses oaths well."

[22] Hyman, *To Try Men's Souls*, 71.

[23] Hening, ed., *Statutes of Virginia*, 9:281-82 (May 1777 sess., "An Act to Oblige the Free Male Inhabitants of this State . . . to Give Assurance of Allegiance").

[24] *Ibid.*, 9:351.

[25] *Ibid.*, 9:549; *Papers of Jefferson*, 2:219, 222.

[26] *Ibid.*, 10:22-23; *Papers of Jefferson*, 2:590. For an eloquent denunciation of such oaths, see *Historical Memoirs from 12 July 1776 to 25 July 1778 of William Smith*, ed. by William H. W. Sabine (New York, 1958), 22, 410-412, 415.

justified by the military necessity of cutting Dunmore off from provisions and intelligence supplied by local Tories; it applied to those who had taken Dunmore's oath of allegiance to the British Crown.[27]

Strong medicine became stronger still when the governor's Council in August 1777 ordered militia commanders to remove beyond military zones and to restrain all persons who refused to take the oath of loyalty to the American cause or who were merely suspected of disaffection. The order "affected a good many people, and the assembly, at its meeting in the fall, fearing that the executive had acted unconstitutionally, passed a special act of immunity."[28] The immunity statute, framed by a committee of which Jefferson was a member, "indemnified" and "exonerated" the governor and members of his council from any suits brought by or on behalf of any persons who had been evacuated and interned.[29] Virginia thus retroactively constitutionalized the executive act that ordered the internment of political suspects and nonjurors.

Three years later, when an invasion was anticipated, Governor Jefferson, known for his scrupulous constitutional conscience, received from the legislature "extraordinary powers." One provision of the statute declared:

> That the governor be authorized, with advice of council . . . to commit to close confinement, any person or persons whatsoever, whom there may be just cause to suspect of disaffection to the independence of the United States, and of attachment to their enemies; or to cause any such persons to be removed to such places of security as may best guard against the effects of their influence and arts to injure this community, and benefit the common enemy.[30]

Although Jefferson did not order the internment of any part of the population in "places of security," Jefferson did exercise his power to imprison the disaffected or politically suspect, and many languished in jail without a hearing or even a court-martial. In one case, twenty-five Tories in the Henrico jail complained to the governor that they had been confined for six months without trial or bail. In another

[27] Eckenrode, *Revolution in Virginia*, 140-42, 184.

[28] *Ibid.*, 185.

[29] Hening, ed., *Statutes of Virginia*, 9:373-74 (Oct. 1777 sess. chap. VI, "An Act of Indemnifying the Governour and Council . . . for Removing and Confining Suspected Persons during the Late Publick Danger"); *Papers of Jefferson*, 2:119.

[30] Hening, ed., *Statutes of Virginia*, 10:309-15 (May 1780 sess., chap. XXXV, "An Act for Giving Farther Powers to the Governor and Council").

case, a man protested that he had been under military arrest for six-teen days without being able to secure a copy of the charges against him.[31] Tories, whether in thought or in deed, had no civil liberties; they were not free to state their opinions, nor did they receive due process of law. The protections of Virginia's glorious Declaration of Rights did not apply to them, nor were they better off in other states. Claude Van Tyne summed up the matter when he declared, "The freedom of Speech was suppressed, the liberty of the press destroyed."[32]

Congress and especially the states dealt effectively with those who opposed the American Revolution, even if only by expressing their opinions. On the other hand, supporters of the Revolution could say or publish whatever they pleased; and they poured bile on public policies and politicians. In 1779 Congress discovered that, unlike a state legislature, it had no way of coping with the excesses of a free press. Every state legislature regarded itself as a successor to the House of Commons, nearly omnipotent, accountable only to its electorate, and jealous of its prerogatives, which it might protect by punishing breaches of parliamentary privilege. Although Congress served as the government of the United States, it had no formal constitution until the ratification of the Articles of Confederation in 1781, and even then it could not coerce anyone except members of the armed forces. Congress acted through its constituent members, the states; its delegates were accountable to the state legislatures that chose them. The state legislatures may have been miniature parliaments, but not Congress. It directed the war and conducted foreign policy yet could not control the press or influential publicists.

Thomas Paine, the pamphleteer of the American Revolution, served as secretary to Congress's Committee on Foreign Affairs. He knew many state secrets and revealed one in an article in the *Pennsylvania Packet* of Philadelphia. France, readers learned, had provided clandestine aid to the American cause long before its alliance with the United States. The revelation embarrassed and angered both France and the Congress. John Dunlap, the printer of the *Pennsylvania Packet*, also printed the *Journals* of Congress. But for that fact he was under no obligation to obey a Congressional summons. Stung by the protests of the French minister, Congress sought some sort of satisfaction by instructing Dunlap and Paine to "attend immediately at the bar of this house."[33] The two men appeared, despite the in-

---

[31] Eckenrode, *Revolution in Virginia*, 243-44.
[32] Van Tyne, *Loyalists*, 66.
[33] *Journals of the Continental Congress*, 13:30, Jan. 6, 1779.

capacity of Congress to compel them. Dunlap named Paine as the author and Paine confessed. Congress could do no more than remove Paine as secretary and find someone else to print its *Journals*. Dunlap continued to publish his newspaper as he pleased, and Paine moved across the street as secretary of the Pennsylvania Assembly.[34]

Six months later Dunlap's *Pennsylvania Packet* printed a slashing attack on Congress written by "Leonidas," a penname for Dr. Benjamin Rush, the famous physician who had been a signer of the Declaration of Independence. Leonidas tore into Congress for issuing continental money that depreciated in value and for covering up "the grossest frauds" in the management of public finances, even sharing in the "plunder" of the country. Elbridge Gerry of Massachusetts, a member of Congress, outraged by the "infamous" publication, moved that Congress summon Dunlap for interrogation. Gerry promptly confronted opposition from other members who, having their own fish to fry, opposed the motion by declaiming on the virtues of a free press.[35]

Merriwether Smith of Virginia read to Congress from the *Packet*, "thought it contained some good things," and closed by observing, "When the liberty of the press shall be restrained, take my word for it, the liberties of the people will be at an end." By restraint he meant subsequent punishment, not prior censorship, but his inconsistency was clear enough given Congressional measures against Tory presses. Thomas Burke of North Carolina also opposed Gerry's motion, on the ground that Congress should not dignify the newspaper or the author of the article by taking notice of either. John Penn of the same state claimed to believe that the author meant well. He too opposed restraining the press, but he added a practical consideration: "Gentlemen talk of imprisoning the Printer or the Author. I will undertake to say, if you have the power, which I doubt, and were to imprison them for six months, they would come out greater Men than they went in. What was it made Wilkes so great and popular a Man, but the imprisonment he suffered?" Henry Laurens of South Carolina, who had seconded Gerry's motion, angrily recorded that the same "three Worthies" on a previous occasion had vehemently objected to a publication but now opposed doing anything when "a

[34] I am indebted to Dwight L. Teeter's article, "Press Freedom and the Public Printing: Pennsylvania, 1775-1783," *Journalism Quarterly* 45 (1968):445-51, covering the Tom Paine affair, as well as the "Leonidas" affair mentioned immediately below.

[35] Henry Laurens, "Notes of Proceedings," July 3, 1779, in Edmund C. Burnett, ed., *Letters of the Members of the Continental Congress* (Washington, D.C., 1928), 4:295-96.

complaint was made of gross affronts to Congress by one of their own Printers."[36] In the final vote, however, everyone, Laurens included, excepting only Gerry, opposed the motion to summon Dunlap. Congress did not on that occasion vote by factions.[37]

In the period between the Declaration of Independence and the ratification of the First Amendment (1776-1791), America had its first opportunity to develop a legal system and a society in which all men were free to express their opinions, however unpopular, on any subject, short of direct and immediate incitement to crime. No doubt America during this period, as earlier, was as free as, and probably freer than, any other place in the world. Yet the American states did not take the opportunity of abandoning or seriously limiting the oppressive common law of seditious libel.

On the contrary, twelve of the thirteen original states, all but Connecticut, expressly adopted the common-law system after separating from England. Virginia did it by statute in 1776: "The common law of England shall be the rule of decision, and shall be considered in full force until the same shall be altered by the legislative power of the colony."[38] New Jersey did it by a provision in its Constitution of 1776: "The common law of England, as well as so much of the statute law, as have been heretofore practiced in this colony, shall remain in force, until they shall be altered by a future law."[39] The independent republic of Vermont at first adopted the common law as it was "understood in the New England states," but three years later, in 1782, followed the prevailing model of adopting "so much of the common law of England, as is not repugnant to the constitution, or to any act of the legislature of this State."[40] No state abolished or altered the common law of criminal defamation in general or seditious libel in particular, and no state court ruled that the free press clause of its state constitution rendered void the prosecution of a libel.

The Revolution generated the most creative constitutional achievements in history, including the world's first written constitutions and bills of rights that limited all branches of government. Virginia included in its Declaration of Rights, which preceded that of any other

---

[36] *Ibid.*, 296-97.

[37] *Journals of the Continental Congress*, 14:799-800, July 3, 1799.

[38] Hening, ed., *Statutes* 9:127.

[39] New Jersey Constitution, sect. 22, in Francis Newton Thorpe, ed., *The Federal and State Constitutions, Colonial Charters, and Other Organic Laws* (Washington, 1909, 7 vols.) 6:2598.

[40] For a survey of all the states, see Ford W. Hall, "The Common Law: An Account of Its Reception in the United States," *Vanderbilt Law Review* 4 (June 1951):497-800.

state, a provision "That the freedom of the Press is one of the greatest bulwarks of liberty, and can never be restrained but by despotic
Governments."[41] Presumably the second clause meant that a free state
should not restrain the freedom of the press. Virginia established a
pattern for all American free press clauses: it gave no hint of what it
meant by freedom of the press or by the word "restrained." Its free
press clause, as noted, did not apply to Tory opinions, nor did its
other constitutional protections, nor did those of other states. Virginia's free press clause served as a model for that of North Carolina,
although North Carolina substituted a namby-pamby "ought" for the
word "can."[42] "Ought," which was hardly enforceable, reflected an
ideal, not a prescription or a command. The word "ought" instead
of "shall" appeared in the revolutionary constitutions of seven of the
nine states that had a free press clause, including Vermont, thereby
expressing a hope rather than a constitutional injunction. None used
"shall."

Delaware, Maryland, Georgia, and South Carolina devised the
briefest free press clauses. The first two, in identical language, provided "That the liberty of the press ought to be inviolably preserved."[43] Georgia and South Carolina had incomplete clauses; the
first provided, "Freedom of the press and trial by jury remain inviolate forever," the second, "That the liberty of the press be inviolably preserved."[44]

The Massachusetts provision, which New Hampshire copied ver-
batim, constituted a third model. It had a rhetorical flourish that
preceded its flabby ending: "The liberty of the press is essential to
the freedom in a state; it ought not, therefore, to be restricted in this
commonwealth."[45] The flourish came from Blackstone's discourse.
"The liberty of the press," he declared, "is indeed essential to the nature of a free state." *Cato's Letters* contained a similar thought. It
was an eighteenth century cliché.[46]

[41] Section XII, Virginia Declaration of Rights of 1776, in Thorpe, ed., *Constitutions*, 7:3814.
[42] Section XV, North Carolina Declaration of Rights of 1776, in *ibid.*, 5:2788.
[43] Section XXIII, Delaware Declaration of Rights of 1776, in Bernard
Schwartz, ed., *The Bill of Rights: A Documentary History* (New York: Chelsea House, 1971, 2 vols.), 1:278; Section XXXVII, Maryland Declaration of
Rights of 1776, in Thorpe, ed., *Constitutions*, 3:1690.
[44] Section LXI, Georgia Constitution of 1777, in Thorpe, ed., *Constitutions*,
2:785; Section XLIII, South Carolina Constitution of 1778, in *ibid.*, 6:3257.
[45] Section XVI, Massachusetts Declaration of Rights of 1780, in *ibid.*, 3:1892;
Section XXII, New Hampshire Declaration of Rights of 1784, in *ibid.*, 4:2456.
[46] Sir William Blackstone, *Commentaries on the Laws of England* (London,
1769), book 4, chap. 11, 151; John Trenchard and Thomas Gordon, *Cato's
Letters* (London, 1755, 4 vols.), no. 15 (1720), 1:96.

The case of Pennsylvania was special, because its 1776 Declaration of Rights exhibited the world's first instance of freedom of speech elevated to a constitutional right: "That the people have a right to freedom of speech, and of writing, and publishing their sentiments; therefore, the freedom of the press ought not to be restrained."[47] "Ought not" seems hardly binding. Its use showed good intention, not the mandatory obligation of "shall not." Pennsylvania's case was also special because in the main body of the state's constitution, as distinguished from its prefatory Declaration of Rights, the state added a second and unique free press clause: "The printing presses shall be free to any person who undertakes to examine the proceedings of the legislature, or any part of the government."[48] That opened every branch of government to criticism and the doors of the Assembly to the public, allowing printers to publish debates without prior approval, which was necessary in the past, and without breaching parliamentary privilege. We do not otherwise know what Pennsylvania meant by "freedom of speech" or press. But the state's suppression of Loyalist speech during the Revolution suggests that speech was no freer there than in other states. Peaceable Quaker meetings were harassed and intimidated, homes were broken into, scores of people imprisoned and even exiled from the state. Those persecuted included not only individuals *suspected* of overt acts against the war effort, but also those "who talked too freely about the mistakes of Congress, or the virtues of the British government; in fact, often their only offense was a refusal of the [test] oath."[49] As will be seen, Pennsylvania's courts from 1782 to the end of the century accepted the doctrine of seditious libel.

Some of our best constitutional authorities have argued that one object of the Revolution was "to get rid of the English common law on liberty of speech and of the press."[50] In fact the Revolution almost got rid of freedom of speech and press for Loyalist opinions, rather than the common law. If the Revolution had gotten rid of the common law on speech and press, state prosecutions for criminal libel would not have occurred, and the Sedition Act of 1798 would not have bloodied the First Amendment. Yet the thesis that the Revolution had a libertarian objective as to speech and press is not without

---

[47] Section XII, Pennsylvania Declaration of Rights of 1776, in Thorpe, ed., *Constitutions*, 5:3083.

[48] Section XXV, Pennsylvania Constitution of 1776, in *ibid.*, 5:3090.

[49] Van Tyne, *Loyalists*, 232. See also 132, 210, 217, and 227.

[50] Henry Schofield, *Essays on Constitutional Law and Equity* (Boston, 1921), 2:251-522; Zechariah Chafee, Jr., *Free Speech in the United States* (Cambridge, Mass., 1948), 20.

supporting evidence. That evidence consists chiefly of, first, a declaration that the states constitutionally protected freedom of speech and press; second, an assumption that such protection superseded the common law; and, third, the hard fact that most states tolerated a press whose caustic conduct belied the existence of the common law. The explanation of the third point is that even in England, where the existence and repressiveness of the law of seditious libel were not in doubt, prosecutions were "occasional," as Madison later wrote, and "the freedom exercised by the press, and protected by public opinion, far exceeds the limits prescribed by the ordinary rules of law."[51] One might reasonably assume that any state that constitutionally guaranteed freedom of the press meant to secure for the press the freedom it actually enjoyed and, moreover, that those constitutional guarantees sanctioned existing press practices. An extraordinary partisanship, vitality, and invective had become ordinary press fare since the mid-1760s. Any state that constitutionally guaranteed the freedom of the press with merely a Blackstonian understanding failed to confront the real world of journalism. No state explicitly adopted the common law on the press or the doctrine of criminal libels, although no state explicitly rejected either. Only two states prosecuted seditious libel after adopting a constitution with a free press clause, but prosecutions for criminal libel fit the law of every state. Drawing a conclusion from the mere fact that a state's constitution had a free press clause is difficult. In major states—Virginia, Pennsylvania, Massachusetts, and New York—prosecutions suggested a compatibility between free government and punishing libel as a crime.

The 1777 constitution of Vermont,[52] admitted to the Union in 1791, copied Pennsylvania's free-speech provision, but the Massachusetts legislature in 1778 rejected the same provision, in a draft of a constitution drawn by John Adams.[53] When Massachusetts finally adopted its constitution, in 1780, it protected only the press in the wishy-washy provision quoted above, despite formal statements from several towns demanding protection for speech, too. Massachusetts had about three hundred towns, each of which voted on every provision of its proposed constitution. The overwhelming majority of the towns approved the free press clause without comment. Lexington, however, was one of the five towns that recommended the substitution of

[51] *The Virginia Report of 1799-1800* (Richmond, Va., 1850), 221.

[52] Article XIV, Declaration of Rights, Vermont Constitution of 1777, in Thorpe ed., *Constitutions*, 7:3741.

[53] Clyde A. Duniway, *The Development of Freedom of the Press in Massachusetts* (New York, 1906), 133-134; Adams, *Works*, 4:227.

"shall not" for "ought not," because "we cannot but think that the words 'it shall not' are more full, expressive, and definite."[54] The Boston town meeting demanded a guarantee of freedom of speech as well as of press in order to protect open political discussion: "The Liberty of Speech and of the press with respect to publick Men and their Conduct and publick measures, is essential to the security of freedom in the States, and shall not therefore be restrained in this Commonwealth."[55] Boston explained that the preservation of all rights depended on freedom of speech, which was even more important than freedom of the press, so that "nothing spoken with design to give information of the State of the Publick should ever be subject to the smalest [sic] restraint."[56] The only other town that also urged both a free speech clause and the use of "shall" for "ought" was Petersham.[57]

Only the town of Milton spoke even indirectly of truth as a defense against a charge of seditious libel. In support of a free speech clause, Milton declared: "For unless this Liberty of Speech is granted, we are apprehensive it may be dangerous in some future time, even in Publick Town meetings, to speak the truth of weak, or wicked Rulers.—and thus the most regular, peaceable and effectual method of calling the servants of the People to account; and of reducing them to private life, may in a great measure be prevented." Milton's stress on truth implicitly suggests that it would have supported reliance on truth as a defense. That no other town endorsed truth as a defense suggests that one basic principle of the Zenger case still hovered on the remote frontiers of American thought. No town proposed the other Zengerian principle, that a jury should be empowered to render a general rather than a special verdict in a prosecution for libel.

Other towns made eccentric recommendations of a wholly different sort. Dunstable, for example, voted unanimously against the free press clause "as there being no restraint thereon it may be made use of to the Dishonor of god by printing herasy [sic] and so forth," as well as injure private reputations.[58] Yarmouth and Boston also thought the free press clause went too far because it appeared "unlimited"

[54] Oscar and Mary Handlin, eds., *The Popular Sources of Political Authority. Documents on the Massachusetts Constitution of 1780.* (Cambridge, Mass., 1966), 660. The other towns recommending "shall" instead of "ought" were Berwick, 728, Boston, 750, Milton, 789, and Petersham, 856.

[55] *Ibid.,* 749-50.

[56] *Ibid.,* 762.

[57] *Ibid.,* 856.

[58] *Ibid.,* 641.

even by liability for private defamation.[59] Not one town objected that the press should also be criminally liable for seditious statements, nor, for that matter, did any town in Massachusetts object to the apparent freedom given to other classes of criminal libel, such as blasphemy and obscenity. On the other hand, not one town criticized the common law or opposed the doctrine of criminal libels. No town really gave extended or serious consideration to the guarantee that the press ought not be "restricted." Whether the people took that literally, or understood it to mean merely no prior restraints, or assumed that the press was responsible in a Blackstonian sense cannot be confidently maintained. On the whole the Massachusetts free press clause showed only the endorsement of a vague principle. And, Massachusetts refused to extend constitutional protection to free speech. Only Pennsylvania and Vermont included free speech clauses in their state constitutions. Thus, twelve out of fourteen states left speech without a constitutional guarantee. Also, four states did not constitutionally protect freedom of the press.

If, as distinguished legal scholars and judges assumed, a general and undefined constitutional declaration in favor of freedom of speech or freedom of the press superseded the common law of seditious libel,[60] then one may with equal validity assume from the silence of twelve states that they intended to preserve intact the common law as to speech and that in four states they intended to preserve it as to the press. The point is not that the second assumption is correct. The point rather is that the first assumption rests on mere logical deduction rather than reliable evidence, and it is not more correct than the second.

That twelve states failed to guarantee speech in their constitutions scarcely meant that people adhering to the American cause during the war felt afraid to speak their minds. On the contrary, they were as outspoken in their criticisms of public measures and public officials as if they had had an iron-clad guarantee of the freedom to speak. Any supporter of the Revolution could express himself orally as uninhibitedly as those who wrote for or printed newspapers in states that enjoyed a free-press guarantee. Constitutional guarantees did not set people free; they were already free and behaved and spoke accordingly. They habitually lambasted their leaders, excoriated public policies, and acted as if their governments were their servants. Americans who believed in the patriotic cause knew that they were the sovereigns. The presence or absence of constitutional guarantees did not alter a citizen's propensity to say what he thought.

[59] *Ibid.,* 724, 762.
[60] See above, Preface, for citations.

Of the four states that did not constitutionally protect freedom of the press, two, Rhode Island and Connecticut,[61] had been corporate colonies that had enjoyed the greatest degree of self-government without royal supervision. They did not frame state constitutions; they merely deleted references to Britain from their colonial charters, which served as their constitutions until well into the nineteenth century. Of the eleven original states that framed new state constitutions, only two omitted a free-press clause, New York and New Jersey. Even a casual reading of the newspapers of those states showed that they were as free and animadvertive as the newspapers in the states with free press clauses in their state constitutions. Indeed, the *New-Jersey Gazette*, edited by Isaac Collins, stood in the vanguard of American libertarian thought during the Revolution.

Collins was honest and fearless; moreover, the government of New Jersey needed his services as a printer, enabling him to take journalistic risks. In 1779 he published an anonymous article that satirized the governor of the state, William Livingston, who was a frequent contributor to the *Gazette*. The governor's Council resented the affront; the Council warned that "the Freedom of the Press ought to be tolerated as far as it is consistent with the Good of the People, and the Security of the Government established under their authority." As Collins's biographer said, "Ironically the Americans interpreted the common law of seditious libel much as the British had." The Council then demanded that Collins reveal the name of the author of the offensive article; he refused. In a letter to the Council he replied that if he gave up the name of the author without his permission, he would not only be betraying a trust; he would "be far from acting as a faithful guardian of the press." Fortunately for Collins, the Assembly, which had its own rivalries with the governor and Council, voted seventeen to eleven to support his refusal to comply, thereby setting "an early precedent for freedom of the press in New Jersey."[62]

In 1784 Governor Livingston, writing as "Scipio," attacked Samuel

[61] For a good article on freedom of the press in Connecticut, emphasizing the 1780s, see Bill F. Chamberlin, "Freedom of Expression in Eighteenth-Century Connecticut: Unanswered Questions," in Donovan H. Bond and W. Reynolds McLeod, eds., *Newsletters to Newspapers: Eighteenth Century Journalism* (Morgantown, W. Va., 1977), 247-61. The case of Thomas Seymour involving breach of parliamentary privilege, occurred in 1783, not 1784 as Chamberlin said. Given the fact that the Connecticut press was Federalist or nationalist and that the faction controlled the courts, the fact that no prosecutions for seditious libel can be found should not be surprising; the victims of the press were members of the opposing faction. Printers did not risk punishment when attacking a helpless opposition.

[62] Richard F. Hixson, *Isaac Collins: A Quaker Printer in 18th Century America* (New Brunswick, N.J., 1968), 95-6.

Tucker in Collins's newspaper. Tucker, a Trenton merchant who had been president of the state's provincial congress, bridled at the accusation that he had misused public funds when he held public office, and the Council resented the accusation that it had failed to support an investigation into Tucker's public conduct. Again pressure bore down on Collins to reveal the name of the author. "Scipio" then wrote a five-part series for the *Gazette* in which he defended anonymous articles as essential to the freedom of the press. But the passages of enduring significance focused on the right of the printer to publish the truth in any matter of public concern. Both Collins and Livingston "advocated freedom of expression short of seditious libel," believing that one might publish anything "with a regard for the laws." But neither believed that truth could be criminal, the view championed by James Alexander and Andrew Hamilton in Zenger's case a half century earlier. Livingston, incidentally, had stretched his understanding of freedom of the press in the three decades since he had edited New York's *Independent Reflector*, when he had condemned "treasonable speech." As Scipio he wrote:

> Printers often innocently publish what is false, believing it to be true.—Were they to be liable for such error, I know not what news they could give us, without first applying to the court of chancery for a commission to examine witnesses in foreign parts, to ascertain the facts they find already published in the gazettes from which they select their intelligence.
>
> Suppose, for instance, that a Printer in New-Jersey, meeting with the following article in a Maryland Gazette, "That Patrick M'Murrough had been there executed for a burglary," should re-print it in his newspaper, believing it to be true; Mr. M'Murrough being all the while in full life, and never having committed any burglary— would an action of slander lie for this against the Jersey Printer? I think not. And hence it is that in the English law, notwithstanding its ineffable nonsense of making the printing of truth more atrocious than the printing of lies, still charges every libel in the process against the author of it to be not only *false*, but *malicious*, clearly affording the most violent implication that even a falsity unattended with *malice* (and such ought to be presumed every falsity which the publisher believed to be true) is not culpable. By this it also appears how flatly they contradict their own doctrine, that falsehood is more innocent than truth.[63]

The protection of political expression by a constitutional guarantee did not necessarily augment freedom. The history of Pennsylvania

[63] *Ibid.*, 107-09, citing *New-Jersey Gazette*, March 30, 1784.

shows that the only one of the original states to protect constitutionally both speech and press did not intend to abandon the common law of seditious libel. Nor did Massachusetts. Both states prosecuted criminal publications. We therefore cannot infer that the other seven states that constitutionally protected freedom of the press intended a departure from the common law. The phrase "freedom of the press" as used in their state constitutions possessed no magical supersessionary powers, nor was it self-defining. Evidence does not exist to contradict the assertion that it was used in its prevailing common law or Blackstonian sense to mean a guarantee against previous restraints and a subjection to subsequent restraints for licentious or seditious abuse. The evidence, in fact, shows that the Blackstonian definition, the traditional and the taught one, was the intended one, at least as respects the law and libertarian theory; press practice, however, showed a different story.

But if we assume that in the nine original states, plus Vermont, which constitutionally provided for freedom of the press, there was a broader concept of that freedom than merely the Blackstonian one, the question is, how much broader? Zechariah Chafee declared that freedom of the press "in a general way" was understood to mean "the right of unrestricted discussion of public affairs."[64] Blackstone himself as well as any eighteenth-century constitution-maker would have agreed, but only because all accepted the common-law notion that discussion was "unrestricted" if there was a guarantee against previous restraints. No one regarded the imposition of subsequent punishment for scandalizing the government as a restraint upon the true or proper liberty of the press, if the utterance was "false" and "malicious." The word "unrestricted" did not mean, to the eighteenth-century libertarian, the absence of subsequent punishment for the expression of any opinions that criminally incited. The eighteenth century's general understanding of the law of freedom of the press, or of speech, would have groped with terms that convey the idea of a freedom to write, print, or utter anything that was critical but accurate and well-intentioned, and that fell short of what a court or the community might deem seditious or maliciously libelous, or unpeaceable. Even "Centinel," when defending the vicious attacks of Mucius Scaevola in the *Massachusetts Spy* in 1772, had accepted the concept of criminal publication even as he alleged that the "Roman" essayist had written nothing but the truth with the best of intentions.[65]

[64] Chafee, *Free Speech*, 19.
[65] See above, pp. 161-62.

Beyond the assumption that a simple constitutional affirmation, "the freedom of the press ought not to be restrained," *ex vi termini* superseded the common law, what evidence can be adduced on behalf of the thesis that the Revolution repudiated Blackstone on seditious libel? The resolutions of the Massachusetts towns, quoted earlier, indicated no abandonment of the common law, not even to the extent of making truth a defense to the charge of criminal libel. To the same effect was the essay by Benjamin Franklin in 1789 on the licentiousness of the press, which for practical purposes escaped restraints. If freedom of the press, he declared, meant the liberty to calumniate one another, the legislature should limit it by statute, but if it meant "the Liberty of discussing the Propriety of Public Measures and Political opinions, let us have as much of it as you please." He recommended the cudgel, a good drubbing, and breaking heads as the best remedies for the press's libels on people. He did not express himself, however, on the legal remedy for calumny against the government except to remark, in the same article, that as to writers who affront the government's reputation, "we should, in moderation, content ourselves with tarring and feathering and tossing them in a blanket."[66] Whatever Franklin intended by the remark, it had ugly overtones. More than likely he meant his endorsement of unlimited discussion to be hedged by the qualification that verbal criticisms of the government must be guided by moderation, truth, and good motives. During a long lifetime in politics and publishing, Franklin never went on record as criticizing the concept of seditious libel. On the contrary, he actively supported the prosecution in the Smith-Moore case of 1758 by championing the legislature's kangaroo trial of its victims for breach of parliamentary privilege in the form of seditious libel. In 1782 he wrote that a publisher should regard himself as a "Guardian of his Country's Reputation, and refuse to insert such Writings as may hurt it." In his *Autobiography* he stated that newspapers printing scurrilous reflections on government were an infamous disgrace. Neither he nor his contemporaries abandoned the concept that a republican state can be criminally assailed by mere

---

[66] "An Account of the Supremest Court of Judicature in Pennsylvania, Viz, The Court of the Press," published as a newspaper essay, 1789, and reprinted in Albert Henry Smyth, ed., *The Writings of Benjamin Franklin* (New York, 1905-07), 10:38, 40. James M. Smith, *Freedom's Fetters: The Alien and Sedition Laws and American Civil Liberties* (Ithaca, 1956), 137, interpreted the tar-and-feathers remark as "horseplay." But the whole piece exuded bitterness. The title indicated that one whose reputation had been scandalized in the press had no practical appeal, except private revenge until the legislature acted to supplement the common law. Physical violence against editors was not unusual.

words. In 1798 Federalist advocates of the Sedition Act quoted and drew support from Franklin's 1789 essay.[67] The thesis that the Revolution had as one of its objectives the elimination of the common law on freedom of speech and press also includes among its evidence the declaration to the inhabitants of Quebec by the Continental Congress in 1774.[68] But that document, which specifically endorsed only the diffusion of "liberal sentiments on the administration of government," has been misread.[69] Congress itself revealed its true meaning, as indicated above, just fifteen months later in a recommendation to the states that they take appropriate measures against "erroneous opinions." Other items of evidence seem more persuasive. One is the Virginia Statute of Religious Freedom of 1785.

The preamble to that great statute which Jefferson drafted indicates his indebtedness to Philip Furneaux, because Jefferson and the Virginia legislature explicitly rejected the bad-tendency test of criminality and defined a new test in its place. The statute asserts

> that to suffer the civil magistrate to intrude his powers into the field of opinion and to restrain the profession or propagation of principles *on supposition of their ill tendency* is a dangerous falacy [*sic*], which at once destroys all *religious* liberty, because he being of course judge of that tendency, will make his opinions the rule of judgment, and approve or condemn the sentiments of others only as they shall square with or differ from his own; that it is time enough for the rightful purposes of civil government for its officers to interfere when principles break out into overt acts against peace and good order; and finally, that truth is great and will prevail if left to herself; that she is the proper antagonist to error, and has nothing to fear from the conflict unless by human interposition disarmed of her natural weapons, free argument and debate; errors ceasing to be dangerous when it is permitted freely to contradict them.[70]

[67] Letter to Francis Hopkinson, Dec. 24, 1782, in *Writings of Franklin*, 8:648. *Ibid.*, 1:344 for *Autobiography*. See above, pp. 51-58 for the Smith-Moore case. For Federalist reliance on Franklin, see below, p. 289.

[68] See Smith, *Freedom's Fetters*, 427; Chafee, *Free Speech*, 17; Schofield, *Essays*, 2:522; John Kelly, "Criminal Libel and Free Speech," *Kansas Law Review* 6 (1958):307.

[69] This judgment excludes only Arthur M. Schlesinger, who kept his personal preferences separated from the evidence. In his *Prelude to Independence*, at 189, he realistically observed that as far as freedom of the press was concerned, the declaration of Quebec was intended "purely for export."

[70] *Papers of Jefferson*, 2:546. Italics added.

This statement does refer to "the field of opinion" generally, although in context the statute provided for and explicitly named only freedom of religion. Yet the principles of the statement could, theoretically, apply with equal vigor to speech and press which are related and linked together with freedom of religion in the First Amendment. The new test of criminality adopted by the Statute of Religious Freedom scrapped the bad-tendency test, which was at the heart of the law of criminal libel. The new test prevented the prosecution of words unless they directly, immediately, and actually incited someone to commit a crime: prosecution is proper only when "principles break out into *overt acts.*"

In Virginia, therefore, there seems to be a possibility that the legislature meant that the protection afforded to the freedoms of religion and press superseded the common law of criminal libel. Dumas Malone, Jefferson's biographer, asserted that Jefferson did not intend to limit the freedom of opinion to religion.[71] According to Malone the great statute embodied a broad libertarian theory because Jefferson believed that "freedom of thought was an absolute, and it may be assumed that he applied not merely to religious opinion but to all opinion" the Miltonic maxim that reason and free inquiry "are the only effectual agents against error." Malone was wrong except when he contradicted himself by conceding that Jefferson did not regard "freedom of political expression as an absolute." As Malone wrote, Jefferson recognized the legitimate authority of the states to prosecute the licentiousness of the press.[72] The Virginia legislature did not enact Jefferson's great measure until 1785, although he had drafted it in 1779. In fact he had proposed a constitution for Virginia in 1776 with a religious liberty provision that anticipated his later achievement. The first two drafts of his 1776 religious-liberty clause suggest the narrowness of his thinking on the scope of *political* expression. The initial draft, after declaring that no person should be compelled to frequent or maintain any religious service or institution, added, "but seditious behavior to be punable by civil magistrate accdg to the laws already made or hereafter to be made."[73] On reconsideration he bracketed but did not red pencil the words quoted. In his second draft, his impulse to punish politically unacceptable opinions again revealed itself in the following clause: "but this [the liberty of religious opinion] shall not be held to justify any seditious preaching or

---

[71] *Jefferson and His Time* (Boston, 1948-81, 6 vols.), 1:278.
[72] *Ibid.*, 2:393-94.
[73] *Papers of Jefferson*, 1:337-64, include the three drafts of a constitution composed by Jefferson in May-June, 1776. See *ibid.*, 1:344.

conversation against the authority of the civil government."[74] Again on reconsideration, Jefferson bracketed the quoted words. He apparently groped for a way to insure the unfettered right to propagate religious opinion without relinquishing the power of the state to curb dangerous political expressions and without permitting freedom for seditious opinions under the guise of religious expression.

In the end Jefferson omitted the restrictive clause from the third and final draft, possibly because he recognized that the task at hand was to insure religious liberty rather than to acknowledge the unquestioned power of the state to prosecute seditious libels. The right to religious liberty, moreover, was the one above all others to which he was most deeply devoted, and he was willing to take risks to insure it.

Significantly, Jefferson never applied the overt-acts test to political opinions. Although his own religious faith was deeply held, he felt quite indifferent about that of others. In his *Notes of the State of Virginia*, which he began in 1780, he remarked that whether his neighbor said that there were twenty gods or none "neither picks my pocket nor breaks my leg."[75] But political opinions could pick his pocket or break his leg: he worried about permitting religiously founded opinions "against the civil government"; he supported political test oaths; he denied civil rights to nonjurors; and he was ready to imprison carriers of "traitorous opinions" in time of crisis. His threshold of tolerance for hateful political ideas was less than generous, and he intended his great statute to protect only beliefs about religion. The declaration "that religious faith shall go unpunished," he wrote in 1788, "does not give impunity to criminal acts dictated by religious error."[76] In any case, there is a certain illogic in assuming that the principle of the Statute of Religious Freedom revealed the intention behind Virginia's constitutional protection of the press, which *preceded* the statute by nine years.

Virginia's legislature certainly did not extend the overt-acts test to certain proscribed political utterances. In the same year that it enacted the Statute of Religious Freedom, the legislature passed a law that aimed at prohibiting the creation of any government within the state's boundaries without the legislature's consent; the act provided that, "EVERY person . . . who shall by *writing* or advised *speaking*, endeavour to instigate the people of this commonwealth to erect or establish such government without such assent aforesaid, shall be

[74] *Ibid.*, 1:353.
[75] *Notes on the State of Virginia*, Peden, ed., 159.
[76] To Madison, July 31, 1788, in *Papers of Jefferson*, 13:443.

adjudged guilty of a high crime and misdemeanor."[77] The statute did not bespeak a broad understanding in Virginia that freedom of political speech and press included a right to express any principle that did not "break out into overt acts." On the contrary, Virginia embodied the bad-tendency test of utterances by failing to distinguish mere words from the overt criminal act of attempting by unconstitutional means to erect a new government within the state's territory.

Virginia reenacted the same statute in 1792, when it also passed an "Act Against Divulgers of False News."[78] The new statute of 1792, which covered printers and others who misinformed the people, showed that the legislature believed that it could regulate the press without restraining it; the state constitution guaranteed the freedom of the press and declared that it "can never be restrained except by despotic Governments." The statute showed the acceptance by Virginia's public law of prosecutions for criminal libel and, in the later words of a member of the Assembly, "it is known to the people that in a prosecution for libel in Virginia, under the state laws, you can neither plead nor give in evidence the truth of the matter contained in the libel."[79] In other words, Virginia even rejected the bedrock of the Zenger case, that truth is a defense.

No state got rid of the common-law concept of seditious libel. No state gave statutory or constitutional recognition to the overt acts test embodied in the preamble of Virginia's 1785 statute. No state adopted truth as a defense during the period 1776-1789. If an objective of the Revolution was to repudiate *in toto* the Blackstone-Mansfield exposition of the common law's restrictions on freedom of expression, how very strange that Americans of the revolutionary generation did not say so. Excepting a dissident reaction to the Oswald prosecution in Pennsylvania in 1782, the statements closest to repudiating seditious libel accepted the justice of punishing false opinions or malicious scandals against the government. Furthermore, all the evidence purporting to prove an intention to supersede the common law and provide for an unrestricted freedom of discussion is logically and legally

[77] Virginia Code, 1803, chap. CXXXVI, quoted in *Dennis* v. *U.S.*, 341 U.S. 494, 521 n. 3. Italics added. See also Thomas F. Carroll, "Freedom of Speech and of the Press in the Federalist Period: The Sedition Act," *Michigan Law Review* 18 (May 1920):633, citing the same statute in Hening, *Statutes of Virginia*, 12:41-43 and Shepard, *Laws of Virginia*, 1:187.

[78] Chapter CXII, in *A Collection of all such Acts of the General Assembly . . . as are now in Force* (Richmond, Davis, 1794), Evans #27999, 219.

[79] Archibald Magill in *The Virginia Report of 1799-1800 . . . Including the Debates and Proceedings Thereon in the House of Delegates of Virginia* (Richmond, Va., 1850), 75.

reconcilable with Blackstone's view that opinions are free but subject to prosecution for falsity, malice, bad tendency, and the like.

The history of the reception of the common law during the Revolution tends to establish the acceptance of the Blackstonian definition of liberty of press and speech. Twelve states, including all nine guaranteeing a free press, provided by constitution or statute that the common law of England before the Revolution was to operate with full force unless inconsistent with or repugnant to some other statutory provision.[80] For example, New York, the home of Zenger's case, repudiated its principles. The state constitution of 1777 expressly adopted the common law as of the date of the outbreak of the war with England.[81] In the states like New York where no protection to freedom of speech and/or press was afforded, there is not even the basis of an implication that it was the intention to get rid of the idea that a republican form of government may be criminally libeled by the opinions of its citizens. As for the states that constitutionally protected freedom of speech and/or press, one may argue that the law of criminal utterances was inconsistent with or repugnant to the constitutional guarantee, a simple declaration on behalf of free expression. But such an argument must be based on inferences from modern libertarian premises and would lack the support of evidence from the 1776-1791 period. The evidence goes the other way.

Two states, in the midst of affording a constitutional guarantee to freedom of religion, provided that its exercise could not justify libeling the government. North Carolina's article on religious liberty (1776) contained this qualification: "Provided, that nothing herein contained shall be construed to exempt preachers of treasonable or *seditious discourses,* from legal trial and punishment."[82] If preachers were not exempt from the law of seditious libel, others were not either. South Carolina's equivalent clause (1778) stated: "No person whatever shall speak anything in their religious assembly irreverently or *seditiously* of the government of this State."[83] If one could not in church speak seditiously of the state, he could not do so elsewhere. To the same effect, though not as explicitly, are the qualifying clauses of the religious freedom provisions in the first constitutions of New

---

[80] Ford W. Hall, "The Common Law: An Account of Its Reception in the United States," *Vanderbilt Law Review* 4 (June 1951):797-800.

[81] Article XXXV, in Thorpe, ed., *Constitutions,* 5:2637.

[82] Section XXXIV, North Carolina Constitution of 1776, in *ibid.,* 5:2793. Italics added.

[83] Section XXXVIII, South Carolina Constitution of 1778, in *ibid.,* 6:3257. Italics added.

York,[84] New Hampshire,[85] Massachusetts,[86] Georgia,[87] and Maryland.[88] The last, for example, provided (1776) that no one "under colour of religion . . . shall disturb the good order, peace or safety of the State, or shall infringe the laws of morality." At common law, an utterance tending to disturb the peace of the state was seditious. New York, New Hampshire, Massachusetts, and Georgia used similar language, prohibiting exercises of religion repugnant to the public peace or safety.

Thus, if some scholars[89] may infer that the Virginia Statute of Religious Freedom laid down a new test of criminality which applied to speech and press as well as religion, then by analogous implication, seven other states, five of which constitutionally protected "the freedom of the press," preserved as to speech and press, as well as religion, the common law of criminal libel.

Another body of evidence, the Cushing-Adams correspondence of 1789, seemingly points to a broad understanding of freedom of speech and press, although not to an abandonment of the concept of seditious libel. In 1789 William Cushing, who had been an influential member of the convention that framed the Massachusetts constitution, was serving his twelfth year as chief justice of his state. He addressed a long, thoughtful letter to John Adams, giving his interpretation of their state constitution's free-press clause which had been originally drafted by Adams. The clause affirmed, "The liberty of the press is essential to the security of freedom in a state; it ought not, therefore, to be restrained in this commonwealth." Cushing worried about the question whether a publication aspersing the conduct of officeholders could be punished under the free-press clause, "when such charges are supportable by the truth of fact."[90] Cushing called this clause "very general and unlimited," and asked, "What guard or

[84] Section XXXVIII, New York Constitution of 1777, in *ibid.*, 5:2637.
[85] Article V, Bill of Rights, New Hampshire Constitution of 1784, in *ibid.*, 4:2454.
[86] Article II, Declaration of Rights, Massachusetts Constitution of 1780, in *ibid.*, 3:1889.
[87] Article LVI, Georgia Constitution of 1777, in *ibid.*, 2:784.
[88] Article XXXIII, Declaration of Rights, Maryland Constitution of 1776, in *ibid.*, 3:1689.
[89] See, for example, Schofield, *Essays*, 2:522; Smith, *Freedom's Fetters*, 428; Kelly, "Criminal Libel," *Kansas Law Review* 6:307; Malone, *Jefferson and His Time*, 1:278.
[90] [Frank W. Grinnell, ed.], "Hitherto Unpublished Correspondence Between Chief Justice Cushing and John Adams in 1789," Cushing to Adams, Feb. 18, 1789, in *Massachusetts Law Quarterly* 27 (October 1942):12. Cushing's letter covers pp. 12-15; Adams's reply of March 7 is at 16. All quotations which follow are from this source. The original manuscripts are in the Cushing Papers, Massachusetts Historical Society.

limitation can be put upon it?" He was certain it did not protect libels upon private reputations, nor did it render immune from prosecution "*injuring* the public or individuals by propagating falsehoods." But he wanted Adams's opinion on his belief that the clause did guarantee a freedom to discuss all subjects and characters "within the bounds of truth." Blackstone, he admitted, had defined the liberty of the press as a freedom from previous restraints and not as a freedom from punishment for the publication of criminal matter.

But the words of our article understood according to plain English, make no such distinction, and must exclude *subsequent* restraints, as much as *previous restraints*. In other words, if all men are restrained by the fear of jails, scourges and loss of ears from examining the conduct of persons in administration and where their conduct is illegal, tyrannical and tending to overthrow the Constitution and introduce slavery, are so restrained from declaring it to the public *that* will be as effectual a restraint as any *previous* restraint whatever.

The question upon the article is this—What is that liberty of the press, which is essential to the security of freedom? The propagating literature and knowledge by printing or otherwise tends to illuminate men's minds and to establish them in principles in freedom. But it cannot be denied also, that a free scanning of the conduct of administration and shewing the tendency of it, and where truth will warrant, making it manifest that it is subversive of all law, liberty, and the Constitution; it can't be denied. I think that the liberty tends to the *security of freedom in a State;* even more directly and essentially than the liberty of printing upon literary and speculative subjects in general. Without this liberty of the press could we have supported our liberties against british administration? or could our revolution have taken place? Pretty certainly it could not, at the time it did. Under a sense and impression of this sort, I conceive, this article was adopted. This liberty of publishing truth can never effectually injure a good government, or honest administrators; but it may save a state from the necessity of a revolution, as well as bring one about, when it is necessary. It may be objected that a public prosecution is the safe and regular course, in case of malfeasance. But what single person would venture himself upon so invidious and dangerous a task against a man high in interest, influence and power?

But this liberty of the press having truth for its basis who can stand before it? Besides it may facilitate a legal prosecution, which might not, otherwise, have been dared to be attempted. When the press is made the vehicle of falsehood and scandal, let the authors be punished with becoming rigour.

But why need any honest man be afraid of truth? The guilty

only fear it; and I am inclined to think with Gordon (Vol. 3 No. 20 of Cato's Letters) that truth sacredly adhered to, can never upon the whole prejudice right religion, equal government or a government founded upon proper balances and checks, or the happiness of society in any respect, but must be favorable to them all.

Suppressing this liberty by penal laws will it not more endanger freedom than do good to government? The weight of government is sufficient to prevent any very dangerous consequences occasioned by *provocations* resulting from charges founded in truth; whether such charges are made in *a legal course or otherwise*. In either case, the *provocation* (which Judge Blackstone says is the sole foundation of the law against libels) being much the same.

But not to trouble you with a multiplying of words; If I am wrong I should be glad to be set right, &c., &c.

Adams replied as follows:

The difficult and important question is whether the truth of words can be admitted by the court to be given in evidence to the jury, upon a plea of not guilty? In England I suppose it is settled. But it is a serious Question whether our Constitution is not at present so different as to render the innovation necessary? Our chief magistrates and Senators &c are annually eligible by the people. How are their characters and conduct to be known to their constituents but by the press? If the press is stopped and the people kept in Ignorance we had much better have the first magistrate and Senators hereditary. I therefore, am very clear that under the Articles of our Constitution which you have quoted, it would be safest to admit evidence to the jury of the Truth of accusations, and if the jury found them true and that they were published for the Public good, they would readily acquit.

The Cushing-Adams correspondence has been quoted at length because it is one of the very rare American expositions of the meaning of freedom of the press before the Sedition Act controversy beginning in 1798; because it is the most detailed and libertarian of those expositions; and because it is scarcely known.[91] What observations

[91] The only writer concerned with the original understanding of freedom of speech and press who used the Cushing-Adams correspondence is John Kelly, "Criminal Libel and Free Speech," *Kansas Law Review* 6 (1958):309, and he neglected to mention the source. See n. 39 above. David A. Anderson, relying on my reproduction of the correspondence, yanks completely out-of-context Cushing's comment about subsequent restraint and leaves the misleading impression that he construed the free press guarantee as excluding subsequent punishment. That would have entailed a repudiation of seditious libel. Cushing and Adams supported prosecutions for seditious libel; they merely advocated truth as a defense. See David A. Anderson, "The Origins of the Free Press Clause," *UCLA Law Review* 30 (1983):528.

will that correspondence yield? First, it is clear that even though Cushing partially repudiated Blackstone when arguing that a guarantee of freedom of the press meant an exclusion of subsequent as well as previous restraints, the chief justice was only going as far as Cato, Alexander, Andrew Hamilton, Bollan, Father of Candor, and a new generation of English writers who were active in the 1780s.[92] Each had a harp with two strings to it: truth should be a defense against a charge of criminal utterance; the jury should decide whether the defendant's words were criminal. As noted earlier, truth as a defense meant a modification of the common law in substance as well as procedure. Unquestionably it would have liberalized the common law by expanding the scope of permissible expression to include even derogatory and scandalous publications if they were true and presumably written for the public good, or at least, without malice.

But truth is a mischievous, often an illusory, standard that defies knowledge and understanding. It cannot always be proved. What is not a fact may be an untruth or a nontruth, an opinion at the very best, and the political opinions of men notoriously differ. The other fellow's are usually false, and "falsity," as Cushing and Adams agreed, was evidence of libel. They did not allow for freedom of *opinion* or for mistakes in facts or reasoning which are so prevalent in political give-and-take. They set a nearly impossible standard, truth, which they would have had jurors judge. A jury is a court of public opinion, often synonymous with public prejudice, and is not an adequate measure of truth, nor are judges. The fault lies in giving fallible men judgment of truth rather than asking them to determine whether the words charged actually led to criminal deeds or whether under the circumstances of time and place the words would have caused the crime but for the effective intervention of the government. Jurors can judge whether the evidence proves the truth of a charge that some official has taken a bribe, but their fallibility is too great to entrust to them a judgment on the truth of an accusation that the government, or one of its policies, or a member of its administration is unjust, tyrannical, or repugnant to the public interest. Accusations of the latter order, not charges of bribes, constituted almost without exception the subject of prosecutions, the very fact that made the doctrine of seditious libel such an oppressive fetter on freedom of expression. The best and most relevant illustration is the entire corpus of prosecutions for seditious libel under the Sedition Act of 1798.

That statute, which nearly abolished freedom of speech and press,

[92] The postrevolutionary English writers will be discussed in Chapter Nine, below.

embodied the reform proposed by Cushing and Adams. As Zechariah
Chafee pointed out, the Sedition Act

> entrusted criminality to the jury and admitted truth as a defense.
> On the other hand, freedom of speech might exist without these
> two technical safeguards.
> The essential question is not, who is judge of the criminality of
> an utterance, but what is the test of its criminality. The common
> law and the Sedition Act of 1798 made the test blame of the gov-
> ernment and its officials, because to bring them into disrepute
> tended to overthrow the state. The real question in every free
> speech controversy is this: whether the state can punish all words
> which have some tendency, however remote, to bring about acts in
> violation of law, or only words which directly incite to acts in
> violation of law.[93]

President Adams willingly signed the Sedition Act and eagerly
urged its enforcement, and Cushing, then an associate justice of the
Supreme Court of the United States, presided over some of the trials
and charged juries on the constitutionality of the statute.[94] Both men
acted in full consistency with the opinions expressed in their correspondence of 1789, because they accepted then, as in 1798-1799, the
concept of seditious libel. They believed then, as Cushing said, that
falsehoods and scandals against the government should be punished
"with becoming rigour." Their libertarianism was founded upon a
brave acceptance of truth as they understood it. Why, asked Cushing,
need an honest man "be afraid of truth? The guilty only fear it." Neither he nor Adams believed that falsehoods or wrong opinions of a
bad tendency warranted free circulation.
    They asserted that the publication of truth could not effectually
injure a good government or an honest administrator, but they would
not take the crucial step of asserting that error of opinion may be
tolerated where reason is left free to combat it, even as to those who
wished to dissolve the Union or change its form of government. Had
Cushing written that a good government or an honest administrator
could not be injured by error of opinion or even by malicious falsehood, he would have evinced a libertarian understanding that was
incompatible with the concept of seditious libel. When President
Adams wrote that United States Attorney William Rawle was unfit
for his job if he did not think that the *Aurora*'s criticism was libelous

---

[93] Chafee, *Free Speech*, 23.
[94] Smith, *Freedom's Fetters*, 97-98, 152, 242, 267, 268, 271, 284, 311, 363, and
371.

and subject to prosecution and when he wrote of Thomas Cooper's criticism that he had "no doubt it is a libel against the whole government, and as such ought to be prosecuted,"[95] he was revealing an attitude that he displayed in the 1770s when fulminating against the seditious character of unpatriotic talk. Even in 1765, when he had urged Edes and Gill to publish their sentiments freely, he counseled that they should go only as far as "can be warranted by the laws of your country." He consistently embraced the opinion that antigovernment talk, which he believed to be unjustified, was seditious. That he supported truth as a defense and would give a free hand to juries showed a libertarianism constricted by an unquestioned premise that words of a bad tendency were criminal.

The frailty of the protection offered to freedom of the press by the Cushing-Adams proposals of 1789 manifested itself when only one Sedition Act jury returned a verdict of acquittal. But neither the juries, the judges, nor the president should be condemned for not believing the truth of the defendants' opinions, because those who were on the side of the prosecution reacted to those opinions by identifying their own politics with truth. They shared, moreover, a belief in the predominant doctrine that opinions can criminally assault government. To be sure, those opinions had to be malicious and false to be criminal, but the doctrine of seditious libel, even modified, implied an extremely narrow concept of freedom of the press.

A final observation must be made on the Cushing-Adams correspondence. It is not a dependable revelation of the intention underlying constitutional guarantees of freedom of the press or speech. Cushing and Adams were proposing, not disposing; moreover they were not representing the constitutional law of Massachusetts as of 1789 or for many years later.[96] From Cushing's bewilderment as to the meaning of the state's free-press clause and his comment that the questions he raised had never been decided, he clearly failed to expose the genral understanding of that clause's meaning in the minds of the 1780 convention that framed it. Cushing had been at that convention; Adams actually wrote the first draft. Adams agreed in 1789 that it "would be" better to construe the clause as Cushing suggested. The two were discussing an "innovation." They were engaged in a reform, not a declaration of the thinking of 1780. At that date, when the constitution was adopted, freedom of the press meant what it had

---

[95] Letters from Adams to T. Pickering, Aug. 1, 1799, and Aug. 13, 1799, in *Works*, 9:5, 13-14.

[96] See below, pp. 213-18, for a discussion of the law of criminal libels in Massachusetts.

always meant. In some respects, such as the validity of truth as a defense or the function of juries in criminal libel cases, its meaning was not clear. As Franklin wrote in 1789, "Few of us, I believe, have distinct Ideas of Its Nature and Extent."[97] Similarly, Hamilton wrote that freedom of the press defied precise definition.[98] But an unquestioned consensus assumed that its freedom did not extend to an immunity against punishment for seditious libel, although the evidence is difficult to dig out because the most deeply rooted assumptions are often not articulated.

One of the few public men of the time who did articulate his assumptions was James Wilson of Pennsylvania. Excepting James Madison, Wilson was probably the most influential Framer of the United States Constitution and as great a legal expert as anyone in the new nation. At the Pennsylvania ratifying convention of 1787 Wilson had occasion, like his fellow Framers in other state ratifying conventions, to deny an Anti-Federalist accusation that the failure to guarantee freedom of the press meant that oppression of opinion was constitutionally possible. Wilson, like many Framers, expressly stated on the subject of the press that "there is given to the general government no power whatsoever concerning it: and no law, in pursuance of the Constitution, can possibly be enacted, to destroy that liberty."[99] But Wilson, unlike his fellow Framers, discussed the subject further. In answer to the charge that federal judges might proceed under federal statutes punishing libels, he replied:

> I presume it was not in the view of the honorable gentleman to say that there is no such thing as libel, or that the writers of such ought not to be punished. The idea of the liberty of the press is not carried so far as this in any country—*what is meant by liberty of the press is that there should be no antecedent restraint upon it;* but that every author is responsible when he attacks the security or welfare of the *government,* or the safety, character and property of the individual.
>
> With regard to attacks upon the public, the mode of proceeding is by a prosecution. . . . Now, Sir, if this libel is to be tried, it must be tried where the offence was committed; for under this Constitution, as declared in the second section of the Third Article, the trial must be held in the State; therefore on this occasion it

[97] "The Court of the Press" (1789), *Writings of Franklin,* 10:37.

[98] *The Federalist,* No. 84, p. 560 of The Modern Library edition, ed. Edward John Earle (New York, n.d.).

[99] Merrill Jensen, ed., *The Documentary History of the Ratification of the Constitution.* Vol. II, *Ratification of the Constitution by the States* (Madison, 1976), 455.

must be tried where it was published, if the indictment is for publishing; and it must be tried likewise by a jury of that state.[100]

Here, in the most explicit language, is James Wilson, a major figure, restating the English or Blackstonian definition of freedom of the press. His statement leaves no doubt that he believed the law of seditious libel to be in force, because he spoke of the legal responsibility of writers who attacked the security or welfare of the government, and he added that for such attacks the remedy was prosecution. He believed that the United States courts had jurisdiction over seditious libel, because Article III, section 2, to which he referred, described the judicial power of the United States. No one at the Pennsylvania convention essayed to deny Wilson's exposition of the law. Thus, in the only state among the original thirteen to guarantee both freedom of speech and press in a constitution drawn before the Federal Bill of Rights, those guarantees did not imply an abandonment of the common law's injunction against criminal libels.

Francis Bailey agreed with Wilson. Bailey, who in 1781 established his Philadelphia newspaper, the *Freeman's Journal*, advocated the orthodox theory of press freedom. He had no quarrel with the law of seditious libel. Any newspaper article, he asserted, "intending to subvert public measures, and undermine the interests of government, is equally a libel . . . these being matters not designed to promote the public good." Bailey failed to distinguish matters designed to promote the public good from those that did not; he did not even assert that a jury should make that distinction by acquitting a defendant who wrote the truth. His conceptual principle was Blackstonian: the press ought to be free "leaving the offender to the ordinary course of law, if his writings have libellous import." Abstract theory probably repelled Bailey, because he understood that "when a press lashes everybody but ME and MY FRIENDS, we enjoy the liberty of the press in perfection. In those cases we say 'a press conducted on the true principles of decency and honours,' but when it touches ME and MY FRIENDS, it is downright licentiousness." His beliefs about the suppressiveness of the law notwithstanding, Bailey regularly printed rancorous assaults on opposition politicians. He could afford to operate a free press because he had the protection of a powerful political party.[101]

[100] *Ibid.* Italics added.
[101] *Freeman's Journal*, June 13, 1782; for the "MY FRIENDS" quotation, *ibid.*, Sept. 11, 1782. Credit for breaking new ground on the Philadelphia press belongs to Dwight L. Teeter, "A Legacy of Expression: Philadelphia Newspapers and Congress During the War for Independence, 1775-1783," unpub.

Pennsylvania had a well-defined two-party system whose parties counterbalanced each other. As long as one could not long dominate the other, no government could safely rely on the common law to silence libelous opposition voices. The restraints of the common law worked effectively only if the government controlled public opinion, or could flout it, or had its support—or could rely on juries to indict and convict. When the two parties just about divided the electorate, the party in power had to apprehend future retaliation if it dared to prosecute its critics. It had to worry too whether it could prosecute successfully. As Dwight L. Teeter wrote, "The pen names of the men who wrote for the newspapers concealed some of Pennsylvania's—and America's—most renowned politicians. Powerful men or men with powerful friends wrote for the newspapers. Political power helped to shield the printers from punishment."[102] Philadelphia was at the center of political power; it was the meeting place of both the state's Assembly and the Continental Congress, whose members used the press to promote their policies and punish their opponents. Political power saved Eleazar Oswald of the *Independent Gazetteer* when in 1782 he crossed foils with the state supreme court.

Oswald's newspaper spoke for the state's conservative party, which backed the nationalist cause in Congress and sought modification of the state's democratic constitution of 1776. The party's leadership, which included James Wilson, John Dickinson, and Robert Morris, contributed to the *Independent Gazetteer* under pennames, but "the public generally knew who the authors were . . ."[103] The public also knew Oswald as a gutsy and pugnacious editor who had served with valor in Washington's army as a lieutenant colonel of artillery; he had learned his craft as a printer from John Holt in New York and William Goddard in Baltimore. Nothing in Oswald's credo for a free press prepared readers for his slashing journalism.[104] In his first

---

dissertation, University of Wisconsin, School of Journalism, Madison, 1966. Teeter published a few articles based on his dissertation. In one, "Decent Animadversions: Notes Toward a History of Free Press Theory," in Donovan H. Bond and W. R. McLeod, eds., *Newsletters to Newspapers: Eighteenth Century Journalism* (Morgantown, W.Va., 1977), 237-45, Teeter based his analysis on a faulty understanding. He mistakenly thought Bailey had contradicted himself merely because Bailey invoked the Pennsylvania free press clause to advocate an unrestrained press yet endorsed the law of seditious libel. He and Blackstone, whom he followed, did not contradict themselves.

[102] Dwight L. Teeter, "Press Freedom and the Public Printing: Pennsylvania, 1775-83," *Journalism Quarterly*, 45 (1968):448-49. On state politics see Robert L. Brunhouse, *The Counter-Revolution in Pennsylvania, 1776-1790* (Harrisburg, Pa., 1942).

[103] Brunhouse, *Counter-Revolution*, 5.

[104] On Oswald see Joseph Towne Wheeler, *The Maryland Press, 1777-1790* (Maryland Historical Society, 1938), 19-36.

issue, in which he attempted a "just Definition of the Liberty of the Press," he sounded respectful of the law. "Some contend for an unbounded liberty," he wrote, but not he. An unbounded liberty would turn the freedom of the press "to the worst Purposes, and occasion more Evil than Good." He did, however, support everyone's right to communicate his sentiments "if delivered with Decency, and under reasonable Regulations."[105] Oswald promptly broke his promise to avoid scurrility and indecency. Within six months of his first issue, the sheriff arrested him on a warrant from the state supreme court.

Chief Justice Thomas McKean, no person to trifle with, sat at the head of that court. He was or became a leading figure in the revolutionary movement in Delaware, a signer of the Declaration of Independence, governor of Delaware, president of the Continental Congress, second only to Wilson in securing Pennsylvania's ratification of the Constitution, chief justice of Pennsylvania for twenty-two years, and Jeffersonian governor for eight.[106] Another member of McKean's court was also a formidable antagonist, George Bryan, a major framer of the state constitution of 1776. The judges belonged to the party that Oswald's paper lambasted with each issue.

McKean, who had a short fuse, exploded when Oswald published an article charging the court with bias and severity. The court ordered his arrest for having published a "seditious, scandalous, and infamous LIBEL" on the court's administration of justice.[107] Released on bail, Oswald showed his contempt by reprinting the offensive article, by lampooning Judge Bryan as "that excrescence," and by damning McKean as another bloody Jefferies.[108] The court rearrested him and raised bail to one thousand pounds. When the date of his trial approached, he wrote to a friend that the chief justice of Pennsylvania had attacked the freedom of the press and that he, Oswald, was "to have a public Trial . . . as a Libeller. The infamous English doctrine of Libels being introduced by the more infamous Judges and Lawyers, in an American Court."[109] In view of the fact that Os-

---

[105] *Independent Gazetteer*, April 23, 1782. In "Decent Animadversions," Teeter omitted Oswald's rejection of an "unbounded Liberty," leaving the impression that Oswald supported it.

[106] On McKean see G. S. Rowe, *Thomas McKean: The Shaping of An American Republicanism* (Boulder, Colo. 1978).

[107] *Independent Gazetteer*, Oct. 1, 1782.

[108] *Ibid.*, Oct. 15, 1782, and Jan. 11, 1783, for Oswald's later account.

[109] Quoted in Teeter, "The Printer and the Chief Justice: Seditious Libel in 1782-83," *Journalism Quarterly*, 45 (1968):235-42, quotation at p. 239, Oswald to Gen. John Lamb, Nov. 26, 1782. Teeter thought that Oswald's remark showed "disgust with seditious libel" and that "Wilkes" (not "Junius Wilkes") in *Independent Gazetteer*, Oct. 19, 1782, showed the same disgust. Oswald did not use the term nor did "Wilkes," who merely believed that the state con-

wald must have heard of some precedents such as Zenger's case or McDougall's, his meaning seems unfathomable, but "Junius Wilkes," one of his contributors, meant to repudiate the very concept of seditious libel. His logic allows no other interpretation. So heroic and unprecedented an accomplishment makes Oswald's case memorable.[110]

Junius Wilkes made a quantum leap over all former libertarians, leaving Cato, James Alexander, Andrew Hamilton, and their successors in a different galaxy of thought. Junius Wilkes did not, however, repudiate the doctrine of libels, only the doctrine of seditious libel. He accepted the legitimacy of criminal prosecutions for libels on the private lives of anyone, including a public official. Maligning the same person in his public capacity presented a wholly different case. Government officials, he observed, were public servants who remained accountable to the people and therefore could not be libeled for their performance in office. Junius Wilkes failed to clench his point by noting the irreconcilability between seditious libel and popular government. He also refused to rely on the defense of truth. Instead he boldly insisted that the constitutional guarantee of a free press should justify publications criticizing the conduct of public officials even if the publications appeared "false and groundless." It is, he said, "a kind of *dammum absque injuria"*—an injury for which no legal remedy existed; theoretically the harm, if any, had been sustained in common with the entire community for its greater good in order to preserve a public right, in this case the freedom of the press. As the author explained the point, which utterly subverted the doctrine of seditious libel, the press might blemish a good reputation but the damage amounted to far less than the evil of restraining the press. The unjustly maligned official should bear his injury rather than allow the public to suffer from a restriction on the press. In any case, Junius Wilkes added, politicians assumed the risks of office and could always answer unjust accusations in the press. When he argued against restraints he meant no subsequent punishment except for libels on private lives. "The danger is precisely the same to liberty, in punishing a person after the performance appears to the world, as in preventing publication in the *first* instance."

The ideas advanced by Junius Wilkes in 1782 prefigured the broad libertarian theory that emerged on a widespread scale after the Sedition Act of 1798. No one before Junius Wilkes had rejected the

---

stitution vested a right to comment on public proceedings, including the conduct of courts. "Wilkes" and "Junius Wilkes" were the pennames of different writers.

[110] *Independent Gazetteer*, Nov. 9, 1782.

principle of subsequent punishment or the standard of falsity as a test of criminality. No one who advocated truth as a defense or who accepted Blackstone straight believed that falsity should go unpunished. Except, perhaps, for the unnamed lawyer who had misinformed Isaiah Thomas's "Centinel,"[111] Junius Wilkes was the first to penetrate beyond Zengerian principles. He was also the first to insist that the public's right to know outweighed the defamation of even a good official.

None of the other articles on freedom of the press that appeared in connection with the Oswald case presented a coherent or reasoned position; Junius Wilkes engendered no progeny. The articles by "Spectator," "Tenax," and "Koster," for example, at best merely revived the principle of truth as a defense but otherwise clung to conservativism.[112] Koster did not even mean to protect political opinions, because his generosity extended only to innocent mistakes of "fact," which he believed should be exempt from punishment. He endorsed criminal prosecution for willful or malicious misrepresentation of "public measures, and public characters." He and Junius Wilkes operated out of different universes of discourse.

"Candid," however, had a radical position but not a reasoned one. He made Koster seem reactionary. Without considered judgment Candid asserted that all criminal prosecutions for libel should be scrapped, though he did not discuss prosecutions for blasphemous or obscene libel. Because he preferred to rely exclusively on civil suits for damages rather than continue the doctrine of libels, one must infer that he rejected seditious libel and even criminal libels on private reputations. He simply declared that criminal prosecutions posed too great a danger to the freedom of the press. However, his case for that freedom made sense because he tied it to the electoral process. The public needed the press to supply the intelligence needed for informed choices. His every other opinion rested on his mere unreasoned say-so.[113]

McKean could order Oswald's arrest but could not try him without an indictment by a grand jury; he could not, however, wrest an indictment from that body, although he tried twice. The grand jury defied him. Some believed that the grand jury thereby rejected "the Doctrine of Libels" as Oswald's paper advised at the eleventh hour, but as Judge Bryan said, writing as "Adrian," witnesses before the

---

[111] See above, pp. 161-62.

[112] *Ibid.*, Oct. 8, 1782, for Spectator, and Dec. 7, 1782, for Koster; Tenax in *Freeman's Journal*, Oct. 30, 1782.

[113] *Independent Gazetteer*, Dec. 14, 1782. Teeter, "The Printer and the Chief Justice," 240, purported to describe Candid's views but confused him with Koster.

grand jury "made out, somehow, that the printer had been misinformed, thence it was inferred, that mistake merely, involved no guilt." Bryan himself believed that Oswald had seditiously libeled the court. McKean and the grand jury went public with their dispute, and the grand jury confirmed Bryan's view of its recalcitrance. The dispute dealt mainly with the question whether the grand jury could interview witnesses not previously approved by the court. More interesting is the fact that Oswald, his lawyer, and the foreman of the grand jury were seen conversing privately in a tavern; moreover, among the witnesses whom the grand jury interviewed, without McKean's approval, were major political figures including James Wilson, the lawyer for one of the defendants to whom Oswald had extended his sympathy when he slammed the court for its bias and severity.[114] Oswald's party outmaneuvered the court in influencing the grand jury.

The Oswald case showed the supreme court's belief that the constitutional guarantee of a free press and the doctrine of seditious libel were compatible, while Junius Wilkes and probably others thought otherwise. The emergence of a sweeping libertarian opinion in Pennsylvania was especially significant and precocious, but infertile.

Within six years McKean nailed Oswald in *Respublica* v. *Oswald*, 1788.[115] A grand jury more compliant than the one of 1782 indicted the editor for a gross libel. Oswald's argument to the contrary received short shrift. An indictment against him charged a gross criminal libel against a private person. Oswald defended himself in his *Independent Gazetteer* by informing the public that his political enemies, including the brother of a member of the state supreme court in which the action had been instituted, had inspired his prosecution. Alluding to "prejudices . . . against me on the bench," he appealed to his jury for a fair trial. More out of hope than accuracy, he added:

[114] *Independent Gazetteer*, Dec. 31, 1782, Jan. 1, 11, and 18, 1783; Jacob Cox Parsons, ed., *Extracts From The Diary of Jacob Hiltzheimer, 1765-1798* (Philadelphia, 1893), 52-54, for remarks by a member of the grand jury; *Pennsylvania Gazette* (Philadelphia), Jan. 8, 1783 for the grand jury's apologia; *ibid.,* Jan. 29 for McKean writing as "Jurisperitus"; *Freeman's Journal*, Jan. 15, 1783, for Bryan as "Adrian," continued in *ibid.,* Jan. 29, 1783; "Aristides," *Pennsylvania Gazette*, Jan. 29, 1783, like Oswald, *Independent Gazetteer*, Jan. 11, 1783, believed the grand jury rejected the doctrine of libels. Teeter, p. 242, makes Aristides reject seditious libel, which he indirectly mentioned as "the doctrine of criminal libels," as he mistakenly observed that Pennsylvania's courts had not received that doctrine. "Impartial," *Freeman's Journal*, Jan. 1, 1783, mentioned recent criminal libel prosecutions.

[115] 1 Dallas (Penn. Reports) 319, 320 (1788), reprinted in Levy, ed., *Freedom of the Press From Zenger to Jefferson*, 132-142.

"The doctrine of libel being a doctrine incompatible with law and liberty, and at once destructive of the privileges of a free country, in the communication of our thoughts, has not hitherto gained any footing in *Pennsylvania*." He supposed his fellow citizens would not allow the freedom of the press to be violated "upon any refined pretence which oppressive ingenuity or courtly study can invent."[116]

McKean ordered Oswald's arrest, promptly tried him without a jury, and convicted him for his seditious contempt of the court. The chief justice ruled that "there is nothing in the constitution of this state, respecting the liberty of the press, that has not been authorized by the constitution of that kingdom [England] for near a century past." He also observed that although every man might publish his opinions, the peace and dignity of society required an inquiry into a writer's motives in order to distinguish between publications "which are meant for use and reformation, and with an eye solely to the public good, and those merely intended to delude and defame. To the latter description, it is impossible that any good government should afford protection and impunity."[117] Oswald's crime, McKean believed, consisted of his wilful attempt to prejudice his jury and dishonor the court. Oswald received a sentence of one month in prison and a ten-pound fine.

As an aftermath to the conviction, Oswald requested the Assembly to prefer impeachment charges against McKean and his associates for procedural irregularities and for violating the liberty of the press. William Lewis, who had prosecuted Oswald, defended the judges before the Assembly in a speech endorsing Blackstone's definition of a free press; Lewis concluded that the "dawn of true freedom" had arisen in England with the expiration of the licensing system. Oswald received considerable support for his accusation of procedural irregularities; no one endorsed his repudiation of the law of criminal libels, although William Findley noted that every person had a right to state his opinion on "public proceedings," and he warned of the danger of allowing judges to punish contempts against themselves. The Assembly resolved that Oswald's charges were groundless.[118]

Pennsylvania adopted a new state constitution in 1790, shortly after

---

[116] *Respublica* v. *Oswald*, 1 Dallas 319, 320 (1788).

[117] *Ibid.*, at pp. 322 and 325.

[118] The record of the impeachment proceedings is in *Respublica* v. *Oswald*, 1 Dallas 319, at pp. 330-337. The *Independent Gazetteer* published many articles on Oswald's behalf but not on the free press or criminal libel issue. No Junius Wilkes came forward, as in 1782. The focus in 1788 fell on the procedural irregularities: no indictment by grand jury, no trial by jury, and conviction by a judge who had a stake in the outcome of the case.

ratifying the First Amendment. James Wilson drafted the new state constitution. The section on speech and press was elaborate, by comparison to the parallel provision of the constitution of 1776. The new section, preceding Fox's Libel Act by two years, allowed the jury to decide whether the accused's statement was libelous as a matter of law; it also preceded Lord Campbell's Act of 1843 by making truth a defense in a prosecution for criminal libel. Previously, of course, the law of criminal libel allowed the jury to decide only whether the accused had in fact made the statement alleged, leaving to the judge the right to decide as a matter of law whether the statement was libelous. And, previously, truth was not a defense because the greater the truth, the greater the provocation and therefore the greater the libel. Pennsylvania's constitution of 1790 was the first to embody these Zengerian reforms, which unquestionably altered the common law of libel as it had been known previously. James Wilson, however, believed that Blackstone's views on libel included mistakes that the Pennsylvania Constitution expunged, making it, he said, "consonant in my opinion to the true principles of the common law."[119]

The provision of 1790 began by guaranteeing the printing presses to anyone examining government proceedings, "and no law shall ever be made to restrain the right thereof." In context, this is Blackstone: no prior censorship. Consider the next clause which uses the Blackstonian language of "free but responsible": "The free communication of thoughts and opinions is one of the invaluable rights of man; and every citizen may freely speak, write, and print on any subject, *being responsible for the abuse of that liberty*. In prosecutions for the publication of papers investigating the official conduct of officers or men in a public capacity, or where the matter published is proper for public information, the truth thereof may be given in evidence."[120] Clearly, Pennsylvania, as well as Delaware, Kentucky, and Tennessee, which had similar provisions in their constitutions of the 1790s,[121] accepted the concept that a republican form of government can be politically libeled and that the offender should be criminally prosecuted.

Even after the constitutional reform of 1790 McKean observed that the constitutional guarantee of a free press merely declared the common law. Charging the grand jury in the trial of William Cobbett for criminal libel, in 1797, the Jeffersonian chief justice asserted:

---

[119] "Lectures on Law," 1791, in *The Works of James Wilson*, Robert Green McCloskey, ed. (Cambridge, Mass., 1967, 2 vols.), 2:652.
[120] Article IX, section 7, Pennsylvania Constitution of 1790, in Thorpe, ed., *Constitutions*, 5:3100. Italics added.
[121] Article I, section 5, Delaware Constitution of 1792, in Thorpe, ed., *Constitutions*, 1:569, and Article XII, sections 7-8, Kentucky Constitution of 1792, in *ibid.*, 3:1274; Tennessee Constitution of 1796, in *ibid.*, 6:3423.

The liberty of the press is, indeed, essential to the nature of a free State, but this consists in laying no previous restraints upon public actions, and not in freedom from censure for criminal matter, when published. Every freeman has an undoubted right to lay what sentiments he pleases before the public; to forbid this, is to destroy the freedom of the press; but if he publishes what is improper, mischievous or illegal, he must take the consequences of his temerity. To punish dangerous or offensive writings, which, when published, shall, on a fair and impartial trial, be adjudged of a pernicious tendency, is necessary for the preservation of peace and good order, of government and religion, the only solid foundation of civil liberty. Thus the will of individuals is still left free; the abuse only of that free will is the object of punishment. Our presses in Pennsylvania are thus free. The common law, with respect to this, is confirmed and established by the Constitution.[122]

Thus, in Pennsylvania, whose constitutional provisions in 1776 and 1790 were the most libertarian in the Union as to freedom of speech and press, the crux of the common law of criminal libels remained in force. McKean's 1797 exposition of the free-press clause might have been issued under the name of Hutchinson, Blackstone, or Mansfield.

The charge by Alexander Addison, presiding judge of the state Court of Common Pleas, in 1798,[123] followed suit as did *Respublica* v. *Dennie* in 1805.[124] The Dennie case ended in an acquittal, but the state's indictment of the Federalist defendant for seditious libel against both Pennsylvania and the United States because of his essay denouncing democracy and President Jefferson hardly bespeaks a repudiation of the common law or a broad understanding of freedom of the press.

Massachusetts, like Pennsylvania, also provided constitutional protection to freedom of the press, but also recognized the law of criminal libels including seditious utterances. Under the rule of the royal governors during the period of the verbal war with England before the battle of Lexington, no restraints upon the Massachusetts press had actually been imposed. The governors and their Councils sought to initiate prosecutions for criminal or seditious libel against several patriot editors, but no grand jury would indict them; public opinion against the government had been so strong that the governors did not even dare to circumvent the grand jury by directing the attorney-

[122] "Trial of William Cobbett," Nov. 1797, in Francis Wharton, ed., *State Trials of the United States during the Administration of Washington and Adams* (Philadelphia, 1849), 323-24.
[123] Selections from Addison's charges are reprinted in Mark Howe, ed., *Readings in American Legal History* (Cambridge, Mass., 1949), 348-358.
[124] 4 Yeates' (Penn.) Reports 267 (1805).

general to proceed by information rather than indictment. Yet, in the free state of Massachusetts, with its constitutional guarantee of liberty of the press, grand juries returned criminal-libel indictments in 1787, 1791, 1798, and 1802, as well as later.

Massachusetts also taxed its press, and by a stamp tax no less. Desperate for revenue, the state fixed on a two-penny stamp tax for every copy of a newspaper or almanac. The legislature did not intend to punish or restrain the press, but printers and editors reacted as if the year was 1765 and the legislature was Parliament. Throughout the state, newspapers shrieked that the tax violated the state constitution's free press clause and threatened economic ruination. The most common argument was that by hurting sales the tax had the effect of preventing some citizens from being informed about public men and measures. The tax provoked such widespread and intense opposition that the legislature repealed it in the same year but replaced it with a tax on advertisements. Despite a comparable reaction from the press, the new tax lasted until 1787 when the legislature repealed it because it brought in a lot of protest and little revenue.[125]

In 1787 Massachusetts indicted several people who encouraged and supported Shay's Rebellion, among them George Brock and Gideon Pond for having published "scandalous, seditious" libels against the government.[126] Although their cases never came to trial, the state did convict Captain Moses Harvey of "seditious and inflammatory words" because he called the legislature "thieves" and urged the closing of the courts. The trial court sentenced him to sit upon the gallows with a rope about his neck, a fifty pound fine, and probation for five years.[127] At about the same time, in April 1787, occurred the most important of these cases. A jury convicted Dr. William Whiting before the Supreme Judicial Court sitting in Great Barrington, the scene of Whiting's crime. No ordinary libeler, Whiting was Chief Justice of the Court of Common Pleas of Berkshire County. Shortly before the fall term of his court, in 1786, he had written an article, signed Gracchus, in which he censured the government for unjust laws and recommended that a virtuous people who lacked redress of grievances should "disturb the government." Whiting did not pub-

---

[125] Clyde Augustus Duniway, *The Development of Freedom of the Press in Massachusetts* (New York, 1906), 136-37, and Gerald Joseph Baldasty, "A Theory of Press Freedom: Massachusetts Newspapers and Law, 1782-91," unpub. M.A. thesis in Journalism, University of Wisconsin, 1974, pp. 12-19.

[126] Duniway, *Freedom of the Press*, 142 n. 1, citing *Suffolk Court (Mass.) Files*, Nos. 104616, 104618, 106011.

[127] *Virginia Independent Chronicle* (Richmond), May 16, 1787, story datelined Boston.

lish the article but read it to several insurgent leaders. When the rebellion broke out, armed men with whom he sympathized closed his court. After the defeat of Shays at Petersham, the government began its arrests. Theodore Sedgwick, the conservative leader of Berkshire, had sent a copy of the Gracchus article to Governor James Bowdoin, who entrusted the case to the state's attorney-general. Whiting denied the charges, but he was dismissed from his judicial post, convicted of writing a seditious libel, and received a sentence of imprisonment for seven months, a one-hundred pound fine, and sureties for good behavior for five years. Bowdoin and his Council denied a petition for a pardon but remitted the prison sentence. No one claimed that the free-press clause of the state constitution stood in the way of a prosecution for seditious libel.[128]

In 1791 Edmund Freeman, a newspaper editor, for having grossly libeled the private life of a member of the legislature, was criminally prosecuted on the theory that his words tended to breach the public peace of the Commonwealth. The prosecutor, Attorney-General James Sullivan, later Jeffersonian governor of the state, maintained that the constitutional guarantee of a free press meant only the absence of a licensing act; he quoted Blackstone at interminable length to prove the point and urged that in this first trial for criminal libel under the state constitution, licentiousness must be distinguished from liberty. The defendant's attorneys, Harrison Gray Otis and R. G. Amory, did not challenge Sullivan's principles. Although not asking for a ruling that truth was a defense, they denied licentiousness or breach of peace on the part of Freeman and sought to prove the accuracy of his publication. Three judges presided at the trial. Judge Nathaniel Sergeant stressed the unlawfulness of words tending to breach the public peace. Judge Increase Sumner offered the jury his opinion that truth was no defense and that the guarantee of a free press notwithstanding, licentiousness, falsehood, and verbal injury to the public were answerable to the law. Chief Justice Francis Dana, and Judge Sumner too, charged the jury in full accordance with prosecutor Sullivan's argument on the definition of liberty of the press, although Dana apprised the jury of the fact that he sympathized with truth as a defense even as he noted that he reserved a ruling on the question.[129] The jury's verdict was not guilty, but as the historian

[128] Stephen T. Riley, "Dr. William Whiting and Shay's Rebellion," *Proceedings of American Antiquarian Society* 66 (1956):119-31, pp. 131-66 include Whiting's essay and letters.

[129] The case is reported in the Boston *Independent Chronicle*. The indictment, the allegedly libelous publication, and Sullivan's introductory address are reprinted in the issue of Feb. 24, 1791. The arguments of defense counsel

of *The Development of Freedom of the Press in Massachusetts* concluded: "a judicial construction of liberty of the press in the state had
been announced, differing in no wise from the opinions of Chief Justice Hutchinson in 1768 or of the Superior Court of Judicature in
1724. In effect it was affirmed that the constitutional provision of
1780 was merely declaratory of the law as it had existed for nearly
sixty years, with an added prohibition of any possible reestablishment
of censorship."[130]

This observation has the substantiation of the indictments for seditious libel against Thomas Adams, editor of the Boston *Independent
Chronicle,* and his brother Abijah, the paper's clerk and bookkeeper.
Thomas already had the honor of being the first important editor indicted by the United States under the Sedition Act. Released on bail,
pending trial, he continued his candid blasts against the Adams administration and the Sedition Act itself.[131] In February of 1799 he
added a new target, the Massachusetts legislature. The legislature, in
repudiating the Virginia Resolutions that condemned the Sedition
Act, had declared that seditiousness of speech and press was punishable on the principles of the common law; moreover, that the state
and federal constitutional protections to freedom of expression had
"generally but one construction": the right to "utter and publish the
truth" by a "rational use and not the abuse" of liberty.[132] Abijah Adams, managing the *Chronicle* during the illness of brother Thomas,
publicly demanded that some Federalist explain how the members of
the state legislature could be faithful to their oaths to support the sovereignty of the Commonwealth if they had rejected the resolutions
of Virginia that claimed a state's right to decide on the constitutionality of the Sedition Act.[133] The government regarded this remark as
a charge that the state legislators had willfully perjured themselves in
taking their oaths of office. A grand jury, at the request of the majority of the legislators, then indicted the Adams brothers at common
law for seditiously libeling the General Court.

---

appear in the issues of March 3 and 10; the trial testimony is not reproduced.
Sullivan's closing is in the issue of March 17 with Sumner's charge. Dana's
charge appears in the issue of March 24 as does Sargeant's.

[130] Duniway, *Freedom of the Press,* 143.

[131] See Smith, *Freedom's Fetters,* 247-253, for a discussion of the background
of the indictment against Thomas Adams under the Sedition Act.

[132] "Answers of the Several State Legislatures . . . Massachusetts," in Jonathan Elliot, ed., *The Debates in the Several State Conventions . . . and Other
Illustrations of the Constitution* (Philadelphia, 1941, 2nd ed., rev.), 4:535, 536.

[133] *Independent Chronicle* (Boston), Feb. 14–Feb. 18, 1799.

The illness of Thomas Adams allowed only Abijah to be tried. George Blake, who became a United States attorney under Jefferson, represented Adams. Blake argued that no indictment could be maintained for a libel against Massachusetts. The law of seditious libel, he contended, not being suited to "the spirit and genius of a Republican Government" founded by consent of the governed, must have been superseded as repugnant to the protection afforded to freedom of the press.[134] Acceptance of the Blackstonian definition would make that protection merely "nominal . . . vague, empty, and delusive," because it would lead the unwary citizen into a wide field of political disquisition only to "abandon him to infamy and destruction." If Adams could be convicted for his remark, then any offensive publication would be punishable in the same manner and degree as if no guarantee of liberty of the press existed, rendering the constitutional clause merely declaratory of the common law. That clause, insisted Blake, existed to render immunity to the strongest censure of the government. A degree of licentiousness, he concluded, was inseparable from genuine freedom of the press, "and the nicest operation of *mental chemistry* could not dissipate the one, without losing in the process some valuable portion of the other."[135]

Blake admitted, however, that the guarantee of a free press did not immunize "wanton, flagrant abuses of the press." No part of his argument, he declared, meant "to show that propriety of an illimited, unqualified indulgence of the rights of speaking, writing, or acting," because the law must protect people's reputations. "No *wanton, malicious* invective" against anyone "can or ought to be suffered to pass with impunity." He approved of indictments for criminal libel, as well as private damage suits, to punish gross calumnies. Without doubt and without exceptions Blake rejected seditious libel for the right reasons, which he elaborated, but he did not reject the remainder of the common law of criminal libel.[136]

Attorney-General Sullivan, with whom Blake had studied law, set his former pupil right on the subject of seditious libel and liberty of the press, arguing that the latter did not imply freedom for the former. Relying on Blackstone, Sullivan advanced the usual argument that the clause on freedom of the press merely declared the common law. He apparently regarded this view as not inconsistent with per-

[134] *Ibid.* The report of Blake's argument, which has been ascribed to Blake himself, continues through the issue of April 29–May 2.
[135] *Ibid.*, 11-15.
[136] *Ibid.* for "wanton, flagrant," and April 15-18, 1799, for the remainder.

mitting truth as a defense, a small advantage enjoyed by the defendant with the court's consent.[137] Chief Justice Dana of the Supreme Judicial Court, in charging the jury, began with the glorious birthright of every American, endorsed Sullivan's argument without reservation, and concluded: "however censurable the libel might be in itself, it could not be more dangerous to the public tranquility, than the propagation of principles which were advanced by the *counsel* in the defense, and through the channel of the same press, as well as before as since the indictment was founded."[138] The records of the court show the following verdict of the jury: "The jury find that the Paper described in the Indictment is a Libel, they do not find the said Abijah guilty of printing, but they find him guilty of publishing the same in manner and form as set forth in the Indictment."[139] Abijah was sentenced to a month in jail, was forced to pay the costs of prosecution, and had to post a bond for subsequent good behavior. In 1802 another publisher, J. S. Lillie, was convicted and sentenced to three months for a libel on Chief Justice Dana.[140]

Unfortunately historians have so neglected the subject of criminal law and freedom of speech-and-press that Duniway's study of Massachusetts is the only work of its kind, leaving us with no systematic body of knowledge about trials in other states. But the Pennsylvania evidence which has been reviewed above proves that Massachusetts is not the only state whose history between 1776 and 1800 gives reason to be skeptical about unsubstantiated declarations that the English law of sedition "was repudiated by every American." The realistic issue is whether any Americans repudiated the common-law doctrine that words alone can criminally assault the government, or whether

[137] My statement summarizing Sullivan's argument is based on Blake's references to it. The *Independent Chronicle* did not report the prosecutor's argument separately. On the permission to Blake to argue truth as a defense, see the *Chronicle* for April 29-May 2. One of the few errors in Duniway's study, *The Development of Freedom of the Press in Massachusetts*, is his implication at p. 146 that the first trial at which truth was permitted as a defense in that state occurred in 1803.

[138] The *Independent Chronicle* did not report Dana's charge to the Jury except for snatches that were interspersed between and in the report of Blake's argument. The lines quoted from Dana appeared in the issue of April 25-29.

[139] The *Chronicle* reported the verdict as "guilty of publishing only," issue of March 4-7, but noted in the issue of March 7-11 that it had been criticized for its report of the verdict, yet stuck to its original statement. I have replied upon Duniway, *Freedom of the Press*, 145, for a statement of the verdict as quoted from the manuscript records of the court, citing Records of the Supreme Judicial Court, February, 1798-August, 1799, pp. 183-186, and *Suffolk Court Files*, No. 108191 (1).

[140] Duniway, *Freedom of the Press*, 146.

any, in a more general sense, repudiated any class of criminal libel. One was the unnamed lawyer who misinformed the pseudonymous "Centinel" in the *Massachusetts Spy* in 1771. The contributors to Oswald's newspaper in 1782, especially "Junius Wilkes" and "Candid" belong on the same list. Oswald himself in 1788 asserted that the doctrine of libels conflicted with liberty. The name of George Blake ends the list. That America produced a few libertarians who went beyond Zengerian principles seems clear, but very few. Equally clear are the more significant facts that no American jurisdiction repudiated the common law doctrine and that most Americans, to the extent that we can tell, accepted it.

CHAPTER VIII

From the First Amendment to the Sedition Act

Did the Framers of the First Amendment intend "to wipe out the common law of sedition, and make further prosecutions for criticism of the government, without any incitement to law-breaking, forever impossible in the United States of America"?[1] The immediate history of the drafting and adoption of the First Amendment's freedom of speech and press clause does not suggest an intent to institute broad reform.

That history is inextricably bound to the history of the framing and ratification of the Bill of Rights, without which the First Amendment would not exist. The omission of a bill of rights was a deliberate act of the Constitutional Convention. The Convention had almost completed its work when it received from the Committee on Style copies of the proposed Constitution and the letter by which the Convention would submit it to Congress. The major task that remained was to adopt, engross, and sign the finished document. The weary delegates, after a hot summer's work in Philadelphia, eagerly wanted to return home. At that point, on September 12, 1787, George Mason of Virginia remarked that he "wished the plan had been prefaced by a Bill of Rights," because it would "give great quiet" to the people. Mason thought that with the aid of state bills of rights as models, "a bill might be prepared in a few hours." He made no stirring speech for civil liberties in general or any rights in particular. He did not even argue the need for a bill of rights or move the adoption of one, although he offered to second a motion if one were made. Elbridge

[1] Zechariah Chafee, Jr., *Free Speech in the United States* (Cambridge, 1948), 21.

Gerry of Massachusetts then moved for a committee to prepare a bill of rights, and Mason seconded the motion. Roger Sherman of Connecticut observed that the rights of the people should be secured if necessary, but because the Constitution did not repeal the states' bills of rights, the Convention need not do anything. Without further debate the delegates, voting by states, defeated the motion 10-0.[2] Two days later, after the states unanimously defeated a motion by Mason to delete from the Constitution a ban on *ex post facto* laws by Congress, Charles Pinckney of South Carolina, seconded by Gerry, moved to insert a declaration "that the liberty of the Press should be inviolably observed." Sherman laconically replied, "It is unnecessary. The power of Congress does not extend to the Press," and the motion lost 7-4. Three days later the Convention adjourned.[3]

In the Congress of the Confederation, Richard Henry Lee of Virginia moved that a bill of rights, which he had adapted from his own state's constitution, be added to the Constitution. Lee was less interested in the adoption of a bill of rights than in defeating the Constitution. Amendments recommended by Congress required ratification by all the state legislatures, not just nine state ratifying conventions. Congress defeated Lee's motion,[4] but the motion showed that, from the start of the ratification controversy, the omission of a bill of rights became an Anti-Federalist mace with which to smash the Constitution. Its opponents sought to prevent ratification and exaggerated the bill of rights issue because it was one with which they could enlist public support. Their prime loyalty belonged to states' rights, not civil rights.

Mason, the author of the celebrated Virginia Declaration of Rights of 1776, soon wrote his influential "Objections to the Constitution," which began, "There is no Declaration of Rights." The sincerity of Mason's desire for a bill of rights is beyond question, but he had many other reasons for opposing the Constitution. Almost two weeks before he raised the issue of a bill of rights on September 12, he had declared "that he would sooner chop off his right hand than put it to the Constitution as it now stands." A bill of rights might protect individuals against the national government, but it would not protect the states. He believed that the new government would diminish state powers and by the exercise of its commerce power could "ruin" the

---

[2] Max Farrand, ed., *The Records of the Federal Convention* (New Haven, 1911, 3 vols), 2:587-88.
[3] *Ibid.*, 2:617.
[4] For Lee's proposals and Madison's opposition, see Merrill Jensen, ed., *The Documentary History of the Ratification of the Constitution* (Madison, 1976), 1:337-39, 343-44.

Southern states; the control of commerce by a mere majority vote of Congress was, to Mason, "an insuperable objection."[5] But the lack of a bill of rights proved to be the most powerful argument against ratification of the Constitution in the Anti-Federalist armory.

Why did the Constitutional Convention omit a bill of rights? No delegate opposed one in principle. As George Washington informed Lafayette, "there was not a member of the Convention, I believe, who had the least objection to what is contended for by the advocates for a Bill of Rights." All the Framers were civil libertarians as well as experienced politicians who had the confidence of their constituents and the state legislatures that elected them. Even the foremost opponents of ratification praised the make-up of the Convention. How could such an "assembly of demigods," as Jefferson called them, neglect the liberties of the people?[6]

On July 26 the Convention had adjourned until August 6 to permit a Committee of Detail to frame a "constitution conformable to the Resolutions passed by the Convention." The committee, consisting of six men including Edmund Randolph of Virginia, James Wilson of Pennsylvania, and Oliver Ellsworth of Connecticut, generously construed its charge by acting as a miniature convention. Introducing a number of significant changes, such as the explicit enumeration of the powers of Congress, the committee, without recommendations from the Convention, decided on a preamble. Randolph left a fragmentary record of the committee's decision that the preamble did not seem a proper place for a philosophic statement of the ends of government because "we are not working on the natural rights of men not yet gathered into society" but upon rights "modified by society and interwoven with what we call . . . the rights of states."[7] According to American revolutionary theory, the natural rights to which Randolph referred were possessed by individuals in the state of nature, which existed before they voluntarily contracted with each other to establish a government in order to secure their rights. In the state of nature, when only the law of nature governed, the theory posited that—as the first section of the Virginia Declaration of Rights stated—"all men are by nature equally free and independent, and have certain inherent rights, of which, when they enter into a state of so-

[5] Farrand, ed., *Records* 2:479 for the statement of Aug. 31, 1787, and 2:640 for "insuperable objection."

[6] Charles Warren, *The Making of the Constitution* (Boston, 1928), 508 (Washington), 67-8 (praising makeup); Jefferson to J. Adams, Aug. 30, 1787, in Lester Cappon, ed., *The Adams-Jefferson Letters* (Chapel Hill, 1959, 2 vols.) 1:196.

[7] Farrand, ed., *Records*, 2:137.

ciety, they cannot, by any compact, deprive or divest their posterity; namely, the enjoyment of life and liberty, with the means of acquiring and possessing property, and pursuing and obtaining happiness and safety."[8] The adoption of the state constitutions having ended the state of nature, there was no need to enumerate the rights reserved to the people—or so the Framers of the Constitution reasoned.

On the other hand they recognized that the existence of organized society and government required the affirmation of certain rights that did not exist in the state of nature but that served to protect natural rights. Trial by jury, for example, was unknown in the state of nature but necessary for the protection of one's life, liberty, and property. Accordingly the Framers recognized a class of rights "modified by society," just as they recognized that the legitimate powers of government that did not belong to the central government of the Union could be called "the rights of the states."

The Committee of Detail recommended some rights ("modified by society"), among them trial by jury in criminal cases, a tight definition of treason to prevent improper convictions, a ban on titles of nobility (a way of guaranteeing against a privileged class), freedom of speech and debate for members of the legislature, and a guarantee that the citizens of each state should have the same privileges and immunities of citizens in other states. In addition the committee introduced the clause guaranteeing to each state a republican form of government. In the minds of the Framers, many provisions of the Constitution had a libertarian character—the election of public officials, the representative system, the separation of powers among three branches of government, and the requirement that revenue and appropriation measures originate in the House of Representatives—a protection of the natural right to property and a bar against taxation without representation. During the controversy over the ratification of the Constitution, when the omission of a bill of rights was the major issue, many Framers argued, as did Hamilton in *The Federalist* #84, "that the Constitution is itself, in every rational sense, and to every useful purpose, a Bill of Rights."[9]

All the rights recommended by the Committee of Detail eventually found their way into the Constitution, but Charles Pinckney believed that the committee had neglected several others that also deserved constitutional recognition. On August 20 he recommended

---

[8] Virginia Declaration of Rights, in Francis Newton Thorpe, ed., *The Federal and State Constitutions, Colonial Charters, and Other Organic Laws* (Washington: Government Printing Office, 1909), 7:3813.

[9] Farrand, ed., *Records*, 2:177-89.

"sundry propositions," including a guarantee of the writ of *habeas corpus*, which protected citizens from arbitrary arrest; an injunction that the liberty of the press should be "inviolably preserved"; a ban on maintaining an army in time of peace except with the consent of Congress; an explicit subordination of the military to the civil power; a prohibition on the quartering of troops in private homes during peacetime; and a ban on religious tests as a qualification for any United States office.[10]

None of these provisions secured what theoreticians regarded as natural rights. The freedoms of speech and conscience were natural rights, but the liberty of the press was probably distinguishable as a right that did not exist in the state of nature. If liberty of the press was a natural right the Convention acted consistently when voting that its protection was unnecessary. Similarly the ban on religious tests, though protecting the right of conscience, constituted another example of what Randolph had called a right "modified by society," not preexisting it. Significantly Pinckney had not recommended a protection of freedom of religion or of speech. Without debate or consideration the Convention referred his proposals to the Committee of Detail, but it made no recommendations on any of them.

On the floor of the Convention Gerry moved that Congress should be denied the power to pass bills of attainder and *ex post facto* laws. The motion passed with hardly any discussion. Bills of attainder and *ex post facto* laws, being legislative enactments, came into existence after the people had compacted to form a government. Banning such enactments, therefore, constituted means for the protection of natural rights, but the bans did not protect natural rights as such. The same may be said of protecting the cherished writ of *habeas corpus* as a device for insuring the personal liberty of an individual wrongfully imprisoned. After the Convention unanimously adopted the Committee of Detail's recommendation for a clause on trial by jury in criminal cases, Pinckney urged the Convention to secure the benefit of the writ as well, and by a vote of 7-3 a *habeas corpus* clause was adopted. Pinckney also moved a prohibition on religious tests, which the Convention summarily adopted by unanimous vote.[11]

Thus, all the protections written into the Constitution were means of vindicating natural rights but no natural rights were constitutionally protected. The overwhelming majority of the Convention believed, as Sherman succinctly declared, "It is unnecessary." Why was it unnecessary given the fact that the Convention recommended a

[10] *Ibid.*, 2:340-42.
[11] *Ibid.*, 2:375-76, 438.

new and powerful national government that could operate directly
on individuals? The Framers believed that the national government
could exercise only enumerated powers or powers necessary to carry
out those enumerated, and no provision of the Constitution authorized the government to act on any natural rights. A bill of rights
would restrict national powers, but, Hamilton declared, such a bill
would be "dangerous" as well as unnecessary, because it "would contain various exceptions to powers not granted; and, on this very account, would afford a colorable pretext to claim more than were
granted. For why declare that things shall not be done which there
is no power to do? Why, for instance, should it be said that the liberty of the press shall not be restrained, when no power is given by
which restrictions may be imposed?"[12]

Hamilton expressed a standard Federalist position, echoing other
Framers and advocates of ratification. Excluding a bill of rights from
the Constitution was fundamental to the constitutional theory of the
Framers. James Wilson, whose influence at the Convention had been
second only to that of Madison, led the ratificationist forces in Pennsylvania and several times sought to explain the omission of a bill of
rights. The people of the states, he declared, had vested in their governments all powers and rights "which they did not in explicit terms
reserve," but the case was different as to a federal government whose
authority rested on positive grants of power expressed in the Constitution. For the federal government, "the reverse of the proposition
prevails, and everything which is not given, is reserved" to the people
or the states. That distinction, Wilson argued, answered those who
believed that the omission of a bill of rights was a defect. Its inclusion
would have been "absurd," because a bill of rights stipulated the reserved rights of the people, whereas the function of the Constitution
was to provide for the existence of the federal government rather
than enumerate rights not divested. Like Hamilton and other Federalists, Wilson believed that a formal declaration on freedom of the
press or religion, over which Congress had no powers whatsoever,
could "imply" that some degree of power had been granted because
of the attempt to define its extent. Wilson also insisted on the impossibility of enumerating and reserving all the rights of the people. "A
bill of rights annexed to a constitution," he added, "is an enumeration
of the powers reserved. If we attempt an enumeration, everything
that is not enumerated is presumed to be given. The consequence is,
that an imperfect enumeration would throw all implied powers into

[12] *The Federalist* No. 84, Modern Library Edition, 559.

the scale of the government; and the rights of the people would be rendered incomplete."[13]

Civil liberties, the supporters of the Constitution believed, faced real dangers from the possibility of repressive state action, but that was a matter to be guarded against by state bills of rights. They also argued, inconsistently, that some states had no bills of rights but were as free as those with bills of rights. They were as free because personal liberty, to Federalist theoreticians, depended not on "parchment provisions," which Hamilton called inadequate in "a struggle with public necessity," but on public opinion, an extended republic, a pluralistic society of competing interests, and a free and limited government structured to prevent any interest from becoming an overbearing majority.[14]

The fact that six states had no bills of rights and that none had a comprehensive list of guarantees provided the supporters of ratification with the argument, made by Wilson among others, that an imperfect bill of rights was worse than none at all because the omission of some rights might justify their infringement by implying an unintended grant of government power. The record was not reassuring; the states had very imperfect bills of rights, which proved to be ineffective when confronted by "public necessity," and the state governments did in fact abridge rights that had not been explicitly reserved.

Virginia's Declaration of Rights, for example, did not ban bills of attainder. In 1778 the Virginia assembly adopted a bill of attainder and outlawry, drafted by Jefferson at the instigation of Governor Patrick Henry, against a reputed cutthroat Tory named Josiah Philips, and some fifty unnamed "associates." By legislative enactment they were condemned for treason and murder, and on failure to surrender were subject to being killed by anyone. At the Virginia ratifying convention, Edmund Randolph, irked beyond endurance by Henry's assaults on the Constitution as dangerous to personal liberties, recalled with "horror" the "shocking" attainder. When Henry defended the attainder, John Marshall, who supported ratification without a bill of rights, declared, "Can we pretend to the enjoyment of political freedom or security, when we are told that a man has been, by an act of Assembly, struck out of existence without a trial by jury, without examination, without being confronted with his accusers and witnesses, without the benefits of the law of the land?"[15]

---

[13] Merrill Jensen, ed., *The Documentary History of the Ratification of the Constitution, Vol. II, Ratification of the Constitution by the States. Pennsylvania* (Madison, 1976-   ), 387-90.

[14] *Federalist* No. 84.

[15] On the Philips attainder, see Leonard W. Levy, *Jefferson and Civil Liberties: The Darker Side* (Cambridge, Mass., 1963), 33-41.

The Framers of the Constitution tended to be skeptical about the value of "parchment barriers" against "overbearing majorities," as Madison said. He had seen repeated violations of bills of rights in every state. Experience proved the "inefficacy of a bill of rights to those occasions when its control is most needed," he said.[16] In Virginia, for example, despite an explicit protection of the rights of conscience, the legislature had favored an establishment of religion, which was averted only because Madison turned the tide of opinion against the bill.[17] As realists the Framers believed that constitutional protections of rights meant little during times of popular hysteria; any member of the Constitutional Convention could have cited examples of gross abridgments of civil liberties in states that had bills of rights.

Virginia's bill was imperfect not just because it lacked a ban on bills of attainder. The much-vaunted Declaration of Rights of Virginia also omitted the freedoms of speech, assembly, and petition; the right to the writ of *habeas corpus;* the right to grand jury proceedings; the right to counsel; separation of church and state; and freedom from double jeopardy and from *ex post facto* laws. The rights omitted were as numerous and important as those included. Twelve states, including Vermont, had framed constitutions, and the only right secured by all was trial by jury in criminal cases. Although all protected religious liberty as well, five either permitted or provided for establishments of religion. Two states passed over a free press guarantee. Four neglected to ban excessive fines, excessive bail, compulsory self-incrimination, and general search warrants. Five ignored protections for the rights of assembly, petition, counsel, and trial by jury in civil cases. Seven omitted a prohibition of *ex post facto* laws. Nine failed to provide for grand jury proceedings, and nine failed to condemn bills of attainder. Ten said nothing about freedom of speech, while eleven were silent on double jeopardy. Whether omissions implied a power to violate, omissions seemed, in Federalist minds, to raise dangers that could be prevented by avoiding an unnecessary problem entirely: omit a bill of rights when forming a federal government of limited powers.

That the Framers of the Constitution actually believed their own arguments purporting to justify the omission of a bill of rights is difficult to credit. Some of the points they made were patently absurd, like the insistence that the inclusion of a bill or rights would be dan-

---

[16] Madison to Jefferson, Oct. 17, 1788, in *The Papers of James Madison*, ed., Robert A. Rutland (Charlottesville, 1977), 11: 297-98. For illustrations of a similar sentiment expressed only by Virginians, see Elliot, ed., *Debates*, 3:70 (Randolph), 298 (Pendleton), and 561 (Marshall).

[17] Anson Phelps Stokes, *Church and State in the United States* (New York, 1951, 3 vols.), 1:356-97.

gerous and, on historical grounds, unsuitable. The last point most commonly turned up in the claim that bills of rights were appropriate in England but not in America. Magna Carta, the Petition of Right of 1628, and the Bill of Rights of 1689 had been grants wrested from kings to secure royal assent to certain liberties, and therefore had "no application to constitutions . . . founded upon the power of the people" who surrendered nothing and retained everything. That argument, made in *Federalist* #84 and by leading ratificationists as sophisticated as Wilson and Oliver Ellsworth of Connecticut, was so porous that it could persuade no one. Excepting Rhode Island and Connecticut, the two corporate colonies that retained their charters (with all royal references deleted), eleven states had framed written constitutions during the Revolution, and seven drew up bills of rights; even the four without such bills inserted in their constitutions provisions normally found in a bill of rights.

To imply that bills of rights were un-American or unnecessary merely because in America power derived from the people denied history. Over a period of a century and a half America had become accustomed to the idea that government existed by consent of the governed, that people created government, that they did it by written compact, that the compact constituted fundamenal law, that the government must be subject to such limitations that are necessary for the security of the rights of the people and, usually, that the reserved rights of the people were enumerated in bills of rights. Counting Vermont (an independent republic from 1777 until its admission to the Union in 1791), eight states had bills of rights—notwithstanding any opinion that such bills properly belonged only in a compact between a king and his subjects. The dominant theory in the United States from the time of the Revolution held that the fundamental law limited all branches of the government, not just the Crown as in England, where the great liberty documents did not limit the legislative power.

When Randolph for the Committee of Detail alluded to the fact that "we are not working on the natural rights of men not yet gathered into society," he referred to the framing of the state constitutions. The constitution of Wilson's state began with an elaborate preamble whose first words established the proposition that "all government ought to be instituted . . . to enable the individuals who compose [the commonwealth] to enjoy their natural rights . . .", and whose preamble was followed by as comprehensive a "Declaration of the Rights of the Inhabitants" as existed in any state. Yet Wilson repeatedly informed Pennsylvania's ratifying convention that rights and liberties could be claimed only in a contract between king and subjects, not when "the fee simple of freedom and government is declared to be in the people."[18] Governor Randolph at the Virginia ratifying convention merely exaggerated when claiming that the Virginia Declaration of Rights "has never secured us against any danger; it has been repeatedly disregarded and violated." But Randolph's rhetoric became unpardonable when he declared that although a bill of rights to limit the king's prerogative made sense in England, "Our situation is radically different from that of the people of England. What have we to do with bills of rights? . . . A bill of rights, therefore, accurately speaking, is quite useless, if not dangerous to a republic."[19] At the Constitutional Convention, however, Randolph had been able to distinguish natural rights from some rights modified by society.

That supporters of the Constitution could ask, "What have we to do with a bill of rights?" suggests a colossal error of judgment, which they compounded by refusing to admit it. Their single-minded purpose of creating an effective national government had exhausted their energies and good sense, and when they found themselves on the defensive, accused of threatening the liberties of the people, their frayed nerves led them into indefensible positions. Any Anti-Federalist could have answered Randolph's question, Wilson's speeches, or Hamilton's #84, and many did so capably without resorting to Patrick Henry's grating hysteria. "Centinel," who answered Wilson in a Philadelphia newspaper, declared that the explanation for the omission of a bill of rights "is an insult on the understanding of the people."[20]

Two wise Americans serving their country abroad in diplomatic missions, coolly appraised the proposed Constitution without the obligation of having to support a party line. John Adams, having received a copy of the document in London, wrote a short letter to Jefferson in Paris. The Constitution seemed "admirably calculated to preserve the Union," Adams thought, and he hoped it would be ratified with amendments adopted later. "What think you," he asked, "of a Declaration of Rights? Should not such a Thing have preceded the Model?"[21] Jefferson, in his first letter to Madison on the subject of the Constitution, began with praise but ended with what he did not

---

[18] Jensen, ed., *Documentary History*, 2:383.

[19] Jonathan Elliot, ed., *The Debates in the Several State Conventions on the Adoption of the Federal Constitution . . . and Other Illustrations of the Constitution* (Philadelphia, 1941, 2nd ed., rev.), 3:191.

[20] Herbert J. Storing, ed., *The Complete Anti-Federalist* (Chicago, 1981, 7 vols.), 2:144.

[21] To Jefferson, Nov. 10, 1787, in Cappon, ed., *Adams-Jefferson Letters*, 1: 210.

like: "First the omission of a bill of rights. . . ." After listing rights he thought deserved special protection, starting with freedom of religion and of the press, Jefferson dismissed as campaign rhetoric Wilson's justification for the omission of a bill of rights and concluded: "Let me add that a bill of rights is what the people are entitled to against every government on earth, general or particular, and what no just government should refuse, or rest on inference."[22]

Adams and Jefferson in Europe were much closer to popular opinion than the Framers of the Constitution who had worked secretly for almost four months and, with their supporters, became locked into a position that defied logic and experience. During the ratification controversy, some Federalists argued that the Constitution protected basic rights, exposing them to the reply that they had omitted the liberty of the press, religious freedom, security against general warrants, trial by jury in civil cases, and other basic rights. If the Framers intended to protect only the rights arising from the existence of society and government and unknown in a state of nature, they were inconsistent. They protected only some of the non-natural rights; the first ten amendments are crowded with such rights which the Framers neglected.

Natural rights, in accordance with American theory and experience, required protection in any government made by compact. At the Convention Madison declared that the delegates had assembled to frame "a compact by which an authority was created paramount to the parties, and making laws for the government of them."[23] Some of the states, when formally ratifying the Constitution, considered themselves to be "entering into an explicit and solemn compact," as Massachusetts declared.[24] During the ratification controversy, publicists on both sides referred to the Constitution as a compact. Chief Justice John Jay, who had been one of the authors of *The Federalist,* observed in *Chisholm* v. *Georgia* (1793) that "the Constitution of the United States is . . . a compact made by the people of the United States in order to govern themselves."[25]

The new compact created a government whose powers seemed intimidating. Article VI, declaring the Constitution, laws made in its pursuance, and treaties of the United States to be the supreme law of the land, anything in the state constitutions to the contrary notwith-

[22] To Madison, Dec. 20, 1787, in *The Papers of Thomas Jefferson,* ed. Julian P. Boyd, et al. (Princeton, 1950), 12:339-42.
[23] Farrand, ed., *Records,* 1:446.
[24] Massachusetts Constitution of 1780, Preamble, in Thorpe, ed., *Constitutions,* 3:1889.
[25] Dallas 419, 471.

standing, seemed to many Anti-Federalists as superseding their state bills of rights and authorizing laws "repugnant to every article of your rights," as "The Impartial Examiner" wrote.[26] Most believed that enumerated powers could be abused at the expense of fundamental liberties. Congress's power to tax for example, might be aimed at the press and was thus, in the words of Richard Henry Lee, "a power to destroy or restrain the freedom of it."[27] Others feared that taxes might be exacted from the people for the support of a religious denomination. Tax collectors, unrestrained by a ban on general warrants, Patrick Henry argued, might invade homes "and search, ransack, and measure, every thing you eat, drink, and wear."[28]

The necessary-and-proper clause, a formidable grant of implied powers, particularly enraged advocates of a bill of rights. They saw that clause as the source of undefined and unlimited powers to aggrandize the national government and victimize the people, unless, as "An Old Whig" declared, "we had a bill of rights to which we might appeal."[29] "A Democratic Federalist" wrote: "I lay it down as a general rule that wherever the powers of government extend to the lives, the persons, and properties of the subject, all their rights ought to be clearly and expressly defined, otherwise they have but a poor security for their liberties."[30] Henry warned that Congress might "extort a confession by the use of torture" in order to convict a violator of federal law.[31] Numerous opponents of ratification contended that Congress could define as crimes the violation of any laws it might legitimately enact, and lacking a bill of rights, accused persons might be deprived of the rights to counsel, to indictment, to cross-examine witnesses against them, to produce evidence in their own behalf, to be free from compulsory self-incrimination, to be protected against double jeopardy or excessive bail, to be exempt from excessive fines or cruel and unusual punishments, and to enjoy other rights traditionally belonging to accused persons. Such an argument was invariably advanced as one among many refuting the Federalist claim that a bill of rights was unnecessary.

If it was unnecessary, Anti-Federalists asked, why did the Constitution protect some rights? The protection of some opened the Federalists to devastating rebuttal. They claimed that because no bill of rights could be complete, the omission of any particular right might

26 Storing, ed., *Complete Anti-Federalist,* 5:185.
27 *Ibid.,* 2:330.
28 Elliot, ed., *Debates,* 3:448-92.
29 Storing, ed., *Complete Anti-Federalist,* 3:37.
30 *Ibid.,* 3:59.
31 Elliot, ed., *Debates,* 3:448.

imply a power to abridge it as unworthy of respect by the government. That argument, in effect that to include some would exclude all others, boomeranged. The protection of trial by jury in criminal cases, the bans on religious tests, *ex post facto* laws, and bills of attainder, the narrow definition of treason, and the provision for the writ of *habeas corpus*, by the Federalists' own reasoning, destroyed their argument. Robert Whitehall, answering Wilson on the floor of the Pennsylvania ratifying convention, noted that the writ of *habeas corpus* and trial by jury had been expressly reserved and in vain called on Wilson to reconcile the reservation with his "favorite proposition." "For, if there was danger in the attempt to enumerate the liberties of the people," Whitehall explained, "lest it should prove imperfect and defective, how happens it, that in the instances I have mentioned, that danger has been incurred? Have the people no other rights worth their attention, or is it to be inferred, agreeable to the maxim of our opponents, that every other right is abandoned?" Stipulating a right, he concluded, destroyed the "argument of danger."[32] Surely, Anti-Federalists said, their opponents might think of some rights in addition to those protected. The ban on religious tests could have reminded them of freedom of religion. Did not its omission, by their reasoning, necessarily mean that the government could attack freedom of religion?

Henry cleverly observed that the "fair implication" of the Federalist argument against a bill of rights meant that the government could do anything not forbidden by the Constitution. Because the provision on the writ of *habeas corpus* allowed its suspension when the public safety required, Henry reasoned, "It results clearly that, if it had not said so, they could suspend it in all cases whatsoever. It reverses the position of the friends of this Constitution, that every thing is retained which is not given up; for, instead of this, every thing is given up which is not expressly reserved."[33] In his influential *Letters of a Federal Farmer*, Lee observed that a clause of the Constitution prohibited Congress from granting titles of nobility. If the clause had been omitted, he wondered whether Congress would have the power to grant such titles and concluded that it would not under any provision of the Constitution. "Why then by a negative clause, restrain congress from doing what it had no power to do? This clause, then, must have no meaning, or imply, that were it omitted, congress would have the power in question . . . on the principle that congress possess the powers not expressly reserved." Lee objected to leaving the rights of the people to "logical inferences," because Federalist principles led to the implication that all the rights not mentioned in the Constitution were intended to be relinquished.[34]

Far from being dangerous, a bill of rights, as "A Federal Republican" stated in answer to Wilson, "could do no harm, but might do much good."[35] Lee, discoursing on the good it might do, observed that having a bill of rights assisted popular "education," because it taught "truths" upon which freedom depends and which the people must believe as "sacred."[36] James Winthrop of Massachusetts, writing as "Agrippa," explained another positive value of a bill of rights. It "serves to secure the minority against the usurpations and tyranny of the majority." History, he wrote, proved the "prevalence of a disposition to use power wantonly. It [a bill of rights] is therefore as necessary to defend an individual against the minority in a republick as against the king in a monarchy."[37]

In sum, the usually masterful politicians who had dominated the Convention had blundered by botching constitutional theory and making a serious political error. Their arguments justifying the omission of a bill of rights were impolitic and unconvincing. Mason's point that a bill of rights would quiet the fears of the people was unanswerable. To have alienated him and the many who agreed with him constituted bad politics and handed to the opposition a stirring cause around which they could muster sentiment against ratification. The single issue that united Anti-Federalists throughout the country was the lack of a bill of rights. No rational argument—and the lack of a bill of rights created an intensely emotional issue because people believed that their liberties were at stake—could possibly allay the fears generated by demagogues like Henry and principled opponents of ratification like Mason. Washington believed that even Mason's "Objections" were meant "to alarm the people."[38] And, when Anti-Federalists in New York demanded a bill of rights, Hamilton alleged, "It is the plan of men of this stamp to frighten the people with ideal bugbears, in order to mould them to their own purposes. The unceasing cry of these designing croakers is, My friends, your liberty is invaded!"[39] The Anti-Federalists capitalized on the Federalist blunder, hoping to defeat the Constitution or get a second convention that would revise it in order to hamstring the national government.

In Pennsylvania, the second state to ratify, the minority demanded

[34] Storing, ed., *Complete Anti-Federalist*, 2:326.
[35] *Ibid.*, 3:86.
[36] *Ibid.*, 2:324-25.
[37] *Ibid.*, 4:111.
[38] To Madison, Oct. 10, 1787, quoted in Robert Allen Rutland, *The Birth of the Bill of Rights, 1776-1791* (Chapel Hill, 1955), 122-23.
[39] Hamilton's "Caesar" letters, October 1788, in Ford, ed., *Essays*, 289.

a comprehensive bill of rights similar to that in their state constitution. Massachusetts, the sixth state to ratify, was the first to do so with recommended amendments. Only two of the recommended amendments, dealing with jury trial in civil suits and grand jury indictment, belonged in a bill of rights. Supporters of the Constitution in Massachusetts had withdrawn a proposed bill of rights on the supposition that Anti-Federalists would use it as proof that the Constitution endangered liberty. Maryland too would have recommended a bill of rights, but the Federalist majority jettisoned it when the Anti-Federalists tried to insert curbs on national powers to tax and regulate commerce. Nevertheless, Federalists grudgingly accepted ratification with recommended amendments to ward off conditional ratification or the defeat of the Constitution. New Hampshire, whose approval as the ninth state made ratification an accomplished fact, urged amendments constituting a comprehensive bill of rights to be adopted after the new government went into operation. Virginia and New York, whose ratification was politically indispensable, followed suit. North Carolina was the fourth state to ratify with a model bill of rights among its recommendations. But the same states also recommended crippling restrictions on delegated powers.

Thus, the Constitution was ratified only because crucial states, where ratification had been in doubt, were willing to accept the promise of a bill of rights in the form of subsequent amendments to the Constitution. State recommendations for amendments, including those of the Pennsylvania minority, received nationwide publicity, adding to the clamor for a bill of rights.

From late 1787 through the following year the proposed Constitution had engrossed the political attention of the country. Excepting the generalized reluctance to yield too much state sovereignty, the failure of the Constitution to provide for a bill of rights provided the most important single objection to ratification. Yet Americans conducted the debate on a bill of rights, during the ratification controversy, at a level of abstraction so vague as to convey the impression that they had only the most nebulous conception of the meanings of the particular rights that they sought to insure; indeed many of the principal advocates of a bill of rights had only a nebulous idea of what it ought to contain. Freedom of the press was everywhere a grand topic for declamation, but the insistent demand for its protection on parchment did not accompany a reasoned analysis of what it meant, how far it extended, and under what circumstances it might be limited. Most opponents of the Constitution genuinely feared the proposed national government yet would have favored ratification if the Constitution had included a bill of rights. However, some Anti-Federalist leaders callously resorted to alarming the people. It was easier than informing them, and the provocation of an emotional climate of fear made the definition of freedom of the press, and other liberties, unnecessary. Merely to denounce the omission of freedom of the press and other liberties was superbly effective and even useful as a mask for less elevating, perhaps sordid, objections to the Constitution concerning such matters as tax and commerce powers. One searches in vain for a definition of any of the First Amendment freedoms in the rhetorical effusions of George Clinton, Elbridge Gerry, Patrick Henry, John Lansing, Luther Martin, George Mason, James Monroe, Edmund Randolph, Spencer Roane, Melancthon Smith, James Winthrop, and other advocates of a bill of rights. Nor do the newspapers, pamphlets, or debates of the state ratifying conventions offer much illumination.

Look, for example, at the members of the Constitutional Convention who either walked out of the proceedings at Philadelphia or remained but refused to sign the Constitution. Gerry of Massachusetts, the first to publish his objections to the Constitution, did not even refer to the omission of a bill of rights or a guarantee of freedom of the press.[40] George Mason of Virginia began his published objections to the Constitution with the generalization, "There is no Declaration of Rights." He did not amplify but regretted that the people were not secured even in the "Enjoyment of the benefits of the common-Law," a remark that seems to accept the Blackstone-Mansfield interpretation of freedom of the press. As for that freedom, Mason simply observed, "There is no Declaration of any kind for preserving the Liberty of the Press."[41] Any free press clause would have appeased Mason, even one consonant with the common law. The New Yorkers, Robert Yates and John Lansing, who had quit the convention in disgust, published their "Reasons of Dissent" without objecting to the absence of a bill of rights; they made no reference to the press.[42] Yates, the probable author of the "Brutus" essays, a major Anti-Federalist production, did not mention freedom of the press there either, nor in his "Sydney" essay, where he declared in passing that although the New York constitution had no bill of rights and needed none, the same consideration did not apply to the national government.[43] Martin of Maryland and Randolph of Virginia, who

[40] Storing, *Complete Anti-Federalist*, 2:4-8.
[41] Objections to the Constitution, in *ibid.*, 9-14.
[42] *Ibid.*, 15-18.
[43] *Ibid.*, 1:358-452, and 6:89-121.

refused to sign the Constitution, also made no reference to freedom of the press in their published statements opposing the new plan.[44] John Francis Mercer of Maryland, another member of the Constitutional Convention who became an Anti-Federalist, began his "Farmer" essays by scorning the contempt shown for a bill of rights by men who had been entrusted with the guardianship of public liberty. He opposed the omission of a free press clause but failed to develop the thought beyond a defense of anonymous publications.[45]

Of the fourteen non-signers who had attended the Constitutional Convention, only Gerry, Mason, Yates, Lansing, Martin, Randolph, and Mercer published explanations of their rejection of the Constitution, and none showed any serious concern for the omission of a bill of rights or of a guarantee of liberty of the press, let alone concern for the need to ensure a broad scope for freedom of political discussion; and none said anything that could be construed to constitute a rejection of the common law restraints upon the press. Not one even recommended the Zengerian principles of truth as a defense to the charge of criminal libel or the right of a jury to return a general verdict on the charge. The omission of a free press clause was an insignificant factor in the opposition of these "Framers" to ratification of the Constitution.

An examination of the ratification controversy in Pennsylvania, the first major state to ratify the Constitution, shows how impoverished was Anti-Federalist understanding of freedom of the press. Philadelphia, where the Constitutional Convention had met, was the largest city in the nation and the capital of the second largest state. It had fifteen newspapers (ten in Philadelphia) and a well-defined two-party system. One party, the Republicans, supported ratification, while the other, the Constitutionalists, so-called because they backed the Pennsylvania Constitution of 1776, got tarred with the name "Anti-Federalists," because they opposed ratification. The Pennsylvania Assembly, having heard a reading of the proposed Constitution on September 18, 1787, provided for the election of delegates to a state ratifying convention that met on November 30. On December 12, 1787, Pennsylvania became the second state to ratify, following Delaware within a week, but the battle in the press continued. Pennsylvania's printers reported developments in other states and contributed profusely to the flow of propaganda on each side. The Anti-Federalists of Philadelphia had the advantage of a fearless printer, Eleazar Oswald, whose press produced more Anti-Federalist tracts than any other in

[44] *Ibid.*, 2:19-98.
[45] *Ibid.*, 5:5-69, quoted words at 9.

the country. On the single day of October 17, 1787, the Philadelphia Anti-Federalists published five major items against ratification. Nowhere else was the ratification controversy on a state and national scale better reported, and in no state, except Virginia, were the proceedings of the state ratifying convention as fully reported. If anything significant appeared in print on the subject of freedom of the press, Philadelphia should have been the place for it.[46]

The first reference to freedom of the press appeared in Oswald's *Independent Gazeteer* over the signature of "Fair Play." The Constitution neglected freedom of the press, he observed, despite the fact that it "ought never be restrained."[47] The phrase "ought never be restrained" sounded as if the writer favored the uttermost scope for political expression, exempt from any governmental restrictions, exempt even from the common-law doctrine of seditious libel. In fact, however, the writer, like so many Pennsylvanians who followed him, had merely paraphrased the language of the state's Declaration of Rights of 1776, which provided that "the freedom of the press ought not to be restrained."

Those words cannot be taken literally. Even Blackstone had stated that the absence of "previous restraints upon publications" guaranteed that "neither is any restraint hereby laid upon freedom of thought or enquiry." Publicizing "bad sentiments destructive of the ends of society," he added, "is the crime which society corrects."[48] And the highest court of Pennsylvania had accepted Blackstone as the yardstick by which to measure the state's free press clause. Neither Fair Play, whose remarks appeared in Oswald's paper, nor any of the other Pennsylvania Anti-Federalists who declared that a free press ought never be restrained, criticized Chief Justice McKean's interpretation of the free press clause in Oswald's case. In Pennsylvania the language of no restraints meant no prior restraints, not freedom from subsequent punishments. At the time of Oswald's 1782 prosecution, several individuals had denounced the court's narrow interpretation, but five years later, at the time of the ratification controversy, no one advocating a federal counterpart to the state's free press clause remembered that the state court believed that it did not bar a prosecution for seditious libel. Perhaps, however, Pennsylvania Anti-Federalists did not fear state prosecutions, because they con-

[46] Merrill Jensen, ed., *The Documentary History of the Ratification of the Constitution*, vol. 2 on Pennsylvania (Madison, Wisc., 1976), 5-6, 30-35, 180.
[47] *Ibid.*, 2:149, quoting issue of Sept. 29, 1787.
[48] *Commentaries on the Laws of England* (London, 1765-69), Bk. 4, Chap. 11, p. 152.

trolled the state government or could thwart it with a recalcitrant grand jury.

When the Pennsylvania Assembly called for the election of delegates to a state ratifying convention, its Anti-Federalist members published a remonstrance.[49] At one point they asked voters to consider "whether the liberty of the press may be considered as a blessing or a curse in a free government, & whether a declaration for the preservation of it is necessary?"[50] The author of the minority address was Judge George Bryan, who had supported Chief Justice McKean's attempt to indict Oswald. Clearly Bryan did not believe that a constitutional declaration in favor of an unrestrained free press modified, let alone repudiated, the common law of seditious libel.

On October 6, 1787, James Wilson, calling for the election of delegates who would support the Constitution at the ratifying convention, delivered a speech in the Statehouse Yard that received national attention.[51] Arguing that the proposed Constitution needed no bill of rights because the new government would have no power that extended to the people's liberties, Wilson declared that although the liberty of the press "has been a copious source of declamation and opposition," the federal government could not abridge it. Because "the proposed system possesses no influence upon the press . . . it would have been merely nugatory to have introduced a formal declaration on the subject."

Wilson's remarks provoked Anti-Federalist replies. "A Democratic Federalist," in the first major response, focused on the fact that the judicial power of the United States, under Article III of the Constitution, extended "to all cases, in law and equity, arising under this constitution." That provision convinced the writer that "the tribunal of the United States may claim a right to the cognizance of all offenses against the general government, and libels will not probably be excluded." The Zenger case, he recalled, proved that men in high power disliked liberty of the press. Instead of concluding that it should be constitutionally guaranteed in a way that would prevent prosecutions for libels, he endorsed the "general rule" that all the rights of the people "ought to be clearly and expressly defined"; but he did not attempt that clear and express definition. He did not even recommend a free press clause. He sought to muster opposition to the Constitution, not improve it.[52]

[49] *Pennsylvania Packet*, Oct. 4, 1787, in Storing, ed., *Complete Anti-Federalist*, 3:11-16.

[50] *Ibid.*, 15.

[51] Jensen, *Documentary History*, 2:167-8.

[52] *Pennsylvania Herald*, Oct. 17, 1787, in *ibid.*, 2:193-4.

A pamphlet by "A Federal Republican" also answered Wilson. The writer contended that the press faced real danger from Congress's delegated power to tax; stamp duties could "as effectually abolish the freedom of the press as any express declaration." His simple solution: "A bill of rights should either be inserted, or a declaration made, that whatever is not decreed to Congress, is reserved to the several states for their own disposal." He explained no further. On the basis of his argument, a clause denying Congress the power to tax the press would have been adequate. He did not speak to the issue of libel prosecutions.[53]

Another Pennsylvania Anti-Federalist, probably William Findley, warned in an essay for Oswald's newspaper: "The Liberty of the Press is not secured, and the powers of Congress are fully adequate to its destruction, as they are to have the trial of *libels*, or *pretended libels* against the United States, and may by a cursed abominable Stamp Act (as the *Bowdoin administration* has done in Massachusetts) preclude you effectually from all means of information. Mr. W[ilson] has given you no answer to these arguments."[54] The writer clearly assumed that Congress had a power to define and punish seditious libels as well as a power to tax the press. He proposed no means of securing the press other than by a constitutional guarantee, yet such a guarantee existed in the state constitutions of Pennsylvania and Massachusetts without having prevented Pennsylvania's attempt to prosecute Oswald for seditious libel, the passage of a stamp tax on the Massachusetts press, or several Massachusetts prosecutions for seditious libel.

During the Pennsylvania ratifying convention's session, Cumberland County published a petition asking the convention to support a bill of rights securing the liberty of the press. The petitioners noted that in the absence of a bill of rights, the supremacy clause made the Constitution and federal statutes the supreme law of the land, thereby superseding the state bills of rights, "nor are the people secured in the privileges of the common law." Although the common law embodied the doctrine of seditious libel and did not even permit truth as a defense, the Cumberland petitioners worried only about the "unlimited power" vested in Congress by the necessary-and-proper clause. If uncontrolled by a bill of rights, Congress might exercise its power "to the total suppression of the press."[55] Perhaps the news of

---

[53] *A Review of the Constitution . . . By a Federal Republican*, Oct. 28, 1787, in Storing, ed., *Complete Anti-Federalist*, 3:65-90, quotations at 81 and 85.

[54] An Officer of the Late Continental Army, *Independent Gazetteer*, Nov. 6, 1787, in *ibid.*, 3:93.

[55] *Carlile Gazette*, Dec. 5, 1787, in Jensen, ed., *Documentary History*, 2: 310-11.

McKean's propensity to prosecute had not reached Cumberland County, which seemed to know little about the potential limitations of its own state's free press clause. The Cumberland petition surely did nothing to clarify the meaning of freedom of the press.

Nor did "A Confederationist," who demanded a constitutional guarantee of the liberty of the press. With such a guarantee in hand, he asserted, he would "carry that declaration [of a free press] . . . as my shield and my constitutional defense."[56] Whether he believed that the declaration of a free press would quash the libel or afford him the benefit of Zengerian principles cannot be known. The editor of *The Complete Anti-Federalist*, Herbert Storing, believed that "A Confederationist" adopted "the more modern view" but that "most of the Anti-Federalists" probably accepted the then standard argument advanced by James Wilson, that the meaning of the freedom of the press did "not preclude the punishment of libel, including seditious libel."[57]

Also during the Pennsylvania ratifying convention, John Smilie, who like William Findley was an Anti-Federalist leader, advocated that a bill of rights be appended to the Constitution. "Suppose," declared Smilie, "Congress to pass an act for the punishment of libels and restrain the liberty of the press, for they are warranted to do this. What security would a printer have, tried in one of their courts?[58] He did not explain what security a printer had in Pennsylvania without a courageous and independent grand jury to protect him from the state supreme court. On the next day, December 1, Robert Whitehall, another Anti-Federalist leader, declared that Congress could "destroy the liberty of the press." Under the copyright clause, he observed, Congress could secure to authors "the right of their writings. Under this, they may license the press, *no doubt;* and under licensing the press, they may suppress it." Whitehall professed to believe that the fear of prior restraint as well as of subsequent punishment was still real. He advocated a free press clause to prevent censorship in advance of publication;[59] Blackstone too had defined freedom of the press as no prior restraints. Once again Smilie added that "Congress have a power to restrain libels."[60]

James Wilson's speech of December 1 at the ratifying convention directly answered Whitehall, Findley, and Smilie. Wilson was not

[56] *Pennsylvania Herald*, Oct. 27, 1787, quoted in Storing, ed., *Complete Anti-Federalist*, 1:97-8 note 6.
[57] *Ibid.*, 1:97-8 note 6.
[58] Jensen, ed., *Documentary History*, 2:441.
[59] Dec. 1, 1787, in Jensen, ed., *Documentary History*, 2:454.
[60] *Ibid.*

being hypothetical as some recent scholars have argued.[61] Addressing issues that the Anti-Federalists had raised, Wilson first asserted that the new government had "no power whatsoever" concerning the press. Nevertheless Smilie had asked whether a printer would have a chance of acquittal if Congress made a law to punish libels and the federal judges proceeded under that law. Wilson "presumed" that Smilie had not meant "there is no such thing as a libel" or that libelers ought not be punished. "The idea of liberty of the press is not carried so far as this in any country." He then defined that liberty as meaning "no antecedent restraint upon it," but that "every author is responsible" if he attacked the government's security or welfare. The "proceeding is by a prosecution." Thus the publication of a seditious or criminal libel would result in the prosecution of its author in the place of publication, meaning a federal prosecution in the state of publication with the federal jury drawn from citizens of that state.[62]

Smilie had assumed that Congress must first pass a law against criminally libelous publications. Wilson, however, assumed the existence of a federal common law of crimes, that is, that the federal courts possessed jurisdiction over non-statutory crimes against the United States. His point was that although libels were subject to federal prosecution, the defendant would not be worse off than a defendant prosecuted in a state court for libeling the state. Wilson went further by contending that the federal defendant would be no worse off even if "the general government . . . had the power to make laws on this subject," which he denied. No Anti-Federalist disagreed on the key point. They did not accept Wilson's contention that Congress lacked power to abridge the press, but they did not contest his claim that the federal courts could prosecute libels against the United States, and no one said that a free press guarantee would operate to prevent such prosecutions.

Long after Pennsylvania ratified the Constitution, the controversy continued as frenetically as before in the state's presses. Three major series of Anti-Federalist newspaper articles had begun appearing in the pages of the *Independent Gazetteer* in October 1787 and two ran until the next spring. The "Centinel" series was one of the most widely reprinted Anti-Federalist productions.[63] Contemporaries thought Cen-

---

[61] David A. Anderson, "Origins of the Press Clause," *UCLA Law Review* 30(Feb. 1983):504, and William T. Mayton, "Seditious Libel and the Lost Guarantee of a Freedom of Expression," *Columbia Law Review* 84:(Jan. 1984), 91, 125 n. 180.

[62] Jensen, ed., *Documentary History*, 2:454-5.

[63] Storing, ed., *Complete Anti-Federalist*, 2:130-213.

tinel to be Judge George Bryan but his son, Samuel, composed the essays. Centinel's ideal free press guarantee was that of his own state's constitution of 1776, and notwithstanding his father's support of McKean in Oswald's case, Centinel declared that in Pennsylvania "the liberty of the press yet remains inviolate." That remark made sense only if a fundamental meaning of a free press was a press free from prior restraints. Centinel lavished encomiums on the press; it was sacred, the scourge of tyrants, the palladium of liberty, but he illumined it not at all. Employing the most commonplace definition of a free press, he called it the right to publish one's "sentiments upon every public measure." Replying to Wilson, Centinel insisted that Congress had "immense authority" to "restrain the printers, and put them under regulation." By way of proof he reasoned that the supremacy clause of the Constitution aborted that state's free press clause, leaving printers subject to the absolute control of Congress. A simple declaration that "the liberty of the press be held sacred" would have appeased Centinel, who wrote not one latitude on the topic without a matching platitude.[64]

"Old Whig" was more measured but not more enlightening. The press, he feared, "may possibly be restrained of its freedom," depriving posterity of the invaluable right to communicate freely on political subjects. He advocated a bill of rights to check "undue power" and enable the judicial branch of the government "to protect us by their judgments." Whether he thought that McKean and Bryan constituted a model bench for the protection of the press cannot be known; but the Pennsylvania court sat closest at hand. Instead of resting conclusions on judicial experience, Old Whig preferred to speculate in an effort to disprove Wilson's allegation that Congress posed no danger to the press. On that point the Anti-Federalists imaginatively refuted Wilson, but not one criticized or rejected Wilson's remarks on the propriety of criminally prosecuting libels against government.[65]

"Suppose," declared Old Whig, that Congress seeking to restrain the press enacted a law "to appoint licensers of the press in every town in America; to limit the number of printers; and to compel them to give security for their good behavior, from year to year, as the licenses are renewed." He could think of nothing to prevent the passage and enforcement of such a national law. He then supposed that some courageous Pennsylvania printer, opposed to prior restraint, would publish without a license. The United States would prosecute

[64] *Ibid.*, 144, 146, 153, 177.
[65] *Ibid.*, 3:17-52, quotation at 20.

him; he would plead the state's constitutional guarantee of freedom of the press only to be told that the congressional licensing act was the supreme law of the land.[66]

Assuming that Old Whig really believed his frenetic forebodings, they proved only his belief that the addition of a free press clause to the Constitution would prevent prior restraints on the press. His remarks implicitly showed an acceptance of Blackstonian principles and an assumption that the judicial power of the United States extended to press violations of the law. On that, Wilson and Old Whig did not differ. That Old Whig and other Anti-Federalists who shared his views really believed that Congress would subject the press to prior restraints after three score years without them confounds belief.

"Philadelphiensis" was a mathematics professor at the University of Pennsylvania given to ipsedixitism, but he expounded at greater length on the liberty of the press than any other writer; unfortunately he obscured the subject as much as any one. Nothing interested Philadelphiensis more than preserving the right of anonymous or pseudonymous publications on the subject of politics. He believed that the Federalist friends of "this despotic scheme of government" realized that their only chance of getting it ratified was by "the abolition of the freedom of the press." His proof consisted of the fact that a Federalist printer in Boston refused to publish articles on the Constitution unless the authors left their names for disclosure on request. "In Boston," Philadelphiensis concluded, "the liberty of the press is now completely abolished" and all other rights would soon be extinguished too. If the new government were established, "a gallows, a gibbet, or at least a dungeon" awaited "such writers as Old Whig, or Centinel." No person in his right mind would expose himself, by giving his name, "to the mercy of a revengeful and probably powerful party."[67]

Philadelphiensis made sense when he wrote that if an anonymous author used false or dangerous arguments, opponents should refute him. He also made sense when he asserted that the advantages of an "unrestrained press" outweighed its disadvantages. Significantly he used the word "unrestrained" in the context of a reference to a model free press clause that he urged as an amendment to the Constitution copied from Pennsylvania's guarantee. He made another revealing remark: "When a government thinks proper, under the pretense of writing a libel, etc. it may imprison, inflict the most cruel and un-

[66] *Ibid.*, 24.
[67] *Ibid.*, 3:99-140, quotations at 102-03. For the controversy over the right of anonymity, see Jensen, ed., *Documentary History*, 13:312-23.

usual punishment, seize property, carry on prosecutions etc. and the unfortunate citizen has no *magna charta*, no *bill of rights*, to protect him. . . ." The hyperbole aside, Philadelphiensis showed both a fear of libel prosecutions and a disregard of the fact that the printer of the newspaper that published his series had been protected from a prosecution for libel by a grand jury, not by the very constitutional provision that he recommended.[68]

In the entire body of Anti-Federalist publications no one had come to grips with any of the real problems connected with the freedom of the press. Prior restraint raised no real problem; subsequent punishment did, whether in the form of breach of parliamentary privilege or punishment for seditious libel or some other form of criminal libel. When McKean had sought to indict Oswald in 1782, a few incisively attacked the law. No one did so in 1787. Reasoned analysis, sustained argument, careful definition, and, above, all, direct confrontation of actual problems were absent from Anti-Federalist discussions of freedom of the press in Pennsylvania. Crediting the Anti-Federalists with a genuine effort to educate the public on the meaning, scope, and limits of freedom of the press, even crediting them with an effort to understand it themselves, proves difficult. Not even writers who warned that the United States could or might prosecute libels argued that a constitutional guarantee of a free press would or should prevent such prosecutions; if anyone implicitly meant that, his readers had no basis for understanding him. No one even said that a constitutional guarantee recognizing the inviolability of a free press would deny or modify the common law of criminal libels, let alone supersede it, and not one Pennsylvania Anti-Federalist urged truth as a defense or the right of a jury to return a general rather than a special verdict. The name of Zenger's case was remembered, not its principles.

Yet, when twenty-one of the twenty-three Anti-Federalist members of the state ratifying convention published for national circulation their "Address & Reasons of Dissent," they proposed among their recommended amendments to the Constitution one based on their own state's free press clause altered in a way that demolished every Wilson contention.[69] The Pennsylvania minority urged, in the crucial enabling clause, that "the freedom of the press shall not be restrained by any law of the United States." The word "shall" expressed an imperative that replaced the namby-pamby "ought" in the state's own free press clause. Far more significant, the phrase "shall

[68] Storing, ed., *Complete Anti-Federalist*, 3:102-05, 125-6, 129.
[69] Jensen, ed., *Documentary History*, 2:623.

not be restrained by any law of the United States" can justifiably be read in so broad a way as to preclude federal prosecutions for libel whether under some act of Congress or a non-statutory common law falling within the judicial power of the United States. Having dealt for months with mud and straw, the Pennsylvania Anti-Federalists, in a document that went to every printer and every newspaper in the nation, transmuted crumbly elements into an impregnable bulwark of a free press. Their proposal lost by a two-to-one majority in their own convention, but the nation at last had a broad libertarian clause to consider.

Elsewhere in the nation, however, Anti-Federalists learned nothing from Pennsylvania's experience and added no more enlightenment about freedom of the press than the Pennsylvanians had until the scales fell from their eyes at the last minute. In New York the Federalist leader, John Jay, called attention to the fact that his state's constitution did not guarantee freedom of the press. Melancthon Smith, an Anti-Federalist leader, replied that without a free press guarantee in the federal Constitution, Congress might tax the press. New York's constitution, he added, needed no free press guarantee because "the common and statute law of England, and the laws of the colony are established in which this privilege is fully defined and secured."[70] Smith might as well have said that New York needed no constitutional guarantee of freedom of the press because Chief Justice James DeLancey's rulings of law in Zenger's case still prevailed. Few Anti-Federalist leaders made an admission like Smith's, which undermined the strategy of demanding either a constitutional guarantee to protect the press or else the defeat of the Constitution.

New York's Anti-Federalists usually tried to refute Federalist claims that no constitutional guarantee was needed because the national government had no power to abridge or restrict the press. "A Republican," for example, referred to the delegated power to secure for a time the exclusive right of authors to their writings. That power, he urged, of "regulating literary publications," subordinated the press to government "controul." The solution he advanced was simply a guarantee "for preserving inviolate the liberty of the press."[71] Another New Yorker, signing himself, "Timoleon," relied on Blackstone to prove that trial by jury was essential to a free government, but he did not trouble to mention Blackstone, let alone disagree with him, on the free press issue. Timoleon feared that Congress could "restrain or

---

[70] *An Address . . . by a Plebeian* 1788, in Storing, ed., *Complete Anti-Federalist,* 6:145.
[71] Jensen, ed., *Documentary History,* 13:479.

suppress" printers by an exercise of the tax power. Guaranteeing the freedom of the press would have allayed his fears.[72]

In the *New York Journal* "Cincinnatus" answered James Wilson with a unique argument. Congress, he observed, could define and punish violations of the law of nations, and it would necessarily have the power to "declare all publications from the press against the conduct of the government in making treaties or in any other foreign transactions, an offence against the law of nations." He contended too that another Peter Zenger could incur the resentment of the government by disclosing transactions that it wanted concealed. Should he be prosecuted his judges could "put the verdict of a jury out of question." Cincinnatus was muddled. Any prosecution for a federal crime had to pass a jury's verdict, and a general verdict of not guilty could not be undone by a federal appellate court. Nevertheless Cincinnatus declared that under the Constitution the judicial power of the United States extended to all controversies to which the United States was a party and that the federal judges could determine both law and fact, making the court "both judge and jury." Cincinnatus feared that if a federal official were censured in print, he "might effectually deprive the printer, or author, of his trial by jury, subject him to something, that will probably very much resemble the Star Chamber." Remembering that juries had saved Zenger and Henry Woodfall, Junius's publisher, he warned that a printer prosecuted for libel "would not be tried by a jury," with the result that the freedom of the press would be annihilated. To evade such a catastrophe, declared Cincinnatus, the Constitution had to be amended by a provision securing the freedom of the press.[73]

Aside from the erroneous character of the entire argument, its extraordinary feature was the failure of Cincinnatus to condemn the prosecution of an alleged libel of the government. He labored under the belief that a free-press clause assured defendants of a trial by jury in criminal libel cases. He did not even advocate truth as a defense, despite his several references to Zenger's case and his knowledge of Chief Justice Mansfield's interpretation of the law of seditious libel in England.

By contrast, Richard Henry Lee of Virginia, one of the titans among the Anti-Federalists, worried that Congress could destroy freedom of the press by taxing it; but Lee really opposed the possession of the tax power by Congress.[74] "A power to tax the press at discre-

[72] *Ibid.*, 535-36.
[73] Storing, ed., *Complete Anti-Federalist*, 6:8-11, Nov. 1 and Nov. 7, 1787.
[74] *Federal Farmer*, in Storing, ed., *Complete Anti-Federalist*, 2:250.

tion," he wrote, "is a power to destroy or restrain the freedom of it."[75] A *state* constitutional protection of the press would avail nothing, because the Constitution composed the supreme law. Like other Anti-Federalists, Lee pretended to assume that a federal free-press clause would limit the tax power. He naively shared Melancthon Smith's view that the common law adequately protected freedom of the press. England was also Lee's model. In England, he declared, the people had obtained Magna Carta, the power of taxation, the 1689 Bill of Rights, "and, as an everlasting security and bulwark of their liberties, they fixed . . . the freedom of the press."[76]

No other Anti-Federalist tract was more widely read or influential than Lee's "Federal Farmer." Apparently to many Anti-Federalists, an unrestrained press meant an untaxed press whose printers were responsible to the law for licentious abuse. That Lee could have located the standard for freedom of the press in English law seems stupefying. That merely shows, however, how Blackstone gripped American thinking. On the issue of freedom of the press, Anti-Federalists fluctuated between hysterical fears and complaisant indifference. Patrick Henry, for example, indulged in the worst sort of demagoguery when contemplating the future if the Constitution should be ratified. Without a bill of rights, the United States government would recreate the Inquisition and Star Chamber, torture citizens to extort confessions, inflict cruel and unusual punishments, and use general warrants to ransack private homes for incriminating evidence. But as to liberty of the press, Henry told the Virginia ratifying convention, "I need say nothing; for it is hoped that the Gentlemen who shall compose Congress, will take care as little as possible to infringe the rights of human nature. This will result from their integrity. . . . They are not however expressly restrained. But whether they will intermeddle with that palladium of our liberties or not, I leave to you to determine."[77] Henry added nothing to anyone's understanding of freedom of the press.

Anti-Federalists in New England, at least during the ratification controversy, seem to have associated freedom of the press with a right to publish political opinions anonymously. Otherwise they showed slight interest in freedom of the press. The popular essays by "John De Witt," which first appeared in the Boston *American Herald*, did not even recommend a free press clause as an amendment to the Constitution, apparently because the author did not regard the proposed

[75] *Ibid.*, 2:229-30.
[76] *Ibid.*, 2:271.
[77] *Ibid.*, 5:249-50.

new government as a threat to the press. He defined freedom of the press as the right to discuss public measures and men, enabling all citizens to lay their sentiments before the public "in a decent manner."[78] De Witt did not explain what he meant, but "in a decent manner" indicated acceptance of the common law on criminal libels. For example, Chief Justice Thomas Cogswell of New Hampshire's Court of Common Pleas, in an Anti-Federalist tract signed "Farmer," declared that because of the essential nature of a free press to free government, it should be constitutionally preserved in a bill of rights and be exempted from taxation. "But," he added, "if individuals will publish indecent pieces, leave them to the law of the land to abide the consequence."[79] Blackstone was not more succinct.

A "Columbian Patriot," probably Boston's Mercy Otis Warren, also identified freedom of the press with freedom from prior retraint. She professed to believe that in the absence of a constitutional protection for the liberty of the press, despots might impose "unjust restrictions" in the first instance followed by "an *imprimator* [sic] on the Press," thereby silencing the "decent" protests of an oppressed people.[80] Thus Mercy Warren joined other Anti-Federalists who had no quarrel with the common law; she accepted a printer's responsibility to the law for indecent publications, presumably scurrilous, scandalous, or seditious in character.

A Bostonian, who signed himself "One of the Common People," had a more realistic concern for the freedom of the press. The unlikelihood of a system of prior restraints did not divert his attention from the more urgent issue, the threat of criminal prosecutions. James Wilson, who had asked why Anti-Federalists thought the Constitution took away the liberty of the press, was his target. The commoner replied:

> Will not the United States Attorney have the power to prosecute any printer for a pretended libel against the United States? Will not a printer be triable for a pretended libel against any foreign minister or consul, or for a libel against any of the individual states, by a federal tribunal? Are not such prosecutions warranted by the following clause in the new constitution? "*All controversies wherein the United States shall be a party, all cases affecting foreign ministers and consuls, and all controversies between a citizen and a state,*" shall be cognizable before a federal tribunal. Cannot congress by virtue of this clause, restrain all publick information of mal-

[78] *Ibid.*, 4:24.
[79] New Hampshire *Freeman's Oracle*, Jan. 11, 1788, in *ibid.*, 4:206-7.
[80] *Observations on the New Constitution* (Boston, 1788), in *ibid.*, 4:276.

administration? And will not congress have *absolute* uncontrouled power over printers, and every other person within the United States territory, where there will undoubtedly be a great city?[81]

That passage appeared in the context of an argument to the effect that a bill of rights proved indispensable as a means of securing conventional liberties like a free press and trial by jury. The writer genuinely feared that the Constitution rendered the state bills of rights superfluous by replacing them with what undoubtedly could become, in his opinion, a dangerous common law of crimes enforceable in the federal courts. He believed that the judicial power of the United States extended to libels against diplomats, states, and the United States. But he failed to explain how an amendment to the Constitution recognizing freedom of the press could restrict the powers of Congress or the jurisdiction of the federal courts. Nor did he consider that his own state's free press clause had not prevented indictments in 1787 against those whose publications supported Shay's Rebellion. If "One of the People" actually believed that a free press clause prevented libel prosecutions, which he clearly feared from the United States courts, he failed to say so. In that he stood like every other Anti-Federalist during the ratification controversy: not one declared that libel prosecutions would be impossible in a constitutional system guaranteeing the freedom of the press.[82]

Among supporters of ratification only a few individuals revealed what they were talking about when mentioning freedom of the press. Ben Franklin was one. At this time, although not in the context of the ratification controversy, he spoke with clarity in the essay, reviewed above, in which he attacked the excesses of the press. He favored as much discussion as possible of "public measures and political opinions," but recommended harsh treatment for anyone calumniating the government or affronting its reputation. During the same period, John Adams and William Cushing in their private correspondence, agreeing that the press was free "within the bounds of truth," relegated falsehood, scandal, and bad motives to the realm of criminal publications. In Pennsylvania, the state's highest court convicted Oswald in 1788 in an opinion holding up Blackstone as the key toward understanding a constitutional guarantee of the liberty of the press. In Massachusetts a jury had convicted Dr. William Whiting of seditious libel in 1787; and in 1791, when Edmund Freeman stood trial for criminal libel, Chief Justice Francis Dana and his associates showed

---

[81] *Boston Gazette*, Dec. 3, 1787, in *ibid.*, 4:121.
[82] Clyde Augustus Duniway, *The Development of Freedom of the Press in Massachusetts* (New York, 1906), 142.

their agreement with Chief Justice McKean and his Pennsylvania associates.

Jefferson, another advocate of ratification, never protested against the substantive law of seditious libel, not even during the later Sedition Act controversy. He directed his protests at that time against national as opposed to state prosecution for verbal crimes. He accepted without question the dominant view of his generation that government could be criminally assaulted merely by the expression of critical opinions that allegedly tended to subvert it by lowering it in the public's esteem. His consistent recognition of the concept of verbal political crimes throughout the Revolution continued in the period of peace that followed.

His draft constitution for Virginia in 1783 proposed that the press "shall be subject to no other restraint that liableness to legal prosecution for false facts printed and published."[83] He wrote this as an amendment to the state's free press clause. His amendment explicitly opened the door to criminal prosecutions. Yet he framed that amendment after considering the contrary opinion of his neighbors and constituents. In their Albemarle County Instructions concerning the Virginia Constitution, they had recommended an expansion of the freedom guaranteed to the press by the Declaration of Rights. "In regard to the freedom of the press," they urged, "which certainly is, as mentioned in the Bill of Rights, one of the great bulwarks of Liberty, we think that the Printers should never be liable for anything they print, provided they may give up authors, who are responsible, but on the contrary that they should print nothing without."[84] Thus the recommendation from Albemarle favored exempting the press from prosecution for any signed opinion or news. Jefferson singled out for prosecution "false facts," or "falsehoods" as he initially phrased his provision, in the face of a more liberal recommendation.

Jefferson endorsed prosecution again in 1788 when urging Madison to support amendments to the new federal Constitution, including a guarantee for freedom of the press. "A declaration that the federal government will never restrain the presses from printing anything they please, will not take away the liability of the printers for false facts printed. The declaration that religious faith shall be unpunished," he offered as added assurance, "does not give impunity to

[83] *Papers of Jefferson*, 6:304. A documentary history of "Jefferson's Proposed Revision of the Virginia Constitution," preceded by an elaborate editorial introduction, is at 6:278ff.

[84] *Ibid.*, 6:288. Jefferson had the Albemarle proposals before him when composing his 1783 revision of the Virginia constitution. *Ibid.*, 282.

criminal acts dictated by religious error."[85] Publication of false facts on political matters seemed the equivalent of an overt crime resulting from a misguided religious conscience. Jefferson's proposal that the press should not be restrained was pure Blackstone. He meant that the press should be free in the English or common-law sense: free from censorship or licensing acts in advance of publication, but responsible for abuse of an unrestrained freedom to publish. Unlike Blackstone, however, Jefferson implicitly opposed the prosecution of accurate information.

Jefferson received a copy of Madison's proposed amendments to the Constitution in 1789. He was disappointed not to see the adoption of his recommendation on the press. Madison had proposed: "The people shall not be deprived or abridged of their right to speak, to write, or to publish their sentiments; and the freedom of the press, as one of the great bulwarks of liberty, shall be inviolable."[86] Jefferson liked that proposal, he said, but "the following alterations and additions would have pleased me. Art. 4. 'The people shall not be deprived or abridged of their right to speak to write or otherwise to publish anything but false facts affecting injuriously the life, liberty, property, or reputation of others or affecting the peace of the confederacy with foreign nations.' "[87] One can imagine how free the press might have been during the controversies over Jay's Treaty, the Louisiana Purchase, or the embargo, had Jefferson's recommendation prevailed and been taken seriously.

Excepting Franklin, James Wilson and Hugh Williamson were the only Framers, among the ratificationists, who troubled to explain their understanding of freedom of the press. Wilson's views, aligning him with Blackstone, refuted any notion that a free-press clause might supersede the common law of seditious libel. Williamson of North Carolina, in an essay, "Remarks on the New Plan of Government," declared in 1788: "There was a time in England when neither book, pamphlet, nor paper could be published without a license from government. That restraint was finally removed in the year 1694; and, by such removal, the press became perfectly free, for it is not under the restraint of any license. Certainly the new government can have no power to impose restraints."[88] Obviously, freedom of the press meant to Williamson what it had meant to Blackstone. Williamson's friend

---

[85] Jefferson to Madison, July 31, 1788, in *ibid.*, 13:442–43.
[86] *Annals of Congress*, 1st Cong., 1st sess., 451.
[87] Jefferson to Madison, Aug. 28, 1789, in *Papers of Jefferson*, 15:367.
[88] Paul L. Ford, ed., *Essays on the Constitution of the United States* (Brooklyn, 1892), 394.

and ally, James Iredell of North Carolina, soon to become a member of the Supreme Court of the United States, helped mastermind ratification strategy in his state. In a pamphlet on the Constitution he referred to England "where the press is as free as among ourselves." In this respect Iredell agreed with Melancthon Smith and Richard Henry Lee.[89]

The only other revealing statements of the period on this topic came from two Virginians who, though not members of the Federal Convention or of the Congress that framed the Bill of Rights, worked closely with the Framers. George Nicholas, one of the leading supporters of Jefferson and Madison in the Virginia legislature, fought for the Statute of Religious Freedom, and later, as attorney-general of Kentucky, would help Jefferson frame the Kentucky Resolutions of 1798 against the Sedition Act. In 1788, at the Virginia ratifying convention, he declared: "The liberty of the press is secured. . . . In the time of King William, there passed an act for licensing the press. That was repealed. Since that time it has been looked upon as safe."[90] Thus Nicholas, like Williamson, accepted Blackstone. John Marshall, the future chief justice, also speaking as a member of the Virginia ratifying convention, asked, "Is it presumable that they [Congress] will make a law to punish men who are of different opinions in politics from themselves? Is it presumable that they will do it in one single case, *unless it be such a case as must satisfy the people at large?*"[91] Marshall's rhetorical question implied his view that minority critics might be suppressed or "punished" if public opinion demanded or if the people went along with Congress. Amid the torrent of words spoken about liberty of the press or free speech before the final ratification of the First Amendment in 1791, no other statements by public men provide or imply a definition of a free press or a position on the question whether the common law of public libels continued in force.

State pronouncements show no greater enlightenment. None of the first nine states to ratify the Constitution recommended an amendment guaranteeing freedom of speech or press. Indeed, the Pennsylvania ratifying convention, led by Wilson and McKean, rejected the minority's proposal for such an amendment, and the Maryland convention took no action on any of the amendments recommended by its committee on amendments, one of which declared, "That the free-

---

[89] Paul L. Ford, ed., *Pamphlets on the Constitution of the United States* (Brooklyn, 1888), 361.
[90] Elliot, ed., *Debates*, 3:247.
[91] *Ibid.*, 3:560. Italics added.

dom of the press be inviolably preserved." The committee had added this explanation: "In prosecutions in the federal courts for libels, the constitutional preservation of this great and fundamental right may prove invaluable."[92] The necessary implication of this statement by Maryland's Anti-Federalist libertarians, is that prosecutions for criminal libel might be maintained in the federal courts under common if not statutory law, and that the free-press guarantee would provide some advantage to the defendant—possibly truth as a defense or a general verdict by a jury.

Of the twelve states to ratify the Constitution before Congress drafted the First Amendment in 1789, only the last three, Virginia, North Carolina, and New York, sought to safeguard the expression of political opinion from violation by the new national government. Although neither Virginia nor North Carolina protected speech in its own constitution, they both proposed a federal bill of rights that included a provision, copied from the Pennsylvania provision of 1776, which began, "That the people have a right to freedom of speech. . . ."[93] Neither Virginia nor North Carolina used the more sweeping language of 1787 by the Pennsylvania minority. But Virginia had her own broad recommendation for inclusion in a federal bill of rights. Virginia urged that "among other essential rights the liberty of Conscience and of the Press cannot be cancelled abridged restrained or modified by any authority of the United States."[94] Virginia's concern for protecting freedom of speech and press against national invasion, though probably genuine, did not match her desire to prevent a concurrent jurisdiction in the national government on the subject of criminal libels. State sovereignty probably dominated Virginia's concern, and perhaps the state's recommendation for an amendment to the United States Constitution in 1788 ought not to be construed too liberally. Consider not only the comments by Nicholas and Marshall, quoted above, but also the Virginia statutes of 1785 and 1792 which punished the advocacy of carving a new government out of Virginia territory and which punished false news.[95] Virginia's law did not even accept Zengerian principles or reject the remote bad tendency test of political opinions; for practical purposes, however, only the law punishing the defamation of private reputations restrained Virginia's press.

[92] *Ibid.*, 2:552.
[93] Charles C. Tansill, ed., *Documents Illustrative of the Formation of the Union of the American States* (Washington, 1927), 1030 and 1047.
[94] *Ibid.*, 1027.
[95] See above, pp. 195–96.

New York accompanied its ratification of the Constitution in 1788 with the recommendation for an amendment worded, "That the Freedom of the Press ought not to be violated or restrained,"[96] although no comparable provision exsited in that state's constitution. As in the case of the other states recommending a guarantee of First Amendment freedoms, no explanatory statement defining the meaning or compass of any of those freedoms accompanied New York's recommendation. Her expressed solicitude for freedom of the press in 1788 cannot be considered as proof of her faithfulness to the principles of the great Zenger case. In New York, as a matter of law, freedom of the press meant what De Lancey or Blackstone had defined it to be, although popular understanding may have assumed that truth was a defense against a charge of criminal libel and that jurors possessed a power not endorsed by the common law.

In 1799 a New York court imprisoned a printer, David Frothingham, for four months and fined him for the crime having copied from another newspaper the criminal innuendo that Alexander Hamilton opposed the republican form of government and worked with the British government to undermine it by trying to buy out the Philadelphia *Aurora*. Hamilton himself instigated the indictment on the theory that the calumny against him had the "dangerous tendency," he said, of destroying the confidence of the people in the leading defenders of the administration. At Frothingham's trial the court refused to allow evidence to prove the truth of his accusation, even though the prosecution consented to permit truth as a defense. Hamilton, the star witness for the state, testified that the Philadelphia *Aurora*, the source of the seditious libel and the country's foremost Jeffersonian newspaper, was hostile to the government of the United States.[97]

Thus, the state recommendations that a free press clause be annexed to the Constitution did not signal a different theory about the compass of freedom of political expression. But, whatever the Anti-Federalists meant in recommending a bill of rights with a free press clause, they transformed political opinion in the nation. In 1787 a consensus had existed to strengthen the national government. In 1788 a new consensus existed: ratify the Constitution with the understanding that a bill of rights be added to it. A failure to fulfill public expectations could easily have aborted the Constitution by turning public opinion

[96] Tansill, ed., *Documents*, 1037.
[97] "Trial of David Frothingham, for a Libel on General Hamilton," New York, 1799, in Wharton, ed., *State Trials*, 649-651. Frothingham's case is narrated at length in James Morton Smith, *Freedom's Fetters: The Alien and Sedition Laws and American Civil Liberties* (Ithaca, 1956), 400-414, on the basis of much new research.

in favor of a second constitutional convention that would have scrapped the Constitution and merely modified the Articles of Confederation. James Madison prevented that by saving the new system.

Madison was one of the Federalists who finally realized that statecraft and political expediency dictated a switch in position. At the Virginia ratifying convention in June 1788, Madison had upheld the usual Federalist arguments for the omission of a bill of rights but finally voted to recommend such a bill in order to avoid previous amendments. He later conceded that the Constitution would have been defeated without a pledge from its supporters to back subsequent amendments. In Virginia Madison's own political position deteriorated because he had opposed a bill of rights. The Anti-Federalists, who controlled the state legislature, elected two of their own, Richard Henry Lee and William Grayson, as the state's first United States Senators. Madison faced a tough contest for election to the House of Representatives, and he feared that the Anti-Federalists might succeed in their call for a second constitutional convention. He needed to reconsider his position on a bill of rights.[98]

Although Madison had periodically apprised Jefferson in Paris on ratification developments, he had not answered Jefferson's letter of December 1787 supporting a bill of rights. On October 17, 1788, the eve of his campaign for a House seat, Madison faced the issue. He favored a bill of rights, he wrote, but had "never thought the omission a material defect" and did not feel "anxious to supply it even by subsequent amendments"; he did not even think the matter important. Still agreeing with Wilson that the delegated powers did not extend to reserved rights, Madison also worried about the difficulty of adequately protecting the most important rights; experience proved that a bill of rights was a mere parchment barrier when most needed. Government, after all, was the instrument of the majority, which could endanger liberty. "What use then . . . can a bill of rights serve in popular Governments?" Its political truths, he conceded, by way of answer, could educate the people, thereby inhibiting majority impulses.[99]

Jefferson's reply of March 15, 1789, had a profound influence on Madison, as Madison's great speech of June 8 would show. An argument for a bill of rights that Madison had omitted, wrote Jefferson, was "the legal check which it puts into the hands of the judiciary."

---

[98] On Madison and a bill of rights at the Virginia convention, see, for example, *Papers of Madison*, 11:130, for speech of June 12, 1788; see *ibid.*, 11: 301-04, Editorial Note, on Madison in Virginia politics.

[99] *Ibid.*, 11:295-300, letter to Jefferson.

Jefferson believed that an independent court could withstand oppressive majority impulses by holding unconstitutional any acts violating a bill of rights. The point was not new to Madison, for he himself, when defending a ban on *ex post facto* laws at the Constitutional Convention, had declared that it would "oblige the Judges to declare [retrospective] interferences null and void."[100] As for the point that the delegated powers did not reach the reserved rights of the people, Jefferson answered that because the Constitution protected some rights but ignored others, it raised implications against them, making a bill of rights "necessary by way of supplement." Moreover, he added, the Constitution "forms us into one state as to certain objects," requiring a bill of rights to guard against abuses of power. To the contention that a bill of rights could not be perfect, Jefferson replied with the adage that half a loaf is better than none; even if all rights could not be secured, "let us secure what we can." Madison had also argued that the limited powers of the federal government and the jealousy of the states afforded enough security, to which Jefferson answered that a bill of rights "will be the text whereby to try all the acts of the federal government." The argument that a bill of rights was inconvenient and not always efficacious did not impress Jefferson. Sometimes, he replied, it was effective, and if it inconveniently cramped the government, the effect was short-lived and remediable, whereas the inconveniences of not having a bill of rights could be "permanent, afflicting, and irreparable." Legislative tyranny, Jefferson explained, would be a formidable dread for a long time, and executive tyranny would likely follow.[101]

Jefferson's arguments, however persuasive, would have been unproductive but for the dangerous political situation, which Madison meant to ameliorate. Four states, including his own and New York, had called for a second convention; its purpose, Madison feared, would be to "mutilate the system," especially as to the power to tax. Omitting that power "will be fatal" to the new federal government. Madison correctly believed that most Anti-Federalists favored an effective Union on condition that a bill of rights bridled the new government. His strategy was to win them over by persuading the first Congress to adopt protections of civil liberties, thereby alleviating the public's anxieties, providing popularity and stability for the government, and isolating those Anti-Federalists whose foremost objective was "subverting the fabric . . . if not the Union itself."[102]

---

[100] Farrand, ed., *Records*, 2:440.
[101] Jefferson to Madison, March 15, 1789, in *Papers of Jefferson*, 14:659-61.
[102] *Papers of Madison*, 11:12, 238, 330-31. See also 307.

In the first Congress, Representative Madison sought to fulfill his pledge of subsequent amendments. His accomplishment in the face of opposition and apathy entitles him to be remembered as "father of the Bill of rights" even more than as "father of the Constitution." Many Federalists thought that the House had more important tasks, like the passage of tonnage duties and a judiciary bill. The opposition party, which had previously exploited the lack of a bill of rights in the Constitution, realized that the adoption of a bill of rights would sink the movement for a second convention and make unlikely any additional amendments that would cripple the substantive powers of the government. They had used the bill of rights issue as a smokescreen for objections to the Constitution that could not be dramatically popularized, and now they sought to scuttle Madison's proposals. They began by stalling, then tried to annex amendments aggrandizing state powers, and finally depreciated the importance of the very protections of individual liberty that they had formerly demanded as a guarantee against impending tyranny. Madison meant to prove that the new government was a friend of liberty; he also understood that his amendments, if adopted, would thwart the passage of proposals aggrandizing state powers and diminishing national ones. He would not be put off; he was insistent, compelling, unyielding, and, finally, triumphant.

On June 8, 1789, he made his long memorable speech before an apathetic House, introducing amendments culled mainly from state constitutions and state ratifying convention proposals, especially Virginia's. All power, he argued, is subject to abuse and should be guarded against by constitutionally securing "the great rights of mankind." The government had only limited powers but it might, unless prohibited, abuse its discretion as to its choice of means under the necessary-and-proper clause; it might, for example, use general warrants in the enforcement of its revenue laws. In Britain, bills of rights merely erected barriers against the powers of the Crown, leaving the powers of Parliament "altogether indefinite," and the British constitution left unguarded the "choicest" rights of the press and of conscience. He urged the following free speech-and-press clause, using the mandatory "shall" which no state constitution had employed and no state ratifying convention had recommended: "The people shall not be deprived or abridged of their right to speak, write, or to publish their sentiments; and the freedom of the press, as one of the great bulwarks of liberty, shall be inviolable." A bill of rights, Madison declared, limited the powers of government, thus preventing legislative as well as executive abuse, and above all preventing abuses of power by "the body of the people, operating by the majority against the minority."

Mere "paper barriers" might fail, but they raised a standard that might educate the majority against acts to which they might be inclined.[103]

To the argument that a bill of rights was not necessary because the states constitutionally protected freedom, Madison had two responses. One was that some states had no bills of rights, others "very defective ones," and the states constituted a greater danger to liberty than the new national government. The other was that the Constitution should, therefore, include an amendment that "No State shall violate the equal rights of conscience, or the freedom of the press, or the trial by jury in criminal cases." Madison offered no explanation for having omitted freedom of speech from this amendment, nor did he explain what he meant by freedom of the press. He did declare, in defense of his proposed restrictions on the states, that they were "of equal, if not greater importance" than the prohibitions against the state enactment of *ex post facto* laws, bills of attainder, or laws impairing the obligations of contracts. He argued that the states would more likely abuse their powers than would the national government "if not controlled by the general principle, that laws are unconstitutional which infringe the rights of the community." He thought that "every Government should be disarmed of powers which trench upon those particular rights" of press, conscience, and jury trial. The amendment was all the more needed, he asserted, because some of the states did not protect these rights in their own constitutions. As for those that did, a "double security" could not reasonably be opposed. When Congressman Thomas Tucker of South Carolina moved to strike the proposed restriction on state powers, Madison carried the House by a two-thirds majority after he argued that this was "the most valuable amendment in the whole list."[104]

To the contention that an enumeration of rights would disparage those not protected, Madison replied that the danger could be guarded against by adopting a proposal of his composition that became the Ninth Amendment. If his amendments were "incorporated" into the Constitution, Madison said, using another argument borrowed from Jefferson, "independent tribunals of justice will consider themselves in a peculiar manner the guardians of those rights; they will be an impenetrable bulwark against every assumption of power in the legislative or executive; they will be naturally led to resist every encroach-

---

[103] Madison's speech, in the *Annals of Congress,* is reprinted in *Papers of Madison,* 12:197-209 and in Bernard Schwartz, ed., *The Bill of Rights: A Documentary History* (New York, 1971, 2 vols.), 2:1023-34. Because Schwartz reproduced all the debates in Congress on the Bill of Rights, I hereafter cite his excellent compilation as a convenience to readers.

[104] *Ibid.,* 1:784.

ment upon rights expressly stipulated for in the constitution."[105] In his speech of June 8 and in the later debates of 1789 on the Bill of Rights, Madison said nothing that warrants the assertion that he "articulated as early as 1789 the theory of liberty on which he based his Virginia Report of 1799-1800.[106]

Although many Federalists preferred to give the new government time to operate before amending the Constitution, some supporters of Madison exulted, largely for political reasons. Hugh Williamson of North Carolina, a signer of the Constitution, informed Madison that the Anti-Federalists of that state did not really want a bill of rights; William R. Davie, who had been Williamson's colleague in the Convention, gleefully reported that Madison's amendments had "confounded the Anties" who really wanted to restrict the powers of Congress rather than enumerate personal freedoms. Edmund Pendleton of Virginia wrote of Madison's amendments that "nothing was further from the wish of some, who covered their Opposition to the Government under the masque of uncommon zeal for amendments." Tench Coxe of Pennsylvania praised Madison for having stripped the Constitution's opponents of every rationale "and most of the popular arguments they have heretofore used."[107]

Notwithstanding the support of correspondents, Madison's speech stirred no immediate support in Congress. Indeed, every speaker who followed him, regardless of party affiliation, either opposed a bill of rights or believed that the House should attend to far more important duties. Six weeks later Madison "begged" for a consideration of his amendments, but the House assigned them to a special committee instead of debating them. That committee, which included Madison, reported in a week. It added freedom of speech to the rights protected

[105] Schwartz, ed., *Bill of Rights*, 2:1027, 1113.
[106] Vincent Blasi, "The Checking Value in First Amendment Theory," *American Bar Foundation Research Journal*, 1977, p. 521 n. 60. Blasi simply cited Madison's June 8 speech without offering a word of summary description, analysis, or proof of his point. Apart from the fact that his *ipse dixit* proves nothing, he was wrong in fact. Blasi used lawyer's tactics in the manipulation of historical data: he was trying to prove a case, not find the truth. A reader unfamiliar with the sources would be unable to tell from Blasi's footnotes that he used the 1799 report to characterize the 1789 speech.
[107] Williamson to Madison, May 24, 1789, *Papers of James Madison*, 12:183-84; Davie to Iredell, June 4, 1789, quoted in Griffith J. McRee, *Life and Correspondence of James Iredell* (New York: 1857-58), 2:260. Davie to Madison, June 10, 1789, in *Documentary History of the Constitution of the United States of America, 1786-1870*. Derived from Records, Manuscripts, and Rolls Deposited in the Bureau of Rolls and Library of the Department of State (Washington, 1894-1905), 5:177. Pendleton to Madison, Sept. 2, 1789, *Papers of James Madison*, 12:368; Coxe to Madison, June 18, 1789, *ibid.*, 12:239.

against state abridgment, deleted Madison's reference to no "unreasonable searches and seizures," and made some stylistic revisions. The committee also streamlined Madison's free speech-and-press clause and added to it his recommendation for securing the rights of assembly and petition. The revised version asserted: "The freedom of speech and of the press, and the right of the people peaceably to assemble and consult for their common good, shall not be infringed." The committee's report was tabled, impelling Madison on August 3 to implore its consideration.[108]

On August 13 the House finally began to consider the reported amendments, and in the course of debate it made some significant changes. Madison had proposed to "incorporate" or intersperse the amendments within the text of the Constitution at appropriate points. He did not recommend their adoption as a separate "bill of rights," although he had referred to them collectively by that phrase. Members objected, however, that to incorporate the amendments would give the impression that the framers of the Constitution had signed a document that included provisions not of their composition. Another argument for lumping the amendments together was that the matter of form was so "trifling" that the House should not squander its time debating the placement of the various amendments. Ironically, Roger Sherman, who still believed that the amendments were unnecessary, deserves the credit for insistently arguing that they should be appended as a supplement to the Constitution instead of being interspersed within it. Thus, what became the "Bill of Rights" achieved its significant collective form over the objections of its foremost proponent, Madison, and because of the desire of its opponents in both parties to downgrade its importance.[109]

The House recast the free exercise of religion clause and its allied clause banning establishments of religion, improving Madison's original language. The House also confined to criminal cases Madison's broad phrasing that no person should be compelled to give evidence against himself. On the other hand the House restored the extremely important principle against unreasonable searches and seizures, dropped by the committee. In another major decision the House decisively defeated Gerry's motion, for the Anti-Federalists, to consider not just the committee's report but all amendments that the several states had proposed; the Anti-Federalists thus failed to introduce crippling political amendments. Finally, the House added "or to the people" in the recommendation by Madison that the powers not delegated to the

---

[108] Schwartz, ed., *Bill of Rights*, 2:1034-42, 1050, 1054-57, 1062.
[109] *Ibid.*, 2:1062-77, 1126.

United States be reserved to the states. On the whole the House adopted Madison's amendments with few significant alterations during the course of its ten-day debate on the Bill of Rights and no further alteration of the free speech-and-press clause.[110]

In the midst of that debate Madison wrote a letter to a fellow Federalist explaining why he was so committed to "the nauseous project of amendments" that some of the party supported reluctantly. Protecting essential rights was "not improper," he coolly explained, and could be of some influence for good. He also felt honor bound to redeem a campaign pledge to his constituents, mindful that the Constitution "would have been *certainly* rejected" by Virginia without assurances from its supporters to seek subsequent amendments. Politics, moreover, made proposing the amendments a necessity to beat the Anti-Federalists at their own game. If Federalists did not support the amendments, Anti-Federalists would claim that they had been right all along and gain support for a second convention. And, Madison wrote, the amendments "will kill the opposition everywhere, and by putting an end to disaffection to the Government itself, enable the administration to venture on measures not otherwise safe."[111]

Madison had, in fact, upstaged and defeated the Anti-Federalists who wanted to cripple the national government. Sensing defeat, Congressman Aedanus Burke of South Carolina cried sour grapes. During the debate on what would become our First Amendment, he argued that the proposals before the House were "not those solid and substantial amendments which the people expect; they are little better than whip-syllabub, frothy and full of wind. . . . Upon the whole, I think . . . we have done nothing but lose our time, and that it will be better to drop the subject now, and proceed to the organization of the Government." The private correspondence of Senators Lee and Grayson of Virginia reveals the explanation for the attitude of their party toward a bill of rights. A few days after Madison had introduced his amendments, Grayson complained to his mentor, Patrick Henry, that the Federalists meant to enact "amendments which shall effect [sic] personal liberty alone, leaving the great points of the Judiciary, direct taxation, &c, to stand as they are." Lee and Grayson had failed in their effort to have the Senate amend the House's proposals by adopting the Virginia ratifying convention's recommendations on direct taxation and the treaty and the commerce powers. Lee then regretted the original Anti-Federalist strategy of opposing the Constitution unless revised by the addition of a bill of rights and

---

[110] *Ibid.*, 2:1088-1114, 1121-38.
[111] To Richard Peters, Aug. 19, 1789, in *Papers of Madison*, 12:346-47.

other amendments. He sorrowfully informed Henry that "the idea of subsequent amendments, was little better than putting oneself to death first, in expectation that the doctor, who wished our destruction, would afterwards restore us to life." Later, after the Senate had approved the amendments that became the Bill of Rights, Grayson reported, "they are good for nothing, and I believe, as many others do, that they will do more harm than benefit."[112]

The Senate, which kept no record of its debates, had deliberated on seventeen amendments submitted by the House. One the Senate killed, the proposal Madison thought "the most valuable": protection against state infringement of speech, press, religion, or trial by jury. The motion to adopt failed to receive the necessary two-thirds vote, although by what margin is unknown. The Senate included many members jealous of state prerogatives and who believed that the Constitution already imposed too many limitations on the states. As a result of the Senate's rejection of the ban on the states, the Constitution offered against state violation no protection whatever to speech, press, and religion. The Senate also weakened the House's ban on establishments of religion. Someone made a proposal that would have critically weakened the free press clause. The Senate voted down a motion to alter the amendment so that freedom of the press should be protected "in as ample a manner as hath at any time been secured by the common law."[113] There is no way of knowing whether the motion was defeated on the ground that it was too narrow or simply unnecessary. Its phraseology reflects a belief in the mind of its proposer that the common law adequately protected freedom of the press; its defeat suggests the Senate's unwillingness to make the amendment embody merely an explicit Blackstonianism. Otherwise the Senate accepted the House proposals, although the Senate combined several, reducing the total number from seventeen to twelve. The first of the twelve dealt with the relation of population to the number of representatives from each state, and the second would have prevented any law going into effect that would have increased the salaries of members of Congress until after the next election. The third amendment as adopted by the Senate read, "that Congress shall make no law, abridging the freedom of speech, or of the press." We do not know why the Senate wanted to limit the prohibition to Congress rather than any officer or agency of the United States, nor do we know why the right originally

---

[112] Schwartz, ed., *Bill of Rights*, 2:1103; Grayson to Henry, June 12, 1789, quoted in William Wirt Henry, *Patrick Henry: Life, Correspondence and Speeches* (New York, 1891), 3:391; Lee to Henry, Sept. 14, 1789, *ibid.*, 3:399; Grayson to Henry, Sept. 29, 1789, *ibid.*, 3:406.

[113] *Journal of the First Session of the Senate*, 117.

urged by Madison ended as a mere restraint on Congress. We do know that New Hampshire introduced the phrasing "Congress shall make no law" in connection with a proposed amendment on religion. The Senate combined the religion clauses with the clauses on free speech, press, assembly, and petition.[114]

The House adamantly refused to accept the Senate's version of its ban on establishments. A conference committee of both houses met to resolve differences. The committee, which included Madison, accepted the House's ban on establishments but otherwise accepted the Senate's version. On September 24, 1789, the House voted for the committee report; on the following day the Senate concurred, and the twelve amendments were submitted to the states for ratification.[115]

Within six months, nine states ratified the Bill of Rights, although of the twelve amendments submitted for approval, the first and second were rejected. The four recalcitrant states which by mid-1790 had not acted on the amendments were Virginia, Massachusetts, Connecticut, and Georgia. The admission of Vermont to the Union made necessary the ratification by eleven states. Connecticut and Georgia refused to ratify. Georgia's position was that amendments were superfluous until experience under the Constitution proved a need. Connecticut believed that any suggestion that the Constitution was not perfect would add to the strength of Anti-Federalism.[116]

In Massachusetts, Federalist apathy to the Bill of Rights was grounded on a satisfaction with the Constitution as it was, and the Anti-Federalists were more interested in amendments that would strengthen the states at the expense of the national government. Nevertheless the Massachusetts lower house adopted all but the first, second, and twelfth amendments, and the upper house adopted all but the first, second, and tenth. Thus both houses of the Massachusetts legislature actually approved what became our First through Seventh Amendments and the Ninth, but a special committee, dominated by Anti-Federalists, urged that all amendments recommended by Massachusetts should be adopted before the state concurred in any amendments. As a result the two houses never passed a bill promulgating ratification of eight amendments.[117] Jefferson, the secretary of state, believed that Massachusetts, "having been the 10th state which has

---

[114] See *ibid.*, 2:1145-58 for the Bill of Rights in the Senate.

[115] *Ibid.*, 2:1159-66.

[116] David M. Matteson, "The Organization of the Government under the Constitution," in Sol Bloom, Director General, *History of the Formation of the Union under the Constitution* (Washington, 1943), 316-19; Rutland, *Birth of Bill of Rights*, 213-18; Schwartz, ed., *Bill of Rights*, 2:1171-1203.

[117] Matteson, "Organization of the Government," 325-27; Schwartz, ed., *Bill of Rights*, 2:1173-76.

ratified, makes up the threefourth [sic] of the legislatures whose ratification was to suffice." He wrote to a Massachusetts official, asking for clarification. The reply was, "It does not appear that the Committee ever reported any bill." In 1939 Massachusetts joined Connecticut and Georgia when they belatedly ratified on the sesquicentennial anniversary of the Constitution.[118]

Ratification of the Bill of Rights by Vermont, in November 1789, left Virginia the last state to act.[119] Its ratification as the eleventh state was indispensable, although the hostility of its Anti-Federalist leaders presaged a doubtful outcome. Senators Grayson and Lee reported to the Virginia legislature that they transmitted the recommended amendments "with grief." They still hoped for a new constitutional convention that would devise "real and substantial Amendments" to "secure against the annihilation of the state governments. . . ." Patrick Henry vainly moved to postpone consideration of the Bill of Rights. The victims of a dilemma of their own making, the Anti-Federalists then sought to sabotage the Bill of Rights and finally, after delaying ratification for nearly two years, irresolutely acquiesced. The Federalists of Virginia, however, eagerly supported the Bill of Rights in the knowledge that its adoption would appease public fears and stymie the amendments supported by the Anti-Federalists. Virginia's lower house, controlled by the Federalists, acted quickly, "and without debate of any consequence" but the opposition dominated the state senate. Not all Anti-Federalists were implacably opposed. Some respected George Mason's opinion. When he had first heard of Madison's amendments he called them "Milk and Water Propositions," not "important & substantial Amendments"; but Mason changed his mind, saying that they gave "much satisfaction," although he still wanted other amendments, including one that prevented commercial regulations by mere majority vote of Congress.[120]

Virginia's senate, as Edmund Randolph reported to Washington, postponed consideration of the amendments, "for a majority is unfriendly to the government." As a member of the lower house reported to Madison, the senate inclined to reject the Bill of Rights, not because of opposition to its guarantees, but from an apprehension

---

[118] Jefferson to Christopher Gore, Aug. 8, 1791, in *Documentary History . . . Department of State*, 5:244; Matteson, "Organization of the Government," 327-28.

[119] Rutland, *Birth of the Bill of Rights*, 217.

[120] On Grayson and Lee, see *Documentary History . . . Department of State*, 5:216-18; on Mason, see *Papers of George Mason*, ed., Robert A. Rutland (Charlottesville, Va., 1970, 3 vols.), 3:1164, 1172, letters of July 31, 1789 and Sept. 8, 1789.

"that the adoption of them at this time will be an obstacle to the chief object of their pursuit, the amendment on the subject of direct taxation." For that reason, Randolph reported to Washington, the Federalists meant to "push" the Bill of Rights; passage would "discountenance any future importunities for amendments."[121]

Virginia's senate at the close of 1789 rejected what became the First, Sixth, Ninth, and Tenth Amendments, at least until the next session, thereby allowing time for the electorate to express itself. The Anti-Federalists still hoped to drum up support for "radical" amendments, as Lee called them. The senators in the majority also issued a statement grossly misrepresenting the First Amendment (then the third). With unbelievable inaccuracy the eight senators asserted as to speech and press, "This amendment does not declare and assert the right of the people to speak and publish their sentiments, nor does it secure the liberty of the press. Should these valuable rights be infringed or violated . . . the people would have no avowed principle in the constitution to which they might resort for the security of these rights."[122]

Madison confidently expected that this Anti-Federalist tactic of scares and deceits would backfire, and it did. For the senators' statement was not only inaccurate on its face; it came from men who with a single exception did not go before the electorate with clean hands. Like Henry and Lee who planned the senators' statement, the senators had records of having voted against religious liberty and in favor of compulsory taxes for the support of religion. By contrast Madison had led the fight in Virginia against a state establishment of

[121] To Washington, Dec. 6, 1789, in *Documentary History . . . Department of State*, 5:222-23; Hardin Burnley to Madison, Nov. 5, 1789, quoted in *ibid.*, 5:214-215; see also Irving Brant, *James Madison, Father of the Constitution* (Indianapolis, 1950), 286 and 491 n. 15.

[122] Edward Carrington to Madison, Dec. 20, 1789, in *Papers of Madison*, 12:462-64. The senators also asserted that the amendment "does not prohibit the rights of conscience from being violated or infringed . . ." whereas the amendment positively stipulated that Congress shall not abridge the free exercise of religion; the senators also alleged that notwithstanding the amendment's provision against laws respecting an establishment of religion, "any particular denomination of Christians might be so favored and supported by the general government, as to give it a decided advantage over others. . . ." *Journal of the Senate of the Commonwealth of Virginia; Begun and held in the City of Richmond, on Monday the 19th day of October . . . 1789* [the bookbinder's title is *Journal of the Senate, 1785 to 1790*] (Richmond, 1828), 62-63, proceedings of Dec. 12, 1789. This is not the place to argue what was then understood to constitute a law respecting an establishment of religion, but despite the present-day controversy over the meaning of an establishment, every historian without exception agrees that a law giving preference to one denomination over others positively was understood to constitute an establishment.

religion and for religious liberty, and his supporters in the Virginia senate had aided him. In the end Madison's confidence proved justified. Jefferson made his influence felt on behalf of the Bill of Rights, and the Anti-Federalists grudgingly gave ground before public opinion. On December 15, 1791, after two years of procrastination, the senate finally ratified without record vote, thereby completing the process of stage ratification and making the Bill of Rights part of the Constitution.[123]

The history of the framing and ratification of the Bill of Rights indicates slight passion on the part of anyone, except perhaps "the people," to enshrine personal liberties in the fundamental law of the land. We know almost nothing about what the state legislatures thought concerning the meanings of the various amendments, and the press was perfunctory in its reports, if not altogether silent. But for Madison's persistence the amendments would have died in Congress. Our precious Bill of Rights, at least in its *immediate* background, resulted from the reluctant necessity of certain Federalists to capitalize on a cause that had been originated, in vain, by the Anti-Federalists for ulterior party purposes. The party that had first opposed the Bill of Rights inadvertently wound up with the responsibility for its framing and ratification, while the party that had at first professedly wanted it discovered too late that it not only was embarrassing but disastrous for those ulterior purposes. The Bill of Rights had a great healing effect, however; it did, as Mason originally proposed, "give great quiet" to people. The opposition to the Constitution, Jefferson informed Lafayette, "almost totally disappeared," as Anti-Federalist leaders lost "almost all their followers." The people of the United States had possessed the good sense, nourished by traditions of freedom, to support the Constitution *and* the Bill of Rights.[124]

What import did the free speech-and-press clause possess at the time of its adoption? More complex than it appears, the clause had several meanings and did not necessarily mean what it said or say what it meant. Its meaning was surely not self-evident. The controversy in the states over the ratification of the Constitution without a bill of rights had revealed little about the substance and scope of freedom of speech-and-press, and the debates by the First Congress, which framed the First Amendment, illumined even less. Congress

---

[123] Madison to Washington, Jan. 4, 1790, *Documentary History . . . Department of State*, 5:230-231. See also, Matteson, "Organization of the Government," 232, and Brant, *Madison*, 286-87, and 491 n. 16 for the voting records.

[124] To Lafayette, April 2, 1790, in *Documentary History . . . Department of State*, 5:240.

debated the clauses on religion, but on the remainder of the First Amendment considered only whether the right of peaceable assembly vested the people with the power to instruct their representatives how to vote. In the course of that discussion, Madison made the only recorded statement on the subject of speech or press. If by peaceable assembly, he said, "we mean nothing more than this, that the people have a right to express and communicate their sentiments and wishes, we have provided for it already. The right of freedom of speech is secured; the liberty of the press is expressly declared to be beyond the reach of this Government. . . ."[125] Any interpretation of the meaning and compass of freedom of speech-and-press drawn from this vague statement would strain credulity. Apathy, ambiguity, and brevity characterize the comments of the few Congressmen who spoke on the First Amendment. The House did not likely understand the debate, care deeply about its outcome, or share a common understanding of the finished amendment.

The state legislatures that ratified the First Amendment offer no enlightenment either. Without the records of their legislative debates, we do not know what the state legislatures understood the First Amendment freedoms to mean. Private correspondence, newspapers, and tracts do not help. Most people undoubtedly cared about protecting freedom of speech-and-press, but no one seems to have cared enough to clarify what he meant by the subject upon which he lavished praise. If definition were unnecessary because of the existence of a tacit and widespread understanding of "liberty of the press," only the received or traditional understanding could have been possible. To assume the existence of a general, latitudinarian understanding that veered substantially from the common-law definition is incredible, given the total absence of argumentative analysis of the meaning of the clause on speech and press. Any novel definition expanding the scope of free expression or repudiating, even altering, the concept of seditious libel would have been the subject of public debate or comment. Not even the Anti-Federalists offered the argument that the clause on speech and press was unsatisfactory because it was insufficiently protective against prosecutions for criminal defamation of the government. Not even they urged that truth could be no libel.

Even if we assume, as did Alexander Meiklejohn, that the Framers really intended to impose upon the national government "an abso-

---

[125] *The Debates and Proceedings in the Congress of the United States* (Washington, 1834 ff.) 1:766, 1st Cong., 1st Sess. Cited hereafter as *Annals of Congress*, the bookbinder's title.

lute, unqualified prohibition"[126]–there shall be *no* law abridging free speech–we should recognize that the Framers cared less about giving unqualified immunity to all speech than they cared for states' rights and the federal principle. Granting, for the moment, an intention to render the national government utterly powerless to act in any way against oral, written, or printed utterances, the Framers meant the clause to reserve to the *states* an exclusive legislative authority in the field of speech and press. Thus, no matter what the Framers meant or understood by freedom of speech or press, the national government even under the unamended Constitution could not make speech or press a legitimate subject of restrictive statutory action. The Framers intended the First Amendment as an added assurance that Congress would be limited to the exercise of its enumerated powers and therefore phrased it as an express prohibition against the possibility that Congress might use those powers to abridge freedom of speech or press. It goes without saying that an express prohibition on power did not vest or create a new power, previously nonexistent, to abridge speech or press, because as Madison declared, the Bill of Rights was not framed "to imply powers not meant to be included in the enumeration."[127] Because the Senate rejected the House-approved amendment to prohibit state abridgment of freedom of speech, the First Amendment left the states free to act against individual expression, subject only to such restraints as might be laid down in state constitutions. The big question persists, however; even had Congress passed, and the states ratified, an amendment imposing upon the states the same prohibition laid by the First Amendment upon the national government, what did the Framers understand by freedom of speech and freedom of press?

No one can say for certain what the Framers had in mind, because enough evidence does not exist to justify cocksure conclusions, even though all the evidence points in one direction. Whether the Framers themselves knew what they had in mind is uncertain. At the time of the drafting and ratification of the First Amendment, few among them clearly understood what they meant by the free speech-and-press clause, and we cannot know that those few represented a consensus. Considerable disagreement existed, for example, on the question whether freedom of expression meant the right to print the truth about government measures and officials if the truth was defamatory or was revealed for unworthy motives. Disagreement existed too

[126] Meiklejohn, *Free Speech and Its Relation to Self-Government* (New York, 1948), 17.
[127] Madison to Jefferson, Oct. 17, 1788, in *Papers of Madison*, 11:297.

about the function of juries in trials for criminal libel. Zengerian principles had few open advocates.

What is clear is that no evidence suggests an understanding that a constitutional guarantee of free speech or press meant the impossibility of future prosecutions of seditious utterances. The traditional libertarian interpretation of the original meaning of the First Amendment is surely subject to the Scottish verdict: not proven. Freedom of speech and press, as the evidence demonstrates, was not understood to include a right to broadcast sedition by words. The security of the state against libelous advocacy or attack outweighed any social interest in open expression, at least through the period of the adoption of the First Amendment. The thought and experience of a lifetime, indeed the taught traditions of law and politics extending back many generations, supplied an *a priori* belief that freedom of political discourse, however broadly conceived, stopped short of seditious libel.

As Maitland observed, "Taught law is tough law,"[128] and its survival power was sufficient to carry it through the American Revolution with its principles unbroken, except for a few feudal relics such as those relating to primogeniture and entail. The fact is scarcely even remarkable because the origins and conduct of the American Revolution had no relation to any hostility to the common law, and surely not to its doctrines of verbal crime which received statutory recognition and were carried to extremes during the Revolution itself. Moreover, the Sedition Act, passed less than seven years after the ratification of the First Amendment, suggests that the generation that framed the amendment did not consider the suppression of seditious libel to be an abridgment of freedom of speech or press. Yet the Framers themselves, whatever they understand freedom of speech or press to mean, had given the public specific assurances again and again that neither speech nor press could be the subject of repressive legislation by a government bereft of authority on that subject.

The injunction of the First Amendment, therefore, did not imply that a sedition act might be passed without abridging the freedom of the press. Even if a sedition act might not be an abridgment, that was not the main point of the amendment. To understand its framers' intentions, the amendment should not be read with the focus only on the meaning of "the freedom of the press." It should also be read with the stress on the opening clause: "Congress shall make no law. . . ." The injunction was intended and understood to prohibit any congressional regulation of the press, whether by means of censorship, a

---

[128] Frederick Maitland, *English Law and the Renaissance*, 18, quoted in Roscoe Pound, *The Formative Era of American Law* (Boston, 1938), 144.

licensing law, a tax, or a sedition act. The Framers meant Congress to be totally without power to enact legislation respecting the press. They intended a federal system in which the central government could exercise only specifically enumerated powers or powers necessary and proper to carry out the enumerated ones. Thus James Wilson declared that, because the national government had "no power whatsoever" concerning the press, "no law . . . can possibly be enacted" against it. Thus Hamilton, referring to the demand for a free press guarantee, asked, "why declare that things shall not be done which there is no power to do?" The illustrations may be multiplied. In other words, no matter what was meant or understood by freedom of speech and press, the national government, even in the absence of the First Amendment, could not make speech or press a legitimate subject of restrictive legislation. In that sense the amendment itself was superfluous. To quiet public apprehension, it offered further assurance that Congress would be limited to the exercise of its delegated powers. The First Amendment could not possibly have enhanced the powers of Congress; it did not add to them a previously non-existing power. The phrasing was intended to prohibit altogether the possibility that Congress might use its powers to abridge speech and press. From this viewpoint, the Sedition Act of 1798 was unconstitutional.

The difficulty of this interpretation springs from the ineptness of the First Amendment's phrasing. The verbs in its various clauses, if taken seriously, pose insurmountable problems. Congress shall make no law abridging the freedom of speech or of the press. "Abridging" is clear enough. It means diminishing or restraining. But "abridging" is the wrong word, if, as seems so certain, those who made and accepted the amendment meant no law regulating the freedom of the press, or no law respecting it. Perhaps they did not say what they meant because a law protecting copyrights is a law regulating or respecting the press. The original Constitution empowered Congress to enact copyright laws. Accordingly, "no law respecting" would have been contradictory. Congress may regulate without abridging, whereas "no law respecting" would have barred any laws on the subject.

That might explain the phrase "no law abridging" but not "nor prohibiting the free exercise" of religion. Rational analysis fails here. Nowhere in the making of the Bill of Rights was the original intent and understanding clearer than in the case of religious freedom. The phrasing was: "Congress shall make no law respecting an establishment of religion nor prohibiting the free exercise thereof." The meaning was: "Congress shall make no law respecting an establish-

ment of religion or the free exercise thereof." The phrasing suggests
the deliberate avoidance of the obvious as a result of the insertion of
a different verb: prohibiting. Congress can pass laws regulating and
even abridging the free exercise of religion without prohibiting it.
Similarly, "no law . . . abridging the freedom of speech or press"
opened the way to laws regulating or respecting free speech or press.
The phrasing of the amendment made little sense given the fact that
Congress proposed and the states ratified with the understanding that
Congress had absolutely no power to pass laws on the press except
copyright laws.

The amendment protected the *freedom* of the press, not the press.
The freedom of the press and of political discourse generally had so
widened in scope that seditious libel had become a narrow category
of verbal offenses against government, government officials, and government policies. To be sure, the legal definition of seditious libel remained what it had been from the time of Hawkins to Mansfield: malicious, scandalous falsehoods of a political nature that tended to
breach the peace, instill revulsion or contempt in the people, or lower
their esteem for their rulers. But prosecutions were infrequent, the
press habitually scurrilous. Governments forbore, realizing that prosecutions might fail or backfire because critics represented strong factions, and, often, influential men. Moreover, public opinion, except
in times of crisis like Shay's Rebellion, tended to distrust an administration that sought to imprison its critics. The press could not have
endured as aspersive and animadvertive as it was without public support. For the most part people understood that scummy journalism
unavoidably accompanied the benefits to be gained from a free press.
People seem also to have understood that critics vented unfavorable
opinions in order to excite a justifiable contempt for the government;
to prosecute those critics seemed to immunize from criticism public
officials who probably deserved to be disliked or distrusted. That was
the teaching of *Cato's Letters* and of the Zenger case. The actual
freedom of the press had slight relationship to the fact that as a legal
concept, freedom of the press was a cluster of constraints. The law
threatened repression; the press conducted itself as if the law scarcely
existed. In 1799 Madison observed that in England despite the common law on the press and "the occasional punishment of those who
use it with a freedom offensive to the government," all knew that
"the freedom exercised by the press, and protected by the public
opinion far exceeds the limits prescribed by the ordinary rules of
law." The English press, said Madison, criticized the ministry "with
peculiar freedom," and during elections for the House of Commons

the calumnies of the press raged. The American press enjoyed at least as much freedom.[129]

When the framers of the First Amendment provided that Congress shall not abridge the freedom of the press they could only have meant to protect the press with which they were familiar and as it operated at the time. They constitutionally guaranteed the *practice* of freedom of the press. They did not adopt its legal definition as found in Blackstone or in the views of libertarian theorists. By freedom of the press the Framers meant a right to engage in rasping, corrosive, and offensive discussions on all topics of public interest. The English common-law definition had become unsuitable, and libertarian theory had not caught up with press practice. Government in the United States derived from the people, who reserved a right to alter it, and the government was accountable to the people. That required a broader legal concept of freedom of the press than existed in England, where the monarch was a hereditary ruler not accountable to the people and the House of Lords too was not elected or accountable. Glimmerings of a broader libertarian theory existed but did not systematically emerge until 1798.

In a sense the constitutional guarantee of freedom of the press signified nothing new. It did not augment or expand freedom of the press. It recognized and perpetuated an existing condition. Freedom of the presss meant, in part, an exemption from prior restraints and continued to mean that. Circumstances, especially in time of war, might make prior restraints necessary, but the eighteenth century did not have to face the problem whether national security required the censorship in advance of publication of any information whose disclosure jeopardized troop movements or supply ships. No one favored the reimposition of a licensing system that awarded or denied official approval for every word seeking print. The more practical problem faced by writers and printers dealt with subsequent punishment for licentious use of the right to publish without prior restraint. The press remained subject to the common law despite a constitutional guarantee, but the threshold of public tolerance had significantly widened. Thus freedom of the press meant more than just freedom from prior restraint. It meant the right to criticize the government, its officers, and its policies as well as to comment on any matters of public concern. The right to criticize and comment no longer implied a decent or temperate fashion. It meant a freedom for foul-tempered, mean-spirited expression. For practical purposes what

---

[129] "Report on the Resolutions," (*The Virginia Report of 1799-1800*), in *The Writings of James Madison*, ed. Gaillard Hunt (New York, 1906) 6:388.

the law called malice did not signify just a nasty disposition; it signified ill-will, an intention to provoke readers or listeners to hope for damage to the public weal or to the government. Within a decade of the ratification of the First Amendment, mild criticism, certainly not scorching billingsgate, resulted in convictions under the Sedition Act, but the public revulsion that shortly manifested itself in Jefferson's election suggests that the Federalists of 1798-1800 misread the free press clause.

Freedom of the press signified not only freedom from prior restraint, but responsibility under the law for damaging publications. It meant too that the press enjoyed a preferred position in the American constitutional scheme because of its special relationship to popular government. The electoral process would have been a sham if voters did not have the assistance of the press in learning what candidates stood for and what their records showed about past performance and qualifications. A free press was becoming indispensable to the existence of a free and responsible government. Even Blackstone conceded, "The liberty of the press is indeed essential to the nature of a free state."[130] Its essentiality derived also from the fact that the press had become the tribune of the people by sitting in judgment on the conduct of public officials. A free press meant the press as the Fourth Estate, or, rather, in the American scheme, an informal or extraconstitutional fourth branch that functioned as part of the intricate system of checks and balances that exposed public mismanagement and kept power fragmented, manageable, and accountable. Freedom of the press had accrued still another function that intimately associated it with a free state, meriting its constitutional protection. The cliché that it was the bulwark of liberty, "essential," as the Massachusetts constitution asserted, "to the security of freedom in a state," meant that the existence of various personal liberties depended at least in part on the vigilance of the press in exposing unfairness, inequality, and injustice. Freedom of the press had become part of the matrix for the functioning of popular government and the protection of civil liberties.

It does not necessarily follow that the Framers desired to give the utmost latitude to expression. The First Amendment did not embody an absolute because not all speech is free speech, or, to put it another way, there are several classes of speech or of publication, some of which were not intended to be categorized under the rubric, "the freedom of speech" or freedom of the press. Did the Framers intend that the federal mails should be open to pornographic materials or

---

[130] *Commentaries*, Bk. 4, chap. 11, 153.

that a speaker should be free to incite violence directly and immediately against the United States? Did they intend that false, malicious, and damaging calumnies against the government should be free? Madison himself was "inclined to think that *absolute* restrictions in cases that are doubtful, or where emergencies may overrule them, ought to be avoided."[131] If the Framers did not intend that all speech, without exception, should be free without exception, the crucial question is, where did they intend to draw the line between that speech which was constitutionally protected and that which was not? The eighteenth century did not provide answers.

Only after the new government had gone into operation and after the ratification of the First Amendment did many of the Framers and their associates speak and act as if freedom of speech and press could be prosecuted in federal courts and be abridged by Congress as well. In this regard the problem whether a federal common law existed deserves attention. Thanks mainly to the state sovereignty sentiment among the Anti-Federalists, the Bill of Rights imposed limitations upon only the national government. But the First Amendment, when read literally, raises questions. What was the significance of the fact that the prohibition on power was imposed exclusively upon Congress instead of upon the government of the United States? Did the specification of Congress imply that restraints were not intended to be imposed upon other federal authorities? Could the executive arm of the government, through the attorney-general's office and the United States marshals, prosecute common-law crimes committed by mere words? Could the federal courts try verbal crimes at common law? Did a federal common law of crimes exist? If it did, the free-speech clause offered merely the shadow rather than the substance of protection by stipulating only a restriction upon Congress.

If a federal common law of crimes existed, then the attorney-general's office might prosecute and the federal courts might try non-statutory crimes against the United States. In other words, the existence of a federal common law meant that the First Amendment could not possibly have been intended to supersede the common law of seditious libel or other branches of the common law of criminal defamation which delimited freedom of expression. *Congress*, in accordance with a literal interpretation of the First Amendment, might not be empowered to enact libel laws—or more precisely, might not abridge freedom of speech or press, but the executive and judicial departments might proceed at common law independently of statutory provisions. The Congress that framed the amendment and the

[131] Madison to Jefferson, Oct. 17, 1788, *Papers of Madison*, 11:299.

states that ratified it approved of phrasing that limited only Congress, not the United States and not "the Government," thus permitting the possibility that the other branches could do what Congress could not. The question, then, is whether the Framers intended the development of a federal common law of crimes. The answer is that the evidence is contradictory.

Charles Warren has shown that Congress intended by the Judiciary Act of 1789 to vest the federal courts with common-law jurisdiction,[132] but it is not clear that their jurisdiction was to extend to criminal as well as civil cases, except, necessarily to crimes committed on the high seas. Congress did, however, delete a phrase that could have restricted criminal jurisdiction to statutory crimes. Even if Congress intended to vest jurisdiction over common law crimes in the federal courts, uncertainty remains whether the courts were to create a federal common law of crimes or apply the common law of the state in which the crime was committed. Either alternative would comprehend the common law of criminal utterances. If we may extrapolate from Warren's research on section 34 of the Judiciary Act of 1789, the probability is that the Framers of the act intended the state common law to be applied.[133] But the first generation of federal judges assumed the existence of a federal common law of crimes. All the early cases, excepting one in which the court split, support the proposition that a federal common law of crimes existed. Yet in 1812 and again in 1816 the Supreme Court rejected that proposition.[134]

Justice James Wilson, an influential Framer of the Constitution, at

---

[132] Charles Warren, "New Light on the History of the Federal Judiciary Act of 1789," in D. B. Maggs *et al.*, eds., *Selected Essays on Constitutional Law* (Chicago, 1938), 3:1246-1254.

[133] I am indebted to my friend, John P. Roche, for this insight which cuts away the ground of the whole controversy whether a federal common law was intended. I doubt, however, that sufficient evidence can be mustered to support the proposition which, though plausible, seems not to have occurred to the federal courts in criminal cases with but one exception. In 1807 U.S. District Judge Pierpont Edwards ruled that in the trial of a common law crime in a federal court, the law of the state in which the crime occurred was to be applied. Edward's ruling is discussed below, p. 345. Although Professor Roche's proposition is without the support of other rulings, it is logically and psychologically sound and fits with what we know of the original intentions of the framers of the Judiciary Act of 1789 as to civil causes at common law.

[134] *U.S. v. Hudson and Goodwin*, 7 Cranch 32 (1812), and *U.S. v. Coolidge*, 1 Wheaton 415 (1816). The best discussion of the problem whether a federal common law of crimes existed is Stephen B. Presser, "A Tale of Two Judges: Richard Peters, Samuel Chase, and the Broken Promise of Federalist Jurisprudence," *Northwestern University Law Review* 73(1978):27-111, especially 46-72.

his state's ratifying convention had endorsed federal prosecutions at common law for criminal libels against the United States. In 1793 he instructed a federal grand jury on the virtues of the common law, which included, he said, the law of nations. The grand jury indicted Gideon Henfield for breaching American neutrality by assisting a French privateer in the capture of a British ship. Alexander Hamilton prepared the indictment, which Attorney-General Edmund Randolph, another Framer, helped prosecute. Wilson, joined by Justice James Iredell and Judge Richard Peters constituted the federal circuit court that tried Henfield's nonstatutory offense. Secretary of State Jefferson, who had urged Henfield's prosecution and endorsed Wilson's opinion on the indictability of the offense, explained that the jury acquitted because Henfield had not knowingly committed the crime.[135] John Marshall, in his *Life of Washington*, described the prosecution as having been based on an offense "indictable at common law, for disturbing the peace of the United States."[136]

In 1793 a federal grand jury indicted Joseph Ravara, a consul from Genoa, for attempting to extort money from a British diplomat. Justice Wilson, joined by Peters, ruled that the circuit court had jurisdiction, although Congress had passed no law against extortion. At Ravara's trial in 1794, Chief Justice John Jay instructed the jury that the offense was indictable at common law, part of the law of the land. The jury convicted.[137] In 1795 a federal court in New York indicted Greenleaf, the editor of the *New-York Journal*, for the common-law crime of criminal libel. The case was dropped, but in 1797 Greenleaf was again indicted for the same crime and convicted by a court presided over by Chief Justice Oliver Ellsworth, an influential Framer of the Constitution and chief author of the Judiciary Act of 1789. In Massachusetts in 1797 Ellsworth ruled in *United States* v. *Smith* that the federal circuit court possessed jurisdiction over crimes against the common law and therefore might try persons indicted for counterfeiting notes of the Bank of the United States, not then a statutory offense.[138]

In the same year a federal grand jury obeyed Justice Iredell's

---

[135] "Trial of Gideon Henfield," 1793, in Wharton, ed., *State Trials*, 49-92.
[136] Quoted in Wharton, ed., *State Trials*, 88.
[137] "Trial of Joseph Ravara," 2 Dallas 297-299 (1793), in Wharton, ed., *State Trials*, 90-92.
[138] On Greenleaf see Julius Goebel, *History of the Supreme Court of the United States. Antecedents and Beginnings* (New York, 1971), 629. Federal Cases #16323, misdated *U.S.* v. *Smith* as 1792. The MSS Final Record of the United States Circuit Courts of Massachusetts, 1790-99, 1:242, 244 (Federal Records Center, Dorchester, Mass.) shows the date as 1797.

charge and indicted a congressman, Samuel J. Cabell, for the common-law crime of seditious libel. Attorney-General Charles Lee prepared a memorandum on "Libellous Publications" in which he first quoted Blackstone and then Mansfield to the effect that the liberty of the press consists in printing without prior restraint, adding, "in this definition I concur with the learned judge."[139] The prosecution was aborted for political reasons.[140] In 1798, before Congress passed the Sedition Act, the United States initiated prosecutions for seditious libel against editors Benjamin F. Bache, who soon died, and John Burke, who skipped the country before Justice William Patterson could try him.[141] In 1799 Ellsworth and Iredell, in separate cases, told federal grand juries that the federal courts had common-law jurisdiction over seditous libel and, in Ellsworth's words, against "acts manifestly subversive of the national government." "The common law of this country," he declared, "remains the same as it was before the Revolution." He added that an indictable offense need be defined only by common law, not statute.[142]

Iredell explained his position at great length in 1799 when he announced to a federal grand jury that the First Amendment declared the common law as expounded by Blackstone. Stating that every government in the world possessed a power to punish seditious libel, Iredell added, "It is unquestionably possessed by all the State governments, and probably has been exercised in all of them: sure I am, it has in some. If necessary and proper for them, why not equally so, at least, for the government of the United States."[143] Turning to the First Amendment, he declared:

> We derive our principles of law originally from England. There, the press, I believe, is as free as in any country of the world, and

[139] July 27, 1797, in Benjamin F. Hall, ed., *Official Opinions of the Attorneys General of the United States* (Washington, 1852), 1:72.

[140] On Cabell's case, see Manning J. Dauer, *The Adams Federalists* (Baltimore, 1953), 154; Adrienne Koch and Harry Ammon, "The Virginia and Kentucky Resolutions: an Episode in Jefferson's and Madison's Defense of Civil Liberties," *William and Mary Quarterly*, 3rd ser., 5(April 1948):152-53; and Levy, ed., *Freedom of the Press from Zenger to Jefferson* (Bobbs-Merrill, 1966), 342-50.

[141] Smith, *Freedom's Fetters*, chap. 10, "Common Law Indictments," 188-220, is an excellent discussion of these cases.

[142] "Trial of Isaac Williams" (1799), reported originally in the *Connecticut Courant*, Sept. 30, 1799, and reprinted in Wharton, ed., *State Trials*, 652-54. The line quoted is at 653.

[143] Charge to the Grand Jury by Iredell, April 11, 1799, in "Trial of the Northampton Insurgents. In the Circuit Court of the United States for the Pennsylvania District," Wharton, ed., *State Trials*, 476.

so it has been for near a century. The definition of it is, in my opinion, no where more happily or justly expressed than by the great author of the commentaries on the laws of England, which book deserves more particular regard on this occasion, because for nearly thirty years it has been the manual of almost every student of law in the United States, and its uncommon excellence has also introduced it into the libraries, and so often to the favourite reading of private gentleman; so that his views of the subject could scarcely be unknown to those who framed the Amendments to the Constitution: and if they were not, unless his explanation has been satisfactory, I presume the amendment would have been more particularly worded, to guard against any possible mistake. His explanation is as follows: . . . [long quotation from Blackstone].

It is believed that, in every State in the Union, the common law principles concerning libels apply; and in some of the States words similar to the words of the Amendment are used in the Constitution itself, or a contemporary Bill of Rights, of equal authority, without ever being supposed to exclude any law being passed on the subject. So that there is the strongest proof that can be of a universal concurrence in America on this point, that the freedom of the press does not require libellers shall be protected from punishment.[144]

The sole dissenting voice in this line of decisions was that of Justice Samuel Chase in *Worrall's Case* (1798), where the common-law indictment alleged the attempted bribery of a federal official. Judge Peters disagreed with Chase's argument that no federal common law of crimes existed, and the jury convicted.[145] Chase, however, changed his opinion in *United States v. Sylvester* (1799), when he presided over a common-law prosecution for counterfeiting and after a guilty verdict imposed a heavy prison sentence.[146]

Before 1812 there were several other cases in which federal courts accepted jurisdiction over common-law crimes. The only cases worth mentioning were those arising in Connecticut where six persons were indicted for the same offense: seditiously libeling the president of the United States in speech or press. The prosecution in four of the cases was ultimately dropped, but the cases of two editors, on demurrer to the jurisdiction of the federal circuit court, were brought together before the Supreme Court. Justice William Johnson, speaking for the "majority," ruled briefly that the question whether the United States courts "can exercise a common law jurisdiction in criminal

144 *Ibid.*, 478-79.
145 *U.S. v. Worrell*, 2 Dallas 384 (1798), in Wharton, ed., *State Trials*, 189-99.
146 *U.S. v. Sylvester* (1799), MSS Final Record, U.S. Circuit Courts, Mass., 1:303.

cases" had been "settled in public opinion" which had long opposed such jurisdiction. Moreover, the Constitution had not expressly delegated to the federal courts authority over common-law crimes. "The legislative authority of the Union must first make an act a crime, affix a punishment to it, and declare the Court that shall have jurisdiction of the offense."[147]

Justice Joseph Story, who had not made known his dissent at the time, did so in a circuit opinion the following year,[148] thus forcing a reconsideration of the rule of the Hudson-Goodwin case; but on the appeal, in *United States* v. *Coolidge*, decided 1816, Justice Johnson, though noting division within the Court, refused to review his own precedent.[149] In both cases it is an extraordinary fact that there were no arguments of counsel. Hence, the great question was decided without reasoned consideration by bench or bar. The decisions of 1812 and 1816, which were probably politically motivated, contrast with the many federal trials of the 1790s for common-law crimes, including the crime of seditious libel. Those nineteenth-century decisions are not worth a farthing as revelations of the true intentions of the Framers. It is noteworthy that Justices Wilson, Paterson, and Ellsworth, who accepted jurisdiction of common law crimes, had been among a select group of the most influential members of the Constitutional Convention of 1787, while Justices Jay and Iredell, who accepted similar jurisdiction, were major figures closely associated with the Framers. Hamilton and Randolph, who played important roles in the government's prosecution of Henfield, were also giants among the Framers. But no one can prove that in 1787 or 1789 any of them intended the existence of a federal common law of crimes. Indeed, any evidence drawn from the period after 1791 probably should be discounted in any determination of the *original* understanding of the First Amendment.

Among the untrustworthy evidence is that relating to the controversy over the Sedition Act of 1798, even though on most questions concerning the meaning of the free speech-and-press clause, one can find a full-dress debate in the *Annals of Congress* for 1798, supplemented by newspaper comments, related tracts and books, the arguments of counsel in Sedition Act trials, the Virginia and Kentucky Resolutions and accompanying debates, and Madison's "Report on

---

[147] *U.S.* v. *Hudson and Goodwin*, 7 Cranch 32, 34 (1812). W. W. Crosskey, *Politics and the Constitution* (Chicago, 1953), 2:782, claimed that Chief Justice Marshall and Justices Story and Washington dissented from Johnson's opinion without noting the fact of their dissent on the record.

[148] *U.S.* v. *Coolidge*, 1 Gallison 488 (1813).

[149] *U.S.* v. *Coolidge*, 1 Wheaton 415 (1816).

the Virginia Resolutions." For the first time our public men of the generation of the Framers expressed themselves with force, clarity, and elaborate detail on the meaning and limitations of freedom of speech and press; on the powers of Congress under the First Amendment; on the reserved powers of the states in reference to seditious and other criminal libels; on the question whether the First Amendment left the common law in force or superseded it; and on the existence of a federal common law of crimes. A full discussion of all these matters may be found in the controversy over the Sedition Act. But as a revelation of prior opinion, the debate of 1798 and after is suspect.

Views expressed during that acrimonious time are untrustworthy because they were distinctly *ad hoc* in character and because partisans were even less motivated by principle and precedent than usual. They argued from personal and party interests. Not a single Federalist in the United States opposed the constitutionality of the Sedition Act, while the only Federalist who doubted the wisdom of the statute was John Marshall.[150] Every Democratic-Republican with the possible exception of James Sullivan believed it to be unconstitutional.[151] Eminent judges of the twentieth century, including Holmes, Brandeis, Black, Douglas, Jackson, Brennan, and others, declared that the statute was unconstitutional.[152] But every member of the Supreme Court in 1798-1800, in rulings on circuit, thought otherwise.[153] By no coincidence all members of the court at that time were Federalists. The Federalists of 1798 were not the Federalists of 1787 or 1791, and the Fifth Congress which passed the Sedition Act was not contemporaneous with the framing and ratification of the Constitution. The Framers and the Fifth Congress had very little in common.

If Federalist statements of 1798-1800 cannot be accepted as evidence of opinion in 1791 or earlier, the pronouncements of the Jeffersonians must also be rejected. If any of the Jeffersonians at any time before 1791, or before the onset of the Sedition Act controversy, had declared some of the opinions which they formed in the party battle of 1798-1800, their later statements would not be as suspect. That they were sincere in 1798 is not to be doubted, but sincerity is not a test of prior intention. Nor is it a test of consistency; many of the Jeffersonians, most notably Jefferson himself, behaved when in power

[150] Smith, *Freedom's Fetters*, 150-155.
[151] For Sullivan's views, see below, 289-93.
[152] See above, Preface.
[153] See the index to Smith, *Freedom's Fetters*, under the names of the individual justices, Ellsworth, Chase, Cushing, Iredell, Paterson, and Washington, for citation to cases.

in ways that belied their fine libertarian sentiments of 1798. James Madison, the most influential of all the Framers, is possibly the one person of outstanding distinction whose record is clean and consistent. Perhaps Albert Gallatin's name should be joined with Madison's, but there is slight proof that any of the libertarian propositions advanced by them during the 1798-1800 period were believed in or thought of by either at an earlier date. Madison's towering authority and integrity, combined with the power of his arguments, could not in any event do more than deadlock the debate, because the admission of his testimony as evidence of prior understanding necessarily requires the admission of Federalist testimony from John Jay, John Adams, James Wilson, William Paterson, Oliver Ellsworth, James Iredell, and others whose opinions on our fundamental law and on the intentions of the Framers merit respect. The result of such a constitutional Donnybrook would be inconclusive, leading to the proposition that we do not know what the First Amendment's freedom of speech-and-press clause meant to the men who drafted and ratified it at the time that they did so. Moreover, they themselves at that time sharply divided and possessed no distinct understanding either. As Zechariah Chafee said on reconsideration, "The truth is, I think, that the framers had no very clear idea as to what they meant by 'the freedom of speech or of the press.' "[164] If, however, a choice must be made between two propositions, first, that the clause substantially embodied the Blackstonian definition and left the law of seditious libel in force, or second, that it repudiated Blackstone and superseded the common law, the evidence points strongly in support of the former proposition. Contrary to Justice Holmes,[155] history favors the notion.

---

[154] Review of Alexander Meiklejohn, *Free Speech: And Its Relation to Self Government*, in *Harvard Lew Review* 62(1949):898.

[155] In *Abrams* v. *U.S.*, 250 U.S. 616, 630 (1919), Holmes, with Brandeis concurring, wrote: "I wholly disagree with the argument of the Government that the First Amendment left the common law as to seditious libel in force. History seems to me against the notion." On an earlier occasion, when times were more settled and Brandeis's influence was not yet felt, Holmes said with greater historical accuracy, in reference to freedom of press clauses: "The main purpose of such constitutional provisions is to prevent all such previous restraints as had been practised by other governments, and they do not prevent the subsequent punishment of such as may be deemed contrary to the public welfare." (*Patterson* v. *Colorado*, 205 U.S. 454, 462 [1907].)

CHAPTER IX

The Gestation of an American Libertarian Theory

The Sedition Act debates are unreliable as evidence of the Framers' original understanding of freedom of speech and press. But the statute provoked American libertarians to formulate a broad definition of the meaning and scope of liberty of expression for the first time in our history. As usual, however, an avant guard movement in free press theory originated in England. The 1783 trial of William D. Shipley, the Dean of St. Asaph,[1] touched off a flurry of libertarian writings. The government prosecuted him for a pamphlet brimming with seditious libel. The judge instructed the jury to base their verdict on whether he published the pamphlet. The jury returned a verdict of "guilty of publishing," but refused to decide on the libelous nature of the pamphlet. Accordingly, Thomas Erskine, the counsel for defense, moved for a new trial on ground that the court should have charged the jury more fully concerning its responsibility. He denied that the press was truly free under prevailing common-law doctrines and procedures:

> For how can it be said that the press is free because everything may be published without a previous licence, if the publisher . . . may be prosecuted by information of the King's Attorney-General, without the consent of the Grand Jury,—may be convicted by the petty jury, on the mere fact of publishing . . . and must then depend upon judges who may be the supporters of the very Administration whose measures are questioned by the defendant, and who

[1] Thomas Bayly Howell, comp., *A Complete Collection of State Trials to 1783*. Continued by T. J. Howell to 1820 (London, 1816-28), 34 vols., 21:846.

must therefore either give judgment against him or against themselves.[2]

As a close reading of his famous argument indicates, Erskine never
actually proposed more than the power of juries to decide the criminality of the accused's statement, but his exhilarating forensics conveyed the impression that the cause of a free press had found a new
David, and the libertarians rallied round him, especially after Chief
Justice Mansfield rejected his motion for a new trial by reaffirming
orthodox doctrines of the common law on seditious libel.[3] In 1784
and 1785, books and tracts appeared by Joseph Towers,[4] James
Adair,[5] Sir Samuel Romilly,[6] Manasseh Dawes,[7] and Capel Lofft,[8]
popularizing the views of Erskine and his great predecessor, Father of
Candor.

The new generation of English libertarians mainly championed
truth as a defense and the power of juries to give general verdicts.
Lofft, a rationalist leader who wrote with considerable power, came
to the verge of repudiating the concept of seditious libel altogether, a
nearly unprecedented step, but drew back from the abyss at the last
moment. Having defended the right to censure public men and
measures severely, and having denied that "the most artful and daring
libeller can shake a Government worthy of public confidence," he
declared that in the code of a free people who share political rights,
have full information on the operations of the government, and freely
investigate its measures, "it would be no surprize if the very title of
Libel were not to be found."[9] Yet when he enumerated his proposed
reforms in cases of Crown libel, he left the common law intact except

[2] "Argument, in the King's Bench, in support of the Rights of Juries," 1784,
in *Speeches of Thomas Lord Erskine. Reprinted from the Five Volume Octavo
Edition of 1810. With a Memoir of His Life* by Edward Walford (London,
1870), 1:190-191. For an analysis of Erskine's argument, see Sir James Fitzjames Stephen, *A History of the Criminal Law of England* (London, 1883, 3
vols.), 2:330-43.
[3] For an analysis of Mansfield's opinion, see William Holdsworth, *A History
of English Law*, 6th ed. (London, 1938-1966, 16 vols.), 10:676-88.
[4] *Observations on the Rights and Duty of Juries, in Trials for Libels*, 1784,
reprinted in Towers, *Tracts on Political and Other Subjects* (London, 1796),
2:1-174.
[5] *Discussions of the Law of Libels As at Present Received* (London, 1785),
97 pp.
[6] *A Fragment of the Constitutional Power and Duty of Juries Upon Trials
for Libels* (London, n.d., [1785]), 16 pp.
[7] *The Deformity of the Doctrine of Libels, and Informations Ex Officio*
(London, 1785), 40 pp.
[8] *An Essay on the Law of Libels* (London, 1785), 110 pp.
[9] *Ibid.*, 60-61.

for the power of the jury to judge an accused's criminal intent and the libelous character of his utterance. Adair, a Whig member of Parliament and a sergeant-at-law, fleetingly endorsed the view, last proposed by Francis Maseres and Jeremy Bentham, that the bad-tendency test of words should be scrapped and that only "actual" or "positive" injuries to the public rather than "presumed" ones should be punished.[10]

Manasseh Dawes, however, was the first to elaborate on the repressiveness of the bad-tendency test and advocate in considerable detail the overt-acts test in cases of political libel.[11] Comparable remarks by Father of Candor, Bentham, Maseres, and Adair had been brief and undeveloped. In 1785 Dawes, a Whig barrister of the Inner Temple, made their view the foundation of his whole discussion of the right of political criticism, as had Furneaux in respect to religious criticism. Dawes even conscripted Coke as an authority for his proposition that sedition can never be committed by words, but only by "violent act,"[12] an achievement in the technique of citing precedents that was worthy of some of Sir Edward's own inventions. Although the tenor of Dawes's remarks clashed fundamentally with the very concept of seditious libel, he at no point explicitly rejected it. The only interpretation of his thesis that allows it consistency is that he would not, contrary to his own assertions, restrict punishment to the commission of overt acts only, but would punish verbal incitements resulting in crime. There is no other way to reconcile his endorsement of the overt-acts test with his concern for the procedures to be followed in all trials for seditious libel. His tract must therefore be construed as a proposal for a new standard of criminality that should be the guide in cases of verbal crime against the government. Dawes may not have been the most radical English libertarian of the seventeenth and eighteenth centuries—that accolade belongs to Bentham, but he was nearly so and the most sensible and most modern-minded of all. Only Maseres, in a tract marred by contradictory propositions, rivalled Dawes as one who might be at home among twentieth-century libertarians who defend freedom for all expression that falls short of advocating and causing, directly and immediately, the commission of crime.

---

[10] *Discussion of the Law of Libels,* 27-28.

[11] *The Deformity of the Doctrine of Libels,* 11-24, 28. Theodore Schroeder, *Constitutional Free Speech Defined and Defended in an Unfinished Argument in a Case of Blasphemy* (New York, 1919), 419-421, claimed wrongly that Robert Morris in 1770, Joseph Fownes in 1773, and Richard Price in 1777 endorsed the overt-acts test, but wholly ignored Manasseh Dawes.

[12] Dawes, *The Deformity of the Doctrine of Libels,* 13.

The efforts of Dawes, Erskine, and indeed of all the English libertarians since Cato were rewarded in 1792 with the enactment of Fox's Libel Act which embodied their one most insistent demand, that the jury be empowered to give a general verdict on the whole matter put in issue in trials of criminal libel. The libertarian value of the reform was promptly demonstrated by unjustifiable verdicts of guilty returned by juries in a mass of cases. By curious coincidence, in England, as in the United States six years later, the largest wave of prosecutions for seditious libel in the nation's history immediately followed the enactment of the libertarian reform. The explanation, of course, lies with the impact of the ideas of the French Revolution upon public opinion in both Britain and America. The governments in both countries, determined to crush their political opposition, regarded criticism as subversion. There are more trials for seditious utterances reported in the *State Trials* for the two years following Fox's Libel Act than the total number reported for the whole of the eighteenth century before that time.[13] Within a year of Fox's Libel Act the attorney-general declared that he had on file two hundred informations for seditious libel.[14]

The most notorious conviction was that against Tom Paine for publishing his *Rights of Man*.[15] Although Erskine's argument in the Dean of St. Asaph's case was reputedly his best from a technical standpoint, his defense of Paine easily ranks as his most libertarian as well as his most unpopular. His argument elaborately described what he believed should be the scope and limits of freedom of the press. He declared at one point:

> The proposition which I mean to maintain as the basis of the liberty of the press, and without which it is an empty sound, is this: that every man, not intending to mislead, but seeking to enlighten others with what his own reason and conscience, however erroneously, have dictated to him as truth, may address himself to the universal reason of a whole nation, either upon the subjects of government in general, or upon that of our own particular country.[16]

Without rejecting the concept that words alone can criminally assault the government, Erskine came as close as he could to the position of Maseres and Dawes. His principles were so broad as to allow the

---

[13] Stephen, *A History of the Criminal Law of England*, 2:362-363.
[14] Sir Thomas Erskine May, *The Constitutional History of England Since the Accession of George III, 1760-1860* (London, 1880), 2:142 n. 2.
[15] *Rex* v. *Paine*, Howell, *State Trials*, 22:357 (1792).
[16] *Ibid.*, 414.

inference that he believed that no words should ever be prosecuted short of their successful incitement to some criminal act. His position had a nearly revolutionary foundation, one that should have been American and which, as a matter of fact, James Madison would espouse fleetingly in 1794 and elaborately in 1799. If, Erskine declared, the ruler is sovereign his subjects cannot criticize him or his government or its policies. If, however, the government served the people merely as their agent, because they possess sovereignty, their political opinions could have no legal or logical limits. They could say whatever they pleased short of producing some breach of the peace. Said Erskine:

> I have insisted at great length on the origin of governments . . . because I consider it to be not only an essential support, but the very foundation of the liberty of the press. . . . If the people have, without possible recall, delegated all their authorities, they have no jurisdiction to act, and therefore none to think or write upon such subjects; and it would be a libel to arraign government or any of its acts, before those who have no jurisdiction to correct them. But . . . no legal argument can shake the freedom of the press in my sense of it, if I am supported in my doctrines concerning the great unalienable right of the people to reform or change their governments. It is because the liberty of the press resolves itself into this great issue, that it has been in every country the last liberty which subjects have been able to wrest from power. Other liberties are held *under* government, but the liberty of opinion keeps governments themselves in due subjection to their duties.[17]

His argument, which the jury rejected, brought libertarian thought to a new crest.

In the same year, 1792, Patrick Duffin and Thomas Lloyd were convicted of seditious libel for having pasted a placard on the door of their debtor's prison alleging that liberty would commence in Great Britain after the abolition of infamous bastilles, as France had shown.[18] A jury voted guilty against John Frost, an attorney, for his remarks, probably uttered when tipsy, that he favored equality, no king, and a better constitution. Frost was disbarred and pilloried as well as imprisoned for his conversation.[19] William Winterbotham, a Baptist minister, commented favorably in his sermons on the French Revolution and condemned oppressive taxes; after a jury convicted

---

[17] *Ibid.,* 437.
[18] *Rex* v. *Duffin and Lloyd,* Howell, *State Trials,* 22:318 (1792).
[19] *Rex* v. *Frost,* Howell, *State Trials,* 22:471 (1793).

him for seditious words, a court sentenced him to four years in prison and steep fines. In this case the jury convicted against the court's recommendation of an acquittal.[20] The cases of Thomas Briellat, William Hudson, Thomas Muir, T. Fyshe Palmer, William Skirving, Maurice Margarot, and Joseph Gerrald in 1793 and 1794 were similar to those already mentioned. In each the juries returned verdicts of guilty for seditious words, oral or printed, that were harmless and hardly even intemperate.[21] In a few cases, those of John Lambert, Alexander Whyte, and Daniel Eaton,[22] the juries voted for acquittals or returned verdicts of "guilty of publishing only," but the English seditious libel trials, like the American ones a few years later, proved conclusively that making juries judges of the criminality of allegedly seditious words did not have the effect of broadening the scope of free discussion, certainly not during times of stress—and there are rarely sedition trials at any other times.[23]

The most notable published protest against these trials was the Reverend Robert Hall's *An Apology for the Freedom of the Press*.[24] At the time of publication, in 1793, Hall was a Baptist minister of Cambridge, England, who admired the works of Joseph Priestly and Jeremy Bentham. Hall took the position that all men should have an absolute liberty of discussing "every subject which can fall within the compass of the human mind," and he meant what he said. Like Furneaux and Jefferson, he denied that the magistrate should have a power to punish the mere expression of opinions, but unlike their statements, which appeared in contexts of defending religious opinions, Hall's particularly concerned political opinions, just as Dawes's or Erskine's. Distinguishing words, sentiment, and opinion from "conduct" or "behavior," he demanded that only the latter be regarded as criminal.[25] He made an otherwise commonplace point that freedom of expression is to be cherished as a step to the truth by noting that

[20] *Rex* v. *Winterbotham*, Howell, *State Trials*, 22:875 (1793).

[21] Each of the cases, with citations to volume 22 of the *State Trials*, is discussed by May, *The Constitutional History of England*, 2:142-150. Muir's case is also discussed in Arthur E. Sutherland, Jr., "British Trials for Disloyal Association during the French Revolution," *Cornell Law Quarterly* 35 (Spring 1949):309-315.

[22] *Rex* v. *Lambert, Perry, and Gray*, Howell, *State Trials*, 22:953 (1793), and *Rex* v. *Eaton*, Howell, *State Trials*, 22:753 (1793).

[23] The most notable acquittals during the 1790's in England were in cases of treason, not sedition. See the discussion of the trials of Hardy and Tooke in Sutherland, "British Trials," *Cornell Law Quarterly* 34:316-328.

[24] Issued as a tract in 1793. I used the reprint in John Foster, ed., *The Miscellaneous Works and Remains of the Reverend Robert Hall* (London, 1846), 159-233.

[25] *Ibid.*, 172.

opinions of social value were frequently mixed with error. Publications, he stated, "like every thing else that is human, are of a mixed nature, where truth is often blended with falsehood, and important hints suggested in the midst of much impertinent or pernicious matter; nor is there any way of separating the precious from the vile, but by tolerating the whole."[26] This observation may seem obvious now, but it was original and cogent in its time, when men as sensible as John Adams and William Cushing could agree even in a moment of calm that falsehood was criminal if published against the government.

In England, when Hall wrote, and in America after the Sedition Act, people were jailed for snatch phrases or sentences culled from lengthy remarks and condemned as false. Hall's thought must be measured for its courage and libertarianism in the context of the repressive prosecutions that swept England when he wrote:

> [Government] being an institution purely human, one would imagine it were the proper province for freedom of discussion in its utmost extent. It is surely just that every one should have a right to examine those measures by which the happiness of all may be affected. . . . Under pretence of its being seditious to express any disapprobation of the *form* of our government, the most alarming attempts are made to wrest the liberty of the press out of our hands. . . . An inquiry respecting the comparative excellence of civil constitutions can be forbidden on no other pretence than that of its tending to sedition and anarchy. This plea, however, will have little weight with those who reflect to how many ill purposes it has already applied; and that when the example has been introduced of suppressing opinions on account of their imagined ill tendency, it has seldom been confined within any safe or reasonable bounds.
> . . . The law hath amply provided against overt acts of sedition and disorder, and to suppress mere opinions by any other method than reason and argument, is the height of tyranny. Freedom of thought being intimately connected with the happiness and dignity of man in every stage of his being, is of so much more importance than the preservation of any constitution, that to infringe the former, under pretence of supporting the latter, is to sacrifice the means to the end.[27]

Erskine himself in his justly celebrated defense of Paine against a charge of seditious libel provided Hall with an immediate model, for the great lawyer had argued, "His [Paine's] *opinions* indeed were adverse to our system; but I maintain that OPINION is free, and that

[26] *Ibid.*
[27] *Ibid.*, 174, 176-177, and 179.

CONDUCT alone is amenable to the law." This statement had been preceded by the declaration that every man ought to be free to publish "what his own reason and conscience, however erroneously, have dictated to him as truth" on all political subjects.[28] Erskine repeated similar views in Frost's trial,[29] but there as in Paine's trial his further remarks modified his seeming endorsement of the overt-acts test. He regarded the calumny of living magistrates as criminal. In the same class he placed contumacious private judgment and words spoken with a premeditated design of "undermining" the government. He also believed that "time or occasion" may mix with words and invest otherwise innocent expressions with an "enormous guilt."[30] Moreover, Erskine's tolerance for political criticism did not extend to religious criticism. In 1797 he abandoned his defense of freedom of the press by prosecuting the publisher of Paine's *Age of Reason*, a defense of Deism which he deemed an unlawful attack upon the Christian religion.[31]

But no man in American history, except the unknown "Junius Wilkes" in 1782, had as yet approached Erskine's libertarianism in the cases of Paine and Frost, let alone matched Dawes and Hall, or even Maseres and Adair, in their defense of freedom of political criticism against the doctrines of seditious libel. Between the publication of the works of Dawes and Hall in England, America adopted the Constitution and the First Amendment. What American tracts or essays had appeared on the subject of speech and press during that time? Franklin's 1789 essay on the press, discussed in the preceding chapter, was of such a character that supporters of the Sedition Act quoted it during the House debate in 1798, and no opponent of the Act even tried to explain that the damaging testimony from Franklin meant other than it seemed. Senator Robert Goodloe Harper, the South Carolina Federalist who coauthored the Sedition Act, declared that Franklin, "this great man, the champion of liberty . . . did not think that the liberty of the press would be abridged by an explicit law for curbing its licentiousness. Supported by this great authority, I can never believe that a law to punish the publication of false, scandalous, and malicious libels, or conviction by a jury is a law 'to abridge the liberty of the press,' as intended by the Constitution."[32]

The only other American contribution was an anonymous tract of

[28] *Speeches of Erskine*, 1:313 and 309.
[29] *Ibid.*, 1:392.
[30] *Ibid.*, 1:309-310 (Paine's trial) and 380 (Frost's trial).
[31] *Rex* v. *Williams*, Howell, *State Trials*, 26:654 (1797).
[32] *Annals of Congress*, 5th Cong., 2nd Sess., 2102, 2169-70.

1789, published in Boston, by "a Friend to Harmony" who addressed himself exclusively to the problem of personal libels against public men.[33] He took the libertarian view that "a law against libels cannot exist without endangering the liberty of the press."[34] The thesis of the tract was that libels, being addressed to public opinion, should be answered in the press, leaving the public to judge the truth. But the writer wholly ignored the problem of libels on the government, making his contribution to libertarian thought on the subject of seditious utterance slight. Nor was the American contribution in formal debates any greater than in publications, for we have seen that, with the important exception of the Pennsylvania minority, the recorded pronouncements of the members of state ratifying conventions who defined freedom of the press were Blackstonian in character.

Nothing in the American newspapers approximated the sweeping libertarianism or trenchant analysis of the limits of a free press that turned up in British theory. Dwight Teeter has claimed that quotations which he reproduced from the *Massachusetts Centinel* and from a couple of Charleston newspapers "are in direct contradiction to the common law of seditious libel."[35] The statement is misleading. Those papers simply believed that a true statement should not be regarded as a criminal libel; none of the papers rejected the crux of the concept of seditious libel, namely that mere words can criminally assault the government. Teeter may, mistakenly, have thought that the advocacy of a right to criticize the government, or its measures or officials, constituted a repudiation of seditious libel. In fact, however, Cato and the Zengerians had consistently advocated such a right and conceded that seditious libel deserved criminal punishment. Neither the right to criticize nor truth as a defense was incompatible with the doctrine of criminal libel. No state had adopted truth as a defense until Pennsylvania in 1790, and no state, not even Pennsylvania, adopted a statute

[33] *Candid Observations on Libels . . . With Some Observations on the Liberty of the Press.* By a Friend to Harmony (Boston, 1789), 22 pp. The only other American tract which I have found is Samuel Stanhope Smith's *A Sermon on Slander delivered at the church on Brattle St., Boston, Oct. 24, 1790* (Boston, 1791), 24 pp. Smith, the Vice President and Professor of Moral Philosophy at Princeton, was concerned with slander as a sin rather than as a crime. He rejected the notion that truth is not slanderous.

[34] *Candid Considerations*, 20.

[35] Teeter, "Legacy of Expression: Philadelphia Newspapers and Congress During the War for Independence," Ph.D. diss. University of Wisconsin, School of Journalism, 1966, pp. 335-36. Teeter cited the *Gazette of the State of South Carolina* (Charleston), Aug. 27, 1783; *South Carolina State Gazette*, Oct. 1, 1785; and *Columbian Centinel* (Boston), April 17, May 18, May 28, June 15, July 6, July 30, and Sept. 24, 1785. I have checked all these issues; they yield nothing like an attack on the concept of seditious libel.

rejecting the crime of seditious or criminal libel. Moreover only the hearsay remarks of "Centinel" in 1772 and the statements by a few Oswald supporters in 1782 recommended repudiation of seditious libel, but they struck no responsive chords; indeed, they were ignored.

The most common libertarian principle of a free press espoused by newspapers revealed their watchdog function as the Fourth Estate. One small town paper, for example, extolled the press as the source from which the people "learn the circumstances of our country, its various interests, and relations. Here too public men and measures are scrutinized. Should any man or body of men dare to form a system against our interests, by this means it will be unfolded to the great body of the people, and the alarm instantly spread through every part of the continent. In this way only, can we know how far our public servants perform the duties of their respective stations."[36] Even that view, however, met dissent from more conventional voices. Another country paper believed that the press should "point out the defects of government" but not of office holders. "Measures and not men are the proper subjects of cognizance to a free press."[37] Philip Freneau's *National Gazette* of Philadelphia deprecatingly reprinted the *Newark Gazette*'s "ill considered opinions" which endorsed the criminal prosecutions of editors who "censure the government or calumniate its officers."[38] Freneau believed that opinions "opposed not only to the constitution but the very essence of government" should go unpunished, although he conceded that a free press functioned "under the restraint of existing laws," which allowed newspapers to "estimate justly the wisdom of leading measures of administration."[39] These representative views showed that the press on freedom of the press ranged from Cato and Zenger to Blackstone.

An American approximation of British libertarianism before 1798 turned up somewhat uncertainly in a congressional debate of 1794. President Washington, having in mind the Democratic societies of western Pennsylvania, referred critically, in a message to Congress, to "certain self-created societies" that had urged resistance against the whiskey excise.[40] The Senate, in a formal response to the President,

---

[36] *Alexandria Virginia Gazette*, Jan. 14, 1790. See also *Virginia Herald and Fredricksburg Advertiser*, Jan. 7, 1790.

[37] *Virginia Gazette and Winchester Advertiser*, Jan. 5, 1791.

[38] *National Gazette*, May 14, 1792.

[39] *Philadelphia Aurora*, July 30, 1794 and Dec. 26, 1794. On June 7, 1792, Freneau's *National Gazette* asserted that Pennsylvania's constitution left the press "perfectly free, and its real abuses punishable only by the laws of the land."

[40] *Annals of Congress*, 3rd Cong., 2nd Sess., p. 792, November 19, 1794.

declared that the activities of these societies had injured the government and helped foment the Whiskey Rebellion. A motion by Senator Aaron Burr to delete this passage in the Senate's response met defeat.[41] In the House, however, the Republicans, after a four-day debate, managed to expunge the reference to "self-created societies." The House simply expressed its great concern that anyone should have misrepresented the government so seriously as to foment an insurrection.[42] A Virginia trio, Representatives William B. Giles, John Nicholas, and James Madison, in conducting their successful fight to water down the statement, expressed the libertarian position.

Giles, who spoke first, declared that the motion intended "to censure the Democratic societies." Defending the right of free association, whether for religious, political, philosophical, or other purposes, he stated that Congress had no constitutional power "to attempt checking or restraining public opinion." If any societies had acted illegally, they were punishable under the law. But the House simply had no "business to pass random votes of censure."[43] The response by William Smith, a South Carolina Federalist, sharpened the issue and made the debate a precursor of the elaborate controversy four years later over the Sedition Act. Smith, alleging that he was a friend to freedom of the press, believed "the dissemination of improper sentiments . . . subversive of good order" a suitable object of the House's reprobation. The matter in question was not the legality of the self-created societies, but the mischievous consequences of their calumnies against the government.[44]

Nicholas, in reply, repeated Giles's point that censure went beyond the powers of the House. In a statement marked by confusion, he declared: "It was wrong to condemn societies for particular acts. . . . I cannot agree to persecution for the sake of opinion."[45] It was a poor libertarian argument that could not distinguish acts from opinions, particularly when the societies stood accused of having provoked an actual insurrection. Later, Nicholas rose to answer a contention that the existence of libel prosecutions proved that calumnious attacks on government were just objects of reprehension. He failed wholly to assault libel prosecutions, thereby revealing how impoverished or stunted was his libertarian thought in comparison to the arguments he was to make only four years later. In 1794 he merely asserted the

[41] *Ibid.*, 794, November 21, 1794.
[42] *Ibid.*, 946-47, November 28, 1794.
[43] *Ibid.*, 900-01, November 24, 1794.
[44] *Ibid.*, 901-02, November 24, 1794.
[45] *Ibid.*, 905, November 24, 1794.

unfairness of comparing the censure of a society with the prosecution of a libel, because in the latter case the accused party had an opportunity to defend himself. The Democratic societies had no such opportunity. They stood accused, said Nicholas, of never having once said a good word about government policies. "If these societies had censured every proceeding of Government, there would have been," he remarked, "the greatest reason for taking some measures." But they had taken no notice whatever of many acts of the government.[46] Aside from his sinister implication about "taking some measures," Nicholas made a confused and fatuous argument.

Giles, in a rambling speech, passingly reflected a genuine libertarian position. "Many people who condemn the proceedings of the Democratic societies, yet will not choose to see them divested of the inalienable privilege of thinking, of speaking, of writing, and of printing. Persons may condemn the abuse in exercising a right, and yet feel the strongest sympathy with the right itself. Are not Muir and Palmer, and the other martyrs of Scotch despotism, toasted from one end of the Continent to the other? And why is it so? These men asserted the right of thinking, of speaking, of writing, and of printing."[47] The significance of this statement lies in Giles's condemnation of the convictions of Thomas Muir and the Reverend T. Fyshe Palmer for the crime of seditious libel. Their notoriously unfair, even brutal, trials in Scotland in 1793 were the result of their outspoken campaign for annual parliaments and universal suffrage.[48] Given the facts of these cases, and the severe sentences, Giles's statement should not be stretched from an obvious censure of the two trials to a repudiation of all trials for seditious libel. Moreover, he never took the trouble of explaining what he meant by freedom of speech and press. Indeed, Fischer Ames, a Federalist, observed in reply that Giles "had been occupied in refuting what nobody had asserted, and in proving what nobody had denied." Ames himself spoke warmly of freedom of speech and press, attacking only, he said, its abuses.[49]

Madison responded that the people, in forming the Constitution, had retained all rights not delegated, making Congress powerless to legislate on certain subjects. "Opinions," he stated, "are not the objects of legislation. You animadvert on the abuse of reserved rights: how far will this go? It may extend to the liberty of speech, and of the press. . . . If we advert to the nature of Republican Govern-

---

[46] *Ibid.*, 911, November 25, 1794.
[47] *Ibid.*, 918, November 26, 1794.
[48] May, *The Constitutional History of England*, 2:145-149.
[49] *Annals of Congress*, 3rd Cong., 2nd Sess., pp. 921, 924, November 26, 1794.

ment, we shall find that the censorial power is in the people over the Government, and not in the Government over the people."[50] That proposition, a few years later, served as the basis for a powerful libertarian argument against the concept of seditious libel. In 1794, however, Madison merely proceeded to restate the seventeenth-century argument that truth would prevail over error, making it unnecessary to proceed against the publications of the societies in question. Although he concluded with merely a limp Miltonic cliché, his brief statement of 1794 suggested his belief, which few Americans had previously expressed, that political opinions should be free. Moreover he provided a profound principle as the basis for that belief. However laconic the remark, it had the potential to transform the concept of free speech.

The Republicans rewrote the offensive passage in the House's response to President Washington, but at no point had the Federalists proposed action against the publications or opinions of the "self-created societies." Publications and opinions did not become subject of repressive legislation until 1798. Only then did the fully libertarian theories emerge.

Before then, a clear opportunity presented itself for the development of the libertarian argument. In 1796 New York had a new "McDougall case." The victim was William Keteltas, a Republican lawyer and member of the local Democratic Society. Keteltas had been present at the unfair and juryless trial of two Irish ferrymen who were convicted for allegedly insulting an alderman by refusing to ferry him off-schedule. Outraged by the proceedings in the Court of General Sessions, Keteltas published a newspaper article denouncing the tyranny of the trial magistrates—the mayor and five aldermen. He demanded a grand-jury investigation and impeachment of the guilty officials by the state Assembly. When the grand jury went fishing and the Assembly took up whitewashing, Keteltas aimed his blistering newspaper comments against the Assembly itself. That august body, smarting from his censure, which it took to be a seditious insult, summoned him to appear before its bar. Keteltas had to answer for his articles, which members condemned as "highly injurious to the honor and dignity" of the Assembly and as "calculated to create distrust and destroy the confidence" of the people in their representatives.[51]

[50] *Ibid.*, 934, November 27, 1794.
[51] Alfred Young brought the Keteltas case to my attention. See his excellent book *The Democratic-Republicans in New York, 1788-1797* (Chapel Hill, N.C., 1967), 380-93. See also *Journal of the Votes and Proceedings of the*

Before the bar of the House, Keteltas admitted authorship of the offensive articles. The Assembly promptly and without debate found him guilty of "a misdemeanor and contempt of the authority of this House." When Keteltas refused to humble himself by admitting his wrong and asking pardon, the Assembly immediately ordered him jailed.[52]

The case presented a perfect opportunity for a libertarian argument in defense of Keteltas. Representative John Bird, a Republican member of the Assembly, raised the issue in the right terms: "Shall we attempt to prevent citizens from thinking? From giving their opinion on acts of the legislature? Shall we stop freedom of the press?"[53] Bird spoke in vain; his questions were ignored or forgotten, and unsupported by any argument in development of the theme. Keteltas became a popular hero among the Jeffersonian faithful in New York, and his case became a cause célèbre. Yet freedom of the press and the right of the citizen to criticize his government played no part in the extensive argument in Keteltas's behalf. Not even Keteltas himself, an experienced politician and lawyer, spoke to the issue, although while in prison he published five articles protesting the "unconstitutional, tyrannical, and illegal" proceedings of the Assembly.[54]

In the last article he discoursed at length on "freedom of speech," but did so exclusively in the context of a discussion of parliamentary privilege. That is, he spoke only of the right of the legislator's freedom of debate. Not once did he allude to his own right, or that of the people, to debate public matters—let alone have the same scope of freedom of political expression as members of the House. He based his defense on the narrow argument that he had not breached any of the privileges of the House and that the House could not lawfully deprive any citizen of his liberty without benefit of grand-jury proceedings and trial by jury. An anonymous supporter, possibly Brockholst Livingston, signing himself "Camillus Junius" after a hero of the ancient Roman Republic, trenchantly put forth the same argument in the press. Although he pronounced himself to be "no friend to the doctrine of libels," he believed it to be "a *perfect* guardian of the press" compared to the power of punishing for breach of parliamentary privilege. Camillus Junius acknowledged that certain verbal

---

General Assembly of New-York 1691-1765 (New York, 1764-66), 19th Sess., March 8, 1796, and Greenleaf's *New York Journal and Patriotic Register*, March 11, 1796.

[52] *Ibid.*

[53] *New York Journal*, March 11, 1796.

[54] *The Argus, or Greenleaf's New Daily Advertiser*, April 4, 5, 7, 8, and 12, 1796.

insults to the House "ought not to pass unpunished." The only remedy, he said, was a jury trial that protected the rights of the accused. "The Courts of criminal jurisdiction are open to prosecutions, which the Attorney-General may commence by information or indictment. A libel tending to asperse or vilify the house of Assembly or any of its members, may be as severely punished in the Supreme Court, as a libel against the government. This, then, . . . is the remedy they should appeal to . . ."[55] The assault on the power of the Assembly to punish citizens for alleged breaches of privilege surely marked a libertarian action. But equally revealing was the absence of discussion of Representative Bird's questions about the right of the citizen to criticize his government.

Keteltas, freed on a writ of habeas corpus as soon as the legislature ended its session, brought an unsuccessful suit for false imprisonment against the speaker of the House. The Assembly supported its speaker by a vote of 88 to 1, and the court ruled against Keteltas. A "Spectator" concluded his report of the trial by remarking: "The freedom of the press is taken away, and personal liberty is no longer secure in the state of New York."[56] Other than Bird's this was the only reference to freedom of the press that emerged from the case.

The libertarians had focused instead on the arbitrary power of the legislature to punish seditious contempts of its authority or reputation. Occasionally, during the colonial period, victims of a provincial assembly had relied on due process to challenge the practice of punishing breaches of parliamentary privilege. The Keteltas case marks the first major criticism of the use of the "privilege" to muzzle offensive publications or remarks. Four years later, however, the Senate of the United States found that a printer's allegedly seditious publications constituted a "high breach of privileges."[57]

Thus, as late as 1794 and 1796, as the Congressional debates on self-created societies and the Keteltas case reveal, American libertarian theory froze into a state of arrested development on the crucial question of the right of the citizen to criticize his government without being accused of a verbal political crime. "Freedom of the press" was invoked, to be sure, but the phrase was not self-defining, its meaning neither self-evident nor static, and its mere utterance *ex vi termini* neither a sovereign remedy nor adequate to support a libertarian the-

[55] *Ibid.*, March 15 and April 6, 1796, reprinted in Leonard W. Levy, ed., *Freedom of the Press from Zenger to Jefferson* (Indianapolis: Bobbs Merrill, 1966), 158-70.
[56] *The Time Piece* (New York), December 22, 1797.
[57] James Morton Smith, *Freedom's Fetters: The Alien and Sedition Laws and American Civil Liberties* (Ithaca, 1956), 294.

ory. Pithy slogans and glittering generalities reflected sentiment and perhaps a principle, but not a theory. Bird's sloganeering, Ketaltas's evasions, Nicholas's inconsistency, and Madison's ultimate reliance on the federal principle together with Milton's truth-shall-prevail-over-error, can scarcely be compared for libertarian qualities, freshness, or boldness, to the arguments of Cato or James Alexander, let alone Junius Wilkes, Thomas Erskine, or Robert Hall.

Not until after 1798 did Americans rival the libertarianism of their English counterparts. The reason for the sudden if belated emergence of a sharply articulated body of "Jeffersonian" thought on freedom of speech and press was the threat that the government of the United States under the Adams administration might attempt to eliminate political criticism, create a one-party press and a monolithic party system, and by controlling public opinion insure a Federalist victory in the elections of 1800. The Sedition Act made criminal "any false, scandalous and malicious" writings, utterances, or publications against the government, Congress, or the president, with intent to defame them, bring them into contempt or disrepute, or excite against them the hatred of the people.

Yet the Federalists in 1798 believed that true freedom of the press would benefit if truth—*their* truth—were the measure of freedom. Their infamous Sedition Act was, in the words of Gilbert and Sullivan, the true embodiment of everything excellent. It was, that is, the very epitome of libertarian thought since the time of Zenger's case. The Sedition Act incorporated everything that the libertarians had demanded: a requirement that criminal intent be shown; the power of the jury to decide whether the accused's statement was libelous as a matter of law as well as of fact; and truth as a defense, an innovation not accepted in England until 1843. By every standard the Sedition Act constituted a great victory for libertarian principles of freedom of the press—except that libertarian standards abruptly changed, because the Republicans immediately recognized a Pyrrhic victory.

In the course of the House debates, advocates of the bill clearly manifested their belief that the political opinion of the opposition party constituted seditious libel, subject to prosecution under the bill.[58] Representative Albert Gallatin of Pennsylvania, an opponent of the bill, accurately summed up the situation when he declared:

> This bill and its supporters suppose, in fact, that whoever dislikes
> the measures of Administration and of a temporary majority in

[58] See, for example, Speech of Rep. Allen of Connecticut, July 5, 1798, *Annals of Congress*, 5th Cong., 2nd session, 2093-2100; speech of Rep. Harper of South Carolina, July 5, *ibid.*, 2102-2103.

Congress, and shall, either by speaking or writing, express his disapprobation and his want of confidence in the men now in power,
is seditious, is an enemy, not of the Administration, but of the Constitution, and is liable to punishment . . . this bill must be considered only as a weapon used by a party now in power in order to
perpetuate their authority and preserve their present places.[59]

Although that explains why the Federalists passed the Alien and
Sedition Acts, questions persist. How were they able to get away
with it, even with majorities in Congress, and why did they enact the
law against seditious libel when it was not legally needed? After all,
the First Amendment did not repeal the English common law on the
press and a federal common law of crimes existed at the time. Politics
provides the answers to the questions.

Federalists of whatever hue shared a sinister understanding that
national security and party supremacy might benefit if the nation
could be first frightened and then panicked. To what extent Federalist leaders felt or feigned the hysteria to which they gave voice is
unknowable. The certain fact is that they exploited a crisis in foreign
relations for the sake of partisan advantage.[60] Chilling stories in the
Federalist press on the imminence of a French invasion and the dangers of subversive activities provoked pathological sentiments. Congressman Robert Goodloe Harper, a coauthor of the Sedition Act,
warned against philosophers who talked about "the perfectability of
mankind." "The philosophers," he declared, "are the pioneers of revolution."[61] Speaker Jonathan Dayton of New Jersey, a Framer of the
Constitution, shrilly warned about the horrors of a Jacobin invasion.[62]
Joseph Hopkinson, the Federalist lawyer who composed the patriotic
anthem, "Hail Columbia," said of the Jacobinical faction in the United
States, "It is the overthrow of your government and constitution, it
is the disorder and ruin of your country, it is your annihilation as a
nation, they seek."[63] Fenno's *Gazette*, a rabid Federalist newspaper,
cautioned parents about "the diffusion of Jacobinical principles, thro'

[59] Speech of July 5, 1798, *ibid.*, 2110. On July 10, Gallatin observed that the
bill's supporters admitted that its true object was "to enable one party to
oppress the other. . . . Is it not their object to frighten and suppress all presses
which they consider as contrary to their views; to prevent a free circulation of
opinion; to suffer the people at large to hear only partial accounts, and but
one side of the question; to delude and deceive them by partial information,
and, through those means, to perpetuate themselves in power?" *Ibid.*, 2162.
See also the speech of Nicholas of Virginia, 2140-2141.
[60] Smith, *Freedom's Fetters*, chap. 1.
[61] *Annals of Congress*, 5th Cong. 2nd sess., pp. 1175-80, March 29, 1798.
[62] *Ibid.*, 1676-78, May 10, 1798.
[63] Hopkinson, *What is Our Situation and What Our Prospects* (Philadelphia, 1798), 29-30.

the medium of children's Books," which corrupted young minds by making them "imbibe, with their very milk," the poisons of atheism and sedition.[64]

Federalists commemorated the Fourth of July in sinister fashion. While the officers of a New York military company drank to the toast "One and but one party in the United States," Federalist partisans in Newburyport, Massachusetts, publicly burned copies of the leading Republican newspaper in New England. On that same festive day the Senate, in the hope of controlling public opinion and crushing the opposition party, passed the bill making it a crime to criticize the government. The sponsor of the bill, Senator James Lloyd, expressed anxiety to George Washington—the bill might not be severe enough to muzzle "the lovers of Liberty, or, in other words, the Jacobins"; moreover, complained Lloyd, "I fear Congress will close the session without a declaration of War, which I look upon as necessary to enable us to lay our hands on traitors."[65] In a similar spirit the president of Yale, in his Fourth of July Sermon, warned that if the author of the Declaration of Independence, then the Vice-President of the United States, were to have his way, the country would "see the Bible cast into a bonfire . . . our wives and daughters the victims of legal prostitution . . . our sons become the disciples of Voltaire, and the dragoons of Marat."[66] Federalists identified the Republican opposition, which they did not accept as legitimate, as revolutionary Jacobins treasonably allied with the foreign enemy.

Hate so obsessed the Federalists and so convinced them that anyone whose opinion differed must be a criminal subversive that they openly reviled even their fellow Congressmen. When, for example, Gallatin discounted the possibility of an invasion, Dayton retorted that because his principles were those of "the furious hordes of democrats which threatened this country with subjugation," Gallatin could calmly watch "our dwellings burning, and might laugh at our calamities and mock when our fears came upon us."[67] When Edward Livingston of New York spoke against a Federalist system of tyranny that would destroy civil liberties, John Allen of Connecticut lashed him for "intimate acquaintance with treason" and claimed that he "vomited" falsehood on "everything sacred, human and divine."[68] The prime victim of abuse was the vice president himself, who ob-

---

[64] *Gazette of the United States* (Philadelphia), June 4, 1800.

[65] Lloyd to Washington, July 4, 1798, quoted in Smith, *Freedom's Fetters*, 110.

[66] Theodore Dwight, *The Nature, and Danger, of Infidel Philosophy* (Hartford, 1798), 9.

[67] *Annals of Congress*, 5th Cong., 2nd sess., pp. 2017-18, June 21, 1798.

[68] *Ibid.*, 2095.

served: "It suffices for a man to be a philosopher and to believe that human affairs are susceptible of improvement, and to look forward, rather than back to the Gothic ages, for perfection, to mark him as an anarchist, disorganiser, atheist, and enemy of the government."[69] To be an alien or even a naturalized citizen equally stigmatized: was not Gallatin himself a Swiss, and were not Priestley, Cooper, Volney, Burk, Duane, Callendar, and other foreign-born scholars and journalists the leaders of swarms of wild Irishmen, political refugees, and French apostles of sedition? It was necessary to "strike terror among these people," as Congressman Harper put it.[70]

Thus, the Sedition Act, the capstone of the new Federalist system, expressed the easy rule of thumb offered by the party organ in the nation's capital, "He that is not for us, is against us."[71] A Boston editor added: "Whatever American is a friend to the present administration of the American government, is undoubtedly a true republican, a true patriot. . . . Whatever American opposes the administration is an anarchist, a jacobin and a traitor. . . . It is *Patriotism* to write in favor of our government—it is Sedition to write against it."[72] Given such a view of things, the Federalists believed that the government could be criminally assaulted merely by political opinions that had the supposed tendency of lowering the public esteem of the administration. Security lay in the elimination of political criticism and the creation of a one-party press, eventually a one-party system.

Incapable of distinguishing dissent from disloyalty, the Federalists easily resorted to legal coercion to control public opinion for party purposes. They controlled the federal courts and many of the state courts; they could have relied upon the common law of seditious libel. In fact there were a few common-law indictments for the crime of seditious libel. A federal grand jury in Richmond presented Congressman Samuel J. Cabell for seditious libel in 1797, and prosecutions for seditious libel were also begun in the federal courts against Benjamin F. Bache of the Philadelphia *Aurora* and John Daly Burk of the New York *Time Piece* in 1798, shortly before the passage of the Sedition Act.[73]

But even in England, where the criminal courts exercised an unquestioned jurisdiction over seditious libels, it was politically advisable in the 1790s to declare public policy in the most unmistakable

[69] Jefferson to T. M. Randolph, May 3, 1798, quoted in Smith, *Freedom's Fetters*, 12.
[70] Quoted in *ibid.*, 142.
[71] *Gazette of the United States*, June 20, 1798.
[72] *Columbian* Centinel, Oct. 5, 1798.
[73] Smith, *Freedom's Fetters*, 95, 183-84, 188-220.

terms by the enactment of sedition statutes. Legislation helped ensure effective enforcement of the law, stirred public opinion against its intended victims, and in every way served party objectives. Accordingly the Federalists, who were very much influenced by British experience and legislation, emulated the British model by resorting to legislation.[74] The statute additionally seemed expedient because the political opposition, which it sought to stigmatize, had insisted that libels against the United States might be tried only by the state courts which were not nearly as trustworthy in some states as the federal courts. Thus the legislation commended itself to the party in every way, regardless of the availability of common-law weapons.

The pressures engendered by the Sedition Act drove Jeffersonians to originate so broad a theory of freedom of expression that they repudiated the concept of seditious libel and advocated the exemption of political opinions from all legal restraints. In the Congressional debates the libertarians did not go that far, although they denounced the Federalist theory of freedom of expression as much too narrow, unwise, and contradictory to the First Amendment. Harrison Grey Otis of Massachusetts had espoused Federalist theory when he delivered a speech based on the following theme: "This freedom . . . is nothing more than the liberty of writing, publishing, and speaking, one's thoughts, under the condition of being answerable to the injured party, whether it be the Government or an individual, for false, malicious, and seditious expressions, whether spoken or written; and the liberty of the press is merely an exemption from all previous restraints."[75] John Nicholas of Virginia denied, however, that there could be any satisfactory way of distinguishing liberty from "licentiousness" without abridging liberty itself; he rejected any distinctions based on "truth" versus "falsehood": offensive criticism of the government would invariably be deemed false. Printers, as a result, "would not only refrain from publishing anything of the least questionable nature, but they would be afraid of publishing the truth, as, though true, it might not always be in their power to establish the truth to

[74] On the English legislation of the 1790s, see May, *The Constitutional History of England*, 2:161-174. The parliamentary debates and the texts of the Treasonable Practices Act and of the Sedition Act of 1795, known together as "The Two Acts," were published in London in 1796 under the title *The History of the Two Acts* and were imported into the United States and advertised under the title *History of the Treason and Sedition Bills lately passed in Great Britain*. For the British influence on Federalist thought, see Manning J. Dauer, *The Adams Federalists* (Baltimore, 1953), 157-59, and Smith, *Freedom's Fetters*, 105.

[75] Speech of July 10, *ibid.*, 2148. For similar statements by other Federalists, see pp. 2097 (Allen), 2102 and 2167-2168 (Harper), and 2112 (Dana).

the satisfaction of a court of justice."[76] As one skeptical scholar has conceded, to distinguish, as Nicholas did, between liberty and license challenged "the prevailing Blackstonian view of the right of free expression. For, to Blackstone and the Federalists, free expression meant, to state the matter simply, no previous restraints but punishment for abuses, a view that presupposes a distinction between liberty and license and the ability of a court to discern and define it."[77]

Gallatin, agreeing with Nicholas, may not have had history on his side but his reasoning now seems persuasively logical. Speaking of the First Amendment, he declared that he and his friends understood it to mean that Congress could not pass *any* law punishing "any real or supposed abuse of the press." He continued:

> The construction given to it by the supporters of the bill was, that it did not prevent them to punish what they called the licentiousness of the press, but merely forbade their laying any previous restraints upon it. It appeared to him preposterous to say, that to punish a certain act was not an abridgment of the liberty of doing that act. It appeared to him that it was an insulting evasion of the Constitution for gentlemen to say, 'We claim no power to abridge the liberty of the press; *that*, you shall enjoy unrestrained. You may write and publish what you please, but if you publish anything against us, we will punish you for it. So long as we do not prevent, but only punish your writings, it is no abridgment of your liberty of writing and printing.'
>
> . . . That amendment [the First] provided against the passing of any law abridging either the liberty of the press or the freedom of speech; and a sound construction must be such as to be applicable to both. But that contended for, to wit, that the only prohibition was that of passing any law laying previous restraints upon either, was absurd, so far as it related to speech; for it pre-supposed that Congress, by the Constitution, as it originally stood, might have passed laws laying such restraints upon speech; and what these possibly could have been, he was altogether at a loss to conceive, unless gentlemen chose to assert that the Constitution had given Congress a power to seal the mouths or to cut the tongues of the citizens of the Union; and these, however, were the only means by which previous restraints could be laid on the freedom of speech. Was it not evident, that, as speech could not be restrained, but

---

[76] Speech of July 10, *ibid.*, 2140-2141.

[77] Walter Berns, "The Freedom of the Press and the Alien and Sedition Laws: a Reappraisal," in Philip B. Kurland, ed., *1970: The Supreme Court Review* (Chicago, 1971), 124. Berns's thesis is that no really broad libertarian theory emerged during the fight against the Sedition Act, *ibid.*, 110, or even during 1799-1801.

might be punished, a Constitutional clause forbidding any abridgment of the freedom of speech must necessarily mean, not that no laws should be passed laying previous restraints upon it, but that no punishment should by law be inflicted upon it?"[78]

By rejecting subsequent restraints, Gallatin should have also rejected the concept of seditious libel, but he did not.

Gallatin also supported Nicholas in answering the Federalist argument that the true liberty of the press was bounded by truth, that the bill reached only falsehoods, and that therefore it did not abridge the only kind of political criticism that the First Amendment protected. Animadversions on the government and its measures, replied Gallatin, almost always intermixed facts and opinions. "And how could the truth of opinions be proven by evidence?" If one who thought, as he did, that the bill was unconstitutional and intended for party purposes, should publish that opinion and were prosecuted for doing so, a jury sympathetic with the administration would not hesitate to judge his opinion ungrounded, "or, in other words, false and scandalous" and therefore malicious.[79]

Gallatin and Nicholas were among the first Americans on record to have rejected "truth" as a defense because it inadequately protected the freedom of political opinion in cases of seditious libel; to put the thought another way, they were the first to discard "false" and "licentious" on grounds that there were not meaningful or usable standards for the guidance of a jury weighing the lawfulness of an alleged verbal crime against the government. In this respect the remarks of the two congressmen were as sound as could be. So, too, was Gallatin's scornful repudiation of the Blackstonian definition of liberty of the press as grossly unprotective. He also accurately observed that the "no prior restraints" concept never applied to freedom of speech,[80]

[78] *Ibid.*, 2160-2161.
[79] *Ibid.*, 2162.
[80] Later writers who have made the same point are Thomas M. Cooley, *Treatise on Constitutional Limitations Which Rest Upon the Legislative Power of the States*, ed., V. H. Lane (Boston, 1903, 17th ed.), 603-604, and W. R. Vance, "Freedom of Speech and of the Press," *Minnesota Law Review* 2(March 1918):250. Vance, however, said correctly, that freedom of speech, as originally understood, was "intended to mean that a citizen's right to express publicly his opinions concerning public men and events was to be unrestricted save as he might render himself liable to civil action for slander or criminal prosecution for treason or sedition in accordance with then existing common law rules" (*Ibid.*). I agree with Vance's statement except as to its reference to treason which the Framers did not regard as a crime that could be committed by words. Vance was also wrong in concluding at 259 that the Framers intended the United States as well as the states to have the power to enact legislation against seditious utterances.

although no one literally meant that it ever could have. The point of the Federalist argument on freedom of speech was not that it meant the absence of prior restraints but that one might say what he pleased subject to his responsibility under the law for malice, falsehood, seditiousness, and the like; in other words, that freedom of speech did not imply exemption from subsequent punishment for the abuse of "licentious" use of that freedom. The intolerable narrowness of this view of freedom of speech is unquestionable today, but it was not publicly questioned in America before Gallatin did so.[81] He exposed the frailty of the argument that freedom of political expression implied freedom for "truth" only; his achievement spurred a "breakthrough" in American libertarian thought, aided by his exposure of the repressive connotations of the Blackstonian "no prior restraints" formula. Professor Walter Berns wrongly asserted that the Jeffersonian party in Congress did not develop a broad libertarian theory except "in one limited respect," their rejection of the distinction between liberty and license.[82] Their new and broad libertarianism was multidimensional, and Gallatin led the way.

Gallatin and his congressional colleagues did not, however, define the scope of permissible political expression. True enough, they hammered away at their main point that under the First Amendment Congress could not enact any law effecting any degree of a restraint on speech or press, and they denied insistently that the federal courts possessed any jurisdiction over seditious libels. But they did not repudiate the concept of seditious libel and did not deny the power of the states to control speech and press. Gallatin, for instance, in the same speech in which he denounced "the law of political libels" as an instrument of tyranny and advocated open discussion as the only proper means of combatting error, admitted that prior to the bill under debate, "the cognizance of offences of this nature had exclusively belonged to the State courts."[83] Nicholas agreed.[84] Nathaniel

---

[81] William Cushing, in his private correspondence with John Adams, in 1789, had questioned the prior restraints concept but only in reference to political "truths." See above, pp. 199, 201.

[82] Berns, "Freedom of the Press," 124. My friend, Professor Berns, who allowed his preconceptions to govern his interpretation of the evidence, has obdurately persisted in thrice repeating the same errors. See his "Free Speech and Free Government," a retrospective essay review of *Legacy of Suppression*, in *The Political Science Reviewer*, 2:217-41 (1972), and his book, *The First Amendment and the Future of American Democracy*, chap. 3, "Free Speech and the Founding Principle (New York, 1976), 80-146, a slightly revised version of his article in *1970: The Supreme Court Review*, cited above, note 72.

[83] Speech of July 10, in *Annals of Congress*, 5th Cong., 2nd session, 2163.

[84] *Ibid.*, 2142.

Macon of North Carolina said of liberty of the press, "The States have complete power on the subject."[85] The last of the principal speakers against the bill made the point unanimous; Edward Livingston of New York declared, "There is a remedy for offenses of this kind in the laws of every State in the Union. Every man's character is protected by law, and every man who shall publish a libel on any part of the Government, is liable to punishment."[86] A moment later, however, Livingston added that there "ought to be" no power to protect the United States Government from verbal abuse; moreover that "when gentlemen speak of slanders against the Government, he knew of no such thing."[87] From the passage in which this statement appears, it seems that Livingston meant that there ought to be no power in the *national* government to protect itself from slander, for he was paraphrasing and answering the Federalist claim that the United States needed the Sedition Act to protect itself against seditious libel. When he alleged that he knew of no slanders against the United States, he was simply denying that the Federalists' illustrations of slanders, drawn from the Jeffersonian press, were slanderous.[88] Quite possibly, of course, the opponents of the Sedition Act argued for an exclusive state jurisdiction over political libels not because they believed in or wanted state prosecutions, but because such an argument was tactically useful as a means of denying federal jurisdiction.[89] Nevertheless, an assertion

[85] *Ibid.*, 2152, and see also 2106.

[86] *Ibid.*, 2153.

[87] *Ibid.*, 2154.

[88] Smith, *Freedom's Fetters*, 149, stated that Livingston meant to repudiate the concept of seditious libel. He claimed that Livingston was discussing "the nature of free speech," which is not so, and like the other Republican speakers, intended his arguments against seditious libel to be applied "to state governments as well as the federal government. . . . They made clear their belief that political libels had been withdrawn from the realm of prosecution by either the state or federal government" (*Ibid.*, 149). Smith stated that until the Sedition Act was brought forward the cognizance of libels belonged exclusively to the state courts, a proposition supported in part by a citation to Gallatin's speech of July 10, at p. 2164 of the *Annals*, 5th Cong., 2nd session. Smith did not quote Gallatin's remark but confidently assured us at p. 148 n. 21 that he "referred not to seditious libels, but to defamatory libels against personal reputations, obscenity, etc." These statements by Smith are insupportable. Gallatin was explicitly discussing seditious libel and no other kind and had just finished quoting the proposed Sedition Act when he stated, "Heretofore the cognizance of *offences of this nature* had exclusively belonged to the State courts . . ." I find no statement by Gallatin that seditious libels could not exist under a free government.

[89] See, for example, the case of the Jeffersonian theorist, Tunis Wortman, in his *Treatise Concerning Political Enquiry, and the Liberty of the Press* (New York, 1800), 229–230, where he alleged that if the coercion of libels be necessary or proper "our state legislatures and tribunals are possessed of sufficient

of state control over speech and press is scarcely compatible with a supposed intention to exempt either from subsequent punishment for abuse.

The Kentucky Resolutions of 1798, drafted by Jefferson, for instance, affirmed that no power over the freedom of speech or press having been delegated to the United States by the Constitution, "nor prohibited by it to the states, all lawful powers respecting the same did of right remain, and were reserved to the states, or to the people; that thus was manifested their determination to retain to themselves the right of judging how far the licentiousness of speech, and of the press, may be abridged without lessening their useful freedom, and how far those abuses which cannot be separated from their use should be tolerated." The Kentucky Resolutions also declared that the federal courts had no jurisdiction over libels, falsehood, and defamation.[90] Neither the Kentucky nor the Virginia Resolutions declared the Sedition Act void because a free, republican government could not punish the press for political criticism. Madison in early 1799 said of the Sedition Act that "from the existence of state law, some inferred that Congress possess a similar power of legislation," an inference of a "concurrent power" which he denounced as a "death-wound on the sovereignty of the States."

The laws for the correction of calumny were not defective, he added, because, "Every libellous writing or expression might receive its punishment in the State courts."[91] In the same lengthy address

---

authority to remedy the evil . . . the States respectively should solely exercise the power of controuling the conduct of their own citizens in such cases. . . ." Yet Wortman opposed the concept of seditious libel and did not support a criminal prosecution for mere words. For a discussion of Wortman, see below, pp. 327-31, and for his opposition to state criminal prosecutions for libel, see especially p. 331 n. 63, below.

[90] Reprinted in Jonathan Elliot, ed., *The Debates in the Several State Conventions . . . and Other Illustrations of the Constitution* (Philadelphia, 1941, 2nd ed., rev.), 4:540-541. Only one of the nine resolutions dealt with First Amendment freedoms and even that one, like the rest, stressed state's rights. Dumas Malone, *Jefferson and the Ordeal of Liberty* (Boston, 1962), 396-97, absurdly stated that Jefferson and Madison in the Kentucky and Virginia Resolutions "denounced the Alien and Sedition Acts as unconstitutional infringements on human rights." For an equally exaggerated statement associating the resolutions with slavery, see Berns, "Freedom of the Press," 142-50. For a conventional view, see Adrienne Koch, *Jefferson and Madison: the Great Collaboration* (New York, 1950), chap. 7.

[91] "Address of the General Assembly to the People of the Commonwealth of Virginia," Jan. 23, 1799, a document accompanying the Virginia Resolutions of 1799, in *The Writings of James Madison*, ed. Gaillard Hunt (New York, 1900-10), 6:333-334. Whether "Every libellous writing" was meant to include libels against the government and Constitution as well as against public officers is not clear from the context of the statement.

Madison rejected the distinction between liberty and licentiousness and denied in passing that the defense of truth protected opinions, but he concerned himself more with the Sedition Act as a "death-wound on the sovereignty of the states." In a memorandum of 1801 President Jefferson gave a related reason for dismissing the prosecution, initiated under his predecessor, against William Duane, the Republican editor of the Philadelphia *Aurora*, who had been indicted under the Sedition Act. Jefferson wished "to secure to the press that degree of freedom in which it remained under the authority of the states, with whom alone the power is left of abridging that freedom the general government being expressly excluded from it."[92] Jefferson cleared away any doubt about his opinion on this issue when he wrote, in 1804:

> Nor does the opinion of the unconstitutionality and consequent nullity of that law [the Sedition Act] remove all restraint from the overwhelming torrent of slander which is confounding all vice and virtue, all truth and falsehood in the US. The power to do that is fully possessed by the several state legislatures. It was reserved to them, and was denied to the general government, by the constitution according to our construction of it. While we deny that Congress have a right to controul the freedom of the press, we have ever asserted the right of the states, and their exclusive right to do so.[93]

Thus even as the Jeffersonians flatly repudiated the Blackstonian and Federalist theories of freedom of speech and press, they had reservations about the unlimited application of their own theory in the realm of state law. Not to represent their theory of freedom of expression as inextricably part of their theory of federalism would be misleading. Although they believed a federal common-law prosecution for seditious libel to be illegal, they believed a similar prosecution in the state courts to be legal; although they argued the unconstitutionality of the Sedition Act, they deemed constitutional a similar statute enacted by a state legislature. They might have regarded such a statute as unwise and dangerous public policy, whether constitutional or not. Yet the hard fact remains: Jefferson, Madison, Gallatin, Livingston, Nicholas, and Macon explicitly endorsed the power of the states to prosecute seditious and other criminal libels, and they did not even argue that such a prosecution must necessarily be based on a statute; that is, they either endorsed the basic concept of the common

[92] Undated memo of 1801, in Paul Leicester Ford, ed., *The Writings of Thomas Jefferson* (New York, 1892-99, 10 vols.), 8:56.
[93] Jefferson to Abigail Adams, Sept. 4, 1804, in *ibid.*, 10:90.

law of libels, the criminal responsibility of the writer or printer for abuse of his rights, or they failed to oppose it. And no one explicitly applied to the *states* the transforming principle that a few espoused, namely that the very concept of seditious libel conflicted with republican government.

CHAPTER X

The Emergence of an American Libertarian Theory

The widely reported speeches of Gallatin, Livingston, Macon, and Nicholas, during the House debates on the Sedition Act, and the states' rejection of the Virginia and Kentucky Resolutions launched the rapid emergence of the new libertarianism in America. In its initial phase it was expressed in brief, disjointed fashion in the rapid fire of legislative give-and-take. Even under such pressures, the Jeffersonians in the General Assembly of Virginia promoted the new libertarianism. In December 1798 the General Assembly debated the proposals, which James Madison wrote and John Taylor of Caroline introduced, that became the Virginia Resolutions of 1798. In those resolutions, Virginia protested the general tendency of the national government to "consolidate the States by degrees into one sovereignty" and, in particular, protested the Alien and Sedition Acts. The resolutions briefly condemned the exercise of a power that the First Amendment prohibited: the United States had unconstitutionally legislated against "the right of freely examining public characters and measures . . . which has ever been justly deemed the only effectual guardian of every other right." In this nothing was new, but the resolutions prompted a grand debate in the Assembly, during which Taylor, William B. Giles, and Robert B. Daniel repeated the arguments of Gallatin and other Republican Congressmen. The Virginians repudiated Blackstone on freedom of the press and his distinctions between liberty and licentiousness and between prior restraint and subsequent punishment. They argued that political opinions must be free from legal restraints and could not be measured or protected by the test of "truth." They also advanced libertarian theory by what

they did not say; they did not argue that the national government had
no power over seditious libels because the state possessed an exclusive
power. They did not even refer to the power of the states to prosecute libels.[1]

Once the Republicans had a chance to take stock, after legislative
debate had ceased, they became more reflective, systematic, and libertarian. In February 1799 the question arose in Congress whether to
repeal the Sedition Act. The House, by a straight party vote, adopted
a majority report that restated Federalist orthodoxy on freedom of
the press, but not until the Republican minority had their say. John
Nicholas of Virginia presented the minority report. It did far more
than bring together in coherent form all the arguments of 1798
against the policy and constitutionality of the Sedition Act; Nicholas
established a conceptual foundation for an explicit repudiation of the
entire body of the common law on freedom of the press and criminal
libels against government:

> The mode of thinking which countenances this law, and the doc-
> trines on which it is built, are derived from a country whose Gov-
> ernment is so different from ours, that the situation of public
> officers ought to be very different. In Great Britain, the King is
> hereditary, and, according to the theory of their Government, can
> do no wrong. Public officers are his representatives, and derive
> some portion of his inviolability from theory, but more from the
> practice of the Government which has, for the most part, been
> very arbitrary. It was, therefore, of course, [intended] that they
> should receive a different sort of respect from that which is proper
> in our Government, where the officers of Government are the
> servants of the people, are amenable to them, and liable to be
> turned out of office at periodical elections.[2]

[1] *The Virginia Report of 1799-1800, Touching the Alien and Sedition Laws;
Together With the Virginia Resolutions of December 21, 1798, Including the
Debate and Proceedings Thereon in the House of Delegates of Virginia* (Rich-
mond, 1850), 26, 94-97, 115-21, and 146, reprinted by Da Capo Press of New
York in 1970 under the general editorship of L. W. Levy.

[2] *Annals of Congress* 5th Cong., 3rd Sess., 3003-3014. Leonard W. Levy, ed.,
Freedom of the Press, from Zenger to Jefferson (Indianapolis, 1966), 172-86,
reprints both the majority and minority reports. W. Berns asserted that the
system of thought that I call the new libertarianism did not emerge in 1798
and appeared only after the states rejected the Virginia and Kentucky Resolutions. Berns, "Freedom of the Press," 135. The minority report was dated Feb.
25, 1799. Delaware, Rhode Island, and Massachusetts issued their replies between Feb. 1 and Feb. 9. Whether Congress had copies of their replies is not
known. New York replied in March, Connecticut in May, New Hampshire in
June, and Vermont in October. I doubt that the first three replies had any
influence on Nicholas. For the state replies, see Jonathan Elliot, ed., *The De-*

The written Constitution of the United States and its First Amendment, Nicholas continued, established a limited government, while England, by contrast, "has no Constitution but what may be altered by Parliament." Our Constitution, he contended, did not adopt or embody the common law on freedom of the press. Not only did a federal common law of crimes not exist, he alleged; England's law of political libels was not even in force in the states. That Nicholas erred is not nearly as important as the fact that he and the Republican minority for whom he spoke believed what he said. He inaccurately claimed that the states did not retain the law of libels in their criminal codes. He thought no one could prove that the states had considered the law of libels consistent with the freedom of the press. "So far as I know," he added, "it has been a dead letter." Nor did Congress follow the common law when it passed the Sedition Act, which required a showing of malice, made truth a defense, and broadened the jury's powers. Nicholas concluded that "this whole doctrine of libels was obsolete. . . . I think it inconsistent with the nature of our Government, that its administration should have power to restrain animadversions on public measures." Excepting Junius Wilkes in 1782, never before had an American repudiated seditious libel as a legal concept, yet the thought soon became commonplace among Republican libertarian theorists.

They soon appeared in print with reflective and systematic expositions of considerable length, in the form of tracts and books. The one exception was the scholarly argument of George Blake, counsel of Abijah Adams when he was tried at common law for seditious libel against the Commonwealth of Massachusetts in 1799. Blake's argument, summarized in a preceding chapter, filled several long columns in each of eight consecutive issues of the Boston *Independent Chronicle*.[3] His thesis was that the concept of seditious libel, being repugnant to the spirit and genius of a republican form of government, could not have been received with the main body of the common law in a state whose constitution guaranteed freedom of the press. Shortly before the publication of Blake's argument, George Hay wrote *An Essay on the Liberty of the Press*.[4] Early in 1800 appeared James

---

bates in the Several State Conventions on the Adoption of the Federal Constitution . . . and Other Illustration of the Constitution (Philadelphia, 1941, 2nd ed., rev.), 4:532-39.

[3] Issues of the *Chronicle* dated from April 8-11 through April 29-May 2, 1799, summarized above, pp. 216-18. Each issue of the *Chronicle* carried a dateline covering a four-day period, the interval between issues.

[4] George Hay [Hortensius, pseud.], *An Essay on the Liberty of the Press. Respectfully Inscribed to the Republican Printers Throughout the United*

Madison's lengthy *Report* for the Virginia House of Delegates on the Alien and Sedition Acts.[5] In the same year Tunis Wortman published his *Treatise Concerning Political Enquiry, and the Liberty of the Press,*[6] and Thomas Cooper did a new edition of his *Political Essays.*[7] In the following year appeared James Sullivan's *A Dissertation upon Constitutional Freedom of the Press in the United States of America*[8] and John Thomson's *An Enquiry, Concerning the Liberty, and Licentiousness of the Press, and the Uncontroulable Nature of the Human Mind.*[9] In 1803 Hay republished his tract of 1799 and a completely new one with a similar title,[10] while St. George Tucker devoted an appendix of his edition of Blackstone's *Commentaries* to the subject of freedom of speech and press.[11]

Nicholas's minority report, Blake's newspaper argument, the tracts by Hay, Cooper, Sullivan, and Thomson, and the book by Wortman are quite rare and little known among historians. Tucker's appendix and to a much greater degree Madison's *Report* are easily accessible, but have infrequently been used. Taken together these are the sources that compose the main body of original and significant Jeffersonian thought on freedom of speech and press.

Hay, a member of the Virginia House of Delegates and son-in-law of James Monroe, became a United States attorney under Jefferson, gained fame as the prosecutor in Burr's trial for treason, and later

---

States (Philadelphia, 1799), 51 pp. I have used the original edition just cited; my references, however, are to the 1803 Richmond reprinting, set in smaller type (30 pp.), but otherwise the same as the original edition. In 1970 Da Capo Press of New York published a facsimile edition of the Richmond copy, under the general editorship of L. W. Levy, bearing the title *Two Essays on the Liberty of the Press;* the second essay is the one cited in note 10 below.

[5] *The Virginia Report*, cited in n. 1 above, this chapter, appeared originally as a tract of over eighty pages. The reproduction in Elliot, ed., *Debates*, 4:546-580, reprinted it under the title, "Madison's Report on the Virginia Resolutions . . . Report of the Committee to whom were referred the Communications of various States, relative to the Resolutions of the last General Assembly of this State, concerning the Alien and Sedition Laws." The *Report* is also available in Hunt, ed., *The Writings of Madison*, 6:341-406, and in a number of early printings. The *Report* was written by Madison in late 1799, adopted by the state legislature on Jan. 11, 1800, and published immediately after.

[6] (New York, 1800), 296 pp.

[7] (Philadelphia, 1800), 88 pp.

[8] Published anonymously "By an Impartial Citizen" (Boston, 1801), 84 pp.

[9] (New York, 1801), 84 pp., reprinted by Da Capo Press, 1970, under the general editorship of L. W. Levy.

[10] *An Essay on the Liberty of the Press, Shewing, That the Requisition of Security for Good Behaviour from Libellers, is Perfectly Compatible with the Constitution and Laws of Virginia* (Richmond, 1803), 48 pp. reprinted 1970; see above, note 4.

[11] (Philadelphia, 1803), I, pt. II, n. G, 11-30 of Appendix.

served on the federal bench. Two-thirds of his first essay on the liberty of the press was a carefully wrought attack on the constitutionality of the Sedition Act. The last third of the essay is of greater interest because he addressed himself to the intentions of the Framers of the First Amendment and the meaning of freedom of political expression. As a libertarian theorist, Hay was an absolutist, one of the earliest of the new-style American radicals for whom the concept of a verbal crime was abhorrent. Jefferson himself was to provide their standard when he declared in his First Inaugural Address, "If there be any among us who would wish to dissolve this Union or to change its republican form, let them stand undisturbed as monuments of the safety with which error of opinion may be tolerated where reason is left free to combat it." Hay might have regarded this statement as too moderate, for he explicitly favored complete freedom for licentiousness, falsehood, and error, even if maliciously motivated and harmful.[12] Of freedom of speech he wrote, "A man may say every thing which his passions suggest; he may employ all his time, and all his talents, if he is wicked enough to do so, in *speaking* against the government matters that are false, scandalous, and malicious" without being subject to prosecution.[13] Although the statement appeared in the context of a passage on the First Amendment, Hay believed in the same scope of freedom under state law.

His second essay on the subject focused on the law of Virginia, and in that context he claimed that no person could be punished for his opinions, however absurd "or immoral in their tendency" on any subject whatever, nor for malicious untruths. One was "safe within the sanctuary of the press" even if he condemned republican institutions, censured the state government and every officer of it, ascribed its measures and their conduct to the basest motives, and lied outright in doing so. These, said Hay, were all matters of public concern affecting the rights and interests of the people, and were therefore placed by the free-press clause of the state constitution "in the open field of discussion" without any limits. Those who had framed that constitution knew "that this field would be often occupied by folly, malignity, treachery, and ambition; but they knew too that intelligence and patriotism would always be on the spot in the hour of danger, and to make *their* entrance at all times easy and secure, it was

---

[12] *An Essay on the Liberty of the Press* (1799), 22-23, 25, and 27 of the 1803 edition. On Hay, see Stephen H. Hochman, "On the Liberty of the Press in Virginia: from Essay to Bludgeon, 1798-1803," *Virginia Magazine of History and Biography*, 84:431-35 (1976).

[13] *Ibid.*, 25.

left open to all."[14] Hay drew the line only at libels of private reputations.

Observing that there were only two kinds of freedom, "absolute" or "uncontrouled" versus "qualified or abridged," Hay attempted to prove as a matter of logic but without the grace of historical evidence that the Framers must have intended the former freedom when guaranteeing freedom of speech and press. A qualified freedom, he explained, meant a privilege, not a right, that might be restrained or regulated by law as the public good might require in the opinion of the legislature. If the Framers meant that, "they meant nothing" and the First Amendment was superfluous, "the grossest absurdity that was ever conceived by the human mind." They meant that all citizens should have the same right to free speech as congressmen themselves had, totally exempt from the control of any law or the jurisdiction of any court. As to the press, the Framers intended "a total exemption from any law making any publication whatever criminal," even if the result was "mischief."[15] Truth and facts had no greater protection under the First Amendment than the worst falsehoods and opinions, regardless of their tendency. The latter were as equally uncontrollable as the former. To rest the defense of the press on truth as a defense protected only the "morally right" and ignored that fact and opinion were often indistinguishable and that opinions were not provable as true. And there existed "many truths, important to society, which are not susceptible of that full, direct, and positive evidence, which alone can be exhibited before a court and jury." A policy of permitting full scope to licentiousness, Hay admitted, might result in harm, but far less harm than would result from any effort to restrain licentiousness.[16]

Hay concluded his essay with a contemptuous glance at the definition of a free press as simply an exemption from previous restraints. If that definition were accepted, he declared, a man might be put to death for what he published provided that no notice was taken of him before he published it. That might be the case in England, "But this definition does not deserve to be transplanted into America." The introduction of "British doctrine" here had no basis. Unlike England, America had a written constitution, a limitation on the legislative power, and a constitutional guarantee of freedom of the press.[17] Such was the character of Hay's 1799 essay.

[14] *An Essay on the Liberty of the Press* (1803), 29.
[15] *An Essay on the Liberty of the Press* (1799), 23-26 of the 1803 edition. Pages 21-30 of Hay's 1799 essay are reprinted in L. W. Levy, ed., *Freedom of the Press*, 187-97.
[16] *Ibid.*, 26-28.
[17] *Ibid.*, 29. See also Hay, *Essay on the Liberty of the Press* (1803), 32.

His second essay, in 1803, did not differ in any vital respects when he traversed much of the same ground, examining state rather than federal law. The only notable change, perhaps, was his much stiffer stand against personal defamation. It remained the only exception to his belief in "absolute" freedom, but in 1803 he accepted the validity of a criminal proceeding, by information or indictment, against a notorious libeler of a private person; earlier he had believed that the injury should be redressable civilly only by a suit for damages. Significantly, however, Hay defined a libel as a false and malicious "defamation of an individual," by which he meant defamation "on private character," not on the public character of an officeholder. Hay could not countenance the concept of seditious libel in any form, however defined, and he emphasized that no citizen should "be punished, for publishing his opinions, however absurd in principle, or immoral in their tendency, on any subject whatever of a general nature, whether religious, philosophical, moral, political, or legal. Not for enforcing and illustrating these opinions, by stating as a fact, what is not true."[18] Walter Berns was mistaken when he wrote that "even Hay, in the second edition of his essay, concedes that the state may punish libels, including libels on the President of the United States."[19]

The *Report* of 1800 by the Virginia House of Delegates contained little on the First Amendment that had not been in Gallatin's speeches, Blake's argument, or Hay's first essay; but because the *Report* came from the hand of the "Father" of the Constitution and of the Bill of Rights it carries an uncommon authority, not on the original meaning of the First Amendment but on the meaning that it ought to have. Madison advanced the following propositions in a characteristically brilliant exposition: that the Sedition Act was unconstitutional; that the United States possessed no jurisdiction over common-law crimes; that a popular, or free, republican government cannot be libeled; that the First Amendment intended to supersede the common law on

[18] Compare the 1799 *Essay*, p. 23, with the 1803 *Essay*, pp. 9-11, 24, 29.
[19] Berns, "Freedom of the Press and the Alien and Sedition Laws: A reappraisal," *1970 The Supreme Court Review*, ed. Phillip B. Kurland, Chicago, 1970), 141, citing 19-20 of the 1803 edition, presumably of the "Hortensius" essay of 1799, reprinted in 1803. Nowhere in 1803 edition of the 1799 essay, nor in the second essay of 1803 on state power in libel cases, did Hay concede that a state can punish libels on the President as President. He conceded only in the second essay of 1803, p. 41, that "the private character of the officers of government" may be protected by libel prosecutions. Berns, in this instance, did not even get his facts right, let alone understand the difference between a criminal prosecution for libeling the private or personal reputation of a public official and a criminal prosecution for libeling his performance in office or his public policies. Usually he failed to distinguish civil and criminal libels.

speech and press; and that the amendment guaranteed an absolute freedom against the federal government, because no authority of the United States could abridge it.

Following an elaborate examination and rejection of the arguments that had been advanced by the Federalists in support of the existence of a federal common law of crimes,[20] Madison next enlarged on the absence of any power in Congress to enact a sedition law. Concluding that such a law could not be constitutionally justified by either the enumerated or implied powers, he turned his attention to the First Amendment and the contention that its protection of the freedom of the press connoted the common-law definition of that term. Were the contention valid, a sedition law that did not establish a prior restraint would not abridge the freedom of the press, and Congress might regulate the press short of abridging it. By way of answer Madison followed Gallatin, Nicholas, Blake, and Hay in denouncing the prior-restraints definition; "this idea of the freedom of the press can never be admitted to be the American idea of it" because a law inflicting penalties would have the same effect as a law authorizing a prior restraint. "It would seem a mockery to say that no laws should be passed preventing publications from being made, but that laws might be passed for punishing them in case they should be made."[21]

At this point Madison discoursed on the "essential difference between the British government and the American constitutions" to support his view. In England, he pointed out, the danger of encroachments on the rights of the people was understood to be confined to the king, while Parliament, being considered as the guardian of those rights against violation from the executive, possessed unlimited power. Under such a government an exemption of the press from prior restraints by licensers appointed by the king was all the freedom that could be achieved. But the case of the United States differed altogether. The people, not the government, possessed "the absolute sovereignty" and placed the legislature as well as the executive under limitations of power by constitutions that were paramount to legislative acts. As a result, the security of the press required that it should be exempt "not only from previous restraint of the executive, as in Great Britain but from legislative restraint also; and this exemption,

---

[20] "Madison's Report on the Virginia Resolutions," Elliot, ed., *Debates*, 4:561-567, or *The Virginia Report*, 211-19. On this point, see also Gallatin's speeches, *Annals of Congress*, 5th Cong., 2nd session, 2137, 2157-2158; Hay's first *Essay on the Liberty of the Press* (1799), 15-18; and the Minority Report by Nicholas, in Levy, ed. *Freedom of the Press*, 185.

[21] "Madison's Report," Elliot, ed., *Debates*, 4:569, or *The Virginia Report*, 220.

to be effectual must be an exemption, not only from the previous inspection of licensers, but from the subsequent penalty of laws. The state of the press, therefore, under the common law, cannot, in this point of view, be the standard of its freedom in the United States."[22]

On the behalf of that conclusion, Madison advanced a second and related theoretical point. In England, with its hereditary and nonresponsible monarch, it was a maxim that the king can do no wrong, and Parliament, two-thirds of whose membership was also hereditary and nonresponsible, claimed omnipotence. America, however, did not hold the executive to be infallible nor the legislature unlimited, and both, being elective, were responsible. Necessarily, therefore, American constitution-makers contemplated a different degree of freedom of the press. An elective, limited, and responsible government required a much greater freedom of animadversion than might be tolerated by a government such as that of Great Britain. And because the electoral process comprised the essence of a free and responsible government, a wide latitude for political criticism was indispensable to keep the electorate free, informed, and capable of making intelligent choices. The relationship of the press to the elective principle required that the press, "checkered as it is with abuses," be exempt from punishment. Abuse was inseparable from the proper use of anything, but wisdom dictated leaving the press's "noxious branches to their luxurious growth, than, by pruning them away, to injure the vigor of those yielding the proper fruits."[23]

To these considerations Madison added another which he thought proved that the common law could not be permitted to explain the terms used in the First Amendment. That amendment also protected freedom of religion, whose English meaning did not limit its meaning in the United States. The "liberty of conscience and freedom of the press," Madison affirmed, "were equally and completely exempted from all authority whatever of the United States."[24] The principle of the First Amendment rather than "a studied discrimination" of its words and phrases should dictate an understanding of it. Some persons, Madison observed, had argued that a notable difference existed in the protections afforded the various First Amendment freedoms. Congress, for example, could make no law *respecting* an establishment of religion but the amendment merely enjoined it against *abridg-*

[22] *Ibid.*, 4:569-70, or *The Virginia Report*, 220. Nicholas and Blake had previously reached the same conclusion that Erskine had first advanced in principle in Paine's case in 1792.

[23] *Ibid.*, 4:570-71, or *The Virginia Report*, 222.

[24] *Ibid.*, 4:576, or *The Virginia Report*, 228.

ing freedom of speech and press, from which fact the conclusion had been drawn that Congress might make a law respecting but not abridging freedom of speech and press.[25] The Federalists, of course, made that argument. They believed that the freedom of the press entailed no right to indulge in seditious libel. Therefore Congress could regulate the press by punishing seditious libel without diminishing the freedom of the press. If Congress could make no laws respecting the freedom of the press, it could not enact copyright laws to protect authors. The able Virginia Federalist, George K. Taylor, concluded that Congress could make laws respecting the press, "provided they do not *abridge* its freedom."[26] Madison, who had drafted the amendment, regarded such reasoning as specious for it would also yield the impossible conclusion that freedom of religion might be abridged by Congress although not prohibited:

> For, if Congress may regulate the freedom of the press, provided they do not abridge it, because it is said only, "they shall not abridge it," and it is not said "they shall make no law respecting it," the analogy of reasoning is conclusive, that Congress may *regulate* and even *abridge*, the free exercise of religion, provided they do not *prohibit* it; and it is *not* said, "they shall make no law *respecting*, or no law *abridging* it."[27]

The amendment, Madison declared, was intended to have the broadest construction on freedom of the press as well as religion. It "meant a positive denial to Congress of any power whatever on the subject."[28]

To buttress his argument Madison noted that freedom of religion and freedom of the press were "both included in the same amendment, made at the same time, and by the same authority." If Congress could regulate one, it could regulate the other, and if the common law fixed the meaning of one, it fixed the meaning of the other. Because the common law did not even recognize the free exercise of religion, and because Congress, Madison alleged, could not regulate that choice freedom, the common law did not provide a standard for freedom of the press; therefore the press could not be the subject of congressional regulation.[29]

[25] See, for example, Justice Iredell's Charge to the Grand Jury, April 11, 1799, in the "Trial of the Northampton Insurgents," in Francis Wharton, ed., *State Trials of the United States during the Administrations of Washington and Adams* (Philadelphia, 1849), 478.
[26] *The Virginia Report*, 136.
[27] "Madison's Report," Elliot, ed., *Debates*, 4:577, or *The Virginia Report*, 229.
[28] Elliot, ed. *Debates*, 4:571, or *The Virginia Report*, 222.
[29] *The Virginia Report*, 229.

Madison's argument leaked at its seams. From the fact that America rejected the common law on religion, one could not logically or historically conclude that it rejected the common law on the press. Most provisions of the Bill of Rights gave constitutional recognition to common-law rights. Moreover, when Madison parsed the clauses of the amendment, he cleverly proved too much, or nothing at all. In effect he said that the amendment did not mean what it said and should not be read too closely, else one might conclude that Congress could regulate and even abridge the free exercise of religion, so long as Congress stopped short of a prohibition. Nor did it follow that the incapacity of Congress to regulate religion meant that it could not regulate the press.

Madison then reversed his reading of the amendment. Having shown to his satisfaction that a careful reading led to the impossible, he made too much of the fact that the same amendment protected the freedoms of press and religion. That chance fact resulted from the Senate's preference for fewer amendments; it simply combined provisions that had originally been separate.

In support of his proposition that Congress had no power over the press, he reviewed the immediate history of the First Amendment, noting that although the Framers of the Constitution had invariably urged that any power exercised over the press would be a "manifest usurpation," the people had demanded express assurance "to prevent misconstruction or abuse" of the powers vested. The purpose of the First Amendment had been to give that assurance by an explicit guarantee that would extend public confidence in the government. Here Madison raised and directly answered a crucial question:

> Is then, the federal government, it will be asked, destitute of every authority for restraining the licentiousness of the press, and for shielding itself against the libellous attacks which may be made on those who administer it?
>
> The Constitution alone can answer this question. If no such power be expressly delegated, and if it be not both necessary and proper to carry into execution an express power; above all, if it be expressly forbidden by a declaratory amendment to the Constitution,—the answer must be, that the federal government is destitute of all such authority.[30]

Contrary to Professor Berns, Madison said nothing in *The Virginia Report* that qualified or diminished his libertarianism. He did not contradict himself by urging national officials to rely on state prosecu-

[30] Elliot, ed., *Debates*, 4:572-573, or *The Virginia Report*, 224.

tions for seditious libel or any other form of criminal defamation. He merely advised that the remedy "for their injured reputations" should be sought in the state tribunals, "which protect their lives, their liberties, and their properties," as Berns noted, but without understanding that Madison meant a *civil* suit for damages, not a criminal prosecution. No printer, writer, or theorist had ever contended that the right to bring a private suit for defamation of character abridged the freedom of the press or that its freedom required the junking of damages awards in civil cases. Earlier in 1799, however, in a different document Madison *had* approved of state prosecutions.[31] By the end of that year he no longer endorsed them.

In other striking passages Madison lent his great authority to the view, becoming prevalent in American libertarian thinking, that the privilege of giving in evidence the truth of the matter contained in political writings was of little value if any.[32] He also depreciated the supposed protection inhering in the requirement that a political libel cannot be proved against an accused without proof of his malicious or criminal intent to defame or bring into contempt, disrepute, or hatred. That intent was simply inferred from the publication, and its punishment necessarily struck at the right of freely animadverting on the government, its measures and officers. To prohibit the intent prohibited the excitement of unfavorable sentiments against the government, and to do that was "equivalent to a prohibition of discussions having that tendency and effect; which again, is equivalent to a protection of those who administer the government, if they should at any time deserve the contempt and hatred of the people, against being exposed to it, by free animadversions on their characters and conduct."[33]

Because no one knew better than Madison what the First Amend-

---

[31] Walter Berns, "Freedom of the Press," 136. Berns wrongly alleged that I failed to note Madison's "qualifications" of his views concerning freedom of the press. Berns believed that Madison used a double standard, allowing the states to bring the criminal prosecutions that he denied to the national government. "This was in accord with the Virginia Resolutions of 1798, where Madison had written that every 'libellous writing or expression might receive punishment in the state courts'" (*Ibid.*, 136). I quoted the same statement by Madison in the first edition of *Legacy of Suppression*, 266, but correctly noted the document in which it appeared. See above, chap. 9, note 91. Apart from Bern's accusation that I misrepresented facts, his main difficulty was an inability to understand the difference between civil and criminal libel and the significance of that difference for freedom of the press. Berns also failed to credit me for pointing out that several of the libertarians used a double standard. Much of his evidence derived from my earlier work, a fact he did not note. "Freedom of the Press," 120–24.

[32] *Ibid.*, 4:575, or *The Virginia Report*, 226.

[33] *Ibid.*, 4:575, or *The Virginia Report*, 227.

ment was intended to mean, the problem naturally arises whether his exposition of 1800 should be regarded as a reliable account of a prior understanding or as a hindsight interpretation that demonstrated the formulation of a new libertarian theory in response to the Sedition Act. The problem cannot be satisfactorily resolved, because the evidence is negative in character. Madison did not explain himself during the period of the framing, except to say that the national government should have no authority whatsoever over speech and press. Yet if Madison's views of 1800 represented his earlier understanding, it passes belief that he would not have revealed himself in private correspondence with Jefferson in 1788, when Jefferson urged him to support a bill of rights. Jefferson recommended a free press clause that would have made printers liable for "false facts."[34] Madison, who still opposed a bill of rights at that time, did not champion a new and broad theory of freedom of the press. He merely expressed the belief that exempting the press from liability for printing "true facts" was "an innovation" meriting consideration, but on consideration he did not advocate Zengerian principles when proposing a bill of rights to Congress in 1789.[35] In October 1788, when replying to Jefferson's argument that the powers of the national government should be restricted by a bill of rights, Madison declared that "absolute restrictions in cases that are doubtful, or where emergencies may overrule them, ought to be avoided"—hardly a viewpoint compatible with a rejection of the common law of criminal libels or the espousal of an unorthodox view of the scope of political opinions.[36]

If Madison's views of 1800 represented his views at the time of the framing, he would not likely have remained silent in the Virginia ratifying convention of 1788 when George Nicholas, one of his closest supporters, defined freedom of the press as the absence of a licensing act. Significantly, no one at the convention, not even the demagogic Patrick Henry and those of his party who clamored for a written guarantee for freedom of the press, took issue with Nicholas's definition.[37] Given the fact that that definition, which was the common law's, was the most widely known and believed, Madison would

---

[34] Jefferson to Madison, July 31, 1788, in Julian Boyd, *et al.*, eds., *The Papers of Thomas Jefferson* (Princeton, 1950–), 13:442.

[35] Madison to Jefferson, Oct. 15, 1788, in Robert A. Rutland, ed., *The Papers of James Madison*, 11:293.

[36] Oct. 17, 1788, in *ibid.*, 11:297.

[37] For the statement by Nicholas, see above, p. 252. For an argument to the effect that his statement demanded no response from Madison, see David A. Anderson, "The Origins of the Press Clause," *UCLA Law Review* 30(1983): 530.

have explained to the First Congress that his proposed amendment for a guarantee of the freedom of the press comprehended a rejection of the common law's restraints and meant to secure a greatly enlarged scope for the freedom—if that is what he believed and wanted Congress to understand. He offered no such explanation, and no one suggested the existence of a novel understanding.

On the other hand, Madison's statement of 1794, made during the Congressional debate on Democratic societies, balances his earlier silence.[38] In the context of a debate touching the First Amendment and in the midst of an explicit reference to the freedoms of speech and press, he declared in passing, "Opinions are not the objects of legislation." The theoretical framework for that declaration consisted of the principle that in a republic, the people censure the government. Thus Madison in 1794 did not merely rely on the First Amendment's injunction that "Congress shall make no law . . ." He construed the amendment's reference to freedom of speech and of the press to mean that opinions enjoyed constitutional protection from government abridgment. Thus he implicitly endorsed the overt acts test and meant that a national law punishing political opinions abridged free expression. The year 1794 was not 1789 or 1791, but its proximity to them and the fact that Madison was the prime Framer could make a difference in understanding the original meaning of the free press clause. Yet Madison did not act alone.

What became the First Amendment was a congressional proposal that the requisite number of state legislatures ratified. In the absence of some proof that Congress and the states in 1789-91 understood and shared the broad meaning that can be retroactively read into the First Amendment from Madison's 1794 statement, the prudential use of evidence inhibits drawing the conclusion that the First Amendment went much beyond Blackstone or that it subverted the core of the doctrine of seditious libel. Moreover, to repeat an important point, the acceptance of Madison's testimony of 1794 as evidence of the understanding of 1789-91 requires the acceptance of the views of John Adams, William Cushing, Oliver Ellsworth, James Iredell, John Jay, Thomas McKean, William Paterson, and James Wilson, among others, who differed from Madison on the meaning of the free press clause. What is most strange, perhaps, creating a stumbling block for those who read 1794 and 1798-1800 back into 1789-91 is the fact that Madison did not, before 1794, say publicly or privately that political opinions should be as free as opinions on religion. Although Madison

[38] See above, pp. 293-94.

deserves credit for having secured the enactment, in 1785, of the Virginia Statute of Religious Liberty, he did not explicitly extend its overt acts test to political opinions until 1799 nor did he make the simple point that popular government cannot be criminally attacked by opinions. When, moreover, he framed the Bill of Rights, he wrote privately that its chief purpose was "to kill the opposition everywhere."[39] That does not sound like someone intent on revolutionizing the common law of seditious libel, nor did the man who told the House that when one defined abstractions such as freedom of the press, "enumeration of simple acknowledged propositions would speed ratification, whereas questionable amendments might be harmful.[40] Given the novelty of the proposition that an irreconcilable conflict existed between political liberty and seditious libel, no one in 1789 could have regarded it as a "simple acknowledged" proposition. Even the Zengerian proposition that truth should be a defense against a charge of seditious libel had no wide acceptance in 1789. The only simple acknowledged principle about freedom of the press in 1789 remained Blackstonian in character: one had freedom to publish whatever he pleased subject to his criminal liability for abusing that freedom.

In 1800 Madison construed the amendment as implying a bar on all federal authority respecting speech or press. That was surely his intention in 1789, but his draftsmanship left much to be desired as an expression of that intention. He did not employ the emphatic language of the Virginia ratifying convention's recommendation that the liberty of the press "cannot be cancelled abridged restrained or modified by any authority of the United States."[41] As he originally introduced the amendment it read, "shall not be deprived or abridged,"[42] but omitted the significant phrase, "by any authority of the United States," which would have included the executive and judiciary, as well as Congress, and would have implied a prohibition on the exercise by the federal courts of any jurisdiction over a common law of criminal libels. As originally drafted, Madison's proposed amendments had separate articles on religion and the press;[43] this

[39] Rutland, ed., *Papers of Madison*, 12:346-47, Aug. 19, 1789.
[40] *Ibid.*, 12:342.
[41] Charles C. Tansill, ed., *Documents Illustrative of the Formation of the Union of the American States* (Washington, 1927), 1027.
[42] *Annals of Congress*, 1:451.
[43] *Ibid.* The separate articles on religion and on speech-and-press were joined together as clauses in the same article or amendment by a select committee of the House to whom Madison's recommendations were assigned, but as passed by the House the clauses were once again separated and made into distinct

weighs against his argument in 1800 that because the same amendment protected the free exercise of religion and the freedoms of speech and press, the inapplicability of the common-law definition of freedom of religion implied the inapplicability of the common-law definition of freedom of speech-and-press. No part of that argument was worthy of Madison. The English common law on freedom of religion could scarcely have been intended, because America had no national church, and also because a long history of American thought and experience on freedom of religion proved a clear rejection of the common law in this respect. But American thought and experience on freedom of speech and press had been the same as England's, indicating that the common-law definition in that respect did apply. If anything, English thought on the necessity for repudiating the common law as to speech and press had been far more vigorous, original, and libertarian than American thought, which tended to be quiescent or acquiescent by comparison.

The mere fact that a common-law right, such as the liberty of the press, received constitutional status in America did not argue that its meaning had changed. The Bill of Rights gave constitutional status to many common law rights without altering their common law meanings. But if freedom of the press did not significantly change in meaning when it received the protection of the fundamental law, why did so many of the states trouble to guarantee it constitutionally? The most probable answer is disconcerting: the history of the writing of American bills of rights does not warrant the presupposition that the process was a very systematic one. In the glorious act of reverting from a state of nature to a civil government by framing a social compact, Americans tended simply to draw up a glittering catalogue of "rights" that satisfied their urge for an expression of first principles. It was a terribly important and serious task executed in an incredibly haphazard fashion that verged on ineptness. Of the eleven original states that framed constitutions, two neglected freedom of the press; four ignored the right of a defendant to be represented by counsel in a criminal trial; six failed to protect the right against unreasonable

articles. The Senate, on receiving the separate articles, rejoined them as clauses of a single article, and the joint committee of House and Senate that finally agreed on the wording of the amendments retained the compressed form. For a convenient collection of the various drafts of the Bill of Rights, from Madison's initial draft through the submission to the states, see Edward Dumbauld, *The Bill of Rights and What It Means Today* (Norman, Okla., 1957), Appendices 5-9, 206-222. For a narrative of the adoption of the First Amendment by Congress, see Milton R. Konvitz, *Fundamental Liberties of a Free People* (Ithaca, 1957), 345-361.

searches and seizures; six omitted a provision against compulsory self-incrimination; six, incredibly, neglected the right to the writ of habeas corpus; six, again, took no notice of a right to indictment by grand jury; and eight made no provision against bills of attainder. The right to trial by jury was probably the only one universally secured by the first American state constitutions, unless freedom of religion be added to the list despite the fact that five states constitutionally permitted or provided for an establishment of religion in the form of tax supports for churches. Too many of the bills of rights gave constitutional status to a variety of common-law rights, unchanged in their meaning, to warrant the belief that the guarantee of a free press originally intended a repudiation of its common-law meaning. In the national Bill of Rights, for example, the guarantees of the right against self-incrimination, indictment by grand jury, and trial by jury in civil and criminal cases simply declared the common law, as indeed was the case concerning numerous provisions of the Bill of Rights.

The conclusion must be that Madison's exposition of 1800 did not constitute a reliable statement of the understanding prevalent at the time of the framing and ratification of the First Amendment. His 1800 exposition, rather, described a major step in the evolution of the meaning of the free speech-and-press clause. That evolution is sharply discernible by comparing Madison's *Report* of 1800, composed at the end of 1799, with his Address of the General Assembly, composed at the beginning of 1799. No one who has read both documents can validly claim that his views did not develop quickly and even change dramatically. In the earlier statement, for example, he counted on state criminal prosecutions to correct seditious libels against public officials; in the later one, he relied only on civil suits for damages. His libertarian arguments in the first were truncated and fleeting but in the second elaborate and well developed. The differences appear as pronounced as his statements in 1788 against a bill of rights and those of 1789 in favor. What he believed in late 1799 did not reflect his beliefs of 1789.

The work of St. George Tucker, having borrowed so heavily and openly from Madison's *Report*, may be best reviewed at this point. Tucker, who served on the highest court of Virginia and then as a federal judge during the last twenty-five years of his life (1752-1827), succeeded the great Chancellor George Wythe in 1790 as professor of law at the College of William and Mary. Tucker used Blackstone's *Commentaries* as his text, but found that most famous of all law books inadequate for American needs. He remedied that situation by publishing, in 1803, a five-volume annotated edition of his own, adapted to American conditions, and containing almost fifteen hundred "notes" one of which was an early legal commentary on the Constitution of the United States. Another, almost thirty pages long, provided a commentary on First Amendment freedoms, in which Tucker repudiated Blackstone's views on the freedoms of conscience and press.

Tucker habitually used the word "absolute" as a prefix to the right of speaking, writing, and publishing, which he described as "unlimited as the human mind," subject to the penalties of the law only for personal defamation. He claimed that the First Amendment freedoms had been purposely undefined so that they could be transmitted to future generations unshackled and unlimited. In his rejection of the constricted concept of freedom in the common law, Tucker enlarged on Madison's comparison of political theory in England and America by noting that in America the government, whether state or federal, served the sovereign people, making indispensably necessary that the people have the broadest freedom of inquiring into and criticizing the conduct of its servant. Freedom in England proved so much narrower because the locus of sovereignty and the relationship between rulers and subjects differed.[44] Tucker's exposition, although adding very little to Madison's, was enormously important to the emergence of an American libertarianism because his absolutist theory of freedom of discussion appeared in his scholarly edition of Blackstone, for many years the standard edition used by the American bench and bar. A more strategically significant place for the repudiation of the Blackstonian concept of "no prior restraints" could not be imagined.

One passage in Tucker requires clarification, because notwithstanding his reiterated endorsements of the "absolute freedom of inquiry," "absolute freedom of discussion," and "absolute freedom of the press," he also seemed, inconsistently, to favor state prosecutions for criminal libels of individuals. He asked whether a remedy existed "for injuries done to the good name and reputation of a man" by a press "stained with falsehood . . . and personal slander." His answer was such that Professor Berns denied that Tucker espoused an absolutist theory of political expression. Tucker, Berns wrote. "made it

---

[44] Tucker, *Blackstone's Commentaries: with Notes of Reference, to the Constitution and Laws of the Federal Government of the United States; and of the Commonwealth of Virginia* (Philadelphia, 1803), vol. I, pt. II, n. G, pp. 11, 15, 16, 17, 20, and 29. Pages 15-21 are reprinted in Levy, ed., *Freedom of the Press*, 318-26.

abundantly clear in a very visible place that the states must punish such words."[45] Tucker's controversial statement asserted that whoever used the press to asperse the conduct of public men must be truthful, because

> The right of character is a sacred and invaluable right, and is not forfeited by accepting a public employment. Whoever knowingly departs from any of these maxims is guilty of crime against the community, as well as against the person injured; and though both the letter and the spirit of our federal constitution wisely prohibit the congress of the United States from making any law, by which the freedom of speech, or of the press, may be exposed to restraint or persecution under the authority of the federal government, yet for injuries done the reputation of any person, as *an individual*, the state-courts are always open, and may afford ample, and competent redress, as the records of the courts of this commonwealth abundantly testify.[46]

Tucker referred to "a crime against the community" for which, presumably, the remedy would be a criminal prosecution, but he did not recommend that. The dominant remedy in Virginia for the wrong to which Tucker referred—injuries to the reputation of a person "as *an individual*"—was merely a civil suit for damages.[47] Without doubt Tucker spoke loosely but not inconsistently. Virginia records show very few criminal prosecutions for libeling private reputations. In any case, if the defendant enjoyed the protections that Tucker urged—proof that he "knowingly" lied and believed that reputation was not an invaluable right—a criminal prosecution would provide ample scope for political opinions.

Tunis Wortman, a New York lawyer prominent in Tammany politics, contributed preeminently to the emergence of an American libertarianism in his book of 1800, *A Treatise Concerning Political Enquiry, and the Liberty of the Press.*[48] From 1801 to 1807 Wortman

---

[45] Walter Berns, "Freedom of the Press," 137.

[46] Tucker, *Blackstone's Commentaries*, pt. II, n. G, pp. 29-30. Italics added.

[47] In the fall semester of 1973 six graduate students in a seminar directed by Professor Harold L. Nelson at the University of Wisconsin, Madison, divided the labor of reading all of Virginia's newspapers for the decade 1780-89. Testing *Legacy of Suppression*, they looked for criticism of public men and measures, discussions of freedom of the press, and reports of prosecutions for any kind of criminal libel. Professor Nelson generously made copies of their research papers available to me. No one found a single instance of prosecution for criminal libel.

[48] (New York, 1800), 296 pp. Reprinted by Da Capo Press of New York in 1970 under the general editorship of L. W. Levy. An abridgment appears in Levy, ed., *Freedom of the Press from Zenger to Jefferson* (Indianapolis, 1966),

served as clerk of the city and county of New York, a position in which he distinguished himself every election day by certifying scores of Irish immigrants as naturalized citizens and marching them off to the polls to vote the straight ticket. But Wortman was also the author of several important tracts, one of which outlined a democratic philosophy of social reform.[49] Albert Gallatin supported the publication of Wortman's great book of 1800 by undertaking to place subscriptions for it among Republican members of Congress. It is, in a sense, the book that Jefferson did not write but should have. Devoid of party polemics and of the characteristically American preoccupation with legal and constitutional problems, it is a work of political philosophy that systematically presents the case for freedom of expression. "The freedom of speech and opinion," wrote Wortman in his preface, "is not only necessary to the happiness of Man, considered as a Moral and Intellectual Being, but indispensably requisite to the perpetuation of Civil Liberty. To enforce and advocate that inestimable right, is the principal object of the present Treatise."[50] The outstanding characteristics of the book are its philosophic approach and its absolutist theses.

Always preoccupied with first principles, Wortman began with the premise of the Declaration of Independence that government, particularly a representative system, is founded for the good of the whole people to secure their liberties. From the right of the people to dissolve their government whenever public opinion deemed essential, Wortman implied the existence of an "unlimited right" in both the individual and society to express political opinions. Any attempt by the government to coerce opinion or abridge the freedom of inquiry "materially violates the most essential principles of the social state."[51] The right of the individual would also be violated, for Wortman believed, "There is no natural right more perfect or more absolute, than that of investigating every subject which concerns us."[52] He drew that right from a psychological explanation of the way the human mind worked in gaining knowledge and forming beliefs.[53]

230-84. Eugene Perry Link, *Democratic-Republican Societies, 1790-1800* (New York, 1942), mentions Wortman at p. 115 as one of the "leading American democrats" of the time. See also Isaac Q. Leake, *Memoir of the Life and Times of General John Lamb* (Albany, 1850), 345. No sketch of Wortman appears in the *Dictionary of American Biography*.

[49] *An Oration on the Influence of Social Institutions upon Human Morals and Happiness* (New York, 1796).

[50] *Treatise Concerning Political Enquiry*, iv.

[51] *Ibid.*, 28-29.

[52] *Ibid.*, 33.

[53] *Ibid.*, 32-43.

It was the "prerogative of intellect" and the nature of the mind to extend its operation into every subject, because thoughts spring uncontrolled and spontaneously in response to environment. The association of ideas leads with astonishing rapidity from subject to subject and reflection to reflection, making it impossible, even stupid, to prescribe bounds to the "empire of thought." Nor would bounds on the formation of opinion be desirable, even if possible, because the mind, given access to knowledge and the habits of reason, could be sufficiently enlightened to overcome passion. From the standpoint of a society interested in the progression of knowledge and truth, intellectual intercourse should remain "entirely unshackled," so that error will be subjected to continued diminution as investigation continues free and unrestricted. But opinions among men vary on all subjects and fortunately so, because diversity engenders argument which tends in the long run to correct errors, remove prejudices, and strengthen perceptions. Thus, the habit of open debates enables society to form the wisest decisions in the management of human affairs, particularly on matters of government.[54] Wortman devoted several chapters to the development of this Jeffersonian thesis that man is capable of wisely governing himself in his political as well as personal and social life, on condition that the expression of opinion be unfettered.[55]

The first half of the book stressed the right of society to freedom of expression. Wortman then turned to the importance of freedom to the individual and to the social benefits of individual freedom. All prospects of general improvement, he argued, depend on the industry and imagination of the individual, whose contribution, in turn, depends on the unlimited liberty of exercising his faculties. But without the "liberty of enquiry, and the right of disseminating our opinions," the individual is crippled. Society suffers with him because his disability diminishes public enlightenment and holds forth the specter that tyranny might replace free government. The alternative is to regard knowledge as a "general fund of which all have a right to participate: it is a capital which has the peculiar property of increasing its stores in proportion as they are used. We are entitled to pursue every justifiable method of increasing our perceptions and invigorating our faculties. We are equally entitled to communicate our information to others." He drew the line only at the "point at which our conduct becomes injurious."[56]

Turning to the problem of willful and false libels against private

[54] *Ibid.*, 122-123.
[55] *Ibid.*, 47-113.
[56] *Ibid.*, 140-148 *passim.*

persons or against the government, Wortman presented in detail the thesis that prosecution is most inadvisable even for an undoubted abuse of freedom of expression that should be regarded as criminal.[57] Coercion, he argued, is a destructive and self-defeating corrective; force can never conquer falsehood, nor is it necessary. The worst misrepresentation of the government cannot result in public disrepect for it, nor in a breach of peace. To believe to the contrary libels society by assuming that the people cannot differentiate truth from error when given the facts. To invoke the penal code against seditious libelers invariably results in the most pernicious consequences to society, far exceeding the dangers of the "most unbounded licentiousness."

"How then," Wortman asked, "shall erroneous opinions or wilful misrepresentations be combated by the wise and provident legislator? The proper answer to this enquiry is, That Government should by no means interfere unless by affording such information to the public as may enable them to form a correct estimate of things." A libel might be willfully false and injurious. "Admitted. But how shall such opinion be destroyed, or its farther propagation prevented? By fair and argumentative refutation, or by the terrible dissuasive of a statute of sedition? By the convincing and circumstantial narrative of the Truth, or by the terrors of Imprisonment and the singular logic of the Pillory?"[58] Falsehood might temporarily triumph, but never for long if the remedy of "Reason and Argument" be relied upon. A society accustomed to thinking, talking, and writing freely will become experienced in judgment; "confidence should be reposed in the wisdom and virtues of the people."[59] Their discernment, strengthened by habits of political discussion, detects and condemns misrepresentations. Only a government whose administration and policies cannot survive investigation needs to resort to the punishment of seditious utterances, although coercion can never vindicate the character of a government or its officers, nor remove an erroneous impression.

For the government to proceed by criminal prosecutions in order "to punish men for their assertions respecting itself, ever has been, and ever will be, subject to the most odious oppression." Sedition laws make it impossible "to attempt to estimate the precise extent of prohibition, or ascertain what we are permitted to speak, and at what point we are compelled to silence." People whose only guilt consists of credulity, zeal, prejudice, or mistaken opinion are victimized by

[57] *Ibid.*, 150-182.
[58] *Ibid.*, 159, 160.
[59] *Ibid.*, 161.

prosecutions, with the resulting destruction of the free formation of public opinion. Prosecutions fail, however, to achieve their underlying purpose of establishing public transquillity, and they can never effect a cure of the complaints that give rise to libels. Indeed, by damming up discontent and removing the possibility of its verbal expression, prosecutions make a resort to violence more likely. The worsening of the situation would compel the government either to fortify its powers by introducing "military despotism" or to relax its suppressive measures. The wise government understands that free speech is a preventative of revolutions. In a representative system of government, which Wortman believed to be functionally dependent upon freedom of political discussion, prosecutions for seditious libel subvert the constitution.[60]

In the final chapters of his book, he addressed himself to legal and constitutional problems in the United States. He traversed minutely the ground covered by Madison and others on the constitutionality of federal sedition laws, the meaning of the First Amendment's freedom of speech-and-press clause, the question whether a federal common law of criminal libel existed, and the invalidity of relevant Blackstonian concepts. In the course of his presentation of the Madisonian argument, Wortman endorsed the overt-acts test[61] and concluded that the entire law of criminal libel was the "offspring of a Monarchy"; it could "never be reconciled to the genius and constitution of a Representative Commonwealth."[62] Contrary to Walter Berns, Wortman did not support the authority of the states to punish criminal libels.[63]

In the whole of Wortman's book there was probably not an argument that could not be traced to some earlier writer, but the same point can be made as to the "originality" of other classics in libertarian literature, from Milton's *Areopagitica* to Mill's *On Liberty*.

[60] This paragraph summarizes 162-192 of Wortman. The quoted lines are at pp. 163 and 170.
[61] *Ibid.*, 253.
[62] *Ibid.*, 262.
[63] Berns, "Freedom of the Press," 139, declared that Wortman qualified his position or contradicted himself by supporting state prosecutions. Berns quoted the statement that I quoted in note 89 of Chapter Nine above, but it does not mean what Berns thought. A careful reading of Wortman shows that he habitually referred to civil suits for damages as "prosecutions." When he spoke of state prosecutions or state coercion he did not mean criminal prosecutions and, therefore, he did not contradict himself or qualify his absolutist position. See Wortman, *Treatise*, 151, 169, and especially 257-60. Berns had difficulty, apparently irremediable, distinguishing private libel suits from state criminal prosecutions.

Wortman's treatise is surely the preeminent American classic, because of its scope, fullness, philosophical approach, masterful marshaling of all the libertarian arguments, and uncompromisingly radical view.

Thomas Cooper's *Political Essays* reinforced the new libertarianism. The book included a two-part essay "On the Propriety and Expediency of unlimited Enquiry," which did not allow Cooper the space in which to develop his ideas. Jefferson called him "the greatest man in America, in the powers of mind and in acquired information." The man was a lawyer, a chemist, a journalist, and a philosopher but his essay on "unlimited Enquiry," although incisive, conveyed no original opinions. To review it would entail too much repetition. Suffice that Cooper brilliantly if briefly opposed prosecutions for seditious libel only to become a victim of the Sedition Act in 1800. President Adams himself spurred his prosecution, and Justice Samuel Chase of the Supreme Court, who presided at his trial, denied him a fair trial under the statute. Cooper represented himself, and his report of his trial is the most effective critique of the operation of the Sedition Act, enhancing libertarianism theory but originating no new points.[64]

The tract written by James Sullivan in 1801 on liberty of the press[65] deserves notice because its author led the Democratic-Republican party in Massachusetts. The party's perennial candidate for governor, he finally gained election in 1807 after many years of service as attorney-general of the state. During the controversy over the adoption of the Constitution he had been closely associated with the Federalists. From his record and a reading of his tract on liberty of the press one would never know that he had become one of the foremost Jeffersonian politicians in New England.[66] As attorney-general, Sullivan had successfully prosecuted Abijah Adams in 1799 for a seditious libel against the state legislature and had advanced the same

[64] *Political Essays* 2d ed. with Corrections and Additions (Philadelphia, 1800). *Account of the Trial of Thomas Cooper, of Northumberland* (Pa.) (Philadelphia, 1800). The best works on Cooper are Dumas Malone, *The Public Life of Thomas Cooper* (New Haven, 1926), and, on his trial, James M. Smith, *Freedom's Fetters: The Alien and Sedition Laws and American Civil Liberties* (Ithaca, 1956), 307-33. For the quotation by Jefferson, see Malone's life of Cooper, 237.

[65] *A Dissertation upon the Constitutional Freedom of the Press in the United States of America.* By an Impartial Citizen (Boston, 1801), 54 pp.

[66] J. T. Adams, "Sullivan, James," *Dictionary of American Biography.* For a full-length study, see Thomas Coffin Armory, *The Life of James Sullivan* (Boston, 1859).

Blackstonian argument as in his earlier prosecution of Freeman, in 1791.[67] His tract of 1801 was considerably more moderate, conspicuously omitting any reference to the "no prior restraints" concept, but in tone and content it was alien to the newly emergent libertarianism of Gallatin, Wortman, Hay, Madison, Tucker, and other Jeffersonians, a fact that may have accounted for the tract's anonymous publication.

Calling himself an "Impartial Citizen," Sullivan wrote a narrowly legalistic analysis that attempted to reconcile freedom of the press and the common law of criminal libel. He defined that freedom as meaning the right to publish any political opinions in the absence of such restraints "as shall prevent a free and necessary communication of ideas, for the preservation of liberty and the support of the principles of the constitution." Sullivan believed that although a few states had accepted the defense of truth, they had not changed the common-law principle of freedom of the press which had been "adopted and uniformly acknowledged in the country; nor do they differ essentially from those [constitutions] of the other states."[68] Sullivan insisted that the existing freedom of the press was broad enough to permit the exposure of an official's weakness, impropriety, bad policies, and even unconstitutional acts, without charging him with crime or defaming his character. He realized that representative government depended upon open political debate as a means of enabling the public to form its opinions on an administration for the purpose of voting; and he would not invoke the common law against any writer whose criticism of the government was mistaken. Anyone had a right to give his opinion, however wrong. "Some men," wrote Sullivan, "may form wrong conclusions with very honest hearts, while others form the same from wrong heads and seditious minds; but there can be no way, in which a just and exact scrutiny can be made, and therefore, there can be no punishment in such cases, without a dangerous infringement on the right of private judgment, in public concerns." People reasoned in different ways; to punish wrong reasoning or error would mean "an end of all free inquiry on the measures of administration."[69]

Sullivan drew a line, however, against seditious libel as he understood it: "But if the false publications proceed from *malice* to the government, or its officers, or from a seditious temper against the powers of the state, and the fact published be in itself false, there can

---

[67] See above, 208 and 211.
[68] *Dissertation upon Freedom of the Press*, 20.
[69] *Ibid.*, 34. See also 31 and 54.

be no reason why the author and publisher should not receive adequate and condign punishment."[70] Criminal prosecution was not warranted in the case of a libel against a officer of the government, even for an act done in his official capacity, on the theory that the libel was against the person privately; the remedy in that case must be the same as in the case of ordinary citizen: a civil suit for damages in the courts of the state in which the libel was published, even if the injured party be an officer of the United States government. But a false and malicious libel against such an officer made "with an intent to subvert the government of the United States, to bring it into hatred or contempt . . . must in itself be a crime against the government, and ought to be punished."[71] In such cases of seditious libel Sullivan would permit truth as a defense.

In his discussion of federal powers against seditious libel, he endorsed the view that a federal common law of crimes necessarily existed as a means of preserving the government of the United States. Whatever had "a tendency to overthrow the constitution and civil authority" he believed to be a crime against the government punishable "without any act of Congress for the purpose."[72] As for the Sedition Act of 1798, he thought that it "was intended to have been passed on proper principles, and the Congress had an undoubted right to pass an act against seditious libels."[73] A power to punish a libel against the government itself derived implicitly from the inherent right of self-protection. To argue, as some had, Sullivan declared, that the state governments would preserve and defend the federal government was absurd, "because a government, depending upon another government for its existence, is merely a corporation—it can have no sovereignty—and can be no band of union for a nation."[74] The Sedition Act of 1798, however, was not drawn on "rules of prudence" nor enforced with a discretion that merited the confidence of the people.[75] In one provision, moreover, it was unwarranted by the Constitution, for it outlawed libels against the president personally as well as libels against him published with intent to injure or subvert the government itself. Only the latter case was constitutionally punishable by the United States; yet some of the actual prosecutions under the act were for libels against the president that belonged to

[70] *Ibid.*, 31.
[71] *Ibid.*, 33.
[72] *Ibid.*, 41.
[73] *Ibid.*, 31.
[74] *Ibid.*, 50.
[75] *Ibid.*, 31.

the exclusive jurisdiction, civil or criminal, of the states.[76] This distinction between a libel on the officer and a libel on the office, or any institution of the government itself, may have been a lawyer's hairsplitting, but it would have prevented a majority of the prosecutions that did in fact occur under the Sedition Act.

Nevertheless, Sullivan's mild criticism of the statute would not warrant classifying him among the new libertarians. He could differentiate fact from opinion and tolerate opinion even if "wrong" or erroneous, a feat that John Adams could not accomplish; but Sullivan's tract placed him apart from the Jeffersonian theorists. His independence of mind led him to an endeavor that holds the same fascination for the reader as for one who watches a man trying to keep his balance while straddling two stools that are placed too far apart. No amount of reasoning could keep Sullivan from falling between the common law of seditious libel and the freedom of the press in his effort to keep both securely under control. He really passed judgment on himself when first he recognized that the virtual impossibility of separating "wrong" but "honest hearts" from "seditious minds" made prosecution a dangerous infringement on liberty, and then went ahead to endorse prosecutions for malicious or seditious utterances against the government. Sullivan's tract deserves to be remembered as an example of the failure to find a middle way between the old Blackstonian views and the newer Jeffersonian ones.

In the same year that Sullivan's tract appeared, John Thomson of New York published his slim book on the press,[77] a trenchant and comprehensive discussion that represented the same viewpoint as Wortman's and inevitably duplicated it in many respects. Thomson began with a cogent analysis of the meaninglessness of the term "licentiousness" when used as a test to gauge the criminality of the press. He concluded that it was an undefinable term used by those "who evidently wished nobody to enjoy the Liberty of the Press, but such as were of their opinion."[78] All opinions should be allowed an equal freedom of expression and none could actually alienate the affections of the people from their government or injure them.[79] "Political opinions," he claimed," could never be destructive of social

---

[76] *Ibid.*, 27-28, 33, 48, 51-52.
[77] *An Enquiry, Concerning the Liberty, and Licentiousness of the Press, and the Uncontroulable Nature of the Human Mind* (New York, 1801), 84 pp. I have been unable to locate biographical data on Thomson. An abridgment of Thomson's book is in Levy, ed., *Freedom of the Press*, 284-317.
[78] *Ibid.*, 7.
[79] *Ibid.*, 8, 77, 79, 84.

order, or public tranquility, if allowed a free operation." The law protected against "actions injurious to the peace of the community";[80] opinion should never be punished, not even if false.

Error, granted Thomson, would circulate widely under a policy of "free and unrestrained Liberty of Speech and Press," but even error had its use as a step toward public enlightenment.[81] To make "truth" the limit of permissible freedom cut society off from the better understanding of truth that developed from collision with error, fixed the understanding of truth at its present stage of development, and ignored the fact that opinions could not be proved: "how are *their* truth or falsehood to be determined? A decision in this case, would be as absurd as deciding which was the most palatable food, agreeable drink, or beautiful color."[82] The real danger did not come from erroneous opinions or misrepresentations of fact, which could be corrected in the public mind by counter-argument. The real danger derived from the "Government interfering in the direction of public opinion,"[83] as Thomson sought to prove by reviewing the recent history of prosecutions for sedition in England and America. "Let not Government interfere," he declared, not even in a case of malicious falsehood. "In no case whatever use coercive measures. . . . Coercion may silence," he concluded, "but it can never convince."[84]

Such was the gist of Thomson's book. In the course of it, he restated that the traditional theory of the responsibility of freedom of expression was responsible for myriad benefits in the realm of art, science, religion, and philosophy as well as in politics and government, benefits that far outweighed its disadvantages. He also rehearsed many of the arguments that Madison, Wortman, and others had recently made. But he added two unjaded, provocative, and libertarian arguments.

The first of these had been suggested rather obliquely as early as 1704 by Matthew Tindal,[85] when he claimed that members of Parliament should not deny to others the right they themselves possessed of publishing their debates. Hay was the first American to contend that a guarantee of freedom of speech meant that citizens should have the same right of unlimited expression possessed by their repre-

---

[80] *Ibid.*, 79.
[81] *Ibid.*, 83.
[82] *Ibid.*, 68.
[83] *Ibid.*, 74.
[84] *Ibid.*, 83. Walter Berns, "The Freedom of the Press," 141, inaccurately declared, "The power of law to deter expression is implicitly admitted by Thomson in various places." Berns gave no examples.
[85] *Reasons against Restraining the Press* (London, 1704), 10.

sentatives.[86] Others had discoursed on the relation between unfettered public discussion and a representative system of government, but not even Madison or Wortman went on to draw the related conclusion that Hay and Thomson did. It was Thomson, however, who buttressed the point with a sustained and reasoned argument.

He noted that the Constitution provided that members of Congress "shall not be questioned," that is, held legally liable, for any speech they might make; their remarks were clothed with an immunity that gave them the right to say whatever they pleased in their legislative capacities. Thomson then reasoned that if legislators needed freedom of discussion, their sovereigns, the people whom they represented, needed it even more. The electorate must pass judgment on the proceedings of Congress and insure that the government operated for the benefit of the government. For the fulfillment of their electoral duties and their responsibility to protect themselves, the people could not be denied access to any viewpoint. Accordingly the agents of the people had no power to abridge the freedom of speech or press. The framers of the First Amendment, Thomson concluded, intended to guarantee that the people possessed "the same right of free discussion" as their agents.[87] His argument was logically, if not historically, convincing; it went far to show the invalidity of the concept of seditious libel in a republican form of government.

Thomson's second unusual thesis was no less thoroughgoing in its implication, far more subtle, and the most interesting in the entire libertarian armory. In essence he held that opinion is not punishable because it is involuntary, an idea traceable to Locke and Jefferson and even to the common-law requirement that a criminal intent must be present before a crime can be said to exist. The idea, whether valid or not, also went far to provide immunity for political expression.[88]

The emergence of a body of libertarian thought among the Jeffersonians did not, however, result in a union of principle and practice when they achieved power. Prosecutions for verbal crime had been reprehended as a shocking betrayal of natural and constitutional rights when the victims were the party faithful. But accession to power stimulated a fresh understanding of the dangers of seditious libel from an uncontrolled opposition press. Measures to protect the government and public opinion suddenly seemed necessary, even

[86] *An Essay on the Liberty of the Press* (1799), p. 26 of the 1803 edition. Cooper made the same point in passing when he asked why the public should not have the same latitude of expression as legislators. *Political Essays*, 76.

[87] Thomson, *Enquiry*, 20, 22.

[88] See Appendix, "The Psychology of Freedom," in my *Legacy of Suppression*, 313-20.

salutary. New York, the home of Wortman and Thomson, as well as of Zenger and James Alexander, was the scene of the first Jeffersonian assault on liberty of the press. The Federalists of New York reacted by revealing that they too had chameleon-like qualities; they played the role of defenders of freedom of expression—against Jeffersonian despoliation.

When Jefferson became president, his most powerful ally in New York, George Clinton, once again became governor of that state after a Federalist interregnum. In 1803 Clinton's administration obtained a common-law indictment for seditious libel against Harry Croswell, editor of an upstate Federalist publication, *The Wasp*. His crime was an accusation that Vice-President Jefferson had paid James T. Callender, an unethical journalist, to denounce Washington as "a traitor, a robber, and a perjurer" and Adams as "a hoary-headed incendiary."[89] Croswell was convicted at a trial presided over by Chief Justice Morgan Lewis, a Jeffersonian Democrat, who followed Clinton as governor. Lewis denied a request that the trial be postponed long enough for the defendant to subpoena Callender as a witness to prove the truth of his accusation against Jefferson. "His honor," says the report of the case, "then read to the jury the opinion of Lord Mansfield, in the case of The Dean of St. Asaph . . . and charged them, that the law therein laid down was the law of this state." Chief Justice Lewis, in other words, instructed the jury that truth was not a defense against a charge of seditious libel, and that its only duty was to find whether the defendant had in fact published the statement charged, leaving to the court the decision whether the publication was criminal as a matter of law.[90] The jury convicted.

On appeal to the highest court of the state, Croswell was represented by Alexander Hamilton, who eloquently championed the cause of a free press in an argument that recalled Andrew Hamilton's defense of Zenger. The great Federalist leader demanded in vain that the court grant Croswell a new trial and the defense of truth, so that the people might know whether President Jefferson had been guilty of the "foul" act attributed to him. Hamilton maintained "that the common law applied to the United States," but construed it to empower the jury to decide the criminality of an alleged libel. Freedom of the press, he declared, "consists in the right to publish, with im-

---

[89] *People v. Croswell*, 3 Johnson's (N.Y.) Cases 336, 337-339 (1804). The best discussions of this case are Julius Goebel, Jr., *The Law Practice of Alexander Hamilton* (New York, 1964), 1:775-806; and Morris D. Forkosch, "Freedom of the Press: *Croswell's Case*," *Fordham Law Review* 33(1965):415-48.

[90] *Ibid.*, 341.

punity, truth, with good motives, for justifiable ends, though reflecting on government, magistracy, or individuals."⁹¹ Without proof of
the defendant's actual malice, not his presumed malice, Hamilton contended, the jury should acquit. Attorney-General Ambrose Spencer,
another member of the Jeffersonian establishment, who had prosecuted Croswell at his trial, argued for the state that a libel was punishable not because of its falsity, "but because of its evil tendency; its
tendency to a breach of the peace" which existed whether true or
false. Blackstone and Mansfield were his guides.⁹²

The Supreme Court of Judicature, reporting its opinions in 1804,
divided equally; if Ambrose Spencer, newly appointed to the court,
had not disqualified himself, the most reactionary views on freedom
of the press would have mustered a majority of the court. Chief Justice Lewis, joined by Judge Brockholst Livingston, whom Jefferson
would appoint to the Supreme Court of the United States in 1806,
followed Mansfield. The opinion of Judge James Kent, a Federalist,
joined by Smith Thompson, a Democrat who had studied law with
Kent, restated Hamilton's argument. Kent, believing that the mere
act of publication could not in itself be criminal, emphasized that
criminality consisted "in a malicious and seditious intention," which
a jury must decide in seditious libel cases as in any cases of crime. To
deny the jury the right of deciding the intent and tendency of the
act deprived the defendant of the substance and security of a jury
trial. Moreover, unless the jury considered the truth of the defendant's statements, it could not determine "the goodness of the motive
in making it" and thereby abridged the means of defense. Kent
wished not to be misunderstood, however; he would not under any
circumstances tolerate libels upon private character or the dissemination of accusations "for seditious and wicked ends." As a result of
this case, the state legislature enacted a bill in 1805 allowing the jury
to decide the criminality of an alleged libel and permitting truth as a
defense if published "with good motives and for justifiable ends."⁹³

The standard embodied in the New York statute slowly spread
throughout the nation as the acceptable one, defining freedom of the
press in criminal libel cases. By the time of the Civil War, most states,

⁹¹ Hamilton's argument is reported in *People* v. *Croswell*, at pp. 352-361.
The quoted words are at pp. 352-353, 357, and 358.
⁹² Spenser's argument is reported in *People* v. *Croswell*, at pp. 348-352, the
quoted words at p. 349.
⁹³ Lewis's opinion is reported in *People* v. *Croswell*, at pp. 394-411; Kent's
at pp. 363-394; the statute of 1805 at pp. 411-413. An abridgment of Hamilton's
argument and of Kent's opinion is available in Levy, ed., *Freedom of the
Press*, 379-99.

whether by constitutional provision, judicial decision, or statutory enactment, followed New York to some extent. In the end, then, modified Zengerian principles prevailed, after their abandonment by libertarians like Madison and Wortman as too restrictive and after their betrayal by other Jeffersonians, such as Morgan Lewis, Thomas McKean, and sometimes Jefferson himself. The New York standard, which retained legal restrictions on the right to criticize the government, represented a point midway between the contradictory positions of the Jeffersonians. That standard accepted the compatibility of free government and prosecutions for seditious libel, and it conditioned the defense of truth: if one did not publish the truth with good motives for justifiable ends, he was as guilty as if he had published malicious falsehoods. Thus, the New York standard constricted the freedom of the press to discuss public affairs. Moreover, "good motives" and "justifiable ends" hardly defined clear and ascertainable standards for the guidance of judges, juries, writers, printers, and booksellers. The infamous Sedition Act of 1798, which did not adulterate or dilute Zengerian principles, better protected the freedom of the press than did the test that emerged from the Croswell case. The Sedition Act made truth a defense without requiring the defendant to prove, additionally, good motives or justifiable ends, and it placed upon the prosecution the burden of proving malice. The prejudiced enforcement of the Sedition Act hamstrung its Zengerian principles, but they existed in that act more clearly and broadly than in the New York test, which modified the common law still less.

We do not know President Jefferson's opinion of New York's prosecution of Croswell for seditiously libeling him, but he probably approved of the Clinton administration's effort to vindicate his name. Indeed it would not be surprising if one day there should be discovered a letter from Jefferson to Clinton advising that the scurrilous Federalist press be muzzled by the common law. Such a letter exists in an analogous case in Pennsylvania, addressed by Jefferson in 1803 to Clinton's counterpart, Governor Thomas McKean, the same McKean who, when chief justice of his state, had ruled that Pennsylvania's clause on freedom of speech-and-press had merely declared the common law.[94] In a letter to the president, McKean observed that the nearly daily seditious libels published in the newspapers against the chief officers of the nation verged on the intolerable. He believed that prosecutions would check their publication, but because the evil occurred on a national scale, he sought the President's advice.[95]

[94] See above, pp. 211-13.
[95] McKean to Jefferson, Feb. 7, 1803, quoted in Dumas Malone, *Jefferson the President: First Term, 1801-1805* (Boston, 1970), 229.

Jefferson answered at once. First informing McKean that patronage appointments would be coming his way, Jefferson then cautioned the Democratic governor to keep confidential his remarks on the subject of libel prosecutions. The Federalists, he noted, having failed to destroy the freedom of the press "by their gag law, seem to have attacked it in an opposite form, that is by pushing its licentiousness and its lying to such a degree of prostitution as to deprive it of all credit." Jefferson had a suggestion for the melioration of the condition of the press: "I have therefore long thought that a few prosecutions of the most eminent offenders would have a wholesome effect in restoring the integrity of the presses." But he warned McKean not to begin a "general prosecution, for that would look like a persecution: but a selected one. The paper I now inclose, appears to me to offer as good instance in every respect to make an example of, as can be selected."[96]

Although we do not know what paper Jefferson enclosed with his letter, singling out his intended victim, it was probably a clipping from *The Port Folio*, a Philadelphia journal of literature and politics edited by Joseph Dennie, an arch-Federalist and onetime secretary to Timothy Pickering, Adams's secretary of state, who had directed the enforcement of the Sedition Act. Dennie made a practice of satirizing Jefferson unmercifully. McKean took no action, however, until two months after the President's letter, when *The Port Folio* published an essay calling democracy "contemptible and vicious" and predicting that it would bring the country to civil war, despotism, and anarchy: "No wise man but discerns its imperfections, no good man but shudders at its miseries, no honest man but proclaims its fraud, and no brave man but draws his sword against its force."[97] The essay led to Dennie's indictment by Pennsylvania for a seditious libel against both the state and national governments. The state charged him with maliciously intending to "condemn the principles of the revolution, and revile, depreciate and scandalize the characters of the revolutionary patriots and statesmen, to endanger, subvert, and totally destroy the republican constitutions and free governments of the United States" and similar crimes.[98] The case was not tried for more than two years.

Judge Jasper Yeates, a Federalist, instructed the jury, which acquitted Dennie, that although the defendant was accountable to the law for an abuse of his constitutional privilege to speak and write

[96] Jefferson to McKean, Feb. 19, 1803, in *The Writings of Thomas Jefferson*, ed. Paul Leicester Ford (New York, 1892-99), 9:451-52.
[97] *Respublica* v. *Dennie*, 4 Yeats' (Penn.) Reports 267 (1805).
[98] *Ibid.*, 268.

freely, "The enlightened advocates of representative republican government pride themselves in the reflection that the more deeply their system is examined, the more fully will the judgments of honest men be satisfied that it is the most conducive to the safety and happiness of a free people."[99] Judge Yeates modeled his charge on Hamilton's argument in the Croswell case. Yeates drew a line against "malicious" publications which have a "tendency to anarchy, sedition, and civil war." He let the jury decide whether the defendant had gone to "unwarrantable lengths" in his essay, but first he fixed an "honest" attempt to inform the public and a "temperate" investigation of the government as the equivalents of good motives and justifiable ends. The Pennsylvania constitution of 1790 had recognized the right of a jury to return a general verdict and truth as a defense without qualifications. The defense of truth applied, according to the constitution, in prosecutions for criminal libel that involved "investigating the official conduct of officers or men in a public capacity" and "matters proper for public information." Dennie's case, in effect, watered down the meaning of the free press clause of the 1790 state constitution by applying to it an equivalent of the New York standard.

The aphorism that taught law is tough law is true here. The common law possessed remarkable tenacity, resisting even the modest Croswell doctrines. In Massachusetts, where the state constitution of 1780 declared that the liberty of the press, being essential to a free state, ought not be restrained, the Supreme Judicial Court ruled in 1808 that the press clause merely declared the common law as defined by Blackstone. In a dictum, however, the court announced an exception to the rule that truth was not a defense; in prosecutions for criminal libel against a public official or a candidate for office, the rule did not apply. That meant that truth, regardless of motives or ends, did not constitute a defense if the criminal libel concerned public matters as distinguished from public officials.[100] Virginia's high court construed the free press clause of that state the same way.[101] In other states, truth constituted a defense in a trial for libeling the government, but not for libeling a government official. Several states adopted constitutional amendments or passed new laws governing libel law in order to supersede judicial decisions that perpetuated Blackstone and Mansfield.[102]

[99] *Ibid.*, 270.
[100] *Commonwealth* v. *Clapp*, 4 Mass. 164 (1808).
[101] *Commonwealth* v. *Morris*, 1 Va. Cases 176 (1811).
[102] See Alfred H. Kelly, "Constitutional Liberty and the Law of Libel." *American Historical Review* 74(1968):432-33; Clyde A. Duniway, *The Development of Freedom of the Press in Massachusetts* (New York, 1906), 158 n. 1.

As late as 1826 the Supreme Judicial Court of Massachusetts, in an opinion by Chief Justice Parker, observed: "The general principle decided is, that it is immaterial to the character of a libel *as a public offence,* whether the matter of it be true or false. . . . Nor does our constitution or declaration of rights abrogate the common law in this respect, as some have insisted. . . . The *liberty* of the press, not its *licentiousness;* this is the construction which a just regard to the other parts of that instrument, and to the wisdom of those who formed it requires. . . . Besides, it is well understood, and received as a commentary on this provision for the liberty of the press, that it was intended to prevent all such *previous restraints* upon publications as had been practised by other governments, and in early times here, to stifle the efforts of patriots towards enlightening their fellow subjects upon their rights and the duties of rulers. The liberty of the press was to be unrestrained, but he who used it was to be responsible in case of its abuse. . . . The common law therefore is left unimpaired by the constitution . . ." except that truth was admissible as a defense in certain cases involving animadversion upon elected officials and candidates for office.[103] In 1827 the legislature of Massachusetts enacted a statute making truth a defense in all criminal libels when published with "good motives and for justifiable ends."[104] The case of Massachusetts shows the staying power of the common-law definition of freedom of the press even when freedom of the press received constitutional recognition. Little or nothing changed. The same case also shows the eventual triumph of the Croswell doctrine of 1804 enunciated by Hamilton and Kent.

Although Jefferson had written in 1804 that he had always asserted an "exclusive" right in the states "to controul the freedom of the press,"[105] he was ready to concede a concurrent right in the United States to prosecute seditious libel at common law when Federalist control of Connecticut stymied state punishment of his critics. A Federalist partisan referred to the prosecutions in the United States courts in Connecticut during Jefferson's presidency as Jefferson's "reign of terror."[106] The story begins with the President's appointment of a trusted political lieutenant, Pierpont Edwards, as United States district judge for Connecticut in 1806. Justice William Pater-

---

[103] *Commonwealth* v. *Blanding,* 3 Pickering (Mass.) 304, 312-314 *passim.*
[104] Laws of Massachusetts, 1827, chap. CVII, printed in Duniway, *Development of Freedom,* 159.
[105] Letter to Abigail Adams, Sept. 4, 1804, quoted in full above, at p. 307.
[106] "Hampden," *A Letter to the President of the United States, touching the Prosecutions under his Patronage, before the Circuit Court in the District of Connecticut* (New Haven, 1808), 28.

son being ill at the time, Judge Edwards conducted the United States Circuit Court alone. In an address to a grand jury handpicked by a Jeffersonian marshal, Edwards asked for common-law indictments against the publishers of libels against the United States, on ground that they would, if not restrained, "more effectually undermine and sap the foundations of our Constitution and Government, than any kind of treason that can be named."[107] The federal grand jurors returned indictments in 1806 for seditious libel against Judge Tapping Reeve of the Connecticut Superior Court for articles he had published in *The Litchfield Monitor*, a Federalist paper; against Thomas Collier, publisher of the *Monitor;* and against Thaddeus Osgood, a candidate for the ministry. A few months later, Barzillai Hudson and George Goodwin, editors of the Federalist *Connecticut Courant* of Hartford, and the Reverend Azel Backus were also indicted. The charge against each of the six defendants was the same: seditious libel of President Jefferson. Backus and Osgood had committed the alleged crime in the course of preaching sermons; the other defendants in newspaper print.[108]

Jefferson, in 1809, informed a friend that the prosecutions "had been instituted, and had made considerable progress without my knowledge, that they were disapproved by me *as soon as known*, and directed to be discontinued."[109] The prosecutions may have been instituted without Jefferson's knowledge, but he learned of them by mid-October of 1806, nearly six months before they were scheduled for trial, and he approved of them until expediency dictated his disapproval many months later. Gideon Granger, Jefferson's cabinet officer from Connecticut who kept a close watch on political developments at home, first apprised him of the facts. To Granger the prosecutions were repugnant: "Where will be the liberty of future generations if the dreadful doctrines maintained by Federalists on this point are to be sanctioned by precedents given by the republican administration?"[110] Jefferson did not reply. Thomas Seymour, a Connecticut Democrat, informed the President that the party faithful

[107] The *Litchfield* (Conn.) *Witness*, April 30, 1806, as quoted by Dumas Malone, *Jefferson and His Time* (Boston, 1974), 5:375; quoted also in variant form by William W. Crosskey, *Politics and the Constitution* (Chicago, 1958), 2:771. Crosskey deserves credit for breaking first ground on this story. Crosskey's account portrays Jefferson in the worst possible light, Malone's in the best.

[108] "Hampden," *A Letter to the President*, 8-12.

[109] Jefferson to Wilson Carey Nicholas, June 13, 1809, in Jefferson's *Writings*, 9:253. Italics added.

[110] Granger to Jefferson, Oct. 9, 1806, quoted by Malone, *Jefferson and His Time*, 5:379.

in Connecticut supported "the prosecutions depending before the Circuit Court in this District for libels against the President and Administration of the General Government." Without naming the indicted parties, Seymour described them as "a Judge, two political priests, and three Federal printers."[111] Moreover, Congressman Samuel W. Dana, a Connecticut Federalist, on January 2, 1807, described the prosecutions to the House of Representatives in order to obtain support for his abortive bill making truth a defense in federal criminal-libel trials.[112] Jefferson himself replied to Seymour in a letter dated February 11, 1807, acknowledging the "prosecutions in the Court of the US" and recommending that if truth be admitted as a defense, the effect could "not lessen the useful freedom of the press." He himself had never troubled to contradict the calumnies against him, he declared, and he would "leave to others"—Judge Pierpont Edwards and the federal jury?—the task of recalling the press to truth.[113] By curious coincidence Judge Edwards then decided that section 34 of the Judiciary Act of 1789 required him to follow state law in common-law trials in the courts of the United States, with the consequence that a Connecticut statute of 1804, allowing truth as a defense, was held to be applicable to the forthcoming trials.[114] This ruling ultimately led to the undoing of the government's position.

The case against Judge Reeve was dropped because he was related by marriage to Judge Edwards, who refused to issue a warrant of arrest. The other trials were scheduled for the April session of the court in 1807. The federal marshal personally selected the petty jurors instead of choosing them by lot as was customary. Defense counsel objected to the proceedings. They stated that they meant to argue that the federal courts had no jurisdiction over crimes at common law; they therefore requested a postponement of the cases until a member of the Supreme Court on circuit duty joined Edwards in the following year. Edwards, however, declared that the public peace of the state would not permit the cases to lie over another year, particularly because the public had a right to have a determination "as to the facts charged." But the discovery of defects in the indictments frustrated his eagerness to try the cases immediately, necessitating a

---

[111] "From the Citizens of Hartford," Seymour and others to Jefferson, December 20, 1806, in W. C. Ford, ed., *Thomas Jefferson, Correspondence Printed from the Originals in the Collections of William K. Bixby* (Boston, 1916), 137, 139.

[112] *Annals of Congress*, 9th Cong., 2nd sess., 247.

[113] Jefferson to Seymour, Feb. 11, 1807, in Jefferson's *Writings*, ed. Ford, 9:30.

[114] "Hampden," *A Letter to the President*, iii.

postponement until the September session of the court. In September Edwards behaved in a manner that caused counsel to express "surprise at the unexpected turn the case had taken." Each of the defendants, except the Reverend Azel Backus, having renewed a demurrer to the jurisdiction of the court, Edwards promptly reserved decision on their demurrers until he should be joined by another judge. The effect of this move postponed the trials until, if necessary, the Supreme Court itself would finally rule on the question of jurisdiction. Backus, however, insisted upon being tried immediately, while Edwards insistently sought to convince him that it would be a hardship on him to have to stand trial before settlement of the jurisdictional point. In the end, Backus's trial was postponed against his wishes.[115]

Quite obviously, Edwards had changed his mind between April and September of 1807 about going ahead with the prosecutions. The explanation for his change of mind reveals why Backus was so eager to be tried for seditious libel. Jefferson had learned for the first time the exact nature of Backus's libel, knew that it could be proved to be true, and commanded Gideon Granger to secure "an immediate dismission of the prosecution."[116] The libel in question concerned "the Walker affair" of 1768, when Jefferson seems to have attempted the seduction of a friend's wife. The incident had become a "public scandal" in 1805, forcing the president to confess, to a member of his cabinet, the "incorrectness" of his conduct: "when young and single I offered love to a handsome lady."[117] Because Backus had the facts on his side and had already subpoenaed the lady's husband as well as James Madison and others from Virginia to testify to the truth of his accusation against the president, the decision to prevent the trial from coming off was understandable. In April of 1808 the government withdrew the prosecutions against Backus and the other defendants excepting Hudson and Goodwin.[118] Their case, prior to trial, was appealed to the Supreme Court for a decision on the question whether federal tribunals possessed jurisdiction over the common-law crime of seditious libel; the Court's decision, handed down in 1812, ruled against federal common law jurisdiction.[119]

Regardless of Jefferson's personal complicity in the Connecticut prosecutions, the very fact that they could have been instituted in

---

[115] *Ibid.*, 14-20, quoting at pp. 16-20 an article from the *Connecticut Courant* (Hartford), Sept. 30, 1807.

[116] Jefferson to W. C. Nicholas, June 13, 1809, in Jefferson's *Writings*, 9:253.

[117] Jefferson to Robert Smith, July 1, 1805, quoted in Malone, *Jefferson and His Time*, 1:448. See *ibid.*, 447-451 for a discussion of the Walker affair.

[118] "Hampden," *A Letter to the President*, 23.

[119] *U.S. v. Hudson and Goodwin*, 7 Cranch (U.S.) 32 (1812).

the federal courts under his own administration suggests that the libertarian arguments of the Sedition Act period were *ad hoc* in character, at least in part. The prosecutions against Croswell and Dennie additionally indicated that Jeffersonian principles respecting freedom of political expression depended upon whose ox was being gored by the common law of seditious libel.[120]

Neither Hay, Wortman, nor Thomson should be regarded as the theorist of Jeffersonianism in power; the honor belongs, rather, to a greater writer than any of them, a man who was the foremost pamphleteer in the English language, a friend of the radicals in England and France as well as in America, a condemned seditionist, Thomas Paine. In 1806, after the indictments for seditious libel had been returned in Judge Edwards's court, Paine published an essay on "Liberty of the Press" in a New York newspaper.[121] He began by criticizing the "licentiousness" of Federalist editors and noted that nothing was more common than "the continual cry of the *Liberty of the Press.*" Undertaking to define the term, because it was being used "without being understood," Paine drew from English history a Blackstonian conclusion that the abolition of previous censorship made the press only as free as speech had always been. He ended:

A man does not ask liberty beforehand to say something he has a mind to say, but he becomes answerable afterwards for the atrocities he may utter.

In like manner, if a man makes the press utter atrocious things he becomes as answerable for them as if he had uttered them by word of mouth. Mr. Jefferson has said in his inaugural speech, that '*error of opinion might be tolerated, when reason was left free to combat it.*' This is sound philosophy in cases of error. But there is a difference between error and licentiousness.

Some lawyers in defending their clients . . . have often given their opinion of what they defined the liberty of the press to be.

---

[120] Worthington Chauncey Ford, summarizing his study of "Jefferson and the Newspaper," concluded, "he had lashed himself into a fine frenzy over the temporary sedition laws as a gag upon free speech and an attack upon a free press, yet would have the state permanently apply the same remedy; he had wished to reform journalism, but his idea of reformation was that of the character in Beaconsfield's novel of the agreeable man—'one who agrees with me'; and he had begun by writing for a sheet of advertisements without news." *Records of the Columbia Historical Society* 8(1905):110. On Jefferson and the press, see L. W. Levy, *Jefferson and Civil Liberties: the Darker Side* (Cambridge, Mass., 1963), *passim.*
[121] *The American Citizen* (N.Y.), Oct. 20, 1806, reprinted in *The Life and Works of Thomas Paine*, ed. William M. Van der Weyde (New Rochelle, 1925), 10:287-290.

One said it was this, another said it was that, and so on according to the case they were pleading. Now these men ought to have known that the term *liberty of the press* arose from a FACT, the abolition of the office of Imprimateur [*sic*], and that opinion has nothing to do with the case. The term refers to the fact of printing *free from prior restraint*, and not at all to the matter printed, whether good or bad. The public at large—or in case of prosecution, a jury of the country—will be judges of the matter.[122]

Paine's views in this respect represented those of the Framers.

But the Framers had a genius for studied imprecision. They were conscious of the need to phrase the Constitution in generalized terms and without a lexicographical guide, for they meant to outline an instrument that would serve future generations. Like Martin Chuzzlewit's grandnephew who had no more than "the first idea and sketchy notion of a face," the Constitution was purposely made to embody first ideas and sketchy notions. Detailed codes, which become obsolete with a change in the particular circumstances for which they were adopted, are avoided by men trained in the common law. They tend rather to formulate principles that are expansive and comprehensive in character. The principles and not their Framers' understanding and application of them are meant to endure. The Constitution, designed by an eighteenth-century rural society, serves as well today as ever because an antiquarian historicism that would freeze its original meaning has not guided its interpretation and was not intended to.

The First Amendment's injunction, that there shall be no law abridging the freedom of speech or press, was boldly stated if narrowly understood. The bold statement, not the narrow understanding, was written into the fundamental law. "It is far better," as Tunis Wortman wrote, "to err on the side of Latitude than on that of Restraint."[123] On this point the Framers would probably have agreed with Wortman. He and Blake, Nicholas, Hay, Madison, Gallatin, Cooper, Tucker, and Thomson originated a libertarian philosophy that sought to define the content of the free speech-and-press clause. They were addressing the future, not the past. Their insistence that they were simply clarifying the past's original understanding reflected an Anglo-American habit of going forward while facing backwards: rights that should exist are established on the fictitious pretense that they have always existed, and arguments are concocted to give to the fiction the appearance of both reality and legality. But

[122] *Ibid.*, 10:289-290.
[123] Wortman, *Treatise*, 205.

there is no evidence to warrant the belief, nor is there valid cause or need to believe, that the Framers possessed the ultimate wisdom and best insights on the meaning of freedom of expression. What they said is far more important than what they meant. It is enough that they gave constitutional recognition to the principle of freedom of speech and press in unqualified and undefined terms.

Bibliography

NEWSPAPERS

American Weekly Mercury (Philadelphia) 1719-1749.
Boston Chronicle 1767-1770.
Boston Evening Post 1735-1775.
Boston Gazette 1719-1798.
Boston News-Letter 1704-1776.
Boston Post-Boy 1734-1775.
Columbian Centinel (Boston) 1790-1820.
Connecticut Courant (Hartford) 1764-1809.
Connecticut Gazette (New Haven) 1755-1768.
Connecticut Journal (New Haven) 1767-1809.
The Daily Advertiser (New York) 1785-1800.
The Freeman's Journal (Philadelphia) 1781-1792.
Independent Gazetteer (Philadelphia) 1782-1796.
Maryland Gazette (Annapolis) 1745-1776.
The Massachusetts Centinel (Boston) 1784-1790.
The Massachusetts Spy (Boston) 1770-1775.
The Massachusetts Spy (Worcester) 1775-1800.
New-England Courant (Boston) 1721-1727.
New-Hampshire Gazette (Portsmouth) 1756-1800.
New York Gazette and Weekly Mercury 1768-1783.
New-York Gazette, or Weekly Post-Boy 1747-1773.
New York Journal (or *Gen'l Advertiser*) 1766-1776.
New York Mercury 1752-1768.
New-York Weekly Journal 1733-1751.
Newport Mercury 1758-1800.
The Pennsylvania Chronicle (Philadelphia) 1767-1774.
The Pennsylvania Evening Post (Philadelphia) 1775-1784.

The Pennsylvania Mercury (Philadelphia) 1784-1792.
Philadelphia Gazette 1738.
Providence Gazette 1762-1800.
The Rhode Island Gazette (Newport) 1732-1733.
South Carolina Gazette (Columbia) 1732-1775; 1792-1793.
The Weekly Rehearsal (Boston) 1731-1735.

ORIGINAL TRACTS, ESSAYS, BOOKS AND COLLECTED WORKS

[Adair, James]. *Discussions of the Law of Libels As at Present Received* (London: T. Cadell, 1785), 97 pp.
Adams, John. *Works; with a Life of the Author,* ed. Charles Francis Adams (Boston: Little, Brown, 1850-56), 10 vols.
Addison, Joseph. See Anon. *Thoughts of a Tory Author* . . .
Alexander, James. Untitled essay on freedom of speech, in *Philadelphia Gazette,* Nov. 17-Dec. 8, 1737, numbers 466-69. (Photostat courtesy of the Historical Society of Pennsylvania)
[Asgil, John]. *An Essay for the Press* (London: Printed for A. Baldwin, 1712), 8 pp.
Anon. *Another Letter to Mr. Almon, in Matter of Libel* (1770), in *A Collection of Scarce and Interesting Tracts* (London: Printed for J. Debrett, 1788, 4 vols., editor unnamed), 4:5-157.
——— *A Second Postscript in a Late Pamphlet, Entitled, A Letter to Mr. Almon, in Matter of Libel,* in *A Collection of Scarce and Interesting Tracts* (London: Printed for J. Debrett, 1788, 4 vols., editor unnamed), 4:158-96.
Anon. *Arguments Relating to a Restraint upon the Press in a Letter to a Bencher, from a Young Gentleman of the Temple* (London: Printed for R. and F. Bonwicke, 1712), 52 pp.
Anon. *Candid Considerations on Libels . . . With Some Observations on the Liberty of the Press.* By a Friend to Harmony (Boston: Printed by E. Freeman and L. Andrews, 1789), 22 pp.
Anon. *Common Sense: or, the Englishman's Journal* (London: Printed by J. Purser and G. Hawkins, 1738), A letter to the editor, Jan. 7, 1738, pp. 331-41, and an editorial, Jan. 21, 1738, pp. 349-54.
Anon. *The Craftsman's Doctrine and Practice of the Liberty of the Press* (London: Printed for J. Roberts, 1732), 61 pp.
Anon. *The Doctrine of Innuendo's Discuss'd; Or the Liberty of the Press Maintain'd* (London: Printed for the Author, 1731), 26 pp.
Anon. *An Enquiry into the Doctrine, Lately Propagated concerning Libels, Warrants, and the Seizure of Papers . . . in a Letter to Mr. Almon from the Father of Candor* (London: Printed for J. Almon, 1764), 135 pp. Facsimile reprint by De Capo Press (1970), gen. ed. Leonard W. Levy.
Anon. "Hampden." *A Letter to the President of the United States, touch-*

ing the Prosecutions under his Patronage, before the Circuit Court in the District of Connecticut (New Haven: Steele & Co., 1808), 28 pp.

Anon. *The Journeyman's Touchstone; or, A Full Refutation of Lord Mansfield's lawless opinions in Crown Libels.* By the Censor General (London: 1771), 93 pp.

Anon. *A Letter Concerning Libels, Warrants, the Seizure of Papers, and Sureties for the Peace of Behaviour . . . With the postscript and Appendix* (London, 1771), 164 pp., in *A Collection of Interesting Political Tracts,* ed., probably, by John Almon. 8 vols. (London, 1773), 1:1-164. Separately paged.

Anon. *A Letter from Candor to the Public Advertiser* (1764), in *A Collection of Interesting Political Tracts,* ed., probably, by John Almon. 8 vols. (London, 1773, reprinting Candor's 3rd ed., 1770), 1:1-40. Separately paged.

Anon. *Letters on the Subject of the Proper Liberty of the Press.* By an Englishman (London: Printed for J. Ridgway, 1790), 58 pp.

Anon. *The Liberty of the Press* (London: J. Innes, Printer, n.d. [*ca.* 1763]), 58 pp.

Anon. *Literary Liberty Considered; in a Letter to Henry Sampson Woodfall* (London: J. Johnson, 1774), 32 pp.

Anon. *A Narrative of a New and Unusual American Imprisonment of Two Presbyterian Ministers: And Prosecution of Mr. Francis Mackemie* (1704), by a Learner of Law, and Lover of Liberty, in Peter Force, ed. *Tracts and Other Papers . . .* , vol. 4, no. 4.

Anon. *The Press Restrained: A Poem* (London: Printed for John Morphew, 1712), 16 pp.

Anon. *State Law: Or, the Doctrine of Libels, Discussed and Examined* (London: Printed by E. and R. Nutt, n.d. [1729], 2nd ed.), 136 pp.

Anon. *The Thoughts of A Tory Author, Concerning the Press: With the Opinion of the Ancients and Moderns, about Freedom of SPEECH and WRITING* (London: Baldwin, 1712), 33 pp. [Uncertainly ascribed to Joseph Addison].

[Austin, Benjamin]. *Mr. Otis' Speech in Congress, on the Sedition law, with remarks by the "Examiner" on this important subject* (Boston, n.d.), [1798], 35 pp.

Bentham, Jeremy. *A Fragment on Government* (London: T. Payne, 1776), 208 pp.

Blackstone, Sir William. *Commentaries on the Laws of England* (London, 1765-69, 4 vols. 1st ed.,).

Bl[o]unt, Charles. *A Just Vindication of Learning and the Liberty of the Press* (London, 1695), 27 pp.

Blount, Charles. *Reasons Humbly Offered for the Liberty of Unlicens'd Printing* (London, 1693), 32 pp.

[Bollan, William]. *The Freedom of Speech and Writing upon Public Affairs, Considered, with an Historical View* (London: S. Baker, 1766),

160 pp. Facsimile reprint by De Capo Press (1970), gen. ed. Leonard W. Levy.

Bollan, William. *Essay on the Right of every Man in a free State to Speak; and Write Freely* (London: Printed by J. Almon, 1772), 49 pp. An abridgment of Bollan's book of 1766.

Brown, John. *Thoughts on Civil Liberty, on Licentiousness, and Faction* (London: Printed by J. Wilke & T. Saint, 1765), 168 pp.

[Burgh, James]. *Political Disquisitions: Or, An Enquiry into Public Errors, Defects and Abuses* (London: E. and C. Dilly, 1775), 3 vols. Chapter VI of vol. 1 and chap. IX of vol. 3 are related to speech and press. A facsimile reprint by De Capo Press (1971), gen. ed. Leonard W. Levy.

Busher, Leonard. *Religious Peace: or A Plea for Liberty of Conscience* (London, 1614; reprinted 1646), in Edward Bean Underhill, ed., *Tracts on Liberty of Conscience and Persecution, 1646-1661* (London: J. Haddon, 1846), pp. 1-81.

Caribbeana (London: T. Osborne, 1741), 2 vols.

Cato's Letters See Trenchard, John.

Chauncy, Charles. *The only Compulsion proper to be made Use of in the Affairs of Conscience and Religion. A Sermon* (Boston: Printed by J. Draper, 1739), 26 pp.

A Collection of Scarce and Interesting Tracts (London: Printed for J. Debrett, 1788, 4 vols., editor unnamed), vol. 4.

[Collins, Anthony]. *A Discourse of Free Thinking* (London, 1713), 178 pp.

―――― *A Discourse of the Grounds and Reasons of the Christian Religion* (London, 1724), 285 pp., preface iii-lxii.

―――― *A Discourse concerning Ridicule and Irony in Writing* (London: Printed for J. Brotherton, 1729), 77 pp.

Cooper, Thomas. *Account of the Trial of Thomas Cooper* (Philadelphia, 1800).

―――― *Political Essays*, 2d ed. with Corrections and Additions (Philadelphia, 1800).

―――― *A Treatise on the Law of Libel and the Liberty of the Press* (New York: Printed by G. F. Hopkins & Son, 1830), 184 pp.

[Cushing, William, and John Adams]. "Hitherto Unpublished Correspondence Between Chief Justice Cushing and John Adams in 1789," [ed. Frank W. Grinnell], *Massachusetts Law Quarterly* 27 (October 1942):12-16.

Dawes, M[anasseh]. *The Deformity of the Doctrine of Libels, and Information Ex Officio* (London: J. Stockdale, 1785), 40 pp.

[Defoe, Daniel]. *A Vindication of the Press* (London: T. Warner, 1718), 36 pp.

Erskine, Thomas Lord. *Speeches of Thomas Lord Erskine. Reprinted from the Five Volume Octavo Edition of 1810. With a Memoir of His Life* by Edward Walford (London: Reeves and Turner, 1870), 2 vols.

Force, Peter, ed. *American Archives: Consisting of a Collection of Authentic Records* (Washington, 1837ff.), 4th series, 6 vols.

—— *Tracts and Other Papers Relating Principally to the Origin . . . of the Colonies in North America* (New York: P. Smith, 1947 ed.), 4 vols.

Ford, Paul Leicester, ed. *Essays on the Constitution of the United States* (Brooklyn: New York Historical Printing Club, 1892).

—— ed. *Pamphlets on the Constitution of the United States* (Brooklyn: New York Historical Printing Club, 1888).

Ford, Worthington, C., ed. *Thomas Jefferson Correspondence Printed from the Originals in the Collection of William K. Bixby* (Boston, 1916).

Fowle, Daniel. *A Total Eclipse of Liberty* (Boston: Printed by D. Fowle, 1755), 32 pp.

Franklin, Benjamin. *The Writings of Benjamin Franklin*, ed. Albert Henry Smyth (New York: Macmillan, 1905-07), 10 vols.

—— *The Papers of Benjamin Franklin*, ed. Leonard W. Labaree (New Haven: Yale University Press, 1959–ser. in progress).

Furneaux, Philip. *Letters to the Honourable Mr. Justice Blackstone, Concerning his Exposition of the Act of Toleration . . . in His Celebrated Commentaries on the Laws of England* (London: T. Cadell, 1770; 2nd ed., 1771).

—— *An interesting appendix to Sir William Blackstone's Commentaries on the laws of England* (Philadelphia: Printed by Robert Bell, 1773).

—— *The Palladium of Conscience* (Philadelphia: Printed by Robert Bell, 1773).

Gorton, Samuel. "Simplicities Defence against Seven-Headed Policy" (1646), in Peter Force, ed., *Tracts and Other Papers Relating Principally to the origin . . . of the Colonies in North America* (New York: P. Smith, 1947 ed.), 4 vols., no. 6.

Hall, Robert. *An Apology for the Freedom of the Press, and for General Liberty* (1793), in John Foster, ed., *The Miscellaneous Works and Remains of the Reverend Robert Hall* (London: H. G. Bohn, 1846), pp. 159-233.

Haller, William, ed. *Tracts on Liberty in the Puritan Revolution, 1638-1647* (New York: Columbia University Press, 1933), 3 vols.

Haller, William, and Davies, Godfrey, eds. *The Leveller Tracts, 1647-1653* (New York: Columbia University Press, 1944).

Hay, George [Hortensius, pseud]. *An Essay on the Liberty of the Press, Respectfully Inscribed to the Republican Printers Throughout the United States* (Philadelphia: Printed by Samuel Pleasants, 1799), 51 pp. Reprinted in Richmond, 1803, in a 30 pp. edition.

Hay, George. *An Essay on the Liberty of the Press, Shewing, That the Requisition of Security for Good Behaviour from Libellers, is Perfectly Compatible with the Constitution and Laws of Virginia* (Richmond: Printed by Samuel Pleasants, 1803), 48 pp.

———— *Two Essays on the Liberty of the Press* (New York: De Capo Press, 1970), gen. ed., Leonard W. Levy. [Reprint of the two preceeding pamphlets.]

[Hayter, Thomas Bishop]. *An Essay on the Liberty of the Press, Chiefly as It Respects Personal Slander* (London, n.d. [late 1750s]), 47 pp.

[Hiltzheimer, Jacob] *Extracts from the Diary of Jacob Hiltzheimer, 1765-1798,* ed. Jacob Cox Parsons (Philadelphia: Fell and Co., 1893).

Hopkinson, Francis. *The Miscellaneous Essays and Occasional Writings of Francis Hopkinson* (Philadelphia: Printed by T. Dobson, 1792), 3 vols.

Hume, David. *Essays Moral, Political, and Literary,* ed. T. H. Green and T. H. Grose (London: Longmans, Green & Co., 1898), 2 vols.

Jefferson, Thomas. *The Papers of Thomas Jefferson,* ed. Julian P. Boyd, *et al.* (Princeton: Princeton University Press, 1950-   , series in progress).

———— *The Writings of Thomas Jefferson,* ed. Paul Leicester Ford (New York: G. P. Putnam's Sons, 1892-1899), 10 vols.

Jensen, Merrill, ed. *The Documentary History of the Ratification of the Constitution* (Madison: State Historical Society of Wisconsin, 1976-   , ser. in progress).

Kaminsky, John P., and Gaspare J. Saladino, eds. *Commentaries on the Constitution: Public and Private* (Madison: State Historical Society, 1981-   ser. in progress). Vol. 13 *et seq.* of *The Documentary History of the Ratification of the Constitution.*

[Keith, George, and Thomas Budd]. *New England's Spirit of Persecution Transmitted to Pennsilvania, And the Pretended Quaker Found Persecuting the True Christian-Quaker, in the Tryal of Peter Boss, George Keith, Thomas Budd and William Bradford . . . 1693. Giving an Account of the most Arbitrary Procedure of that Court* (Philadelphia: Printed by William Bradford, 1693), 38 pp.

Kippis, Alexander. *A Vindication of the Protestant Dissenting Ministers* (London: G. Robinson, 1773), 123 pp.

Livingston, William *et al. The Independent Reflector,* ed. by Milton M. Klein (Cambridge, Mass.: Harvard University Press), 1963.

Locke, John. *Letters on Toleration,* in *The Works of John Locke* (London: W. Otridge, Leigh and Sotherby, 1812, 11th ed., 10 vols.), vol. 6.

———— *An Essay Concerning Human Understanding* (written 1671, first published 1690), (London: Tegg and Co., 1879).

[Lofft, Capel]. *An Essay on the Law of Libels* (London, 1785), 110 pp.

Madison, James. *The Papers of James Madison,* ed. William T. Hutchinson, Robert A. Rutland *et al.* (Chicago: University of Chicago Press, 1962-   , ser. in progress).

———— *The Virginia Report of 1799-1800 Touching the Alien and Sedition Laws* (Richmond, 1850). A facsimile reprint by Da Capo Press (1970), gen. ed. Leonard W. Levy.

—— *The Writings of James Madison*, ed. Gaillard Hunt (New York: G. P. Putnam's Sons, 1900-1910), 9 vols.

[Marshall, John]. *Address of the minority in the Virginia Legislature to the people of that state, containing a vindication of the constitutionality of the Alien and Sedition laws* (n.p., 1799), 16 pp.

[Maseres, Francis]. *An Enquiry into the Extent of the Power of Juries, on Trials of Indictments or Informations, for Publishing Seditious, or other Criminal Writings, or Libels. Extracted from a Miscellaneous Collection of Papers that were Published in 1776, Intitled, Additional Papers Concerning the Province of Quebec* (Dublin: E. Lynch, 1792), 48 pp.

Maule, Thomas. See Philanthes, Theo.

Mayhew, Jonathan. "A Discourse Concerning Unlimited Submission" (1750) in Perry Miller and Thomas H. Johnson, eds., *The Puritans* (New York: American Book Comany, 1938), 277-80.

McPherson, Elizabeth, ed. "Unpublished Letters from North Carolinians to James Madison and James Monroe," *North Carolina Historical Review* 14 (1937):157-69.

Milton, John. *The Works of John Milton*, ed. Frank A. Patterson, *et al.* (New York: Columbia University Press, 1931-38, 18 vols.); vol. 4, ed. William Haller, contains: *Areopagitica* (1644); *A Treatise of Civil power in Ecclesiastical causes* (1659); and *Of True Religion, Heresie Schism, and Toleration* (1673).

Morris, Robert. *A Letter to Sir Richard Aston . . . Containing . . . some Thought on the Modern Doctrine of Libels* (London: Printed for Geo. Pearch, 1770), 68 pp.

Paine, Thomas. *The Life and Works of Thomas Paine*, ed. William M. Van der Weyde (New Rochelle: Thomas Paine National Historical Association, 1925), 10 vols.

Philanthes, Theo [Thomas Maule]. *New-England Persecutors Mauld With their own Weapons . . . Together with a brief Account of the Imprisonment and Tryal of Thomas Maule of Salem, for publishing a Book, entitled, Truth held forth and maintained, &c.* (New York: W. Bradford, 1697), 62 pp.

[Raynor, John]. *A Digest of the Law concerning Libels. By a Gentleman of the Inner-Temple* (Dublin: W. Hallhead, 1778), 139 pp.

Ratcliffe, Ebenezer. *Two Letters Addressed to the Right Rev. Prelates* (London: Printed for J. Johnson, 1773), 123 pp.

[Romily, Sir Samuel]. *A Fragment of the Constitutional Power and Duty of Juries upon Trials for Libels* (London: Society for Constitutional Information, n.d. [1785]), 16 pp.

Smith, Samuel Stanhope. *A Sermon on Slander delivered at the church on Brattle St., Boston, Oct. 24, 1790* (Boston: Printed by Samuel Hall, 1791), 24 pp.

Smith, William. *Historical Memoirs from 16 March 1763 to 9 July 1776 of William Smith*, ed. William H. W. Sabine (New York: n.p., 1956).

Spinoza, Benedict de. *The Chief Works of Benedict de Spinoza*, trans. R. H. M. Elwes (London: G. Bell & Sons. 1883), 2 vols.

[Sullivan James]. *A Dissertation upon the Constitutional Freedom of the Press in the United States of America*. By an Impartial Citizen (Boston: Printed by David Carlisle, 1801), 54 pp.

Thomson, John. *An Enquiry, Concerning the Liberty, and Licentiousness of the Press, and the Uncontroulable Nature of the Human Mind* (New York: Printed by Johnson & Stryker, 1801), 84 pp. A facsimile reprint by De Capo Press (1970), gen. ed. Leonard W. Levy.

Tindall, Matthew. *A Letter to a Member of Parliament, shewing that a restraint on the press is inconsistent with the Protestant religion, and dangerous to the liberties of the nation* (London: Printed by J. Darby, 1698), 32 pp.

———— *A Letter to a Friend: Occasioned by the presentment of the grand jury for the county of Middlesex, of the author, printer and publisher of a book entitled the rights of the christian church asserted* (London, 1708), 24 pp.

———— *Reasons against Restraining the Press* (London, 1704), 15 pp.

Towers, Joseph. *Observations on the Rights and Duty of Juries, in Trials for Libels*, 1784, reprinted in Tower's *Tracts on Political and Other Subjects* (London: Printed for T. Cadell & W. Davies, 1796, 3 vols.), 2:1-174.

[Towers, Joseph]. *An Enquiry into the Question, Whether Juries are, or are not, Judges of Law, as well as of Fact; With a particular Reference to the case of Libels* (London: Printed for J. Wilkie, 1764), 31 pp.

[Trenchard, John, and Thomas Gordon]. *Cato's Letters: Or, Essays on Liberty, Civil and Religious* (London: Printed for J. Walthoe, T. and L. Longman, 1755, 6th ed.), 4 vols. A facsimile reprint by De Capo Press (1971), gen. ed. Leonard W. Levy.

Tucker, St. George. "Of the Right of Conscience; And of the Freedom of Speech and of the Press," in Tucker's *Blackstone's Commentaries: with Notes of Reference, to the Constitution and Laws, of the Federal Government of the United States; and of the Commonwealth of Virginia* (Philadelphia: Published by William Young Birch, and Abraham Small, 1803, 5 vols.), Appendix to Vol 1, Part II, Note G., pp. 1-30.

Underhill, Edward Bean, ed. *Tracts on Liberty of Conscience and Persecution, 1614-1661* (London: Printed for the Hanserd Knollys Society by J. Haddon, 1846).

[Wilkes, John]. *English Liberty . . . containing the Private Correspondence, Public Letters, Speeches, and Addresses of John Wilkes* (London: T. Baldwin, n.d. [1769], 2 vols. in 1), 391 pp.

———— *The North Briton* (Dublin, 1766), 2 vols.

Williams, Elisha. *A Seasonable Plea for the Liberty of Conscience, and the Right of private Judgment, in Matters of Religion, without any Controul from human Authority*. By a Lover of Truth and Liberty

(Boston: Printed by S. Kneeland and T. Green, 1744), 66 pp. Signed "Philalethes" on p. 66.

Williams, Roger. *The Writings of Roger Williams*. Publications of the Narragansett Club (Providence, 1866-74), 6 vols.

[Wilson, James]. *The Works of James Wilson*, ed. by Robert Green McCloskey (Cambridge, Mass.: Harvard University Press, 1967), 2 vols.

Winslow, Edward. *Hypocracie Unmasked, A True Relation of the Proceedings of the Governor and Company of the Massachusetts Bay against Samuel Gorton of Rhode Island* (1646), ed. Howard Millar Chapin (Providence: The Club for Colonial Reprints, 1916).

Winthrop, John. *The History of New England from 1630 to 1649*, ed. James Savage (Boston: Little, Brown & Co., 1853), 2 vols.

Wolfe, Don M., ed. *Leveller Manifestoes of the Puritan Revolution* (New York: T. Nelson & Sons, 1944).

[Woodfall, Henry]. Phileleutherus Anglicanus. *A Summary of the Law of Libel. In Four Letters* (1770) in *A Collection of Scarce and Interesting Tracts* (London: J. Debrett, 1788, 4 vols., editor unnamed), 4:197-221.

Wortman, Tunis. *Treatise Concerning Political Enquiry, and the Liberty of the Press* (New York: Printed by G. Forman, 1800). A facsimile reprint by De Capo Press (1970), gen. ed. Leonard W. Levy.

DEBATES, TRIALS, AND OTHER PUBLIC RECORDS

[Alexander, James]. *A brief Narrative of the Case and Tryal of John Peter Zenger, Printer of the New-York Weekly Journal* (1736) in Livingston Rutherford, *John Peter Zenger . . . Also a Reprint of the First Edition of the Trial* (New York: Peter Smith, 1941).

—— *A Brief Narrative of the Case and Tryal of John Petter Zenger, Printer of the New-York Weekly Journal*, 2nd ed., Stanley Nider Katz, ed. (Cambridge: Harvard University Press, 1972).

Andrews, Charles M., ed. *Narratives of the Insurrections, 1675-1690* (New York: C. Scribner's Sons, 1915).

[Annals of Congress]. *The Debates and Proceedings in the Congress of the United States* (Washington: Gales & Seaton, 1834ff).

Browne, William Hand, et al., eds. *Archives of Maryland* (Baltimore: Maryland Historical Society, 1883-   ), 72 vols., series in progress.

Chandler, Peleg W., ed. *American Criminal Trials* (Boston: T. H. Carter, 1844), 2 vols.

Documentary History of the Constitution of the United States of America, 1786-1870, Derived from Records, Manuscripts, and Rolls Deposited in the Bureau of Rolls and Library of the Department of State (Washington, 1894-1905), 5 vols.

Elliot, Jonathan, ed. *The Debates in the Several State Conventions on the*

Adoption of the Federal Constitution . . . and Other Illustrations of the Constitution (Philadelphia: J. B. Lippincott, 1941, 2nd ed., rev.), 5 vols.

Fleet, Beverly, ed., *Virginia Colonial Abstracts* (Richmond, 1937-52) 34 vols.

Ford, Worthington C., *et al.*, eds. *Journals of the Continental Congress 1774-1789* (Washington, 1904-37), 24 vols.

Fortescue, J. W., ed. *Calendar of State Papers, Colonial Series, America and the West Indies (27 October 1697 to 31 December 1698) Preserved in the Public Records Office* (London: Longmans and Co., 1905).

Greene, Jack P., ed., *The Nature of Colony Constitutions* (Columbia, S.C.: University of South Carolina Press, 1970).

Hall, Benjamin, ed. *Official Opinions of the Attorneys General of the United States* (Washington: U.S. Government Printing Office, 1852), 2 vols.

Hening, William Waller, ed. *The Statutes at Large, Being a Collection of All the Laws of Virginia (1619-1792)* (Richmond: Samuel Pleasants, 1809-23), 13 vols.

Howe, Mark DeWolfe, ed. *Readings in American Legal History.* (Cambridge: Harvard University Press, 1949).

Howell, Thomas Bayly, comp. *A Complete Collection of State Trials to 1783.* Continued by T. J. Howell to 1820 (London, 1816-28), 34 vols.

The Journal of the First Session of the Senate of the United States of America (New York, 1789).

Journal of the Senate of the Commonwealth of Virginia: Begun and held in the City of Richmond, on Monday the 19th day of October . . . 1789 (Richmond, 1828). [Journal of the Senate, 1785 to 1790].

Journal of the Votes and Proceedings of the General Assembly of the Colony of New-York, 1691-1765 (New York, 1764-1766), 2 vols.

Levy, Leonard W., ed., *Freedom of the Press from Zenger to Jefferson* (Indianapolis: Bobbs-Merrill, 1966).

MacKinney, Gertrude, and Charles F. Hoban, eds. *Votes and Proceedings of the House of Representatives of the Province of Pennsylvania (1682-1776),* in *Pennsylvania Archives,* 8th ser. (Philadelphia: J. Severns, 1931-35), 8 vols.

McIlwaine, H. R., and W. L. Hall eds. *Executive Journals of the Council of Colonial Virginia, 1680-1754* (Richmond, 1925-1945), 5 vols.

McIlwaine, H. R., and J. P. Kennedy, eds. *Journals of the House of Burgesses of Virginia, 1619-1776* (Richmond, 1905-15), 13 vols.

McMaster, John Bach, and Frederick D. Stone, eds. *Pennsylvania and the Federal Constitution, 1787-1788* (Philadelphia: Inquirer Printing & Publishing Co., 1888).

Minutes of the Provincial Council of Pennsylvania (Harrisburg, 1838-1840), 3 vols.

O'Callaghan, E. B., ed. *Documentary History of the State of New York* (Albany: Weed, Parsons & Co., 1849-51), 4 vols.

O'Callaghan, E. B., and B. Fernow, eds. *Documents Relative to the Colonial History of the State of New York* (Albany: Weed, Parsons, 1856-87), 15 vols.

Quincy, Josiah, Jr., ed. *Reports of Cases Argued and Adjudged in the Superior Court of Judicature of the Province of Massachusetts Bay, Between 1761 and 1772* (Boston: Little, Brown & Co., 1865).

Rutherfurd, Livingston. *John Peter Zenger, His Press, His Trial and a Bibliography of Zenger Imprints. Also a Reprint of the Edition of the Trial* (New York: Dodd, Mead, 1904).

Saunders, William L., ed. *The Colonial Records of North Carolina (1662-1776)* (Raleigh: P. M. Hale, 1886-90), 10 vols.

Schwartz, Bernard, ed. *The Bill of Rights: A Documentary History* (New York: Chelsea House, 1971), 2 vols.

Shurtleff, Nathaniel B., ed. *Records of the Governor and Company of the Massachusetts Bay in New England (1628-86)* (Boston: W. White, Printer, 1853-54), 5 vols.

Siebert, Frederick S., ed. *Documents Relating to the Development of the Relations Between Press and Government in England in the XVIth and XVIIth Centuries* (n.p., n.d.), mimeo vol.

Storing, Herbert J., ed., *The Complete Anti-Federalist* (Chicago: University of Chicago Press, 1981), 7 vols.

Tansill, Charles C., ed. *Documents Illustrative of the Formation of the Union of the American States* (Washington: Government Printing Office, 1927).

Thorpe, Francis Newton, ed. *The Federal and State Constitutions, Colonial Charters, and Other Organic Laws* (Washington: Government Printing Office, 1909), 7 vols.

Toppan, Robert Noxon, ed. *Edward Randolph* (Boston: Prince Society, 1898-1900, 7 vols.), vol. 4 for the trial of John Wise.

The Virginia Report of 1799-1800, Touching the Alien and Sedition Laws; Together with the Virginia Resolutions of December 21, 1798, Including the Debates and Proceedings Thereon, in the House of Delegates in Virginia (Richmond: J. W. Randolph, 1850). Valuable for the Virginia debates on the Sedition Act, at pp. 22-161, although adding little to the earlier debate on the same subject by the House of Representatives. Madison's *Report* is at pp. 189-237.

Wharton, Francis, ed. *State Trials of the United States during the Administrations of Washington and Adams* (Philadelphia: Carey & Hart, 1849).

SECONDARY SOURCES

Allen, J. *English Political Thought, 1603-1660* (London: Methuen, 1938), 2 vols. Amory, Thomas Coffin. *The Life of James Sullivan* (Boston: Philips, Sampson and Co., 1859), 2 vols.

Anastaplo, George. *The Constitutionalist: Notes on the First Amendment* (Dallas: Southern Methodist University Press, 1971).

—— "Freedom and Speech and the First Amendment," *University of Detroit Law Journal* 42 (1964): 55-73.

—— [Review of *Legacy of Suppression*] *New York University Law Review* 39 (1964): 735-41.

Anderson, David A. "The Origins of the Press Clause," *UCLA Law Review* 30 (1983): 455-540.

Bailyn, Bernard, and John B. Hench, eds. *The Press and the American Revolution* (Worcester: American Antiquarian Society, 1980).

Becker, Carl Lotus. *The History of Political Parties in the Province of New York 1760-1776* (Madison: University of Wisconsin Press, 1909).

Berns, Walter. *The First Amendment and the Future of American Democracy* (New York: Basic Books, 1976).

—— "Freedom of the Press and the Alien and Sedition Laws: A Reappraisal," *1970 The Supreme Court Review*, ed. Philip B. Kurland (Chicago: University of Chicago Press, 1970), pp. 109-60.

—— "Free Speech and Free Government," *Political Science Reviewer* 2 (1972): 217-41.

Beveridge, Albert J. *The Life of John Marshall* (Boston: Houghton, Mifflin, 1919), 4 vols.

Biddle, Francis. *The Fear of Freedom* (New York: Doubleday, 1951).

Blasi, Vincent. "The Checking Value in First Amendment Theory," *American Bar Foundation Research Journal* 1977: 521-649.

Bond, Donovan H., and William R. McLeod, eds. *Newsletters to Newspapers: Eighteenth Century Journalism* (Morgantown, W.Va.: School of Journalism, West Virginia University, 1977).

Bork, Robert H. "Neutral Principles and Some First Amendment Problems," *Indiana Law Journal* 47 (1971): 1-35.

Botein, Stephen. " 'Meer Mechanics' and an Open Press: The Business and Political Strategies of American Colonial Printers," in Donald Fleming and Bernard Bailyn, eds., *Perspectives in American History* 9 (1975): 127-228.

Brandwen, Maxwell. "The Battle of the First Amendment: A Study in Judicial Interpretation," The *North Carolina Law Review* 40 (1962): 273-96.

Brant, Irving. *James Madison, Father of the Constitution* (Indianapolis: Bobbs-Merrill, 1950).

Brown, David Paul. *The Forum: Or, Forty Years Full Practice at the Philadelphia Bar* (Philadelphia: R. H. Small, 1856), 2 vols.

Brown, Robert E. *Middle-Class Democracy and the Revolution in Massachusetts, 1691-1780* (Ithaca: Cornell University Press, 1955).

Bruce, Philip A. *Institutional History of Virginia in the Seventeenth Century* (New York: G. P. Putnam's Sons, 1910), 2 vols.

Buckingham, Joseph T. *Specimens of Newspaper Literature* (Boston: Redding, 1852), 2 vols.

Buckley, Thomas E. *Church and State in Revolutionary Virginia, 1776-1787* (Charlottesville: University Press of Virginia, 1977).

Buel, Richard, Jr. "Freedom of the Press in Revolutionary America: The Evolution of Libertarianism, 1760-1820," in Bernard Bailyn and John B. Hench, eds., *The Press and the American Revolution* (Worcester, Mass., 1980).

Buranelli, Vincent. "Peter Zenger's Editor," *American Quarterly* 7 (1955): 174-81.

—— *The Trial of Peter Zenger* (New York: New York University Press, 1955)

Bury, J. B. *A History of Freedom of Thought* (Home University ed., Oxford University Press, 1952 printing).

Carroll, Thomas F. "Freedom of Speech and of the Press in the Federalist Period: The Sedition Act," *Michigan Law Review* 18 (May 1920): 615-51.

Chafee, Zechariah, Jr. *Free Speech in the United States* (Cambridge: Harvard University Press, 1948).

—— *Three Human Rights in the Constitution of 1787* (Lawrence: University of Kansas Press, 1956).

Chamberlain, Bill F. "Freedom of Expression in Eighteenth Century Connecticut," in Bond and McLeod, eds., *Newsletters to Newspapers*, pp. 247-61.

Champagne, Roger J. *Alexander McDougall and the American Revolution* (Schenectady: New York State American Revolution Bicentennial Commission in conjunction with Union College Press, 1975).

Clarke, Mary Patterson. *Parliamentary Privilege in the American Colonies* (New Haven: Yale University Press, 1943).

Clyde, William C. *The Struggle for the Freedom of the Press from Caxton to Cromwell* (London: Oxford University Press, 1934).

Cobb, Sanford H. *The Rise of Religious Liberty in America* (New York: Macmillan, 1902).

Cohen, Henig. *The South Carolina Gazette* (Columbia, S.C.: University of South Carolina Press, 1953).

Colbourn, H. Trevor. *The Lamp of Experience: Whig History and the Intellectual Origins of the American Revolution* (Chapel Hill, N.C.: University of North Carolina Press, 1965).

Cook, Elizabeth Christine. *Literary Influences in Colonial Newspapers* (New York: Columbia University Press, 1912).

Cooley, Thomas M. *Treatise on the Constitutional Limitations Which Rest Upon the Legislative Power of the States*, ed. V. H. Lane (Boston: Little, Brown, 1903, 7th ed.).

Corwin, Edward S. "Freedom of Speech and Press under the First Amendment: A Resume," in *Selected Essays on Constitutional Law*, Douglas B. Maggs *et al.*, ed., (Chicago: The Foundation Press, 1953, 5 vols.), 2:1060-1068.

Cranston, Maurice. *John Locke, A Biography* (London: Longmans, Green, 1957).

Crosskey, William W. *Politics and the Constitution* (Chicago: University of Chicago Press, 1953), 2 vols.

Dargo, George. *Roots of the Republic: A New Perspective on Early American Constitutionalism* (New York: Praeger, 1974).

Dauer, Manning J. *The Adams Federalists* (Baltimore: Johns Hopkins Press, 1953).

Davidson, Philip. *Propaganda and the American Revolution, 1763-1783* (Chapel Hill: University of North Carolina Press, 1941).

DeArmond, Anna Janney. *Andrew Bradford, Colonial Journalist* (Newark, Del.: University of Delaware Press, 1949).

Dillon, Dorothy Rita. *The New York Triumvirate* (New York: Columbia University Press, 1949).

Dumbauld, Edward. *The Bill of Rights and What It Means Today* (Norman, Okla.: University of Oklahoma Press, 1957).

——— "State Precedents for the Bill of Rights," *Journal of Public Law* 7 (1958): 323-44.

Duniway, Clyde Augustus. *The Development of Freedom of the Press in Massachusetts* (New York: Longmans, Green, 1906).

Emerson, Thomas I. "Colonial Intentions and Current Realities of the First Amendment," *University of Pennsylvania Law Review* 125 (1977): 737-60.

——— *The System of Freedom of Expression* (New York: Random House, 1970).

Finkelman, Paul. "The Zenger Case: Prototype of a Political Trial," in Michal R. Belknap, ed., *American Political Trials* (Westport, Conn.: Greenwood, 1981).

Fitzgerald, Percy. *The Life and Times of John Wilkes* (London: Ward and Downey, 1888), 2 vols.

Ford, Paul Leicester, ed. *The Journals of Hugh Gaine, Printer* (New York: Dodd, Mead, 1902), 2 vols.

Forkosch, Morris D. "Freedom of the Press: *Croswell's Case*," *Fordham Law Review* 33 (1965): 415-48.

Fraenkel, Osmond K. *Our Civil Liberties* (New York: Viking Press, 1944).

Frank, Joseph. *The Levellers* (Cambridge: Harvard University Press, 1955).

Gegenheimer, Albert Frank. *William Smith* (Philadelphia: University of Pennsylvania Press, 1943).

Goebel, Julius, Jr., and T. Raymond Naughton. *Law Enforcement in Colonial New York* (New York: The Commonwealth Fund, 1944).

Haiman, Franklin S. *Speech and Law in a Free Society* (Chicago: University of Chicago Press, 1980).

Hall, Ford W. "The Common Law: An Account of Its Reception in the United States," *Vanderbilt Law Review*, 4 (June 1951): 791-825.

Hanson, Lawrence. *Government and the Press, 1695-1763* (Oxford: Oxford University Press, 1936).

Henry, William Wirt. *Patrick Henry: Life, Correspondence, and Speeches* (New York: Charles Scribners Sons, 1891), 3 vols.

Hixson, Richard F. *Isaac Collins: A Quaker Printer in 18th Century America* (New Brunswick, N.J.: Rutgers University Press, 1968).

Hoffman, Daniel H. "Contempt of the United States: The Political Crime that Wasn't," *American Journal of Legal History* 25 (1981): 343-60.

—— *Governmental Secrecy and the Founding Fathers: A Study in Constitutional Controls* (Westport, Conn.: Greenwood Press, 1981).

Holdsworth, Sir William S. *A History of English Law,* 6th ed. rev. (Boston: Little, Brown, 1938-66), 16 vols.

Howe, Mark DeWolfe. "Juries as Judges of Criminal Law," *Harvard Law Review* 52 (February 1939): 582-616.

—— "The Psychology and Language of Freedom," in *Progress and Survival: Present-Day Revelance of Eighteenth Century Thought.* A pamphlet reproducing papers delivered at a conference sponsored by the American Council of Learned Societies (n.pg., n.d., n.pb.).

Hudon, Edward G. *Freedom of Speech and Press in America* (Washington D.C.: Public Affairs Press, 1963).

Hulme, Harold. *The Life of Sir John Eliot* (New York: New York University Press, 1957).

—— "The Winning of Freedom of Speech by the House of Commons," *American Historical Review* 61 (July 1956): 825-53.

Hurst, Willard. "Treason in the United States," *Harvard Law Review* 58 (1944-45): 226-72, 395-444, and 806-57.

Huxford, Gary. "The English Libertarian Tradition in the Colonial Newspaper," *Journalism Quarterly* 45 (1968): 677-86.

Hyman, Harold M. *To Try Men's Souls: Loyalty Tests in American History* (Berkeley, Cal.: University of California Press, 1959)

Jacobson, David L. *The English Libertarian Heritage* (Indianapolis: Bobbs-Merrill, 1965).

Jones, Matt Bushnell. *Thomas Maule, The Salem Quaker and Free Speech in Massachusetts Bay* (Salem: The Essex Institute, 1936), 42 pp. Reprinted from Essex Institute Historical Collections, vol. 72, no. 1, January 1936.

Jones, Thomas. *History of New York During the Revolutionary War,* ed. E. F. deLancey (New York: New York Historical Society, 1879), 2 vols.

Jordan, W. H. *The Development of Religious Toleration in England* (Cambridge: Harvard University Press, 1934-40), 4 vols.

Judson, Margaret. *The Crisis of the Constitution* (Rutgers: Rutgers University Press, 1949).

Kalven, Harry. "The New York Times Case: A Note on the Central Meaning of the First Amendment," *1964 Supreme Court Review,* ed.

Philip B. Kurland (Chicago: University of Chicago Press, 1965), pp. 199-222.

Kelly, Alfred. "Constitutional Liberty and the Law of Libel," *American Historical Review* 74 (1968): 429-52.

Kelly, John. "Criminal Libel and Free Speech," *Kansas Law Review* 6 (1958): 295-333.

Kendall, Nellie D., ed. *Willmore Kendall Contra Mundum* (New Rochelle, N.Y.: Arlington House, 1971).

King, Lord. *The Life and Letters of John Locke* (London, H. G. Bohn, 1858 ed.).

Koch, Adrienne, and Ammon, Harry, "The Virginia and Kentucky Resolutions: An Episode in Jefferson's and Madison's Defense of Civil Liberties," *William and Mary Quarterly* 3rd ser., 5 (1948): 145-176.

Konkle, Burton Alva. *The Life of Andrew Hamilton, 1676-1741* (Philadelphia: National Publishing Co., 1941).

Konvitz, Milton R. *Fundamental Liberties of a Free People* (Ithaca: Cornell University Press, 1957).

Krislov, Samuel. *The Supreme Court and Political Freedom* (New York: The Free Press, 1968).

Kurland, Philip B. "The Irrelevance of the Constitution: The First Amendment's Freedom of Speech and Freedom of Press Clauses," *Drake Law Review* 29 (1979-80): 1-13.

Lawhorne, Clifton. *Defamation and Public Officials* (Carbondale, Ill.: University of Southern Illinois Press, 1971).

Leake, Isaac Q. *Memoir of the Life and Times of General John Lamb* (Albany: J. Munsell, 1850).

Leder, Lawrence H. *Liberty and Authority: Early American Political Ideology, 1689-1763* (Chicago: Quadrangle Books, 1968).

Levy, Leonard W. "Did the Zenger Case Really Matter?" *William and Mary Quarterly*, 3rd Ser., 17 (1960): 35-50.

——— *Jefferson and Civil Liberties: The Darker Side* (Cambridge: Harvard University Press, 1963).

——— *The Law of the Commonwealth and Chief Justice Shaw* (Cambridge: Harvard University Press, 1957).

——— *Origins of the Fifth Amendment: The Self-Incrimination Clause* (New York: Oxford University Press, 1968).

——— *Treason Against God: A History of the Offense of Blasphemy* (New York: Schocken Books, 1980).

Lincoln, Anthony. *Some Political and Social Ideas of English Dissent, 1763-1800* (Cambridge, Eng.: The University Press, 1938).

Link, Eugene Perry. *Democratic-Republican Societies, 1790-1800* (New York: Columbia University Press, 1942).

Lorenz, Alfred L. *Hugh Gaine: a Colonial Printer-Editor's Odyssey to Loyalism* (Carbondale, Ill.: Southern Illinois University Press, 1972).

Malone, Dumas. *Jefferson and His Time* (Boston: Little, Brown, 1948-81), 6 vols.

—— *Jefferson the Virginian* (Boston: Little, Brown, 1948).

—— *The Public Life of Thomas Cooper* (New Haven: Yale University Press, 1926).

Marcuse, Herbert. "Repressive Tolerance," in Robert Paul Wolff *et al.*, eds., *A Critique of Pure Tolerance* (Boston: Beacon Press, 1965), pp. 80-117.

Masson, David. *Life of Milton* (London: Macmillan, 1858-1880), 6 vols.

Matteson, David M. "The Organization of the Government under the Constitution," in Sol Bloom, Director General, *History of the Formation of the Union under the Constitution* (Washington: United States Sesquicentennial Commission, 1943), 141-508.

May, Thomas Erskine. *The Constitutional History of England Since the Accession of George III, 1760-1860* (London: A. C. Armstrong & Son, 1880), 2 vols.

Mayton, William T. "Seditious Libel and the Lost Guarantee of Freedom of Expression," *Columbia Law Review* 84 (Jan. 1984): 91-142.

McAnear, Beverly, ed. "James Parker *versus* New York Province," *New York History* 32 (1941): 321-30.

McCoy, Ralph E., ed. *Freedom of the Press: an Annotated Bibliography* (Carbondale, Ill.: Southern Illinois University Press, 1968).

—— *Freedom of the Press: a Bibliocyclopedia, 10-Year Supplement (1967-1977)* (Carbondale, Ill.: Southern Illinois University Press, 1979).

McCrady, Edward. *The History of South Carolina under the Royal Government 1719-1776* (New York: Macmillan, 1899).

McRee, Griffith J. *Life and Correspondence of James Iredell* (New York: Appleton, 1857-58), 2 vols.

Meiklejohn, Alexander. *Free Speech and Its Relation to Self-Government* (New York: Harper, 1948).

—— "The First Amendment Is an Absolute," *1961 Supreme Court Review*, ed. Philip B. Kurland (Chicago: University of Chicago Press, 1961), pp. 245-66.

—— *Political Freedom: The Constitutional Powers of the People* (New York: Harper, 1960).

Middleton, Kent, and Roy M. Mersky, eds. *The Freedom of Expression: A Collection of Best Writings* (Buffalo: William Hine, 1981).

Miller, John C. *Crisis in Freedom: The Alien and Sedition Acts* (Boston: Little, Brown, 1952).

—— *Origins of the American Revolution* (Boston: Little, Brown, 1943).

Miner, Ward L. *William Goddard Newspaperman* (Durham, N.C.: Duke University Press, 1962).

Morgan, E. M. "The Privilege Against Self-Incrimination," *Minnesota Law Review* 34 (1949): 1-45.

Mott, Frank Luther. *A History of American Magazines, 1741-1850* (New York: Appleton, 1930).

Mott, Rodney L. *Due Process of Law* (Indianapolis: Bobbs-Merrill, 1926).

Bibliography

Murphy, Paul L. "Near v. Minnesota in the Context of Historical Developments," *Minnesota Law Review* 66 (1981): 95-160.

Nash, Gary B. *The Urban Crucible* (Cambridge: Harvard University Press, 1979).

Neale, J. E. "The Commons' Privilege of Free Speech in Parliament," in R. W. Seton-Watson, ed., *Tudor Studies* (London: Longmans, Green, 1924), 258-86.

Nelson, Harold L. "Seditious Libel in Colonial America," *American Journal of Legal History* 3 (1959): 160-72.

Nimmer, Melville B. "Is Freedom of the Press a Redundancy: What Does it Add to Freedom of Speech?" *Hastings Law Journal* 26 (1975): 639-58.

Nobbe, George. *The North Briton* (New York: Columbia University Press, 1939).

Ould, Herman, ed. *Freedom of Expression. A Symposium . . . to Commemorate the Tercentenary of the Publication of Milton's "Areopagitica"* (London: Hutchinson International Authors, 1944).

Paterson, James. *The Liberty of the Press, Speech, and Public Worship* (London: Macmillan, 1880).

Patterson, Giles J. *Free Speech and a Free Press* (Boston: Little, Brown, 1939).

Pomerantz, Sidney I. "The Patriot Newspaper and the American Revolution," in Richard B. Morris, ed., *The Era of the American Revolution* (New York: Columbia University Press, 1939), 305-31.

Postgate, Raymond. *That Devil Wilkes* (New York: The Vanguard Press, 1929).

Pound, Roscoe. *The Formative Era of American Law* (Boston: Little, Brown, 1938).

Presser, Stephen B. "A Tale of Two Judges: Richard Peters, Samuel Chase, and the Broken Promise of Federal Jurisprudence," *Northwestern University Law Review* 73 (1978): 27-111.

Pritchett, C. Herman. *The American Constitution* (New York: McGraw-Hill, 1959).

Radin, Max. "Freedom of Speech in Ancient Athens," *American Journal of Philology* 48 (1927): 215-30.

Rea, Robert. *The English Press in Politics, 1760-1774* (Lincoln: University of Nebraska Press, 1963).

Realey, Charles B. "The *London Journal* and Its Authors 1720-1723," *Bulletin of University of Kansas*, vol. V, no. 3 (December 1935).

Riddell, William Renwick. "Libel on the Assembly: A Prerevolutionary Episode," *The Pennsylvania Magazine of History and Biography* 52 (1929): 176-92, 249-79, and 342-60.

Robbins, Caroline. *The Eighteenth Century Commonwealthman* (Cambridge: Harvard University Press, 1959).

Robinson, Laura. *Free Speech in the Roman Republic* (Baltimore: Johns Hopkins University Press, 1940).

Roche, John P. "American Liberty: An Examination of the 'Tradition' of Freedom," in M. R. Konvitz, and C. Rossiter, eds., *Aspects of Liberty: Essays Presented to Robert E. Cushman* (Ithaca: Cornell University Press, 1958), pp. 129-62.

Rowe, G. S., *Thomas McKean: The Shaping of American Republicanism* (Boulder, Colo.: Colorado Associated University Press, 1962).

Rosenberg, Norman L. "The Law of Political Libel and Freedom of the Press in Nineteenth Century America: An Interpretation," *The American Journal of Legal History* 17 (1973): 336-52.

Rossiter, Clinton. *Seedtime of the Republic* (New York: Harcourt, Brace, 1953).

Rude, George. *Wilkes and Liberty* (Oxford: Oxford University Press, 1962).

Rutland, Robert Allen. *The Birth of the Bill of Rights, 1776-1791* (Chapel Hill: University of North Carolina Press, 1955).

Schlesinger, Arthur M. *Prelude to Independence: The Newspaper War on Britain, 1764-1776* (New York: Knopf, 1958).

Schofield, Henry. "Freedom of the Press in the United States," in Schofield's *Essays on Constitutional Law and Equity* (Boston: Published for Northwestern University Law School, by the Chipman Law Publishing Co., 1921, 2 vols.), 2:510-571.

Schroeder, Theodore. *Constitutional Free Speech Defined and Defended in an Unfinished Argument in a Case of Blasphemy* (New York: Free Speech League, 1919).

—— *A Free Speech Bibliography* (New York: H. W. Wilson, 1922).

Schuyler, Livingston Rowe. *The Liberty of the Press in the American Colonies before the Revolutionary War* (New York: T. Whittaker, 1905), 85 pp.

Schwartz, Bernard. *The Great Rights of Mankind: A History of the American Bill of Rights* (New York: Oxford University Press, 1977).

Shapiro, Martin. *Freedom of Speech: The Supreme Court and Judicial Review* (Englewood Cliffs, N.J.: Prentice Hall, 1966).

Siebert, Frederick S. *Freedom of the Press in England, 1476-1776* (Urbana: University of Illinois Press, 1952).

Slafter, Edmund F. *John Checkley; or, the Evolution of Religious Tolerance in Massachusetts Bay* (Boston: Prince Society, 1897), 2 vols.

Smith, Horace Wemyss. *Life and Correspondence of the Reverend William Smith* (Philadelphia: S. A. George & Co., 1879), 2 vols.

Smith, James Morton. *Freedom's Fetters: The Alien and Sedition Laws and American Civil Liberties* (Ithaca: Cornell University Press, 1956).

Smith, Jeffery A. "Impartiality and Revolutionary Ideology: Editorial Policies of the *South Carolina Gazette*, 1732-1775," *The Journal of Southern History* 49 (1983): 511-26.

—— "Legislative Privilege and Colonial Journalism: a Reappraisal," *Journalism Quarterly* 64 (Summer, 1984): 97-103.

Smith, Joseph Henry. *Appeals to the Privy Council from the American Plantations* (New York: Columbia University Press, 1950).

Spaulding, E. Wilder. *His Excellency, George Clinton* (New York: Macmillan, 1938).

Spinrad, William M. *Civil Liberties* (Chicago: Quadrangle Books, 1970).

Stephen, Sir James Fitzjames. *A History of the Criminal Law of England* (London: Macmillan, 1883), 3 vols.

Stephen, Leslie. *History of English Thought in the Eighteenth Century* (London: Smith, Elder, 1876), 2 vols.

Steven, David Harrison. *Party Politics and English Journalism, 1702-1742* (Chicago: University of Chicago Press, 1916).

Sutherland, Arthur E., Jr., "British Trials for Disloyal Association during the French Revolution," *Cornell Law Quarterly* 34 (Spring 1949): 309-15.

Teeter, Dwight L. "Decent Animadversions: Notes Toward a History of Free Press Theory," in Donovan H. Bond and W. R. McLeod, eds., *Newsletters to Newspapers*, pp. 237-45.

———— " 'King' Sears, the Mob and Freedom of the Press in New York, 1765-76," *Journalism Quarterly* 41 (1964): 539-44.

———— "Press Freedom and the Public Printing: Pennsylvania, 1775-83," *Journalism Quarterly* 45 (1968): 445-51.

———— "The Printer and the Chief Justice: Seditious Libel in 1782-83," *Journalism Quarterly* 45 (1968): 235-42.

Terwilliger, W. Bird. "William Goddard's Victory for the Freedom of the Press," *Maryland Historical Magazine* 36 (1941): 139-49.

Thayer, Theodore. *Pennsylvania Politics and the Growth of Democracy, 1740-1776* (Harrisburg: Pennsylvania Historical and Museum Commission, 1953).

Thomas, Isaiah. *The History of Printing in America* (Worcester: Isaiah Thomas, Jr., 1810), 2 vols.

Thomson, Mark A. *The Secretaries of State, 1681-1782* (Oxford: The Clarendon Press, 1932).

Vance, W. R. "Freedom of Speech and of the Press," *Minnesota Law Review* 2 (March 1918): 239-260.

Van Tyne, Claude H. *The Loyalists in the American Revolution* (New York: Macmillan, 1902).

Veeder, Van Vechten. "History of the Law of Defamation," in *Select Essays in Anglo-American Legal History*, comp. and ed. by a Committee of the Association of American Law Schools (Boston, 1909, 3 vols.), 3:446-73.

Walett, Francis J. "The Massachusetts Council, 1766-1774," *William and Mary Quarterly*, 3rd ser., 6 (1949): 605-27.

Wallace, David D. *Constitutional History of South Carolina* (Abbeville, S.C., 1899).

Wallace, John William. *An Address Delivered at the Celebration by the*

New-York Historical Society, May 20, 1863, of the Two Hundredth Birth Day of Mr. William Bradford (Albany: J. Munsell, 1863).

Warren, Charles, "New Light on the History of the Federal Judiciary Act of 1789," in D. B. Maggs, *et al*, eds., *Selected Essays on Constitutional Law* (Chicago: The Foundation Press, 1938, 5 vols.) 3:1246-1254.

―――― *The Supreme Court in United States History* (Boston: Little, Brown, 1923), 3 vols.

Werkmeister, Lucycle. *The London Daily Press, 1772-1792* (Lincoln: University of Nebraska Press, 1963).

Whipple, Leon. *Our Ancient Liberties* (New York: The H. Wilson Company, 1927).

Williams, J. B. *A History of English Journalism* (London: Longmans, Green & Co., 1908).

Wittke, Carl. *The History of English Parliamentary Privilege*, Ohio State University Bulletin, vol. 26, no. 2 (Columbus, 1921).

Yodelis, Mary Ann. "Boston's First Major Newspaper War: A 'Great Awakening' of Freedom," *Journalism Quarterly* 51 (1974): 207-12.

―――― "Courts, Counting House and Streets: Attempts at Press Control, 1763-1775," *Journalism History* 1 (1974): 11-15.

UNPUBLISHED STUDENT PAPERS

Baker, James Wesley. "Freedom of the Press in South Carolina in 1773," University of South Carolina (1975).

Baldasty, Gerald J. "Freedom of Expression and Seditious Libel in Virginia, 1785-86," University of Wisconsin, Madison (1973).

―――― "A Theory of Press Freedom: Massachusetts Newspapers and Law, 1782-1791," Master's thesis. University of Wisconsin, Madison (1974).

―――― "The Virginia Newspapers and Freedom of the Press," in Cleo Among the Media, AEJ History Division (Summer 1974), pp. 22-26. Mimeo.

Beldon, Thomas M. "Seditious Libel and Freedom of Expression in Three Virginia Newspapers: 1787-1788," University of Wisconsin, Madison (1973).

Brown, Norman R. "Freedom and Restraint of the Press in Colonial South Carolina 1763-1766," University of Wisconsin, Madison (1963).

Capers, T. Stacy. "Freedom and Restraint of the Press during the Decade Before Lexington, South Carolina 1767-1770," University of Wisconsin, Madison (n.d.).

Chamberlin, William F. "The Connecticut Press of the 1780s: Vicious in Spite of the Law," University of Washington (1975).

Clark, David. "Freedom of the Press in Pennsylvania as Reflected in the

Chronicle and the *Gazette*, 1767-1770," University of Wisconsin, Madison (1963).

Garcia, Hazel. "Another Look at the Revisionist Historians: A Research Report," University of Wisconsin, Madison (n.d.).

Greenberg, Helaine. "Virginia Newspapers and Freedom of Expression in 1789 and 1790," University of Wisconsin, Madison (1973).

Jones, Douglas C. "Restraints of the Press, Boston, 1767-1770," University of Wisconsin, Madison (n.d.).

Katagiri, T. "Freedom of the Press in South Carolina, 1771-1774," University of Wisconsin, Madison (1963).

Kendrick, Rosemary. "Thomas Cooper: Early Libertarian Writer on Press Freedom," University of Wisconsin, Madison (1965).

Knights, Peter R. "Restraints upon Colonial Newspapers: Massachusetts-Bay Boston 1771-1773," University of Wisconsin, Madison (1963).

Raleigh, E. C. "Newspaper Practices From the First Amendment to the Alien and Sedition Acts 1791-1798," University of Wisconsin, Madison (1964).

Shotwell, John M. "Freedom of the Press in the Old Dominion: Virginia Newspapers 1782-1791," University of Wisconsin, Madison (1973).

Sharp, Erwin A. "Freedom of the Press in Virginia 1788-1789," University of Wisconsin, Madison (1973).

Simpson, Roger A. "Benjamin Franklin: Prudent Editor of *The Pennsylvania Gazette*," University of Wisconsin, Madison (1960).

Thomas, Greta. "Freedom and Restraint of the Press in Colonial New York (1763-1766)," University of Wisconsin, Madison (1963).

UNPUBLISHED DOCTORAL DISSERTATIONS

Dyer, Alan Frank. "James Parker, Colonial Printer, 1715-1770," Ph.D. diss., University of Michigan (1977).

Teeter, Dwight L. "A Legacy of Expression: Philadelphia Newspapers and Congress During the War for Independence," Ph.D. diss., University of Wisconsin, Madison, School of Journaliam (1966).

Yodelis, Mary Ann. "Boston's Second Major Newspaper War: Economics, Politics and the Theory and Practice of Political Expression in the Press, 1763-1775," Ph.D. diss., University of Wisconsin, Madison, School of Journalism (1971).

Index

Seditious Libel *(cont.)*
19; New York, 21, 35-48, 75-81; North Carolina, 61, 72-73; Pennsylvania, 22-25, 48-59, 73 74; South Carolina, 56-60, 74-75; Virginia, 18-20, 60, 71-72 AMERICAN STATES AND, 185-93, 196; in Cushing-Adams correspondence, 198-203; and First Amendment, 274, 281, 298; Jeffersonians and danger of, 337-47; Massachusetts and, 191, 213, 214-19; New York and, 253, 254; patriots and, 62-63, 175-76; Pennsylvania, 206-13; and Sedition Act, 185, 201, 297-98; states versus federal jurisdiction, 274-79, 304-7; Virginia, 177-81, 183, 193-96 ENDORSED BY: Alexander, 133; Cato, 111; Jefferson, 307; Livingston, 138-39; Smith, 245; Wilson, 279 THEORISTS ON: Alexander, 133; Asgil, 104; Bentham, 167-69; Blount, 100-101; Bolingbroke, 115-16; Bollan, 131, 154-55; Busher, 101; "Candor," 147-48; Cato, 111; Collins, 108; *Common Sense* essays, 134; Dawes, 283-87; Defoe, 104-5; Erskine, 285-86, 288 89; "Father of Candor," 148-49; Francklin, 166; B. Franklin, 119-20, 192; "Friend to Harmony," 290; Furneaux, 163-66; Gallatin, 297-98, 302-3; Hall, 287; Hamilton, 132; Hay, 312-15; Iredell, 277-79; Jefferson, 307; Jeffersonians, 307; Kippis, 166-67; Livingston, 138-39; Locke, 97-100; Lofft, 283; Madison, 293-94, 306n, 319-20; Maseres, 160, 167; Mayhew, 137-38; Milton, 93-97; Montesquieu, 34, 153; G. Nicholas, 252, 321; J. Nicholas, 311; Ratcliffe, 166; Robinson, 93; Smith, 245; Spinoza, 89-90; Sullivan, 333-35; Swift, 104-5; Thomson, 335-38; Tindal, 102-3, 336; Toland, 115; "Tory Author," 107-8; Walwyn, 92, 152; E. Williams, 137; R. Williams, 92 93, 152; Williamson, 251, 259; Wilson, 204-5, 241, 275-76, 279; Wortman, 329-31; Young Gentleman of the Temple, 105-6; Zenger defense, 128-34
Seizure, 325
Self-incrimination, 22, 260, 325
Sergeant, Nathaniel, 215
Sewell, Jonathan, 70
Seymour, Thomas, 344-45
Shapiro, Martin, Preface
Shays's Rebellion, 214, 271
Sherman, Roger, 224, 260; on Bill of Rights, 221
Shipley, William D., 282
Sidney, Algernon, 9
Siebert, Frederick S., 6n, 14
Skirving, William, 287
Slye, Gerard, 21
Smilie, John, 240
Smith, James Morton, Preface, 64n

Smith, Jeffery A., 52n, 83-84, 122n
Smith, Melancthon, 235, 245, 247, 252
Smith, Merriwether, 182
Smith, William (New York), 138, 172; attacks libel law, 160-61
Smith, William (Pennsylvania), 38-40, 52-58, 130
Smith, William (South Carolina), 292
Smith-Moore case, 51-58
Society of Cincinnati, 77
"Son of Liberty," 64, 76, 85
"South Briton," 159
South Carolina: colonial seditious libel cases, 59 60, 74-75; free press clause, 184; reception of common law, 197-98
South Carolina Gazette, 59, 74, 75, 122; and *Cato's Letters,* 113
"Spectator," 209, 296
Speech, freedom of: and the American Revolution, 185; in ancient Greece, 4; in Anglo-American history, 3; Bollan on, 154-55; in colonial America, 16, 85-86; colonial patriots, 83; Federalists on, 304; Framers' understanding of, 266-69, 272-74, 280; and Kentucky Resolutions of 1798, 306; Pennsylvania Declaration of Rights, 185; as right of subjects, 103, 107, 137, 142
Spellman, Henry, 18
Spencer, Ambrose, 339
Spinoza, Benedict de, 89, 152-53
Stamp Act, 64, 85, 87
Stationers' Company, 6
Steele, Richard, 105
Stephen, Sir James Fitzjames, Preface
Storing, Herbert, quoted, 240
Story, Joseph, 279
Sullivan, James, 215, 312; on freedom of the press, 217-18, 332-35; on Sedition Act of 1798, 280, 334-35
Sumner, Increase, 215
Swift, Jonathan, 104-5
Sydney, Algernon, 132

Taylor, George K., 318
Taylor, John, 309
Tea Act, 69
Teeter, Dwight L., 85, 182n, 205n, 206, 207n; quoted, 290
"Tenax," 209
Thomas, Isaiah, 69, 83, 114, 161
Thompson, Smith, 339
Thomson, John, 312, 347, 348; on freedom of the press, 335-38
Time Piece, 300
Timoleon, 245
Timothy, Lewis, 122, 123
Timothy, Peter, 59, 60
Tindal, Matthew, 102-3, 336
Toland, John, on freedom of the press, 115
"Tory Author." *See* Addison, Joseph

Leonard W. Levy, whose *Origins of the Fifth Amendment* was awarded the Pulitzer Prize in history, is formerly Earl Warren Professor of Constitutional History at Brandeis University and Andrew W. Mellon All-Claremont Professor of Humanities and History at the Claremont Graduate School. His other writings, many of which have also won awards, include *Blasphemy*, *The Establishment Clause*, *Freedom of the Press from Zenger to Jefferson*, *Original Intent and the Framers' Constitution*, *The Palladium of Justice*, and *Jefferson and Civil Liberties*. He lives in Ashland, Oregon.

Gilbert Osofsky, *Harlem: The Making of a Ghetto*
Edward Pessen, *Losing Our Souls*
Glenn Porter and Harold C. Livesay, *Merchants and Manufacturers*
John Prados, *The Hidden History of the Vietnam War*
John Prados, *Presidents' Secret Wars*
Patrick Renshaw, *The Wobblies*
Edward Reynolds, *Stand the Storm*
Louis Rosen, *The South Side*
Richard Schickel, *The Disney Version*
Richard Schickel, *Intimate Strangers*
Richard Schickel, *Matinee Idylls*
Richard Schickel, *The Men Who Made the Movies*
Budd Schulberg, *Moving Pictures*
Edward A. Shils, *The Torment of Secrecy*
Robert Shogan, *Bad News*
Geoffrey S. Smith, *To Save a Nation*
John David Smith, *Black Judas*
Robert W. Snyder, *The Voice of the City*
Bernard Sternsher, ed., *Hitting Home: The Great Depression in Town
    and Country*
Bernard Sternsher, ed., *Hope Restored: How the New Deal Worked
    in Town and Country*
Bernard Sternsher and Judith Sealander, eds., *Women of Valor*
Peter S. Temes, *Against School Reform*
Athan Theoharis, *From the Secret Files of J. Edgar Hoover*
James Tooley, *The Miseducation of Women*
Nicholas von Hoffman, *We Are the People Our Parents Warned Us Against*
Norman Ware, *The Industrial Worker, 1840–1860*
Robert Weisbrot, *Maximum Danger*
Mark J. White, ed., *The Kennedys and Cuba*
Tom Wicker, *JFK and LBJ: The Influence of Personality upon Politics*
Robert H. Wiebe, *Businessmen and Reform*
T. Harry Williams, *McClellan, Sherman and Grant*
Miles Wolff, *Lunch at the 5 & 10*
Randall B. Woods and Howard Jones, *Dawning of the Cold War*
American Ways Series:
    John A. Andrew III, *Lyndon Johnson and the Great Society*
    Roger Daniels, *Not Like Us*
    J. Matthew Gallman, *The North Fights the Civil War: The Home Front*
    Lewis L. Gould, *1968: The Election That Changed America*
    D. G. Hart, *That Old-Time Religion in Modern America*
    John Earl Haynes, *Red Scare or Red Menace?*
    Kenneth J. Heineman, *Put Your Bodies Upon the Wheels*
    R. Douglas Hurt, *Problems of Plenty*
    D. Clayton James and Anne Sharp Wells, *From Pearl Harbor to V-J Day*
    John W. Jeffries, *Wartime America*
    Curtis D. Johnson, *Redeeming America*
    Maury Klein, *The Flowering of the Third America*
    Larry M. Logue, *To Appomattox and Beyond*
    Jean V. Matthews, *The Rise of the New Woman*
    Jean V. Matthews, *Women's Struggle for Equality*
    Iwan W. Morgan, *Deficit Government*
    Robert Muccigrosso, *Celebrating the New World*
    Daniel Nelson, *Shifting Fortunes*
    Thomas R. Pegram, *Battling Demon Rum*
    Burton W. Peretti, *Jazz in American Culture*
    David Reynolds, *From Munich to Pearl Harbor*
    Hal K. Rothman, *Saving the Planet*
    John A. Salmond, *"My Mind Set on Freedom"*
    Gene Smiley, *Rethinking the Great Depression*
    William Earl Weeks, *Building the Continental Empire*
    Kevin White, *Sexual Liberation or Sexual License?*
    Mark J. White, *Missiles in Cuba*

European and World History
Geoffrey Blainey, *A Short History of the World*
Laurie Winn Carlson, *Cattle: An Informal Social History*
John Charmley, *Chamberlain and the Lost Peace*
Donald T. Critchlow and Agnieszka Critchlow, eds., *Enemies of the State*
John K. Dickinson, *German and Jew*
Lee Feigon, *China Rising*
Lee Feigon, *Demystifying Tibet*
Lee Feigon, *Mao*
Mark Frankland, *The Patriots' Revolution*
Lloyd C. Gardner, *Spheres of Influence*
David Gilmour, *Cities of Spain*
Raul Hilberg, *The Politics of Memory*
Raul Hilberg, et al., eds., *The Warsaw Diary of Adam Czerniakow*
Gertrude Himmelfarb, *Darwin and the Darwinian Revolution*
Gertrude Himmelfarb, *Marriage and Morals Among the Victorians*
Gertrude Himmelfarb, *Victorian Minds*
Thomas A. Idinopulos, *Jerusalem*
Thomas A. Idinopulos, *Weathered by Miracles*
Allan Janik and Stephen Toulmin, *Wittgenstein's Vienna*
Elie Kedourie, *The Chatham House Version*
Warren F. Kimball, *Forged in War*
Hilton Kramer and Roger Kimball, eds., *The Betrayal of Liberalism*
Ronnie S. Landau, *The Nazi Holocaust*
Primo Levi, *The Search for Roots*
Carmel McCaffrey and Leo Eaton, *In Search of Ancient Ireland*
Filip Müller, *Eyewitness Auschwitz*
Clive Ponting, *1940: Myth and Reality*
David Pryce-Jones, *The Closed Circle*
A.L. Rowse, *The Elizabethan Renaissance: The Life of the Society*
A.L. Rowse, *The Elizabethan Renaissance: The Cultural Achievement*
Scott Shane, *Dismantling Utopia*
Paul Webster, *Petain's Crime*
John Weiss, *Ideology of Death*

Literature, Arts, and Letters
Roger Angell, *Once More Around the Park*
Walter Bagehot, *Physics and Politics*
Sybille Bedford, *Aldous Huxley*
Stephen Vincent Benét, *John Brown's Body*
Ira Berkow, *The Minority Quarterback*
Isaiah Berlin, *The Hedgehog and the Fox*
F. Bordewijk, *Character*
Robert Brustein, *Cultural Calisthenics*
Robert Brustein, *Dumbocracy in America*
Robert Brustein, *The Siege of the Arts*
Anthony Burgess, *Shakespeare*
Philip Callow, *Chekhov*
Philip Callow, *From Noon to Starry Night*
Philip Callow, *Son and Lover: The Young D. H. Lawrence*
Anton Chekhov, *The Comic Stories*
Bruce Cole, *The Informed Eye*
James Gould Cozzens, *Castaway*
James Gould Cozzens, *Men and Brethren*
Theodore Dalrymple, *Life at the Bottom*
Clarence Darrow, *Verdicts Out of Court*
Floyd Dell, *Intellectual Vagabondage*
Theodore Dreiser, *Best Short Stories*
Joseph Epstein, *Ambition*
Robert Thomas Fallon, *A Theatergoer's Guide to Shakespeare*
André Gide, *Madeleine*
Gerald Graff, *Literature Against Itself*
John Gross, *The Rise and Fall of the Man of Letters*
Olivia Gude and Jeff Huebner, *Urban Art Chicago*
Raul Hilberg, *The Politics of Memory*

Irving Howe, *Politics and the Novel*
Irving Howe, *William Faulkner*
Aldous Huxley, *After Many a Summer Dies the Swan*
Aldous Huxley, *Ape and Essence*
Aldous Huxley, *Collected Short Stories*
Vladimir Kataev, *If Only We Could Know!*
Roger Kimball, *Experiments Against Reality*
Roger Kimball, *Lives of the Mind*
Roger Kimball, *Tenured Radicals*
Hilton Kramer, *The Twilight of the Intellectuals*
Hilton Kramer and Roger Kimball, eds., *Against the Grain*
Hilton Kramer and Roger Kimball, eds., *The Survival of Culture*
F. R. Leavis, *Revaluation*
F. R. Leavis, *The Living Principle*
F. R. Leavis, *The Critic as Anti-Philosopher*
Marie-Anne Lescourret, *Rubens: A Double Life*
Primo Levi, *The Search for Roots*
Sinclair Lewis, *Selected Short Stories*
Lynne Munson, *Exhibitionism*
Carl Rollyson, *Reading Susan Sontag*
Carl Sandburg, *Poems for the People*
Arthur Schnitzler, *Night Games*
Budd Schulberg, *The Harder They Fall*
Budd Schulberg, *Moving Pictures*
Ramón J. Sender, *Seven Red Sundays*
Karl Shapiro, *Creative Glut*
Peter Shaw, *Recovering American Literature*
James B. Simpson, ed., *Veil and Cowl*
Tess Slesinger, *On Being Told That Her Second Husband Has Taken
    His First Lover, and Other Stories*
Red Smith, *Red Smith on Baseball*
Donald Thomas, *Swinburne*
B. Traven, *The Bridge in the Jungle*
B. Traven, *The Carreta*
B. Traven, *The Cotton-Pickers*
B. Traven, *General from the Jungle*
B. Traven, *Government*
B. Traven, *March to the Montería*
B. Traven, *The Night Visitor and Other Stories*
B. Traven, *The Rebellion of the Hanged*
B. Traven, *Trozas*
Anthony Trollope, *Trollope the Traveller*
Ivan Turgenev, *Literary Reminiscences*
John Tytell, *Ezra Pound*
Rex Warner, *The Aerodrome*
Rebecca West, *A Train of Powder*
Wilhelm Worringer, *Abstraction and Empathy*
The Shakespeare Handbooks by Alistair McCallum
    Hamlet
    King Lear
    Macbeth
    Romeo and Juliet

Theatre and Drama

Linda Apperson, *Stage Managing and Theatre Etiquette*
Antonin Artaud, *Artaud on Theatre*
Robert Brustein, *Cultural Calisthenics*
Robert Brustein, *Dumbocracy in America*
Robert Brustein, *Reimagining American Theatre*
Robert Brustein, *The Siege of the Arts*
Robert Brustein, *The Theatre of Revolt*
Stephen Citron, *The Musical from the Inside Out*
Robert Thomas Fallon, *A Theatergoer's Guide to Shakespeare*
Louis Fantasia, *Instant Shakespeare*
Trevor R. Griffiths, *The Ivan R. Dee Guide to Plays and Playwrights*

Irina and Igor Levin, *Working on the Play and the Role*
Keith Newlin, ed., *American Plays of the New Woman*
Louis Rosen, *The South Side*
Bernard Sahlins, *Days and Nights at The Second City*
David Wood, with Janet Grant, *Theatre for Children*
Plays for Performance:
  Aristophanes, *Lysistrata*
  Pierre Augustin de Beaumarchais, *The Barber of Seville*
  Pierre Augustin de Beaumarchais, *The Marriage of Figaro*
  Georg Büchner, *Woyzeck*
  Anton Chekhov, *The Cherry Orchard*
  Anton Chekhov, *Ivanov*
  Anton Chekhov, *The Seagull*
  Anton Chekhov, *Three Sisters*
  Anton Chekhov, *Uncle Vanya*
  Thomas Dekker, *The Shoemaker's Holiday*
  Euripides, *The Bacchae*
  Euripides, *Iphigenia in Aulis*
  Euripides, *Iphigenia Among the Taurians*
  Euripides, *Medea*
  Euripides, *The Trojan Women*
  Georges Feydeau, *Paradise Hotel*
  Carlo Goldoni, *The Servant of Two Masters*
  Henrik Ibsen, *A Doll's House*
  Henrik Ibsen, *Ghosts*
  Henrik Ibsen, *Hedda Gabler*
  Henrik Ibsen, *The Master Builder*
  Henrik Ibsen, *When We Dead Awaken*
  Henrik Ibsen, *The Wild Duck*
  Heinrich von Kleist, *The Prince of Homburg*
  Marivaux, *The Dispute*
  Christopher Marlowe, *Doctor Faustus*
  Molière, *The Bourgeois Gentleman*
  The Mysteries: Creation
  The Mysteries: The Passion
  Luigi Pirandello, *Enrico IV*
  Luigi Pirandello, *Six Characters in Search of an Author*
  Budd Schulberg, with Stan Silverman, *On the Waterfront* (the play)
  Mary Shelley, *Frankenstein*
  Sophocles, *Antigone*
  Sophocles, *Electra*
  Sophocles, *Oedipus at Colonus*
  Sophocles, *Oedipus the King*
  August Strindberg, *The Father*
  August Strindberg, *Miss Julie*

Philosophy
Philosophers in 90 Minutes by Paul Strathern
  Thomas Aquinas in 90 Minutes
  Aristotle in 90 Minutes
  St. Augustine in 90 Minutes
  Berkeley in 90 Minutes
  Confucius in 90 Minutes
  Derrida in 90 Minutes
  Descartes in 90 Minutes
  Dewey in 90 Minutes
  Foucault in 90 Minutes
  Hegel in 90 Minutes
  Heidegger in 90 Minutes
  Hume in 90 Minutes
  Kant in 90 Minutes
  Kierkegaard in 90 Minutes
  Leibniz in 90 Minutes
  Locke in 90 Minutes
  Machiavelli in 90 Minutes